NEW ORLEANS

By the 1850s New Orleans was already an established city. The first St. Charles Hotel (domed building, left of center), Gallier Hall and the First Presbyterian Church (left, foreground), and the first Odd Fellows Hall (domed building in foreground) are visible in this 1852 view of the city as it appeared from the top of St. Patrick's Church. Courtesy, The Historic New Orleans Collection.

NEW ORLEANS

TEXT BY JOHN R. KEMP
PICTURE RESEARCH BY JOHN H. LAWRENCE
"PRESERVING THE PAST" BY MARY LOU CHRISTOVICH
"PARTNERS IN PROGRESS" BY JOHN CHASE AND JOHN WILDS
INTRODUCTION BY CHARLES L. DUFOUR
ADVISORY EDITOR, SAMUEL WILSON, JR., F.A.I.A.

SPONSORED BY
THE PRESERVATION RESOURCE CENTER
OF NEW ORLEANS

WINDSOR PUBLICATIONS, INC.
WOODLAND HILLS, CALIFORNIA

Published 1981
Printed in the United States of America

First Edition

Library of Congress Cataloging in Publication Data

Kemp, John R., 1945-
    New Orleans, an illustrated history

    Sponsored by the Preservation Resource Center
of New Orleans.
    Bibliography: p. 312
    Includes index.
    1. New Orleans (La.)—History.   2. New Orleans
(La.)—Description.   I. Preservation Resource
Center of New Orleans.   II. Title.
F379.N557K45   976.3′35   81-52019
ISBN 0-89781-035-X   AACR2

CONTENTS

New Orleans is a city rich in architectural treasures, one of the greatest being the Old City Hall—or Gallier Hall—designed by James Gallier in the 1840s. Regarded as one of America's foremost examples of the Greek Revival style, the hall is a spendid reminder of the energy and grace of the antebellum period. Courtesy, The Historic New Orleans Collection.

FOREWORD

New Orleans is, as it has often been remarked, the most "European" city of the United States. Founded by the French in 1718, ruled by Spain from the 1760s until 1803, and its population increased by influxes of German, Irish, and Italians as well as Anglo-Americans from other areas of the country, the city has retained a distinctive European atmosphere and a French *joie de vivre*. Although under the flag of Bourbon France for less than 50 of its first years, the French cultural heritage has been a dominant influence on its character. Until the middle of the nineteenth century, its newspapers were generally published in both French and English, laws were written in both languages, and legal documents and records of the early years are found in French probably more often than in English. During the Spanish period, Spanish became the official language for court records and other legal papers, but the language and customs of the people remained essentially French.

Of the buildings built during the French regime, only the old Ursuline Convent, designed in 1745, remains almost intact. The colonial city was nearly destroyed by the conflagrations of 1788 and 1794 and in its rebuilding, the architects and builders were almost all French—Guillemard, Andry, Lafon and Hilaire Boutte—and the architectural style of the new buildings was predominantly French. After the fires, the Spanish authorities enacted new building ordinances that required buildings to be of brick or of "brick between posts," covered with at least an inch coating of plaster or stucco. Roofs were to be of tile or slate, and flat or terrace roofs became common. The wrought-iron work of the Canary Islander Marcellino Hernandez, as seen in the balcony railings of the Cabildo, the Orue-Pontalba House (now the rebuilt home of Le Petit Theatre du Vieux Carre) and a few others, is perhaps the finest contribution of Spain to the architecture of New Orleans.

The noted architect, Benjamin H. Latrobe, observed in 1819 that "Americans are pouring in daily, not in families, but in large bodies. In a few years therefore, this will be an American town. What is good and bad in the French manners and opinions must give way and the American notions of right and wrong, of convenience and inconvenience, will take their place. ... One cannot help wishing that a *mean,* an *average* character of society may grow out of the intermixture of the French and American manners." Latrobe, as an English-born, American architect, regretted the changes being introduced by the incoming Americans with their red brick buildings in contrast to the picturesque French and Spanish stuccoed buildings of the colonial city. "We shall introduce many grand and profitable improvements but they will take the place of much elegance, ease and some convenience," Latrobe added.

The city has grown and changed over the more than two and a half centuries of its existence, and it has developed into a modern, thriving metropolis, the nation's second port. Its fascinating history has been recorded in many books, articles, paintings, and photographs. Over the years several publications devoted to the growth and to those who made it possible have appeared and form an invaluable source of information to those interested in the city's history. Among these were Jewell's *Crescent City Illustrated*, published in 1872; *New Orleans and the New South,* in 1888; *The City of New Orleans: The Book of the Chamber of Commerce and Industry of Louisiana,* in 1894; and *New Orleans, the Crescent City,* in 1903-04. Numerous guidebooks and surveys have provided additional information about this unusual city and the series, *New Orleans Architecture,* published by the Friends of the Cabildo, associates of the Louisiana State Museum, documents the city's distinctive architecture.

Not since the books named above, published between 1872 and 1904, has such a volume appeared that not only presents a concise history of the city, but also gives the history of many of the principal business concerns that have contributed to the city's growth and prosperity. In sponsoring this publication, the Preservation Resource Center adds another facet to its efforts to preserve the city's rich heritage of history and architecture.

Samuel Wilson, Jr., F.A.I.A.

Entitled Nouvelle Orleans, *this somewhat romanticized 19th-century painting depicts the city as it would look from a ship entering the port. Courtesy, The Historic New Orleans Collection.*

INTRODUCTION

New Orleans is *sui generis:* among American cities, it is one of a kind. A city geographically in the South—indeed, the Deep South—New Orleans is not a Southern city in the sense that Atlanta, Houston, and Dallas are Southern cities.

New Orleans, according to the 1840 census, became the third city in the nation, after New York and Baltimore, to reach a population of 100,000. Well into the 20th century, New Orleans continued to be the South's largest city; but it has since lost that honor, and in 1981 had fallen substantially behind other booming Southern cities.

During its long history, New Orleans had its share of picturesque rogues, clever rascals, and flamboyant demagogues. Corruption—long rooted in the political life of New Orleans—has often reached proportions of which Tammany Hall might have been proud. Yet for all of its foibles and failings, New Orleans is the envy of its richer and more aggressive sister-cities of the South. These cities, of course, will deny this vehemently.

Why should Atlanta, Dallas, or Houston envy New Orleans, all three of which outstrip her in many ways? It is simply because New Orleans has something that wealth cannot buy nor progress bring. New Orleans is a state of mind, a way of life. For charm, cuisine, and culture; for tradition, tomfoolery, and tragedy; for pestilence, plague, and politics; for floods, fires, and factions; for hurricanes and history, New Orleans has no rival in the United States.

Accordingly the history of New Orleans is colorful, complex, and always exciting, and in his text, John Kemp has capably exploited these characteristics.

Kemp gives a panoramic view of the history of New Orleans, narrating the story in admirable fashion from before Jean Baptiste Le Moyne, Sieur de Bienville, founded the city to the present and Mayor Ernest "Dutch" Morial. One will not find here an excess of details, for Kemp's goal was to survey New Orleans' past within designated limitations of space.

But the whole story is here. Kemp's style is smooth, clear, and direct. He has something to say and says it well; and he has given good pace to his narrative. That he has researched his subject in its many facets is readily evident. Kemp has delved deeply into existing secondary sources as well as using letters, newspapers, diaries, and interviews from which he has drawn skillfully.

The reader moves swiftly through the colonial period when New Orleans was the capital, first of French, then of Spanish, Louisiana. The Louisiana Purchase, the Battle of New Orleans, the lush era that followed the coming of the steamboat on the lower Mississippi, the rise of the plantation economy, and the boom days leading up to the Civil War are all well presented. So, too, is the Reconstruction period, with the carpetbaggers in command; and the rise of the Louisiana Lottery Company, which drained off millions of dollars annually from men, women, and even children. The author has a good, succinct description of the momentous segregation decision of the United States Supreme Court in the New Orleans case of *Plessy v. Ferguson.* When the doctrine of "separate but equal" received the blessing of the Supreme Court, the way was open for racial segregation in the South and

Kemp relates how black voters were disenfranchised by the "grandfather clause" written into the new Louisiana Constitution of 1898.

The history of New Orleans up to this point has been told by many writers in the past. But New Orleans' entry into the 20th century and the political history of the city between 1900 and 1925 has been treated, primarily, only in special studies rather than in narrative histories of the city. Kemp has told the story of Martin Behrman's 17 years in City Hall with clarity—no easy task considering the complexity of New Orleans' political wheeling-and-dealing in the rough-and-tumble era of Ring rule. The research he conducted for his biography of Behrman, published some years ago, has clearly stood him in good stead.

The rise to power of Huey Long, against the backdrop of the Great Depression, is deftly sketched in one of the most interesting sections of Kemp's narrative. Long not only held more power in his hands than any politician in Louisiana—before or since—but he also used power to achieve his goals without the slightest regard to niceties. His assassination cut short Long's already-meteoric rise on the national scene.

Kemp concludes his history with a survey of the decades from the end of World War II to the present. He ably describes the "Chep" Morrison years in City Hall and racial desegregation which was a stormy highlight of Morrison's career. He evaluates the city's progress during the administrations of Victor Schiro, "Moon" Landrieu, and "Dutch" Morial to end the story that really began 300 years ago (come April 9, 1982), when La Salle, standing on the bank of the Mississippi near the Gulf of Mexico, claimed Louisiana for Louis XIV.

Charles L. Dufour

In 1682 Rene Robert Cavelier, Sieur de La Salle, claimed for France the vast territory drained by the Mississippi River. He named it Louisiana in honor of King Louis XIV. Courtesy, The Historic New Orleans Collection.

CHAPTER I
"ROME AND PARIS
HAD NOT SUCH CONSIDERABLE BEGINNINGS"

The Mississippi River, the great divider of the United States into east and west, was born at the conclusion of the Ice Age, when melting glacial water etched a great valley southward across the continent to its point of escape into the Gulf of Mexico. Today the river rises from small streams that feed Lake Itasca in northern Minnesota, flowing 2,350 miles and draining — with its tributaries — all or part of 31 states, accounting for more than a third of the total runoff of the continental United States.

As the Mississippi cascades and winds its way toward the Gulf, it travels from a temperate to a subtropical climate and from an elevation of about 1,400 feet to sea level at its mouth. The upper Mississippi flows through central Minnesota from lake to lake, cutting through glacial debris at such descriptively named towns as Grand Rapids and Little Falls. During the winter the river is often clogged by ice and thick, hazardous fogs settle on the cold waters of the unfrozen parts during warm spells. Below St. Paul, Minnesota, the river valley widens and the grade decreases as the river becomes a major spillway for the continental ice sheet stretching northeast and northwest.

The Mississippi's major tributary, the Missouri — more than 2,000 miles itself — joins 17 miles north of St. Louis, Missouri. Here the river width increases to 3,500 feet and when the Ohio River joins at Cairo,

Illinois, the river expands to 4,500 feet. The lower Mississippi meanders in great loops across broad alluvial plains dotted by marshes, oxbow lakes, and remnants of the river's former channels. Natural levees, built up from sediment carried and deposited in times of flood, border much of the river, making it higher than the surrounding areas. Breaks in the levees often flood the bottomlands.

Below the confluence of the Mississippi, Arkansas, and Red rivers, the Mississippi enters a birdsfoot-like delta, fanning out and into the Gulf through small and large distributaries (such as the Atchafalaya River and Bayou Lafourche). The main stream continues southeast through the delta, entering the Gulf through several mouths including Southeast and South passes.

The present delta has been built outward by sediment carried by the main stream during the last five centuries. Geologists recognize three earlier deltas, and believe that the river is in the process of abandoning its present course—diverting through the Atchafalaya River—perhaps even in the face of man's greatest technological skills employed to contain it. For here is clearly seen the true power—and indifference—of the river: in a posture of perfect neutrality, the river takes no responsibility for New Orleans, nor for the other cities along its banks, essential though it was and is for their vitality. The stream has been one of the key participants in a compelling drama which, although the setting was only the place where the Mississippi meets the sea, has had worldwide effects and engaged the imaginations of some of modern history's most significant thinkers and doers.

Europeans had been aware of the Mississippi River Valley since the early 1500s, but no attempt had been made to colonize it. The first European to discover the mouth of the Mississippi was probably Alonso Alvarez de Pineda during his exploration of the northern Gulf Coast in 1519. He called the great river the Rio del Espiritu Santo. In 1527 Panfilo de Narvaez, a wealthy Spaniard living in Cuba, set sail from Spain to take possession of Florida and any other land he might want. After a series of disasters and desertions, Narvaez and his small fleet left from the western coast of Florida for Mexico. Soon after sailing past the mouth of the Mississippi, a storm wrecked the

fleet. The few survivors wandered on foot through the swamps and forests for almost 10 years before reaching a Mexican settlement. An account of Narvaez's tragedy, and more important, a description of the coastline, was written later by one of the survivors, Alvar Nunez Cabeza de Vaca.

Another Spaniard, Hernando de Soto, who was intrigued by Vaca's account of the Gulf Coast, landed at Tampa Bay in May 1539. But Soto's expedition was doomed to failure, just as his predecessors' had been. After three years of misery and wandering through present-day Florida, the Carolinas, Alabama, Tennessee, Arkansas, Missouri, and Louisiana, Soto died in May 1542, somewhere on the Mississippi near Arkansas.

While the Spanish were the first to see the mouth of the great river, it was the French—already a formidable presence in the Great Lakes area—who first attempted to settle the Mississippi. In 1682 Robert Cavelier, Sieur de La Salle, became the first known European to reach the mouth of the Mississippi by descending the river. On April 6, after almost two months of traveling, exploring, and visiting with Indian tribes along the way, La Salle and his followers reached the mouth of the river with its brisk currents and vast grassy wetlands. On the morning of April 9, a cross was erected on a chosen spot and after honor was paid to God and the king, La Salle took possession of the territory named for Louis XIV, ". . . as far as its mouth at the sea, or Gulf of Mexico, and also to the mouth of the River of Palms, upon the assurance we have had from the natives of these countries, that we are the first Europeans who have descended or ascended the said river."

It was an acquisition with few parallels in world history, one which caused historian Francis Parkman to remark on the irony of "a feeble human voice inaudible at half a mile" claiming "the fertile plains of Texas; the vast basin of the Mississippi, from its frozen northern springs to the sultry borders of the Gulf; from the woody ridges of the Alleghenies to the peaks of the Rocky Mountains—a region of savannas and forests, sun-cracked deserts, and grassy prairies, watered by a thousand rivers, [and] ranged by a thousand warlike tribes."

Determinedly, La Salle returned to France to organize a new expedition to plant a colony at the mouth of the Mississippi. At that location, he thought he would be able to reap the riches of the interior as well as that in the nearby Spanish shipping lanes.

La Salle and the settlers left France for Louisiana in July 1684. But by accident or by decision, the three small ships bypassed the Mississippi and ended up on the beaches near present-day Galveston, Texas. Two of the ships were lost and the third left the settlers stranded on the beach and returned to France. Three years later, with his dream of a Mississippi colony shattered, La Salle decided to return to Canada. On foot and without charts, the explorer and a small party left the settlement for their long journey. After weeks of wandering, La Salle was killed by his own men. A few survivors made their way back to Canada, but those settlers staying behind at the Texas settlement vanished, falling victim either to Indians or to the Spanish.

During the early 1690s prominent Canadians unsuccessfully urged Louis XIV and his ministers to build a colony in Louisiana. The famous Italian-born explorer Henri de Tonti sent his own request for a Mississippi colony to the king in October 1697. But Tonti's suggestion, like the others, was ignored. The pressure from Canada persisted, however, and finally gained the interest of Louis Phelypeaux, the Comte de Pontchartrain and minister of marine for Louis XIV. France had several good reasons for colonizing Louisiana: namely, to protect and expand her colonial possessions; to contain westward movement by the British on the Atlantic Seaboard, for they had already established trade contacts with the Indians along the Mississippi River; and finally, to serve as a base for raids on the prosperous Spanish sea trade passing through the Gulf.

The French government dispatched Canadian Pierre Le Moyne, Sieur d'Iberville, with his younger brother, Jean Baptiste Le Moyne, Sieur de Bienville, and five small ships on September 24, 1698, to establish a permanent settlement in Louisiana.

On January 24, 1699, Iberville and his expedition anchored off Santa Rosa Island near the mouth of Pensacola Bay. The Spanish, however, had beaten the French to the area with the establishment of a settlement at Pensacola a month before. The Spanish commandant went out to meet the French. He was cordial to the

Frenchmen, but refused to let the intruders enter the bay. Iberville raised anchor and sailed west to Mobile Bay, where he set up a temporary base at Dauphin Island. From the island the explorers sailed further westward, exploring the barrier islands of the Mississippi Sound. Iberville decided to set up his new base at Ship Island and dispatched his younger brother, Bienville, to explore the mainland.

On February 13 Bienville and a small party reached the coast where they encountered a handful of Biloxi Indians who fled at the approach of the white men. Bienville's men were able to capture a few of the sickly ones who could not run fast enough. The Frenchmen offered their infirmed guests the comfort of grass mats to sleep on, but the mats caught fire during the night and the Indians were dispatched to the Great Spirit. Bienville's party later captured a woman of the Biloxi tribe and the same day the Frenchmen came upon a Bayagoula (also spelled Bayougoula) raiding party en route to attack the Mobile Indians. From the Bayagoulas, Bienville learned of a great river, called the Malbanchia, located about a hundred miles to the west. With this Bienville hurried

The Louisiana Territory and its principal river, the Mississippi, dominate this early 18th-century map of North America by Guillaume de L'Isle. (THNOC)

The Canadian-born Le Moyne brothers, Pierre, Sieur d'Iberville, and Jean Baptiste, Sieur de Bienville, entered the mouth of the Mississippi to explore the lower Mississippi Valley and investigate the possibility of colonizing the area. Pierre is on the left, Jean Baptiste is on the right. (THNOC)

back to Ship Island and Iberville.

On February 27 Iberville set out with two *traversiers* and his men to find the Mississippi. After five days of enduring blinding rain and high winds and seas, the Frenchmen found the river on March 3. But Iberville wanted definite proof that he had rediscovered La Salle's river.

Moving upstream the explorers encountered an Indian hunting party that guided them to the Bayagoula village. Here Iberville learned that Tonti had left a letter with the Mougoulachas Indians when he had descended the river in 1686 looking for La Salle's ill-fated expedition. Upon reading the letter, Iberville found the assurance he wanted and wrote, "There is no doubt that the Mississippi is the Malbanchia."

Iberville had fulfilled part of his mission: to rediscover the Mississippi. Now, he turned his attention to the second part of his instructions — building a settlement to protect the Mississippi from other European explorations. Consistent with this purpose, Iberville decided to build Fort Maurepas on Biloxi Bay about a hundred miles northeast of the mouth of the Mississippi.

In May 1699 Iberville made the first of several voyages to France bringing supplies and new settlers to the struggling colony. Iberville warned the king, and his advisors who had opposed the Louisiana venture, that unless France established a strong colony there, "the English colony which has become very consid-

erable will grow in such a manner that in less than one hundred years, she will be strong enough to seize all America and drive out all other nations."

Iberville's fears evidently were not unfounded, for the British had already dispatched an expedition to scout a site for a colony on the Mississippi. On September 15, 1699, Bienville and a small band of Frenchmen were paddling on the Mississippi in two small canoes when they encountered the English corvette *Carolina Galley* at anchor in the river. Bienville approached the ship, told her captain she was in French territory, and ordered him to leave. Should the Englishmen refuse, Bienville said, he would use force. The bluff worked and the 12-gun corvette weighed anchor while its captain threatened to return with a greater force. Bienville, his five men, and two canoes were, of course, in no position to force the ship to leave. But the bend in the river, some dozen miles below present-day New Orleans, where Bienville sent the British downriver shaking their fists, is still known today as English Turn *(Detour des Anglais* or *Detour aux Anglais).*

When Iberville returned to the colony and heard of the British expedition, he quickly ordered the building of Fort de Mississippi on the first high spot above the mouth of the river. This cypress-log fort with four cannons and fifteen men was the first French post in what is now the state of Louisiana. By 1707, however,

the little fort, that was to have defended France's claim to the Mississippi, had been abandoned.

Direct confrontation with the English, however, was the least of the Frenchmen's problems. With English traders pushing westward from the Atlantic Coast, several Indian tribes — including the Caddos, Tunicas, and Muskhogeans, as well as the Choctaws and Chickasaws — were caught between the two European powers vying for dominance in North America. For the French, maintaining diplomatic relations with the Indians was a constant, and not always successful struggle in the face of English intrigues among the tribes. When the numerous tribes were not busy raiding each other, they were killing either Frenchmen or Englishmen depending on which colonial power was exerting the most pressure at the time. During peaceful periods, they provided food for the settlers, hides for the fur trade, and wives for lonely frontiersmen. For many generations the Indians of southeast Louisiana provided foodstuffs for the markets of New Orleans, including fish, game, and one of the seasonings they introduced to Creole cookery: filé, used so often in gumbos.

Iberville's strategy with the Indians, es-pecially the antagonistic Chickasaws, was to convince them of British intentions to enslave them and take their lands. Bienville went one step further in his attempts to keep the powerful Chickasaws in line, by threatening to arm the Choctaws, the Illinois, the Mobilians, and other tribes and encouraging them to make war on the Chickasaws. To further ensure their peaceful cooperation, Iberville wrote to the vicar general of the bishop of Quebec imploring him to dispatch missionaries to live among the Choctaws and Chickasaws.

Nor were the English and the Indians the only problems the French colonists encountered in their Louisiana colony. Critical food shortages constantly reminded the Le Moyne brothers of their dependence on supplies from France and the goodwill of the Indians. Complicating matters further, the early settlers — mainly frontiersmen — were far more interested in trapping and trading than in planting crops. Food shortages in 1709 and 1710 were so severe that the colonists survived on Indian corn, and at one point, Bienville sent many of his soldiers to live among the Indians for survival.

Diseases — especially malaria and swamp fever — also caused terrific losses among the colonists. When Iberville returned from one of

A detail of a map by Thomas Jeffreys from the 1770s shows the site of Fort de la Boulaye, which once stood southwest of Lake Borgne. The fort was an early Mississippi River settlement. (THNOC)

his trips to France in 1701, he found Fort Maurepas decimated by disease, prompting him to gather the survivors, take them to Mobile River, and establish Fort Louis de la Mobile (later moved and renamed Fort Louis de la Louisiane) 55 miles from the mouth of Mobile Bay. Iberville himself died of yellow fever he contracted in Havana in 1706, leaving Bienville as the acting governor of the Louisiana Territory.

For all of these reasons, the early Louisiana settlements remained thinly populated. The most serious barrier to establishing a viable colony, however, remained that of enticing women to reside in the wilderness and raise families.

Despite a shipment of young women to the colony in 1704, the population steadily decreased. That year the population consisted of 180 men, 27 French families with 10 children, 11 Indian slave children, and 4 priests. Four years later it was only 122 men, 24 colonists, 25 children, 28 women, and 80 Indian slaves. Conditions were so adverse, it was reported, that even some French soldiers had deserted to

the English in the Carolinas.

Under these circumstances the colony was of minimal value to France, a situation that the ministry of Louis XIV finally set about remedying and which, in turn, led to the founding of New Orleans. Ironically, it was internal conflict between the French and the French-Canadians at Fort Louis that finally prompted royal intervention.

Bienville, in command since the death of Iberville in 1706, had been having personal problems with commissary Nicolas de La Salle and Father Henri Roulleaux de La Vente, the pastor of the Mobile settlement. Both La Salle and Father de La Vente loathed the Le Moyne brothers and sent numerous letters to their superiors complaining about Bienville, whom the priest called a "rogue." The Canadians, La Salle wrote, "are shiftless and libertines who care only to run the woods." Bienville, in return, leveled his own charges against the commissary and priest. La Salle, he said, constantly tried to undermine the commandant's authority; while the priest, he said, illegally conducted marriage ceremonies between white men and

Among the Indians Iberville had to contend with in the early 1700s were the Choctaws, shown here dressed as warriors carrying scalps. Drawing by A. De Batz. Courtesy, Smithsonian Institution, National Anthropological Archives.

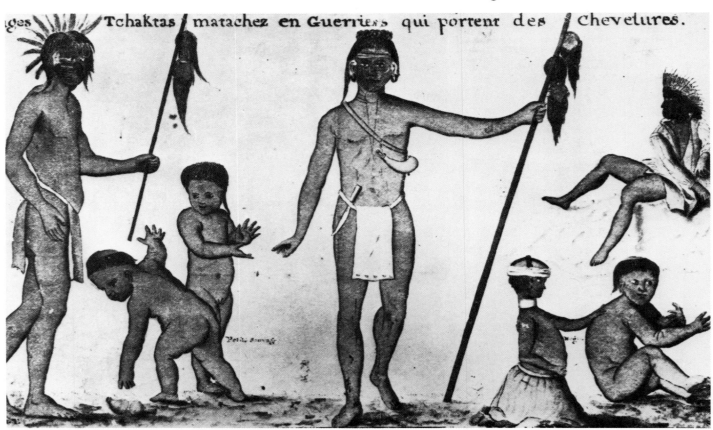

Indian women. He also charged the priest with baptizing children naked in the outdoors, which, he said, resulted in the deaths of several youngsters.

After months of charges and countercharges sailing between France and Louisiana, the French ministry decided to make a change. Louis XIV removed both Bienville and La Salle from office. As replacements, Nicholas Daneau, Sieur de Muy was sent to be governor and Jean-Baptiste-Martin d'Artaguiette d'Iron to be commissary. Daneau de Muy died on the way over and d'Artaguiette arrived in early 1708, immediately setting about investigating the charges leveled by all parties. A month later, d'Artaguiette wrote Pontchartrain not only exonerating, but actually praising Bienville for his efforts under difficult circumstances. Most of all d'Artaguiette pressed the king to realize the importance of Louisiana to France. Its location on the Gulf of Mexico and the Mississippi River was ideal for commerce and the exploitation of the vast and immeasurably wealthy interior of North America.

In 1712 the king, unhappy with the negligible growth in the crown colony and his treasury depleted by the War of Spanish Succession (1701–1714), granted Antoine Crozat a 15-year exclusive charter to Louisiana. Crozat, a wealthy French merchant, was not new to the business of colonial trade. He held stock in the Guinea Company, with its profitable African trade, and in the Asiento Company which carried on a lucrative slave trade between Africa and the New World. Under the terms of the charter, Crozat gained all commercial rights to "Louisiana" south of the Illinois district possessed by the Crown including all the area between Mexico and the Carolinas. Crozat could mine and export ores and precious stones; control all trade in the colony; have full use of all Crown-owned buildings and property in the colony; and the exclusive right to import slaves from Africa. In return Crozat was to colonize and develop the region under the laws, edicts, and ordinances of France.

Crozat was particularly interested in mining the colony and establishing trade with Mexico. So in 1710 he appointed Antoine de La Mothe Cadillac, who supported Crozat's ideas on commerce, to replace Bienville, who favored an agricultural colony, as governor. Cadillac arrived in 1713, carrying a letter from the Crown instructing him to investigate La Salle's earlier charges against Bienville. This initiated a feud between the two men that lasted Cadillac's entire term in Louisiana and that eventually resulted in his removal as governor. Bienville, wounded that he was not made the permanent governor, wrote to the Comte de Pontchartrain, denouncing all charges of wrongdoing. He asked for a pay raise, a promotion, and a new assignment. A year later he got his reply: "Behave yourself and you will get your reward." But neither man seemed able to comply with this edict. Cadillac wrote to France, accusing Bienville of causing trouble among the inhabitants and working against Crozat's interests in the colony. Bienville responded to his superiors that Cadillac criticized him only because he had refused to marry Cadillac's daughter.

The new governor was not long in Louisiana before he managed to alienate almost everyone. His arrogance toward local Indian tribes caused an uprising among the proud Natchez that Bienville had to smooth over. Nor did Cadillac have any kind words for the Louisiana settlers, whom he described as "the dregs of Canada, or the colony." After several years of such acrimony, both Crozat and the Crown realized that Cadillac was not the right man for the job. So Cadillac was recalled, leaving Bienville as the acting governor.

Bienville, however, was replaced quickly with Jean Michiele, Seigneur de Lepinay et de La Longueville, who arrived in March 1717 with Marc Antoine Hubert, the colony's new commissary. The new governor wasted little time before he, like his predecessor, was at odds with Bienville. Lepinay, however, did not last as long as Cadillac and was recalled after only six months. In a letter to France, Hubert claimed Lepinay surely would have destroyed the colony if he had not been removed from office. Bienville was in charge once again.

At about this time Crozat, never even having seen his colony, decided to divest himself of Louisiana which had cost him over 2 million livres in five years. In his letter to the ministry of marine, the merchant-nobleman reflected on the failure of his Louisiana venture to produce the wealth he had imagined: "My three principal projects: discovery of mines of gold and silver, the establishment and maintenance of workers for plantations of tobacco, [and] com-

merce with Spain were dissipated." Crozat asked the Crown to revoke the charter and release him from its responsibilities. On August 13, 1717, Philippe, Duc d'Orleans, and regent for the young Louis XV (Louis XIV had died two years earlier), relieved Crozat from his obligations.

While Crozat took a financial battering in Louisiana, it was the colony that had been truly victimized. Crippled by the laws and regulations of France, by Crozat's monopoly, and by low prices for furs, Louisiana had continued to be a problem rather than an asset. The French throne did not have to wait long before John Law, an adventurous Scotsman, forwarded a new scheme. Law, after founding the "Banque Generale" of France in 1716, convinced the Duc d'Orleans that Louisiana had potential for great wealth if administered properly. He then formed the Company of the West in 1717, a joint-stock company, and sold shares at 500 livres. Rapidly, the value of the shares climbed

to as much as 8,000 livres. On September 6, 1717, the company was granted an exclusive charter to Louisiana, including the Illinois country — an area that had not been part of Crozat's earlier grant. Under the terms of the charter the company promised to send 6,000 settlers and 3,000 slaves to the colony within 10 years. In 1719 the Company of the West was combined with all other French colonizing companies into the Company of the Indies, which promised even greater things for Louisiana. In addition to Louisiana, the new company received charters and special privileges in Africa, Argentina, St. Domingue (Santo Domingo), China, and the East Indies.

Law's Louisiana venture was, perhaps, the biggest and most successful public-relations scheme ever perpetrated on the European people up to that time. Handbills and posters inundated southern Germany, Switzerland, and France encouraging everyone to emigrate to Louisiana, the land of inestimable oppor-

tunities. (There actually were "inestimable opportunities" for some, namely the company's wealthy investors who were given "concessions" of thousands of acres that later were developed into important plantations up and down the river.) Thousands of Germans and Swiss did grab at the opportunity to leave their poverty behind and to make a fresh start in what had been described as a bountiful land.

The success of Law's campaign is also suggested by the variety of colonists attracted. There were the sons of the lesser nobility in France who came to the colony to seek their fortunes, as well as artisans in all of the trades, and even hard-working German farmers who provided the colony with fresh food. (Many of the Germans who remained settled on the west bank of the Mississippi several miles above New Orleans in an area later called the *Cote des Allemands,* or simply *Des Allemands.* German family names gradually gave way to Gallic

spellings and pronunciations, such as *Zweig* (twig) to *LaBranche* or *Himmel* to *Hymel.* The descendants of these Gallicized Germans still live in the area.) Undesirables were also given the opportunity to go and make a new beginning. For a time, convicts and prostitutes were given their freedom if they would marry and go to Louisiana, but the regent ordered this practice stopped in early 1720. Another group, the "casket girls," so-called because each carried a government-issued chest of clothing and linen, came to marry the men who had arrived before them.

The result of this influx during the first four years of Law's control was that the colony's population grew from about 400 to over 8,000, including African slaves. The use of African slaves as opposed to Indian slaves, who were purchased from warring Indian tribes, had proven more satisfactory to the colonists. Indians — both in Louisiana and those shipped to

Below
Antoine Crozat's heavy financial losses in Louisiana from 1712 to 1717 led to a revocation of his charter and the formation of the Company of the West. (THNOC)

Facing page
Le Page Du Pratz, who arrived in the Louisiana colony the year New Orleans was founded, chronicled the plant and animal life of the region and made observations on life in the colony in general. These illustrations of a wildcat, a wood rat, a skunk, and a tree appeared in a history by Le Page. (THNOC)

LETTRES PATENTES

EN FORME D'EDIT,

Portant Establissement d'une Compagnie de Commerce, sous le nom de *Compagnie d'Occident.*

Donné à Paris au mois d'Aoust 1717.

Regiftrées en Parlement.

A PARIS,
DE L'IMPRIMERIE ROYALE.

M. DCCXVII.

LETTRES PATENTES

EN FORME D'EDIT,

Portant Establissement d'une Compagnie de Commerce, sous le nom de Compagnie d'Occident.

Donné à Paris au mois d'Aoust 1717.

Regiftrées en Parlement.

LOUIS PAR LA GRACE DE DIEU ROY DE FRANCE ET DE NAVARRE : A tous prefens & à venir, SALUT. Nous avons depuis noftre avenement à la Couronne travaillé utilement à reftablir le bon ordre dans nos Finances, & à reformer les abus que les longues Guerres avoient donné occafion d'y introduire; Et nous n'avons pas eû moins d'attention au reftabliffement du Commerce de nos Sujets , qui contribue autant à leur bonheur, que la bonne adminiftration de nos Finances. Mais par la connoiffance que Nous avons pris de l'eftat de nos Colonies fituées dans la partie Septentrionale de l'Amerique , Nous avons reconnu qu'elles avoient d'autant plus befoin de noftre protection que le Sr Antoine Crozat auquel le feu Roy noftre tres honoré Seigneur & Bifayeul avoit accor-

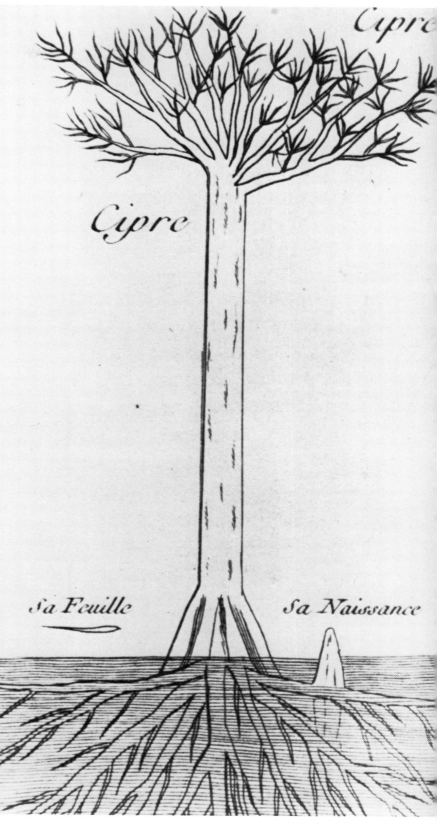

West Indian islands—were of little value to their captors. Those kept in Louisiana usually ran away, while those shipped to the islands pined away until they died.

The Negro trade had not been sanctioned officially until Crozat's 1712 charter. The Company of the West, and its successor, the Company of the Indies, reportedly imported more than 2,000 black slaves by 1731. By 1724 the slave and free-black populations had increased to such numbers that the Crown enacted the *Code Noir*, or Black Code, a far-reaching set of laws that was an adaptation of the code being used in Santo Domingo. The *Code Noir* restricted, protected, and defined the activities of slaves and free blacks. It forbade the practice of any religion other than Roman Catholicism, going so far as to order Jews expelled from the colony. The code prohibited marriage or concubinage between whites and blacks. Slaves could not hold property nor could they be a party to civil suits. Striking a master, his family, or even a free Negro could bring the death penalty for a slave. Although the code was spe-

Although it is believed that slaves were brought to Louisiana as early as 1708, the slave trade was not officially sanctioned until 1712. Slaves were counted in the population of Louisiana. (THNOC)

cific in its regulations, officials were lax in enforcing many of its provisions, especially those concerning coupling between the races.

Because of the *Code Noir,* Negro slaves enjoyed considerably more freedom in colonial Louisiana than their counterparts did in the British colonies. In fact the last article of the code is often considered a precursor to portions of the United States Constitution and its amendments:

We grant to manumitted slaves the same rights, privileges, and immunities which are enjoyed by freeborn persons. It is our pleasure that their merit in having acquired their freedom shall produce in their favor, not only with regard to their persons, but also to their property, the same effects which our other subjects derive from the happy circumstances of their having been born free.

One of Law's major goals was building a permanent settlement on the Mississippi both to cement France's claim to the river valley and to provide the company with a major port where French vessels could fill their holds with the expected riches of Louisiana. A site for the town — to be called New Orleans after the Duc d'Orleans — was chosen 30 leagues upriver at an Indian portage shown to Iberville in 1699. Bienville had pushed for this location because of its elevation and its proximity to Lake Pontchartrain through Bayou St. John, along which French settlers had located since 1708.

Land-clearing at the New Orleans site began in the spring of 1718 under the supervision of Bienville. By the end of the year very little land had actually been cleared of its thick, jungle-like growth, and only a few palmetto huts had been constructed. In 1719 a flood wiped out all that stood, causing company officials to consider moving the town upriver, an idea that was discarded. Very little progress was made in developing New Orleans for the next three years.

The "casket girls" (so called because their belongings were held in small, government-issued chests) were said to be wards of the Ursuline nuns in Louisiana until they found suitable marriage partners. (THNOC)

LE
CODE NOIR,
OU
RECUEIL
DES REGLEMENS
rendus juſqu'à préſent.
CONCERNANT le Gouvernement, l'Adminiſtration de la Juſtice, la Police, la Diſcipline & le Commerce des Negres dans les Colonies Françoiſes.
Et les Conſeils & Compagnies établis à ce ſujet.

A PARIS,
Chez PRAULT, Imprimeur-Libraire; Quai de Gêvres.

M. DCC. LXVII.
AVEC PRIVILEGE DU ROL

The growing slave population of Louisiana caused Bienville to enact the Code Noir (Black Code), which defined the activities in which both slave and free blacks could participate. The code was adopted from a similar code in use in Santo Domingo. (THNOC)

Bienville had returned to the colony at Mobile where he was preoccupied with internal quarrels. But Father Pierre Francois-Xavier de Charlevoix, visiting the primitive settlement in 1721, described what he believed was New Orleans' special destiny:

I have the best grounded hopes for saying that this wild and deserted place, at present almost entirely covered with canes and trees shall one day . . . become the capital of a large and rich colony. . . . Rome and Paris had not such considerable beginnings, were not built under such happy auspices, and their founders met not with the advantages of the Seine and the Tiber, which we have found the Mississippi, in comparison of which, these two rivers are not more than brooks.

Bienville apparently agreed with the good father on the importance of the Mississippi Valley, for in 1719 he moved the capital of Louisiana from Mobile to Biloxi and finally, in 1722, New Orleans became the capital, remaining so until well into the American era.

In March 1721 chief engineer Pierre Le Blond de La Tour dispatched Adrien de Pauger to supervise construction of New Orleans. Despite uncooperative company officials, snakes, mosquitoes, and heavy rains, Pauger and 10 soldiers had cleared enough land in less than a month to plot three streets facing the river. Nine months later, the town had 470 inhabitants. But nature ravaged the settlement again in September 1722 when a hurricane struck, destroying most of the town's buildings. This was in fact fortunate, since none of the original buildings were aligned with the engineer's plan and would have had to be demolished in any case.

The earliest-known complete plan of New Orleans was signed by La Tour and dated April 23, 1722. This plan comprised the section of New Orleans now known as the *Vieux Carre* (Old Square, or French Quarter) that remained the legal extent of the city until the end of the 19th century. Hugging the east bank of the Mississippi on a large crescent bend, the early town was laid out in a grid pattern surrounding a riverfront parade ground called the Place d'Armes (now Jackson Square). Behind the square was space for the parish church. The Church of St. Louis (later St. Louis Cathedral) was first designed by Pauger in 1724 and construction completed in 1727. (The present-day St. Louis Cathedral is the third edifice to stand on that spot.) Following La Tour's plan this time, soldiers, Canadians, Frenchmen, and Negro slaves built sturdier houses and public buildings. The new structures were built of framed timbers with a *bousillage* of clay and moss stuffed between the timbers; the exteriors were covered with wide clapboards. After the first brick kiln was built on the Indian trail leading from the town to Bayou St. John in 1724, bricks-between-posts would replace the clay and moss. The kiln also manufactured roof tiles for the church, government, and other major buildings. (Although early plans of New Orleans indicated pallisades around the town, little effort was made to fortify it until the Natchez Indian massacre in 1729. But even then only part of a moat was completed. Wooden fortifications were not built around the town until 1760 at the height of the French and Indian War.)

Naming the streets of early New Orleans was a masterpiece of 18th-century diplomacy. Bourbon, Orleans, Burgundy, and Royal streets were named for the royal family of France; while the Conti, Chartres, and Conde families were cousins to the Bourbons and Orleans.

The early dwellings of New Orleans were not very substantial structures and were often destroyed by hurricanes and floods. (THNOC)

(Conde Street used to be that section of Chartres stretching from Jackson Square to Esplanade Avenue before it was changed in 1865.) St. Peter Street was named in honor of one of the ancestors of the Bourbon family. The saint-king Louis IX was not forgotten: hence St. Louis Street. Toulouse and Dumaine streets were named for Louis XIV's royal bastards. Louis XV's father, the Duc de Burgundy, was also remembered. By 1728 the settlement, despite its shaky beginnings, was a village. On April 24, 1728, a young Ursuline nun, who had just arrived in New Orleans, described the colonial capital in a letter to her father in France:

Our city is very pretty, well constructed and regularly built. The people have worked and still work to perfect it. The streets are very wide and are laid out in straight lines. The main street is nearly a league in length. The houses are very well built of "collombage et mortier." They are white washed, paneled and filled with sunlight. The roofs of the houses are covered with tiles [shingles] which are pieces of wood in the shape of slate. . . . It suffices to say that there is a song sung openly here in which the words proclaim that this city is as beautiful as Paris.

While New Orleans was taking shape, Bienville once again was having problems with his detractors, most notably with the engineers La Tour and Pauger. The Company of the Indies sent Sieur Jacques de La Chaise and the Sieur de Sauvoy to the colony in 1723 to investigate. The two envoys arrived at Ship Island in early April, but Sauvoy soon died, leaving La Chaise to conduct the inquiry. La Chaise's initial reports to the company were complimentary to Bienville, but later deteriorated as the two became enemies. La Chaise accused Bienville of showing favoritism to the Canadians over native French settlers. Even more devastating was La Chaise's charge that Bienville intentionally tried to undermine the company's economic efforts in the colony, in the hope that the king would revoke the company's charter and give Bienville freer reign to do as he pleased. The weight of these complaints against Bienville became too much to bear for the directors of the company. At their request, the regent, in the name of Louis XV, ordered Bienville back to France and instructed Pierre Dugue de Boisbriant to travel from the Illinois country and take command at New Orleans.

Bienville and his brother, Chateauguay (who had been with Bienville in Louisiana) arrived in France in August of 1725. Bienville's nephews in Louisiana petitioned the regent to reinstate

Below
A year after its founding New Orleans was still a small settlement on a large river as indicated by this 1719 view of the town. (THNOC)

Right
The original city of New Orleans, which now comprises most of the Vieux Carre, was laid out in a regular grid pattern around a central square (the Place d'Armes), now called Jackson Square. (THNOC)

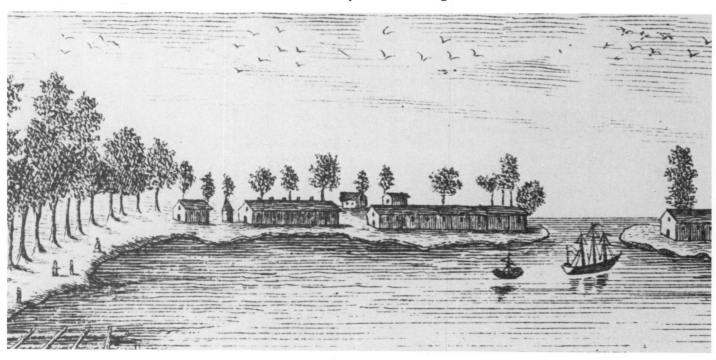

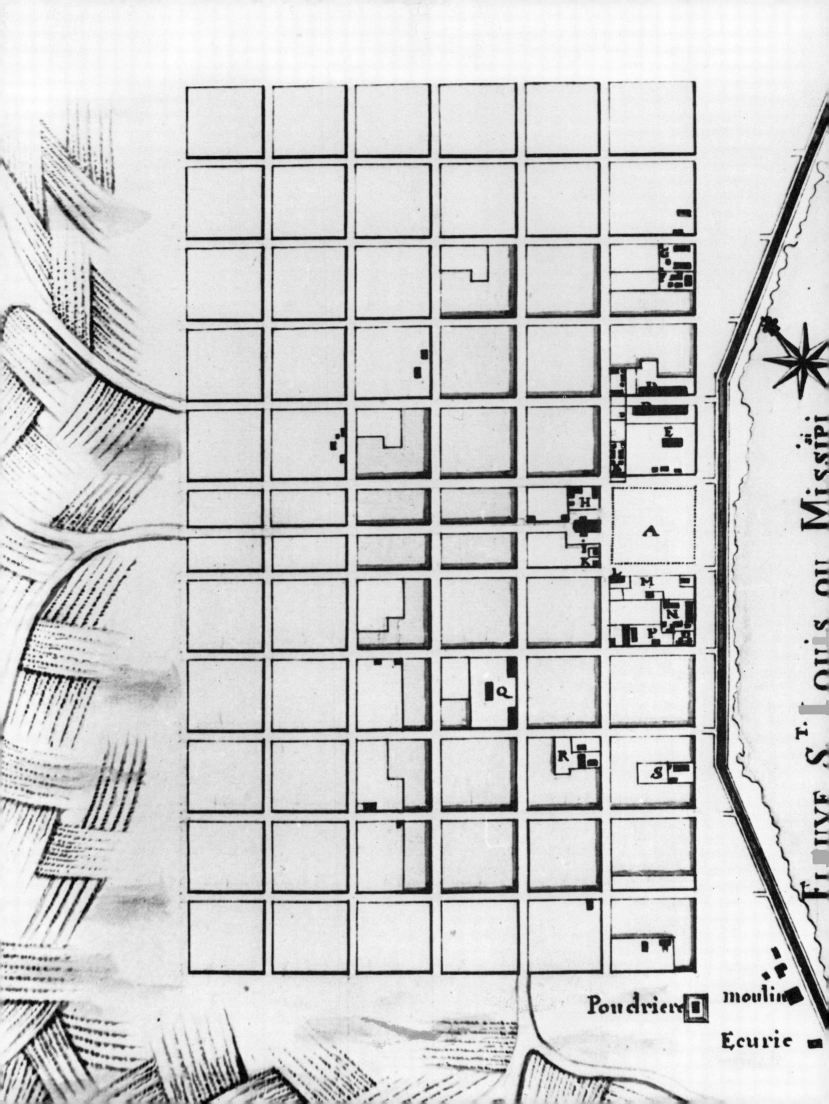

Fleuve St Louis ou Missipi

Poudrier

moulin

Ecurie

their uncle, but to no avail. The regent pensioned Bienville and forbade him, along with Chateauguay, to return to Louisiana.

As if the Company of the Indies did not have enough trouble in Louisiana with Bienville and a feud between the Jesuits and Capuchins over jurisdictional rights, the company's financial condition in France was even worse. By early 1720 Law's so-called "Mississippi Bubble" was in deep financial trouble. All reports from the colony reaching the company's stockholders were bad: Colonists who had come dreaming of a new life were suffering and dying, crops failed, and the promised silver and gold mines did not materialize. The company had received little return on the vast sums of money invested, and the expected trade with the Spanish and English failed to develop to any great extent. Investors began withdrawing gold and silver deposits from the bank, leaving France flooded with paper money. The government tried to avert disaster by printing more money, but the country was on the verge of bankruptcy. An order went out — but was ignored — prohibiting anyone from holding more than 300 livres in gold and silver. Thousands of investors lost their fortunes — including Law, who narrowly escaped being stoned to death by angry mobs in the streets of Paris. For a brief period Law received a pension from the French government, but later he traveled to England and then back to the Continent, where he died in obscurity in 1729.

Soon after the collapse of 1720, the Company of the Indies reorganized and, with fresh money, tried to revitalize the Louisiana venture, but still the profits were not forthcoming. After 1723 the company lost interest in Louisiana because other colonies (for example India where the company held a similar financial arrangement with the Crown) were providing greater return. Finally, after word reached Paris that Fort Rosalie (near present-day Natchez) had been wiped out by Natchez Indians in November 1729, and of the ensuing Indian war, the company's directors threw up their hands. They had had enough. In early 1731 the Crown granted the company's request to be relieved of its reponsibilities in Louisiana.

Despite the company's financial failure in Louisiana, it did succeed in firmly planting the colony's roots in the lower Mississippi Valley. It had founded the city of New Orleans which, because of its position near the mouth of the Mississippi, was destined to become one of the most important ports in North America. In addition, the population of the colony had grown from less than 1,000 in 1717 to over 7,000 by 1731. But most importantly, the company gave the colony an economy — industry, commerce, and trade conducted by company agents and planter-merchants.

The industry and manufacturing in French colonial Louisiana was small-scale. Plantations produced bricks, candles, faience, tiles, lumber, pitch and tar, and barrels, surpluses of which were an important part of Louisiana's export trade. Records indicate that during the colony's early years it had already built up an assortment of artisans and tradesmen, including bakers, armorers, carpenters, locksmiths, harnessmakers, millwrights, barbers, coopers, stonemasons, gold and silversmiths, tanners, tailors, blacksmiths, shipbuilders, cabinetmakers, toolmakers, a wig-maker, and a baker.

Because the usual objects of European colonization — commodities such as gold, silver, and spices — did not materialize, commerce and trade became colonial Louisiana's primary industry. During the first 60 years of the colony's existence, Louisianians maintained a moderately successful import and export trade with France, the Spanish in Florida, the West Indies, the Illinois country, and the British colonies on the Atlantic. Ships carrying commodities to and from these points encountered numerous difficulties, however. Storms, poorly built

After the hurricane of 1722 flattened the settlement at New Orleans, Adrien De Pauger, working with plans from chief engineer Le Blond de La Tour, laid out the streets of New Orleans in a grid-like pattern. (THNOC)

ships, privateers and pirates, and the repeated skirmishes between the colonial powers, not to mention the financial solvency of the colonial entrepreneurs, hampered the young colony's growth. Nonetheless, goods got through. Ships from France brought spices, cloth, cutlery, utensils, wines, food, and other items, including luxury goods. Louisianians sent France tobacco, indigo, lead, sassafras, quinine, naval stores, and lumber. To the West Indies, which became increasingly important to Louisiana's trade after 1720, went lumber, meats, bricks, tiles, corn, beans, naval stores, and tallow. Ships returned with sugar, coffee, rum, rare woods, drugs, cocoa, tanned leather, spices, tortoise shell, syrup, and other "goods," including slaves.

Louisianians at times conducted a small amount of trade with their Spanish neighbors in Florida and the English along the Atlantic Seaboard. Although trade with these colonies was illegal, Louisianians continued to smuggle in British goods even when France and England were at war with each other. British colonials had manufactured goods to sell and the French colonists desperately needed them.

New Orleans and other French Gulf Coast ports were also the exchange points connecting Europe and the West Indies with the wild and rugged back country and upper regions of the Mississippi River. From the Illinois country came lead, furs and hides, flour, corn, beef, pork, tallow, lard, tobacco, leather, lumber, and beeswax. The lower Mississippi and its tributaries also exported tobacco, indigo, cotton, lumber, tallow, and vegetables. Boats, pack trains, and traders returned up the treacherous river loaded with manufactured goods such as liquor, furniture, tools, farming equipment, and items used to trade with the Indians.

After the Company of the Indies withdrew from Louisiana in 1731, the colony was once again under royal control. The governor was Etienne de Perier, who had replaced Boisbriant in 1726. His administration had been plagued by Indian troubles, especially with the Chickasaws and with the Natchez massacre in 1729. In 1732 the Crown asked 52-year-old Bienville to come out of retirement to be governor of Louisiana for the fourth time. Upon his return to the colony, Bienville immediately set about rejuvenating the spirits of the demoralized colony. Soldiers were put to work repairing military equipment and rebuilding barracks. Civilians gathered food and repaired buildings that had been damaged or simply permitted to decay. Then Bienville turned to reestablishing diplomatic relations with the Indians.

Lumbering was just one of the industries in colonial Louisiana. Surplus products from such industries were important sources of export from the colony. (THNOC)

The British had been successful in enticing the Chickasaws and other tribes into their camp and were making headway in alluring the Choctaws. Bienville thought that the best way to teach the Chickasaws a lesson would be to attack their strongholds. With the help of Choctaws, who had been won back by the French, the veteran Canadian launched a coordinated offensive in the summer of 1736. After four years of intermittent bloodshed during which Bienville had been unable to subdue the Chickasaws, he finally signed a peace treaty with them in 1740. Bienville once again was relieved of office in May 1743, but this time at his own request. He sailed for France, never to return to Louisiana.

His replacement was Pierre-Cavagnial de Rigaud, Marquis de Vaudreuil, the brash, arrogant, and flashy son of a former governor of Canada. Vaudreuil's administration in Louisiana has become best known for its colonial-styled Versailles elegance, high society, and corruption. Although popular with the colony's elite, the "Grand Marquis," as Vaudreuil was nicknamed, and his wife were loathed by those outside the inner-circle coterie. Reports reaching France accused the governor of selling military supplies to the highest bidder while issuing inferior goods to the troops; granting monopolies to a favorite few; and forcing merchants to sell goods owned by the governor and his wife at fixed prices.

Vaudreuil inherited Bienville's problems with the Chickasaws with whom peace was fragile at best. When the French were unable to match the quality of British trading goods, the Chickasaws, and a few Choctaws, once again went over to the British. In 1747, and again in 1748, the Indians marched south, raiding and burning white settlements along the Mississippi. Many settlers were killed and others fled to New Orleans for protection. By 1752 Vaudreuil had had enough. He sent a large force against the Indians, burned their villages, and destroyed their crops. The French had little trouble with the Chickasaws thereafter. Military morale and discipline, however, declined to a new low and public morality degenerated to a point that in 1751 Vaudreuil promulgated strict police regulations governing the behavior of the general populace.

Trade and commerce began to languish in the colony during Vaudreuil's administration, while the volume of smuggled British goods increased. But also during this period an addition was made to the Louisiana economy that would have far-reaching importance. Jesuits in Santo Domingo sent sugarcane to their Louisiana colleagues to see how it would grow along the Mississippi. Experiments with the plant had been conducted as early as 1742, but it was not until 1751 that sugarcane plantations began modest production that would grow into such an important industry for the state.

In 1752 Vaudreuil was rewarded for his services with an appointment as governor of Canada. He was succeeded in Louisiana by Louis Billouart, Chevalier de Kerlerec, a capable navy veteran who had the misfortune to be governor of Louisiana during the French and Indian War, when France lost most of its colonial empire. Unlike Vaudreuil, Kerlerec enjoyed considerable success in regaining an alliance with the Choctaws and other Indian tribes of colonial Louisiana. Although Kerlerec lost many of his troops to the war raging in North America, he managed to strengthen the colony's defenses. He built a wall around the city of New Orleans in 1760, and placed a ship at the mouth of the Mississippi to be sunk in case of a British invasion.

But like Bienville, Kerlerec had problems with infighting. Beginning in 1759 a group of officers and officials plotted to have him removed from office. After four years, the conspiracy finally was broken and the conspirators were sent to France, where they were held as guests of the Crown in the Bastille. Kerlerec also had constant problems with his commissary, Vincent-Pierre-Gaspard, Sieur de Rochemore, and Rochemore's successor, Nicolas-Denis Foucault who, like his predecessor, schemed against the governor. Moreover, he inherited the ongoing feud between the Jesuits and Capuchins. The Jesuits eventually were expelled from the colony.

In 1763 Kerlerec, who had served the Crown and the colony well, returned to France, where his enemies were waiting. He was thrown into the Bastille, but his few friends finally secured his release shortly before he died.

When Kerlerec boarded the ship for France, he and other Louisianians had no way of knowing Louisiana was no longer a French possession. Unbeknownst to all but a select few, it had been passed to Spain a year before.

Facing page
This French view of New Orleans-area Indians in a trade canoe from the west bank of the Mississippi is one of the very few depictions of Louisiana Indian activity to survive from colonial times. The picture is dated 1726.

The First Louisianians

Caddos, Tunicas, Natchez, Atakapas, Chitimachas, and Muskhogeans today are strange-sounding words with only a little relevance to present-day Louisianians. But to the Le Moyne brothers—Bienville and Iberville—and the early French settlers in colonial Louisiana, these words had extreme significance as the names of the six Indian family groups in what is now the state of Louisiana. During the early years of French colonization on the Gulf Coast, these tribes—the Bayougoulas (often spelled Bayagoulas), the Mougoulachas, the Chitimachas, Acalopisas, Tunicas, and Natchez Indians—often gave assistance to the French that meant the difference between survival and death. They provided food, knowledge of the terrain, clothing, and, at times, shelter and companionship for the struggling Louisiana colonists.

Some accounts report that almost 13,000 Indians inhabited what is today the state of Louisiana when the French arrived in 1699. Most of them built their villages along the bayous, rivers, and lakes in southern and southeastern Louisiana. Today's metropolitan New Orleans was once the territory of the Muskhogean family, whose scattered tribes occupied areas now known as the Florida and River parishes, from West Feliciana and Point Coupee parishes to the mouth of the Mississippi. From two of these tribes, the Bayougoulas and Mougoulachas, Iberville learned in 1699 the location of the Mississippi River and of an Indian portage on the Mississippi close to Lake Pontchartrain which later became the site of the city of New Orleans.

Until recently, knowledge of these pre-European aborigines was limited to the first-hand accounts of clerics, explorers, military officers, government officials, and settlers. Today professionally trained archaeologists, searching ancient village sites and burial grounds, are unlocking the secrets of these ancient people.

The Canadians and Frenchmen found the culture of the Indian tribes of south Louisiana to be well defined, but still quite primitive. Their somewhat circular villages (which lacked protective palisades) were composed of round huts built of poles and thatched with grass, palmetto leaves, or other vegetation and arranged around a ceremonial lodge and open space. Their possessions generally comprised little more than a few bowls, baskets, jars, bedding, and weapons. The usual sustenance consisted of corn, beans, sweet potatoes, pumpkins, berries, nuts, fish, as well as the wild game they killed with their bows and cane arrows, spears, and reed blowguns. Transportation for the Indians of southeastern Louisiana was limited to walking or riding in a dugout canoe made from a cypress log.

The Indians' clothing, of course, was adapted to the seasons. They wore robes of animal skins during the cold winter months; but during the hot season, which was a considerable portion of the year, men wore only breechclouts. Women usually wore full-length dresses, but on occasion they joined the menfolk with the simple but colorfully decorated breechclout made of bark. Some tribes permit-

ted the men to wear nothing at all during extremely warm weather. By all accounts, the Indians of Louisiana were fond of colorful clothing, and most tribes took great delight in tattooing and painting designs on various parts of their bodies. Some tribes followed the custom of shaping the heads of their children by fastening a flat piece of wood to the forehead and another to the back of the head with leather straps. As the child's head grew, the wood and bindings forced the head to grow flat and oval-shaped.

Louisiana's early Indian tribes had a strong sense of morality and were deeply religious. They resisted the Biblical teachings of the early French missionaries, clinging tenaciously to their own gods and beliefs. Sometimes these beliefs and customs proved to be too much even for the Europeans who were themselves no strangers to death and mutilation in the name of God and the king.

Andre Penigault, a master carpenter who recorded Iberville's expedition to Louisiana, described a scene among the Taensa tribe:

A frightful thunderstorm suddenly arose: lightning struck their temple, burned all their idols, and reduced their temple to ashes. Immediately the savages ran out in front of their temple making horrible shrieks, tearing out their hair, and raising their arms aloft. Facing their temple, they invoked the Great Spirit, like men possessed, to extinguish the fire; then they seized dirt and smeared it on their bodies and their faces. Fathers and mothers brought their children and strangled them and cast them into the fire. . . . In spite of all our efforts they succeeded in throwing seventeen of them into the fire; and had we not hindered them, they would have thrown more than two hundred.

Most of the Indian tribes kept their religious beliefs to themselves. The Yazoos believed in the Great Spirit Minguo-Chitou. The Tunicas had nine gods: heaven, earth, the sun, fire, thunder, and the four points of the compass. The Chitimachas and most other tribes had numerous gods of varying importance with an entire set of ceremonies and beliefs surrounding each. The Caddos had a curious belief in their teachings which followed closely the story of the Great Flood in the Judeo-Christian Bible. According to the Indian legend, there once was a flood which destroyed the people except for a few that the Great Spirit led to a high hill. The people of the world today were descendants of those few survivors.

By the mid-1700s the native Louisiana tribes were no longer a threat to the French. Instead, the French became embroiled with the English in a life and death struggle for colonial domination in North America with two mighty southern Indian nations—the Choctaws and Chickasaws—caught in the middle of the bloody diplomacy.

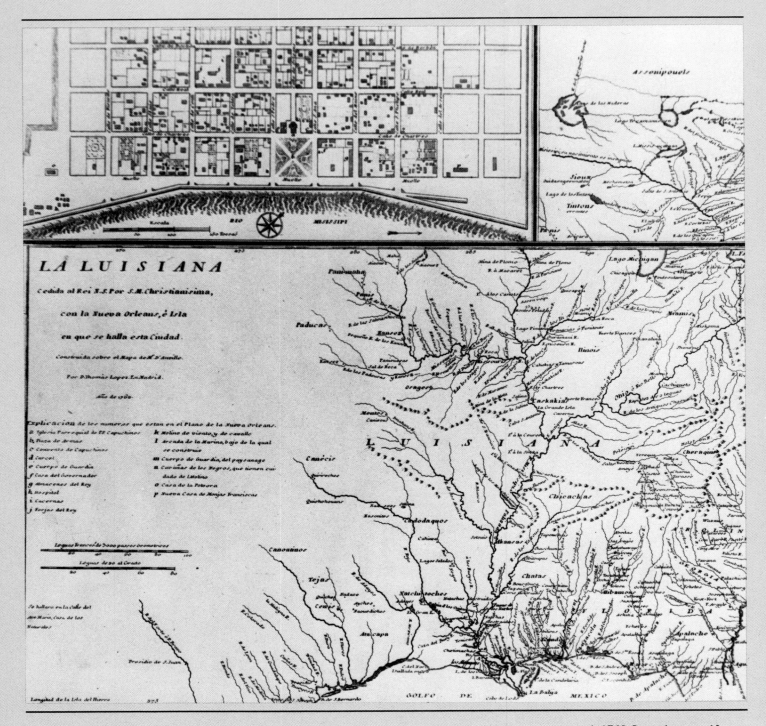

A 1762 Spanish map of La Luisiana. The Spanish were interested in Louisiana mainly because it provided a buffer to westward expansion by English colonies on the Eastern Seaboard. (THNOC)

For almost a century and a half, the three major European colonial powers in North America—France, England, and Spain—had been expanding their borders and claims further into the western wilderness. By the early 1750s both France and England were claiming one area, the Ohio Valley. A military confrontation developed in North America in 1754 and spread to Europe in 1756. Sides were quickly chosen by the European continental powers as the fighting spread to India, the Mediterranean, and the East and West Indies. In 1762 Spain entered the war in an unsuccessful attempt to turn the balance of power in favor of France. The "Seven Years War," as it was known in Europe, or the "French and Indian War," according to the British colonists in America, would realign the colonial structure throughout the world.

The war ended in 1763 with the Treaty of Paris. Defeated France was forced to cede to Great Britain all of its territory in North America, including Canada and Louisiana east of the Mississippi. It kept two small islands in the St. Lawrence River and later regained two of its rich West Indian sugar islands—Guadeloupe and Martinique—as well as some of its holdings in India and Africa. By treaty the British returned to Spain the Philippine Islands and Cuba, which had been captured by the British, in return for both East and West Florida.

New Orleans and Louisiana west of the Mississippi were not included in the treaty concessions. Louis XV of France had given western Louisiana and the "Isle of Orleans" the year before to his cousin Carlos III, king of Spain, through a secret treaty signed in 1762 at Fontainebleau, France. France had been able to convince Spain and Britain that New Orleans was on an island, and therefore was not part of the eastern bank of the Mississippi. As proof they pointed to maps showing the city on a narrow finger of land surrounded completely by water. According to the French, and later the Spanish, the "island" was bordered to the south by the Mississippi and to the north by lakes Pontchartrain and Maurepas. The lakes and the Mississippi were connected by Bayou Manchac, which connected with the Amite

River and then emptied into Lake Maurepas. The island's aqueous border to the east was formed by the lakes emptying into Lake Borgne and then into the open Gulf.

Louis XV apparently decided to cede Louisiana for both economic and political reasons. Louisiana had cost the Crown a considerable amount of money with little in return. In addition, the commercial class in France wanted nothing to do with the colony after the burst of the "Mississippi Bubble." Under these circumstances, Louis began to use the colony as a pawn to achieve his purposes in the war over colonial territory. First in 1761 France offered to give Louisiana to Spain if Carlos III would grant France a loan and enter the war against England. The Spanish monarch wanted Louisiana, but he refused France's conditions. In the meantime, Spain offered to act as a mediator for England and France, but the British refused, accusing Spain of openly aiding France. The situation changed drastically when England declared war on Spain on January 2, 1762. During the rest of that year, British troops brought havoc to Spain's colonial possessions. By August France wanted peace with Britain; but peace was impossible while Spain was still fighting them. Again the French monarch offered Louisiana to his Spanish cousin, but this time to end the fighting—not to enter it. A month later the offer was looking better to King Carlos after Havana had fallen to the British. English troops were already in Florida, and if they should reach Louisiana as well, the British would soon walk through the front door to the riches of New Spain. So Spain accepted France's offer of Louisiana, hoping to limit the expansion of the British, whose territory already extended west to the Mississippi River.

With the signing of the Treaty of Fountainebleau and the Treaty of Paris the following year, Louisiana's days as a French colony ended. Louisiana west of the Mississippi and the Isle of Orleans were Spanish, while Louisiana east of the Mississippi belonged to the British.

Although Louisiana and New Orleans officially belonged to Spain as of 1762, Louisian-

Antonio de Ulloa arrived in New Orleans in 1766 as the first Spanish governor of Louisiana. His arrival and ensuing policies brought much displeasure to the strongly loyal French colonists living in the territory. (THNOC)

ians were ignorant of this fact until October 1764. The transfer was announced to the stunned colonists by Jean Jacques-Blaise d'Abbadie, who had succeeded Governor Kerlerec in 1763. The economy of the colony during this period suffered not only as a result of France's continued neglect, but also because West Indies merchants refused to trade with the colony until its position in either the French or Spanish colonial system was clarified. Events over the next four years continued to deteriorate, giving rise to the much-celebrated, and often romanticized Revolution of 1768, which has been described as the first revolt on American soil against a foreign monarch. The news of the transfer prompted a mass meeting in New Orleans to decide upon a course of action. At the suggestion of Attorney General Nicolas Chauvin de Lafreniere, Jean Milhet — the richest man in New Orleans — was chosen to go to the French court in Paris and petition the king to keep Louisiana. In Paris Milhet enlisted the aid of Bienville, now in his eighties. But even with the venerable Bienville at his side, Milhet could not change the mind of Louis XV's minister of state, the Duc de Choiseul, who had been instrumental in convincing the king to give up Louisiana in the first place. Choiseul offered his regrets, but said there was nothing he could do.

All hope vanished when word reached the colony that Don Antonio de Ulloa, a respected Spanish scientist and captain of the royal navy, had been appointed the first Spanish governor of Louisiana. Unfortunately, communications with the colony were sketchy and Louisianians were apprehensive about the changes the Spanish would bring. Perhaps some of their fears would have been quieted had they known Ulloa's initial instructions from Carlos III:

I have decided that in this new acquisition, for the present, no change in the system of government shall be undertaken and consequently, that in no way shall it be subject to the laws and practices observed in my dominion of the Indies, but that it shall be regarded as a separate colony, even with respect to all trade between them.

On July 10, 1765, Ulloa wrote to the Superior Council in Louisiana, stating he expected to arrive in the near future. Eight months passed, however, before the new governor set foot on Louisiana soil, and when he did drop anchor on March 5, 1766, he came utterly ill-prepared for the task. Waiting to greet the new Spanish governor was Captain Charles Philippe Aubry, the highest-ranking official in the colony since the death of d'Abbadie. Ulloa had brought with him only three civil officials and 90 Spanish troops under the mistaken impression that French troops in Louisiana would join his forces. On the advice of Aubry, Ulloa delayed taking formal possession of the colony until extra troops could be sent to man the various garrisons; these troops never arrived. This led to the bizarre situation of Ulloa attempting to govern the colony through Aubry.

The predominantly French population, already angered by the cession of their colony and a worsening economy, bristled at the tactless Ulloa, who found himself with a multitude of problems. He infuriated the colonists by leaving New Orleans and staying for seven months at La Balize near the mouth of the river where he awaited his Peruvian fiancee. Ulloa added to his problems when he married her at La Balize instead of in New Orleans.

From the beginning Ulloa was engaged in a power struggle with the Superior Council. In addition, the Crown had a change of mind and imposed on Louisiana mercantile regulations similar to those being enforced in other dominions. The commercial edict of May 6, 1766, restricted foreign commerce to a few Spanish colonies and Spain, Martinique, Santo Domingo, and France. Smuggling was to be stopped and the governor would fix all import and export prices. Another edict promulgated in March 1768 restricted trade to certain Spanish ports. Under pressure from the Superior Council, Aubry did not enforce the unpopular edicts and Ulloa backed down. (Louisianians from the early days of the colony had enjoyed almost free trade through the neglect of France or an inability to stop it in the case of the Company of the Indies.) Compounding Ulloa's problems was a lack of money and support from Spain. The government, as well as the merchants and planters, slipped deeper into debt because Spain failed to send silver currency to the colony. The value of paper currency declined rapidly and Ulloa implored his superiors to send silver to pay the government's debts.

By the end of 1767 finances in the colony were near chaos. In a letter to his superior — the governor of Havana — Ulloa expressed grievous concern:

Having described to Your Excellency on previous occasions the miserable and critical state in which this colony finds itself through lack of funds, I have nothing more to add, because the longer the delay the more the want and troubles increase.

Six months later, Ulloa sent a stronger letter of warning to Havana. The financial situation had become so desperate in the colony that dangerous clouds of trouble were lurking. He reminded his superior that Louisianians were new subjects of the Crown. "Their fealty has not become deep-rooted nor their confidence been won, [that] distrust cannot fail to be widespread."

By 1768 Lafreniere, along with a dozen or so important business, military, and political leaders in the colony, had had enough of Ulloa. They conspired to rid the colony of him and the Spanish. To do so they needed the masses behind them. Lafreniere was the leader and voice of the revolt. To enlist the aid of the newly arriving Acadians, the conspirators told them that Ulloa had planned to sell them into slavery. John Law's Germans living upriver were told that Ulloa had no intention of paying the money owed them by the Spanish. When Ulloa learned what the rebels were saying, he sent an envoy to pay the Germans; but before the envoy could carry out his assignment, he was arrested by the conspirators.

The night before the guns guarding the entrances to the city had been spiked. On the morning of the 28th, upon learning that Ulloa had rejected the Superior Council's demands, about a thousand armed colonists, including Acadians and Germans residing upriver from New Orleans, marched into the city. Ulloa and his wife took refuge on the Spanish frigate *El Volante* and later transferred to the French ship, *Le Cesar*. On November 1 they set sail for Havana. Ulloa's three civil officials, however, Esteban Gayarre, Martin Narvaro, and Jose de Loyola, were held by the rebels as security for debts owed to the colonists by the Spanish government.

Having forced Ulloa to leave in a bloodless coup, the rebels asked the French monarch to take Louisiana back into his fold. Again they were refused. One rebel, Pierre Marquis, a colonel general of the colonial militia, suggested Louisiana be declared a republic. His idea was given some consideration by the Spanish king and his ministers, but it was dismissed. Most of the petitioners declared their loyalty to France.

Both Ulloa and Aubry urged their superiors to punish the rebels, and especially Lafreniere. In a letter to the governor of Havana, dated December 8, 1768, Ulloa said he could not return to Louisiana under the existing circumstances. Moreover, he wrote, his initial and subsequent instructions from the Crown were not enforceable since the colonists were not loyal to Spain. But the colony's fate was not destined to be left in the hands of the rebels. It had been decided in Spain that however insignificant Louisiana might be in the Spanish empire, the Crown could not allow its prestige to be tarnished by a handful of rebels. Besides, the colony was still of value to the empire as a buffer to the westward-expanding English colonists on the Atlantic Seaboard.

All doubts about Louisiana's immediate fate were removed from the rebel's minds on July 24, 1769, when the Spanish fleet dropped anchor at the mouth of the river. On board was General Alexander (Alejandro) O'Reilly — a native Irishman in the Spanish service — with 2,600 Spanish troops under his command.

O'Reilly, like so many of his countrymen, left Ireland to join the Spanish, French, or any other army with an excuse to fight England. His father, Thomas O'Reilly, had been a lieutenant in "Reilly's Dragoons" in the Spanish army. Alexander distinguished himself during the French and Indian War, first in the Austrian army, then in the French, and later as a lieutenant colonel in the Spanish army. During the war he led a brigade that captured Chares and Pancorro in Portugal, which was allied with England. After the war and several promotions later, O'Reilly reorganized the government and army in Cuba, founded a military academy at Avila in Spain, and became military governor of Madrid, where he saved Carlos III from angry mobs during the Madrid riots of 1765. A grateful king promoted the Irishman to the rank of lieutenant general; and when the king decided to suppress the revolt in his new Loui-

DON ALESSANDRO
O'REILLY

siana colony, O'Reilly was his man for the job.

When word reached New Orleans of O'Reilly's arrival, Lafreniere and two rebel ring-leaders asked Aubry for a letter of introduction to O'Reilly so they could explain their actions and profess their obedience to the Spanish Crown. They implored the king's representa-tive not to treat the colony as a conquered land. O'Reilly heard their arguments, treated them cordially, and sent them back to New Orleans confident that all would be well. O'Reilly ar-rived in New Orleans with full force on August 18. Salutes were fired, down came the flag of France, and up went the Spanish colors. During formal ceremonies in the Place d'Armes, Aubry handed over the keys to the city to Spain.

O'Reilly wasted little time. Three days after his arrival in the city, he ordered the arrest and trial of the 12 leaders of the conspiracy. On October 24 O'Reilly handed down the court's decision: Six, including Lafreniere, were to be executed, and the others were to be im-prisoned and have their property confiscated. (One of the rebel leaders sentenced to death already had died in a Spanish prison ship while awaiting trial.) In an act of conciliation, O'Reilly granted a general amnesty to everyone else who had signed the petition expelling Ulloa or who had participated in the revolt. The next day Lafreniere and four of his fellow conspira-tors were shot to death by a firing squad close to the present-day site of the old U.S. Mint building at the foot of Esplanade Avenue. From one pro-rebel account came Lafreniere's dying words: "To die for our king—to die French-men—is there anything more glorious?" An-other account has Lafreniere sounding the call of liberty: "I do not fear death . . . the cry of liberty has been heard, it will conquer later."

With the revolt suppressed and its leaders either dead or imprisoned, "Bloody" O'Reilly, so-called by future generations of Louisianians, went about reorganizing the colony with an almost free hand given to him by the Crown. He improved the colony's fortifications and met with the chiefs of the various Indian tribes. He ordered a census taken which placed the population of New Orleans at 3,190 inhabitants and the entire colony at 13,500. (The popula-tion had more than doubled since the early 1740s.) The new settlers included several thou-sand Acadians who began arriving from Nova Scotia during and shortly after the French and

Indian War. O'Reilly abolished the Superior Council and created the Cabildo, or town coun-cil (the building on Jackson Square got its name for the council, or *cabildo,* which met within its walls). He also issued the "Ordinances and In-structions of Don Alexander O'Reilly" or "O'Reilly's Code," as it was called, which was a combination of Spanish laws and regulations used in other Spanish colonies, his own regula-tions, and a variation of the French *Code Noir* of 1724.

To help economic matters, O'Reilly eased commercial and trade regulations, recommend-ing free trade with Spain and Havana, and tem-porarily suspended import and export duties. Although smuggling remained illegal, he looked the other way at illegal trade with the British in West Florida when it was beneficial to the economy of the colony. He also abolished the remnants of the Indian slave trade. By mid-February 1770, O'Reilly was satisfied that he had done all that was necessary to fix Louisiana in Spain's colonial orbit. A month later, O'Reilly turned the colony over to his suc-cessor, Don Luis de Unzaga y Amezaga, and left for Spain, where he arrived by way of Havana at the end of May. For his service in Louisiana, O'Reilly was promoted to director-general of the Spanish infantry.

Unzaga, who had been colonel of the Reg-

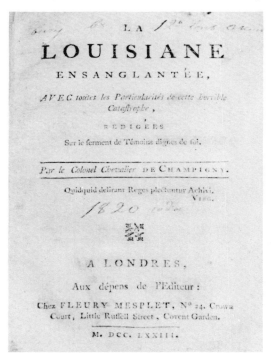

iment of Havana before coming to Louisiana, carried on O'Reilly's goal of making Louisiana a loyal Spanish colony. He endeared himself to French Louisianians by marrying a local girl of the St. Maxent family; ironically, she was a relative of one of the rebels executed by his predecessor. He too overlooked illegal trade with the British in West Florida and along the Gulf Coast. Unzaga, like some of his French predecessors, had problems with religious disputes in the colony, especially squabbles between the Spanish and French Capuchins. It was during his administration that the American Revolution broke out. Although the fighting was in the distant old Northwest and Atlantic Seaboard, Unzaga gave considerable aid and supplies to the Americans. Unzaga, weary from his years in office, wrote repeatedly to his superiors, pleading with them to let him retire and return to Spain. But instead of a most deserved retirement, he was named captain general of Caracas.

On January 1, 1777, Unzaga was succeeded by one of the most colorful, capable, and popular figures in Louisiana's colonial history: 29-year-old Bernardo de Galvez, colonel of the Louisiana Regiment. Galvez was the scion of a distinguished Spanish family. His father, Don Matias de Galvez, served as captain general of Guatemala and viceroy of Mexico. His uncle, Don Jose de Galvez, was Carlos III's secretary of state and president of the Council of the Indies.

Galvez, who had served under O'Reilly in Algiers, was popular among Louisiana colonials because of his amiable nature and his ability to deal with and understand the personality of the predominantly French Creoles. Like his predecessor Unzaga, Galvez married a Louisiana Creole, Felicie de St. Maxent d'Estrehan. (Apparently Unzaga's example was followed by several other high-ranking Spanish officials in the colony. Don Esteban Miro, a military officer and a later governor of Louisiana, married Marie Celeste Elenore de Macarty. Jacinto Panis, another military officer who would be important in future military expeditions against the British in West Florida, wedded the widow of one of the men executed by O'Reilly.)

Soon after Galvez's arrival in the colonies, he began rebuilding the city's defenses and constructing naval craft to take control of the Mississippi in case Spain was drawn into war with Great Britain. In subsequent months he increased the number of men bearing arms from 437 to almost 1,500, adding to the ranks new recruits arriving from Mexico and the Canary Islands. He also secured the loyalty of local Indian tribes. In another move guaranteed to find favor among colonials, Galvez reduced export duties and held meetings with planters to discuss their problems. This young governor also permitted trade with the British in West Florida. But most of all Galvez gained prominence in the annals of Louisiana history for his aid to the Americans rebelling against England and his daring invasions of British West Florida.

After the Treaty of Paris of 1763, the British were quick to settle Florida and Louisiana east of the Mississippi. This included the former French territory stretching from Baton Rouge through what today is the Florida Parishes north of Lake Pontchartrain to the Perdido River east of Mobile. The British divided these colonies into West and East Florida. Today the predominantly Anglo-Saxon look of this area is in marked contrast to the unmistakable Gallic-Hispanic one found south and west of Lake Pontchartrain.

Spanish Louisiana contributed heavily to the cause of the British-American colonists in their revolt against Great Britain. Beginning during the term of Governor Unzaga, and increasing under Galvez, the Spanish sent quantities of supplies and munitions to the American rebels.

The Spanish also permitted an American agent, Oliver Pollock, to conduct the affairs of the rebel government in New Orleans. Oliver Pollock played a prominent role in the American Revolution, but has received little more than a footnote in history. Pollock came to William Penn's colony from his native Ireland in 1760. While still in his early twenties, he became a trader with many business dealings in the Spanish West Indies. During a voyage to Cuba after the French and Indian War, he befriended a Spanish official and fellow Irishman, Alexander O'Reilly. The fortunes of business took Pollock to New Orleans in 1768, where he renewed his friendship with O'Reilly. Not long after his arrival Pollock rescued the colony during a food shortage by selling a shipment of flour to O'Reilly almost at cost. Being on the good side of O'Reilly, and his successor Unzaga, meant special favors for Pollock which certainly were good for business. In less than five years, Pollock had amassed considerable wealth and had trading interests stretching from upper and lower Louisiana to the West Indies. When the American Revolution broke out, the Continental Congress appointed Pollock to be its purchasing agent in New Orleans. With the help of Unzaga, and later Galvez, Pollock was able to send large quantities of supplies to the American forces. Pollock's shipments have been credited with enabling George Rogers Clark's successful campaign against the British in the old Northwest.

Pollock's devotion to the American cause also resulted in his financial ruin. The Continental Congress badly needed the supplies Pollock sent, but it was slow in sending money to pay for them. The American agent used his own money until that ran out and then borrowed heavily from the Spanish Crown and private citizens in the colony. Deep in debt and with no money coming from the American Congress, Pollock might have been thrown into debtor's prison had it not been for Galvez, who personally underwrote Pollock's loans. In desperation Pollock wrote the Congress asking for money to pay his debts, but nothing came. Not until after the Revolution did the United States finally repay part of Pollock's claims.

During the war Galvez warned the British not to molest American ships on the Mississippi River: "Whoever fights on the river will incur the disapproval of my sovereign, and in consideration of my duty, I would have to oppose to the extent of my power." But at the same time Galvez disrupted English commerce and shipping whenever possible as well as permitting Americans to take refuge in New Orleans, even after some had pillaged settlements in British West Florida.

The most notorious of these American raiders was James Willing, the black sheep of a prominent Philadelphia family and the brother of a business partner of Robert Morris (a member of the First Continental Congress and financial wizard of the American Revolution). Before the Revolution, James Willing settled in Natchez, where he failed as a merchant. When the Revolution began, Willing tried unsuccessfully to get residents of the Natchez area to rise in revolt against the British. He pulled up stakes and returned to Philadelphia, where he convinced Congress to support his leading an expedition against West Florida. With Con-

gress's blessing, Willing and about 30 men boarded the gunboat *Rattletrap* in January 1778, beginning their infamous invasion of British West Florida.

Willing's expedition did absolutely nothing to further the cause of the Revolution. He plundered Natchez and plantations in the lower Mississippi Valley, capturing the British gunship *Rebecca*. When the expedition reached New Orleans, Galvez extended his hospitality and protection to Willing and his men. But the Revolution was a long way from Willing's mind. He sold his ill-gotten booty in New Orleans and instead of sending the proceeds to the American forces, he and his men spent it all on high living. When the money ran out, Willing and his men launched another raid on the Baton Rouge area, where they were repulsed by armed citizens. Willing and his "rebels" returned to New Orleans, living there off of Pollock's dwindling resources.

Meanwhile, both Pollock and Galvez had had about enough of Willing. Pollock sent repeated messages to Congress asking that Willing be recalled. At one point Pollock threatened Congress with stopping all supplies to the war effort until Willing left. Shortly thereafter, Willing departed for Philadelphia, but along the way he was captured by the British and taken to New York as a prisoner. He escaped and was recaptured, and eventually was traded in a prisoner exchange.

But in Louisiana and West Florida, Willing had done much harm to both the American cause and Galvez's designs on the neighboring British territory. Willing's actions in West Florida drove many of its residents, some of whom were considering joining the American cause, deeper into the Loyalist camp. Moreover, the British strengthened their defenses in the colony, especially along the Mississippi River, the border between Spanish Louisiana and British West Florida. Of course Galvez's motives for helping the Americans were not entirely altruistic. He and Spain welcomed the chance to do whatever they could to help break up the British colonial empire in North America.

In 1779 Galvez, hearing reports of massive troop buildups in Mobile and Pensacola, sent envoy Jacinto Panis to the two British settlements; his ostensible mission was to discuss Louisiana's neutrality rights in Britain's conflict

Spanish governor Bernardo de Galvez (right) was a great friend of the American colonists in the Revolutionary War, sending them supplies and military goods. His engagement of the British at Pensacola (facing page) was one of several campaigns against the British in their Florida territory. From Cirker, Dictionary of American Portraits, Dover, 1967. (THNOC)

with its colonies, but his true purpose was to gather military intelligence information in the two port towns. In July 1779 word reached Galvez that war had been declared between Spain and Great Britain. His British counterparts in West Florida, however, had not received the news. Galvez had learned earlier, through intercepted letters, that the British were concentrating troops in West Florida to attack New Orleans as soon as war came. But Galvez struck first and through a series of brilliant military maneuvers, he and his approximately 650-man army of Spanish regulars, Mexicans, Canary Islanders, free-people-of-color, Anglo-Americans, Acadians, and French Louisianians, captured Fort Bute (located where the Mississippi River meets Bayou Manchac) and Baton Rouge in September 1779; Natchez in October 1779; Mobile in March 1780; and Pensacola in May 1781. With the fall of Pensacola to Galvez, the British surrendered

the entire province of West Florida. Both Floridas passed to Spanish control with the Peace of Paris in 1783 which also ended the American Revolution.

Galvez's success against the British in the Floridas brought him great fame and reward from the king of Spain. He was able to add the words "Yo Solo" — meaning "I alone" — to his coat of arms for his bravery and courage in capturing Pensacola. In 1785 he was named viceroy of New Spain and departed for his new post in Mexico early the following year. Only a few months later, however, he contracted a fever and died in Mexico City.

Besides their role in the American Revolution, Galvez and his second-in-command and later governor, Esteban Rodriguez Miro, are remembered in Louisiana history for the assistance they gave to immigrants. They gave refuge to the increasing number of Acadians searching for homes in Louisiana, many of

whom settled north of New Orleans, or along Bayou Teche and Bayou Lafourche. Anglo-Americans fleeing the war in the British colonies were given land, tools, and a new start. To get more colonists, Galvez—through his influential uncle, Don Jose de Galvez—induced several hundred Canary Islanders, or "Islenos" as they are called today, to come to Louisiana. They settled in *Terre-aux-Boeufs* below New Orleans (now St. Bernard Parish), along Bayou Lafourche northwest of New Orleans and at the northern tip of the Isle of Orleans along Bayou Manchac. Galvez also welcomed approximately 500 Malagans who founded New Iberia on Bayou Teche in about 1779. Like their French and Spanish neighbors, these new settlers provided New Orleans with much-needed foodstuffs, building materials, and products for commerce.

The census of 1785 showed that the colony had doubled in size since 1769. The Isle of Orleans had in excess of 25,000 inhabitants, while New Orleans had grown to almost 5,000. The population of the *Cote des Allemands et Acadiene* was placed at approximately 4,500.

Miro carried on and expanded Galvez's commercial policies and as a result, trade between Louisiana and the Americans in the upper Mississippi and Ohio valleys increased dramatically. Greater numbers of flatboats loaded with agricultural products, timber, and naval stores, arrived in New Orleans from upriver. Some days dozens of American boats could be seen in the harbor, far outnumbering the ships of other nations, including Spain. The two regions increasingly became dependent on each other economically. Although the situation was lucrative to the Spanish in New Orleans, it set into motion events that would end Spain's domination in the colony.

Also during Miro's administration, the most devastating disaster in the city's history up to

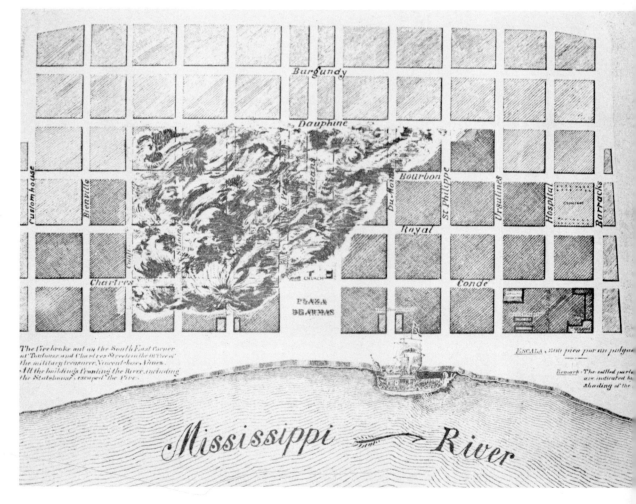

that time began at 1:30 p.m., March 21, 1788 — the Great Fire of 1788. According to legend, a candle ignited a curtain in the home of a Spanish official. The fire spread rapidly, but the clergy would not allow the fire bells to be rung because it was Good Friday. Also, the predominantly French-speaking population could not understand orders being shouted by Spanish-speaking officials. (Mexico City's *Gaceta de Mexico* reported that the fire in New Orleans was further fueled by gunpowder stored in private homes contrary to official orders.)

In less than six hours, almost a thousand buildings and their contents reportedly were destroyed by the fire. Approximately four-fifths of the city was reduced to ruins. One of the few buildings spared by the flames was the Ursuline Convent, which still stands today as the oldest surviving colonial building in the French Quarter. The Parish Church of St. Louis, the Presbytere, O'Reilly's Cabildo, and the building that housed the *corps de garde* and the jail were destroyed.

In a report to his superiors, Miro described the misery he found throughout the city's charred ruins:

. . . night momentarily removed the sight of so many misfortunes, but the dawn the following day brought a worse one, that seeing along the road, crying and sobbing and in most abject misery, so many families who, a few hours before, enjoyed considerable riches and conveniences. Their cries, weeping and pale faces told the ruin of a city which in less than five hours had been transformed into an arid and horrible wilderness; the work of seventy years since its foundation.

After clearing away the ruins, Miro fell quickly into rebuilding New Orleans. With the financial help of Don Andres Almonester y Roxas, public and government buildings were rebuilt including the Church of St. Louis and the Presbytere. Also, a butcher's arcade was built on the levee across from the Place d'Armes — the beginning of today's famous French Market.

The calamity in New Orleans did not go unnoticed by the outside world. Miro's efficiency in handling the aftermath of the disaster gained recognition for him and the city in the *London Chronicle* which described New Orleans as the "most regular, well-governed, small city in the western world."

As a springtime forest fire brings new growth, so the Great Fire of 1788 brought new growth to New Orleans. While the rubble was being cleared away in the city, Madame and Don Beltram (Bertrand) Gravier decided to subdivide their plantation into city blocks and sell them off to people who no longer wanted to live in the crowded Vieux Carre. The Gravier Plantation, located on the upriver side of the city, became New Orleans' first suburb, called Faubourg Ste. Marie (St. Mary), at the site of today's Central Business District.

Royal Surveyor Carlos Trudeau drew up the plans for the subdivision on April 1, 1788, dividing the plantation into squares separated by three cross streets and cross-sectioned by four perpendicular roadways with one oblique street splintering off at an angle. The cross streets today bear such familiar names as Magazine, Camp, and St. Charles streets. The perpendicular ones, running to the river, are called Poydras, Girod, and Julia. The oblique street was named Gravier in honor of the developers. Americans and other immigrants would continue to flock to Faubourg Ste. Marie, which became known as the American Sector because of its predominantly American population and Greek Revival architectural style so common in the Atlantic-Seaboard states.

The heavy weight of war, diplomacy, the fire in 1788, and over 20 years in America had tired Miro. He was ready to go home to Spain and, in 1791, he finally got his wish. He had been a popular and able governor during his tenure in Louisiana. But his successor would prove to be colonial Louisiana's most skilled. He was Don Francisco Luis Hector, Baron de Carondelet, a native of Flanders in the Spanish service.

Carondelet earned his place in Louisiana history for his remarkable achievements in New Orleans. He established the city's first theater in 1792 on St. Peter Street and divided the city into four wards, placing them under the administration of an *Alcalde de Barrio,* similar to a city borough. Also in 1792 he established and edited the city's first newspaper, *Le Moniteur de la Louisiane,* and created the city's first police department in 1796. About a dozen *se-*

renos patrolled the streets at night to keep order and herald the time. He also ordered the lighting of city streets at night by oil lamps suspended from ropes and tied diagonally across street intersections. He ordered the city's fortifications rebuilt and oversaw the digging of the Carondelet Canal which not only drained the rear sections of the city, but also provided a navigable waterway for commerce from the city's rear gates to Bayou St. John and hence to Lake Pontchartrain.

New Orleans suffered three devastating hurricanes and two more fires during Carondelet's administration. The fire of 1792 did not inflict heavy damages, but the 1794 fire destroyed over 200 buildings, including once again the jail and the *corps de garde*. After the 1794 fire Almonester y Roxas financed the construction of the new Cabildo from the destroyed *corps de garde*. Carondelet reported that the fire of 1794 had not destroyed as many buildings as the 1788 fire, but the financial losses were far greater. After three hurricanes and three fires, little was left of the original French settlement.

With a good portion of the city reduced to ashes once again, Carondelet, acting on the

After the fire of 1788, the plantation of Marie and Bertrand Gravier was divided into squares. It became the Faubourg Ste. Marie (St. Mary). (THNOC)

petition of attorney general Miguel Fortier, drew up a stringent new building code for the city. All new buildings with more than one story located in the heavily populated sections of the city had to be built of brick or adobe, using either red or yellow tiles for the roof. Wooden roofs were forbidden and houses had to be constructed close to the sidewalks, or *banquettes*. New Orleans began taking on the appearance which has become so well known to generations of residents and visitors. Neat brick and *colombage* structures lined the *banquettes* abutting each other with passageways to scenic and comfortable rear patios. Balconies, with wrought-iron railings from local forges, decorated the facades of many new buildings. Within a few years, wealthy American and other English-speaking merchant-planters would build their Greek Revival homes in the American Sector or among the Spanish styles

in the Old Quarter. Eventually a mixture of the styles would produce a new and vernacular architecture to suit the culture and climate of New Orleans.

When Carondelet was not at work making New Orleans a modern and viable city, he was busy with political problems. In 1793 the French Revolution, raging in far-off France, came knocking at the gates of New Orleans. Although the revolution got under way in 1789, New Orleanians paid little attention to it until Louis XVI was beheaded in 1793 and Spain and France declared war on each other shortly after the execution. Many French New Orleanians got caught up in the revolutionary rhetoric and zeal, and finding their own despot to behead seemed to be the popular idea. Although French New Orleanians had little to complain about since Spain had brought them only prosperity, mobs marched through the

Among the improvements made during Carondelet's administration was the installation of oil lamps on the city's streets. The lamps were lit each day by paid workers. (THNOC)

streets calling Carondelet a *cochon de lait* (a suckling pig) and shouting such slogans as the "Liberty, Equality and Fraternity" ones so popular in France at the moment. They sang revolutionary airs. Pamphlets and letters from France and the Jacobin Society in Pennsylvania were sent to New Orleans, urging the colonists to rise in rebellion.

Fearing a bloody uprising in New Orleans and the lower Mississippi Valley, Carondelet acted quickly and sternly. He sent for more troops to keep order and issued a proclamation forbidding writings and meetings in which the French Revolution or the political affairs of France were discussed. Violators of his regulations could be fined heavily or sent to cool their revolutionary heels in a Havana prison. Thus Carondelet was able to maintain order. He later gave refuge to French aristocrats fleeing chaos and bloodshed in France.

The governor also had troubles with restless and westward-expanding Americans, or "Kaintocks" as they were called by the Creoles. Since Miro's time, New Orleans had become essential to the commerce of Americans living in the West. It would not have taken much to

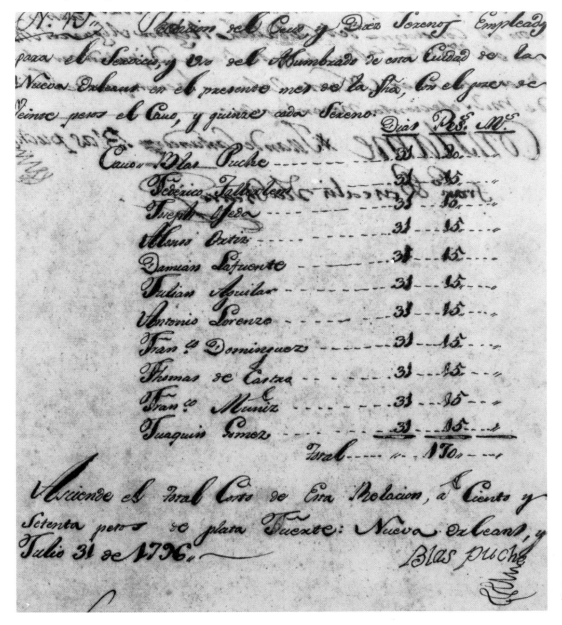

This receipt for payment to lamplighters shows that the government paid for this service. (THNOC)

convince Americans that New Orleans should be annexed to the United States and "Citizen" Edmond Charles Genet, France's ambassador to the young nation, was just the man for the job. Genet, with a full war chest, conspired to raise an army of western Americans — with the famed George Rogers Clark at its head — to march on New Orleans. But before the expedition could be launched, Genet had managed to alienate President George Washington, Secretary of the Treasury Alexander Hamilton, and Secretary of State Thomas Jefferson. Jefferson was about to ask France to recall Genet when word arrived that Genet's revolutionary party in France was out and a more radical element was now in power. The radicals, or Jacobins, also wanted Genet home, but the shrewd diplomat knew what fate awaited him in France. If he returned, he surely would lose his head. He therefore sought, and got, political asylum in the United States, where he settled down in New York and married the governor's daughter.

Genet's aborted invasion did not lessen the tensions between Spanish Louisiana and the United States. During the decades following the American Revolution, the unofficial alliance between the young nation and Spain steadily worsened. Statements made by American leaders during and after their Revolution, assuring Spain that the United States had no designs on Louisiana, were no longer convincing to Spanish officials by the early 1790s. Two major points divided the two nations: navigation of the Mississippi and the northern boundary line between Spanish West Florida and the United

The Treaty of San Lorenzo (also known as the Pinckney Treaty because of its American signer Thomas Pinckney) granted the United States free navigation of the Mississippi River and allowed American merchants to deposit their goods at the port of New Orleans for shipment. The treaty expired in 1802 and was a factor in the negotiations with France that led to the Louisiana Purchase. (THNOC)

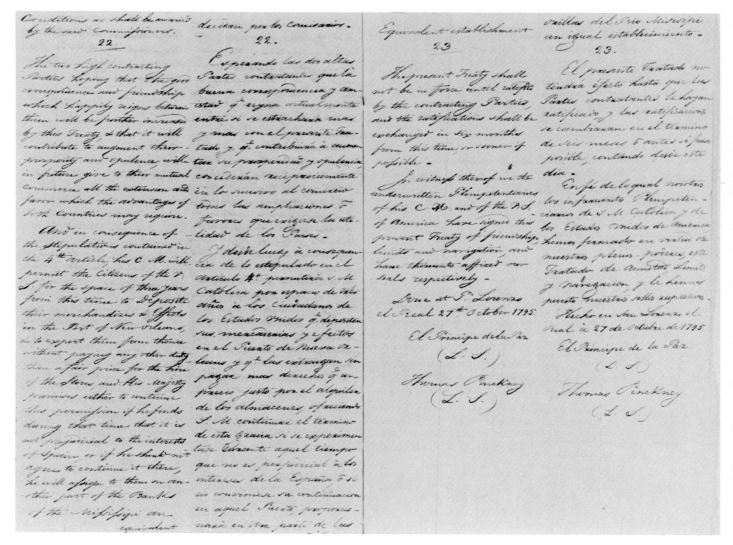

States. According to the 1783 Peace of Paris ending the American Revolution, Great Britain gave the infant nation the right of free navigation of the river, a right Spain claimed England had no right to give since the mouth of the Mississippi clearly was within Spanish territory. As to the West Florida border, the United States contended the 31st parallel (present northern border between the State of Mississippi and the toe of the Louisiana boot) formed its boundary with Spanish West Florida. Spain, however, insisted the border was much further north above Natchez.

Although suspicions and hostilities increased, American commerce on the river continued to grow. Spanish officials occasionally seized American flatboats on the river and the Americans answered with rattling sabres and threats of invasion. Trade with the Americans was officially ordered to stop in 1784, but Governor Miro disregarded those orders because of the colony's need for American commerce. In 1787 a royal decree legalized the trade but put a 25-percent duty on their cargoes, although the duties gradually decreased in following years. The fire of 1788 boosted trade in New Orleans and American flatboats arrived in increasing numbers with loaded decks. By the end of the century, almost three-fourths of the ships and vessels to use the port would belong to Americans.

Governor Carondelet, having problems with the French Revolution and his own citizens in New Orleans, urged his government's cooperation with the United States. By so doing, he hoped to stave off English intervention in the growing separatist sentiments of many Americans living in the trans-Appalachian West. Spanish Louisiana had greater fear of powerful English presence in the region than it did the weaker Americans.

Finally in 1795 Spain and the Americans signed the Treaty of San Lorenzo (also known as the Pinckney Treaty) in which Spain granted the Americans free navigation of the Mississippi with the right of deposit at New Orleans for three years. Moreover, Spain recognized the American's border claim with West Florida. Although the right of deposit legally expired in 1798, the privilege continued until October 1802 when Juan Morales, the Spanish intendant at New Orleans, ordered it stopped.

In the meantime, Carondelet's administration in Louisiana came to an end on August 5, 1797. He was followed by Brigadier General Manuel Luis Gayoso de Lemos, the former governor of the Natchez district. Carondelet was off to his new post as president of the Royal Audience of Quito.

The list of Carondelet's achievements in New Orleans is long, but one of the most important events during his tenure was one with which he had nothing to do. In 1796 Etienne Bore harvested a sugarcane crop on his plantation upriver from New Orleans near present-day Audubon Park. Although earlier Louisianians had planted cane and produced sugar, Bore has been credited with raising sugar production to the level of making it a profitable industry. Bore had believed that sugar produc-

The tiled roofs on some colonial New Orleans houses were flat and served as elevated patios. These took advantage of breezes from the river and also provided a view of the growing city. (THNOC)

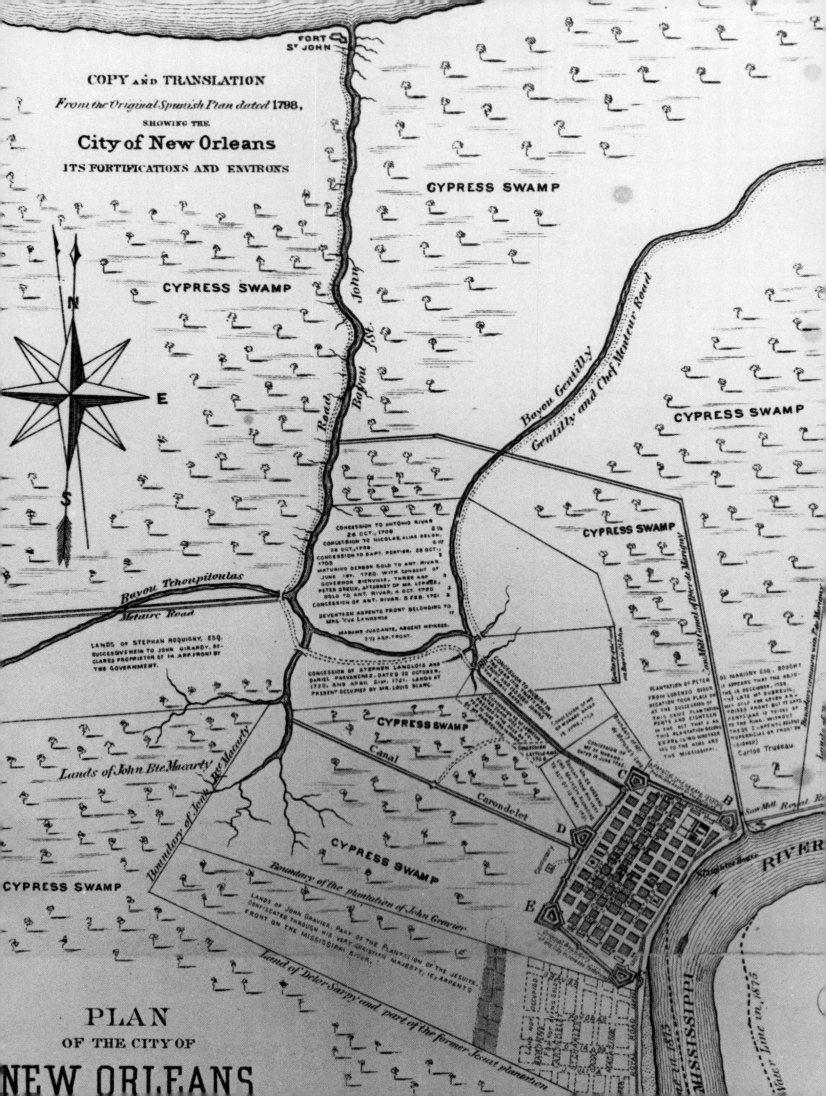

COPY and TRANSLATION

From the Original Spanish Plan dated 1798,

SHOWING THE

City of New Orleans

ITS FORTIFICATIONS AND ENVIRONS

CYPRESS SWAMP

CYPRESS SWAMP

CYPRESS SWAMP

CYPRESS SWAMP

CYPRESS SWAMP

CYPRESS SWAMP

CYPRESS SWAMP

CYPRESS SWAMP

FORT St JOHN

Bayou St. John

Road

Bayou Gentilly and Chef Menteur Road

Bayou Tchoupitoulas

Metaire Road

LANDS OF STEPHAN ROQUIGNY, ESQ. SUCCESSIVE HEIR TO JOHN GIRARDY, DECLARED PROPRIETOR OF 14 ARP. FRONT BY THE GOVERNMENT.

Lands of John Bte Macarty

Boundary of John Bte Macarty

Canal

Carondelet

Boundary of the plantation of John Gravier

LANDS OF JOHN GRAVIER, PART OF THE PLANTATION OF THE JESUITS, CONFISCATED THROUGH HIS VERY CHRISTIAN MAJESTY, 15, ARPENTS FRONT ON THE MISSISSIPPI RIVER.

Land of Delor Sarpy and part of the former Jesuit plantation

RIVER

MISSISSIPPI

Water Line in 1875

Carlos Trudeau

C

B

D

E

PLAN

OF THE CITY OF

NEW ORLEANS

tion had to be large-scale to be profitable. He planted larger quantities of cane and built a bigger sugar house. With the help of an experienced sugar maker, Bore sold his 1796 crop for a considerable profit, marking the beginning of an important industry for Louisiana.

Gayoso was popular among New Orleanians, but his administration was to be cut short when he died of a fever in July 1799. He became the only colonial governor to be buried beneath the floor of St. Louis Cathedral. During his two years in office, Gayoso served well, spending most of his time dealing with the increasing number of American immigrants. Moreover, Gayoso had the honor of entertaining the only royalty New Orleans had ever seen. Louis Philippe, Duc d'Orleans and later king of France, visited the city with his two brothers, the Duc de Montpensier and the Comte de Beaujolais. All three were great-great-grandsons of New Orleans' namesake, Philippe, the Duc d' Orleans, and were keeping the Atlantic between themselves and the new authorities governing France after the revolution, who would dearly have loved the young men's royal heads. New Orleanians were thrilled by the royal visits and did all they could to make their guests feel at home in the would-be Paris on the Mississippi.

After Gayoso's unexpected death, Francisco Bouligny and Nicholas Maria Vidal took charge until a new governor could be sent to the colony. Officials in Cuba dispatched the Marques de Casa-Calvo to serve as acting governor until a permanent appointee could be sent from Spain. The man finally chosen, brigadier general Don Juan Manuel de Salcedo, had a brief and undistinguished career in Louisiana. Old and perhaps senile, the governor left many government matters to his son, who was more concerned with his own profit than the good of the colony.

Salcedo was Louisiana's last Spanish governor, for in the meantime, the colony had been retroceded to France in 1800 through the secret Treaty of San Ildefonso. Napoleon, who had forced the treaty upon Spain, let the Spanish continue to administer Louisiana until he chose a convenient time to occupy it. Little did New Orleanians realize, but a chapter of their history was about to come to an end. Louisiana soon would be no longer a colonial possession of a European power.

By the end of Spanish rule in 1803, New Orleans had come a long way; from its shaky beginning as a remote outpost in the French empire to a major North American city. The population of New Orleans in 1803 has been placed at anywhere from 8,000 to 11,000 people. One estimate accounted for approximately 10,000 residents — 5,000 whites, 2,000 free-people-of-color, and 3,000 slaves. The city could boast of well-constructed brick and stucco-covered buildings and a good harbor. The busy quays held cargoes of all types and descriptions from the interior of North America, the West Indies, and Europe, while merchants, roustabouts, and draymen went about their work. New Orleans had become an international city where the English-speaking culture clashed head-on with the Creole of Louisiana.

New Orleans by this time already had gained a reputation as a gay and colorful city with Mardi Gras balls dating back to the French era. By the end of the Spanish period the affluent Creoles had taken on all the trappings of their European counterparts, Americans were assuming a leading role in the city's commerce, and a large population of free-people-of-color — increased by refugees from the slave revolts in the West Indies — gained prominence in many walks of life in New Orleans. The *gens de couleur libres,* often labeled mulatto, quadroon, or a host of other designations for their percentage of European to African heritage, had developed a sophisticated society, which to a degree paralleled white society. The fabled beauty of the women has become an important part of the city's legend.

By the end of the colonial period, the elements of New Orleans' future fame were already in place. Visitors to 20th-century New Orleans enjoy the mystique of the colonial survivals — the Cabildo, the Ursuline Convent, and the Gallic street names. The Creole food, with its combined French, Spanish, Indian, and African influences, is known throughout the world. *Gris gris, voodoo,* and *banquette* are words that conjure up thoughts of the city's colonial past. Visitors to the city spend hours and days peering down the long passageways into the damp but serene patios with their thick growths of vegetation, looking for a glimpse or a sound of a long-gone colonial New Orleans, and are not disappointed.

There is on the Globe one single spot, the possessor of which is our natural and habitual enemy. It is New Orleans, through which the produce of three-eighths of our territory must pass to market. . . . The day France takes possession of New Orleans . . . from that moment we must marry ourselves to the British fleet and nation."

So wrote President Thomas Jefferson in a now-famous letter to Robert Livingston, American minister to France, when he learned in 1802 that Spain had secretly retroceded Louisiana to the French two years earlier. The situation was a serious one, and Jefferson's reaction to it was extreme, for well he knew that joining with England would have allied the United States with the one country it distrusted more than France. But pressures from the emerging territories in the West, which needed the use of the Mississippi Gulf port for trade with the East Coast and Europe, and from Napoleon's imperial wars were requiring a resolution to the disposition of the Louisiana problem. War between France and the United States would be narrowly averted by the Louisiana Purchase of 1803, which doubled the territory of the United States and ensured its future position as a world power.

In an attempt to avoid war with France, Livingston had been instructed to enter into negotiations with Napoleon to buy the Isle of Orleans and

West Florida. He made little headway at first. "There never was a government in which less could be done by negotiation," he wrote to Jefferson, "There is no people, no legislature, no counsellors. One man (Napoleon) is everything. He seldom asks advice, and never hears it unasked."

Napoleon had more immediate concerns than what to do with his backwater frontier land across the ocean. For more than three years after its acquisition in 1800, he had allowed Spain to continue to govern Louisiana. Tensions between the Spanish in New Orleans and the Western Americans increased during this period, especially because of the expansion of United States shipping activity on the Mississippi. By 1802 ships flying the American flag greatly outnumbered the ships of other nations, even Spain and France. American seamen, enjoying the tawdry delights of the city's riverfront saloons and bordellos, were quick to express their resentment toward Spanish officials with a word, gesture, and sometimes a fist fight.

In late 1802 Juan Morales, the acting Spanish intendant at New Orleans, closed the river to American ships. When this news reached Jefferson in January of 1803, he sent his friend James Monroe (who would become the fifth President) to assist Livingston with his negotiations. Jefferson wrote to Livingston in Paris: "Every eye in the United States is now fixed on the affairs of Louisiana. Perhaps nothing since the revolutionary war has produced more uneasy sensations through the body of the nation."

Later that month the President informed the British *charge d'affaires* that the United States would never relinquish its claim to free navigation of the Mississippi River, so essential to the development of the West, and would resort to war if necessary to insure access. In February a Senate resolution that would have authorized Jefferson to occupy portions of the Isle of Orleans failed. But another resolution calling for the outfitting of 80,000 militiamen was passed.

Since war with Great Britain was seemingly imminent, Napoleon made a decision that sur-

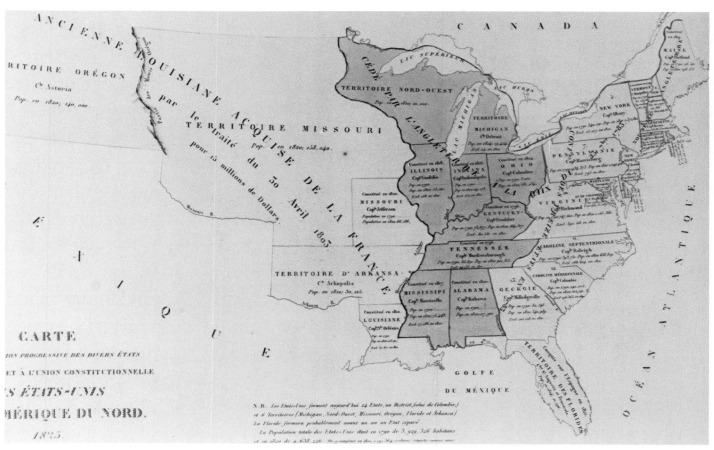

prised the United States. He agreed not only to sell the Americans the land they had requested, but all of Louisiana. This decision probably had less to do with the protracted negotiations than with Napoleon's need for money to continue his imperial wars. He also doubted his ability to hold the territory against a British — or even an American — attack. If France couldn't control the Mississippi, Napoleon would much rather see it in the hands of the United States than his ancient rival England. In issuing the order to sell to his minister of the treasury, Barbe-Marbois, Napoleon wrote:

They [the British] shall not have the Mississippi which they covet. . . . I renounce Louisiana. It is not only New Orleans that I cede: it is the whole colony without reserve. . . . I renounce it with the greatest regret; to attempt obstinately to retain it would be folly.

On April 12, 1803, during a dinner party given by Livingston to celebrate Monroe's ar-rival in Paris, Barbe-Marbois arrived and shocked the Americans with the announce-ment that Napoleon was willing to sell all of the Louisiana Territory. Negotiations over the price, in which Monroe joined Livingston, lasted for more than two weeks. The United States finally agreed on April 29 to pay $11.25 million for the land, and to assume French debts of $3.75 million incurred to American citizens during the recent wars, bringing the total price of the transaction to $15 million. The treaty was dated April 30, although it was actually signed on May 2. Livingston's remarks at the signing would prove prophetic: "We have lived long, but this is the noblest work of our lives. . . . From this day the United States take their place among the powers of the first rank."

Napoleon's comments after the sale would likewise come true: "This accession of territory affirms forever the power of the United States, and I have just given England a maritime rival that sooner or later will lay low her pride." Had the English been able to foresee the future, they

With Livingston and James Monroe in Paris, and Jefferson in Washington, news of the negotiations and instructions were accomplished by letter. Because of the highly secret nature of the negotiations, this particularly sensitive passage from one of Livingston's let-ters to Jefferson was written in a numerical code. (THNOC)

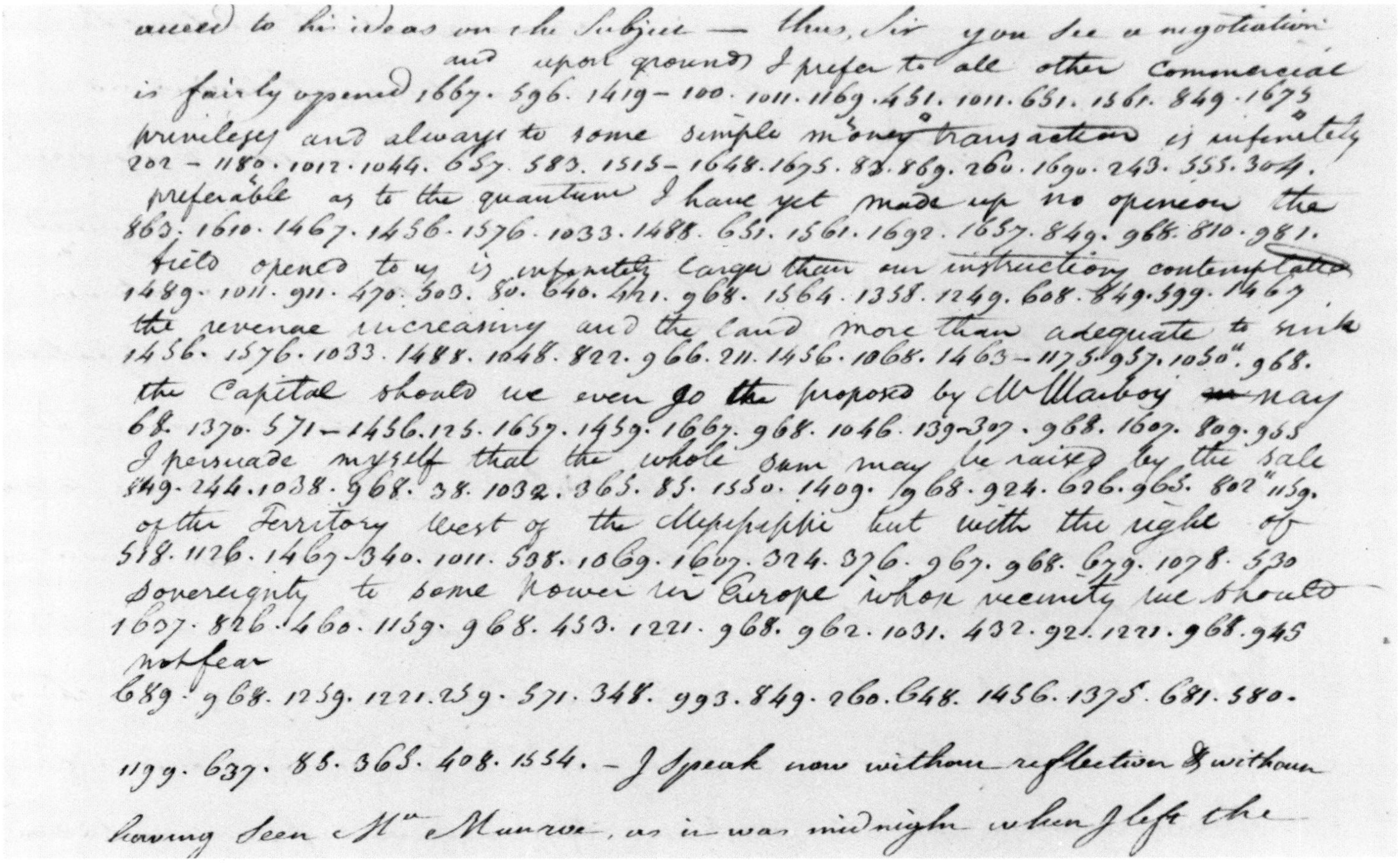

might have gone forward with their own plans to invade New Orleans, which were to be carried out with the resumption of the war between France and Great Britain. Livingston learned of the invasion plan a week after the signing of the treaty, and he quickly informed London of the Louisiana Purchase.

When the time came to actually pay France the approximately $15 million for Louisiana, however, the United States found itself embarrassed: the fledgling country simply did not have that much money in its treasury. But arrangements were made to sell bonds to the banking houses of Baring in London and Hope in Amsterdam to pay Napoleon. The total cost of the Louisiana Purchase, including interest and claims against the government, eventually came to $23,527,872.

Acquiring sufficient funds was not the only problem that Louisiana presented its American purchasers. The extent and exact boundaries of the vast territory had never been clearly delineated. When Livingston asked the French foreign minister Talleyrand for information, he replied, "I can give you no direction; you have made a noble bargain for yourselves and I suppose you will make the most of it."

Not all Americans were happy with the Louisiana Purchase. Jefferson's opponents in Congress argued that the Constitution had made no provisions for acquiring land in such a way or for administering it. New Englanders complained that a large sum was being paid for land that would only benefit Americans living in the West. They were also reluctant to have a rival in New Orleans for their own port cities.

The reaction to the purchase in New Orleans itself was, for the most part, positive. Pierre Clement Laussat, the envoy sent by Napoleon to officiate the return of the colony from France to Spain, however, could not believe the rumors he had heard about the purchase. He wrote to his superiors describing the "incredible falsehoods." The Americans in the city were wild with joy over the news, he wrote, while the Spanish residents expressed pleasure that New Orleans would not be returned to the French. Many of the French Creoles, who were looking forward to a reunion with France, were now in despair, he continued, and were considering selling their possessions and moving away. Laussat soon received word that the rumors were indeed true and he was ordered to receive the colony from Spain and hold it for the United States.

At the time of the Louisiana Purchase, New Orleans was still in a way a frontier city, but yet unlike any other frontier city in the nation. The population in 1803 had risen to more than 10,000 with another 3,000 residents living below the city. The population consisted primarily of Creoles, Anglo-Americans, free-people-of-color and Negro slaves, and a few Indians.

The city's West-Indian flavor, contrasted, for example, with its Roman Catholic religious ceremonies, must have been a strange sight from the more conservative Eastern-Seaboard Protestants moving into the city to open commercial establishments or plantations along the Mississippi River and connecting waterways. During the early years of the American period, New Orleans became well-known for its dens of vice along Tchoupitoulas Street and in the infamous Swamp, a collection of brothels, saloons, and gambling halls where life was not worth a *picayune* (about 6 cents) — the price of a drink. The Swamp, a favorite place for the Kaintock flatboat men of Mike Fink fame and the dregs of the *demi-monde*, was located behind the American Sector of the city at the end of Girod Street near Liberty Street and the Protestant Cemetery, or in the general area of today's Louisiana Superdome. There was perhaps no other city in the Union where a spectator could watch a religious procession wind through the streets, visit a colorful Mardi Gras ball in one of the many white ballrooms, or the famous biracial Quadroon Ballroom, or per-

The French minister of the treasury, Barbe-Marbois, was ordered by Napoleon to negotiate the sale of the Louisiana Territory with the Americans. (THNOC)

haps wander over to Congo Square in the rear of the old city to watch the French-speaking slaves enjoy a day off, singing, beating the drums, rattling the bones, or dancing the Calinda, Bamboula, or the Counjaille (or Counjai), many of which were later made famous in music by New Orleans composer Leon Gottschalk.

New Orleans already had begun to grow beyond its original boundaries with the construction of Faubourg Ste. Marie. Later other Faubourgs would be added, such as Marigny and Treme. By 1810 New Orleans was the largest city in the South, boasting a population of over 24,000 residents, and it was the fifth-largest city by population in the nation. Between 1804 and 1810 the population of the city increased dramatically as French Creoles, free blacks, and slaves fled to the city, escaping revolutions in the French West Indies. In 1809 alone over 5,700 emigrants sought refuge in New Orleans. The mass influx of white and black West Indians caused serious housing, economic, and racial problems for the young American government.

New Orleans could boast of an active opera and theater and many fine homes in the Old Quarter and suburbs, as well as some of the fine plantation houses above and below the city. But according to some visitors, New Orleans was dirty, unhealthy, and decayed, even though it had practically been rebuilt after the fires of 1788 and 1794.

This painting depicts the signing of the Louisiana Purchase treaty on May 2, 1803. (THNOC)

Visiting the city shortly before the purchase, Perrin du Lac, a visiting Frenchman, noted his findings in the Crescent City:

Nothing equals the filthiness of New Orleans. . . . The city, the filth of which cannot be drained off, is not paved and probably never will be in the hands of the Spaniards. Its markets which are unventilated are reeking with rottenness. Its quay is adorned with fish that rot there for want of purchasers. Its squares are covered with the filth of animals which no one takes the trouble to remove.

Another Frenchman, C. C. Robin, had much of the same to say about conditions in the city. The streets of the city, he said, were, in some places, impassable even to carriages:

There were chasms where carriages would be broken to pieces if they attempted it. The pedestrians could take refuge on the sidewalks or banquettes, built along the houses. . . . In many places they are broken and covered with mud, so that one must be an expert in the art of equilibrium in order to follow these pieces of wood without slipping.

Robin, however, was very optimistic about Louisiana's future: "In the New World there are as yet very few of those useless families that permit themselves the time of doing nothing. The universal desire to acquire wealth insures that no profession is despised as long as it makes money."

The Louisiana Territory was vast but sparsely settled with approximately 50,000 inhabitants, excluding Indians. Most of the residents lived in the present-day state of Louisiana, primarily in and around New Orleans. The huge acquisition would later be divided and subdivided to form 15 other states, or parts of states, in the nation.

Shortly after the purchase, the federal government started reorganizing the territory. On March 26, 1804, Congress divided the purchase into the Territory of Orleans (present state of Louisiana minus the Florida Parishes, which were annexed in 1810, and an area near the Sabine River) and the Louisiana Territory which comprised the rest of the acquisition. John Quincy Adams and other New Englanders objected, stating that the Constitution made no provision for determining how the people of a purchased territory would govern themselves. When the time came for Jefferson to name a governor to the Territory of Orleans, he first considered two men: the popular Marquis de Lafayette and James Monroe. Jefferson finally named William Charles Cole Claiborne to the post after both Monroe and Lafayette declined. One of Claiborne's first official duties came on December 20, 1803, during ceremonies in New Orleans when he and General

James Wilkinson took possession of Louisiana — just 20 days after disappointed French Commissioner Pierre Clement Laussat had received the colony from Spain.

Claiborne, Virginia-born and two years away from his 30th birthday, had been the governor of the neighboring Mississippi Territory when Jefferson sent him to New Orleans to accept Louisiana from the French. The new governor, a Protestant who could not speak a word of French, faced a difficult task in making Louisianians Americans. The people felt they were being slighted because the territory was not made a state immediately. The American legal system was confusing to them; they resented the ban on importing slaves, a practice that they had enjoyed since Galvez's days, and rumors persisted that Louisiana would soon be returned to either France or Spain. Claiborne also wrote to Jefferson praising the people of Louisiana, but warning him that certain Americans, namely Edward Livingston, a scion of the plutocratic New York family, Irish-born Daniel Clark, and others were trying to turn the local population against him.

In March 1805 Congress created the first legislature for the Territory of Orleans. A year later Claiborne was writing to Jefferson again

complaining of his problems with that assembly: "I always thought that an early extension of the Representative system in this Territory was a hazardous experiment; and of this I am now convinced."

New Orleans city government retained Laussat's mayor and municipal council system in varying degrees until the territorial legislature incorporated the city on February 17, 1805. Laussat's mayoral appointment, Etienne Bore, had continued in office until he was replaced in 1804 by James Pitot. The city charter of 1805 called for the election of a 14-member board of aldermen, presided over by a recorder and mayor, both of whom were appointed by the governor. The board of aldermen elected the city treasurer and the mayor appointed most other city officials. The board of aldermen, which was based on American municipal concepts, among its many functions, fixed prices and passed ordinances. The mayor, as the city's chief magistrate, presided over the council and headed the city's police and fire departments.

Under the new 1805 charter, Claiborne appointed John Watkins mayor, and later James Mather. In 1811 the city charter was amended to provide for the election of the mayor by property-owning white males. Nicholas Girod, a French-speaking Creole, became the city's first elected mayor in 1812. (Girod would gain fame in Louisiana for his offer of sanctuary to Napoleon, who was brooding away in exile on the island of St. Helena. In 1821 Girod and his supporters collected money to buy the schooner *Seraphine* which was to sail to Napoleon's rescue; but before the ship could depart New Orleans, word reached the city that Napoleon had died.)

The city government created by the 1805

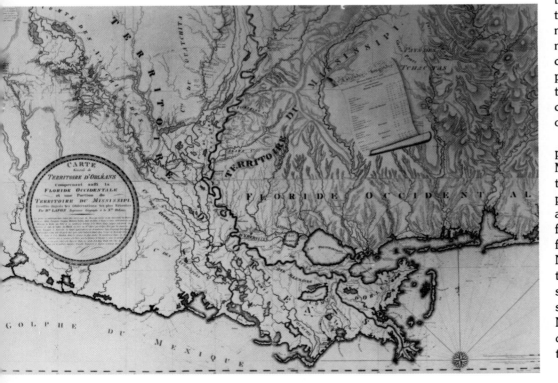

charter also set out to clean up New Orleans. Cockfights were outlawed and the military was ordered to stop using the levees as latrines. The police force was reorganized, newly arrived ships were inspected for diseases, and additional streetlights were installed. Roads and bridges were repaired and a new meat market was built. More firefighting equipment was purchased and a building code was enacted. (The council passed an ordinance requiring each household to keep two buckets on hand in case of fire.) In 1808 the city council enacted an ordinance compelling theater owners to submit all plays to the mayor's office for review before performing them for the public. This law was passed at the request of Mayor Mather because of a "lewd" play he attended at the St. Philip Street Theatre.

The first decade or so of the American era in New Orleans was a period historian John Clark described as one of "excitement, uproar, flux, boom and bust, disasters, disappointments, and achievements." Thousands of people died in the yellow-fever epidemics of 1804, 1807, 1808, 1811, and 1813. American and foreign sailors frequently slugged it out on the levees and in taverns, while Creoles lavished their contempt on Anglo-Americans. Collector of Customs William Brown absconded in 1809 with $150,000 in customs receipts and a year later a slave insurrection just above the city in St. John the Baptist Parish was suppressed. The heads of many of the leaders of the revolt were mounted on poles along the levee for

other slaves to see and take heed.

Aside from the purchase itself, the events that left the most significant impressions on the collective imagination in those years were the Aaron Burr conspiracy of 1805–1807; Jefferson's Embargo Act of 1807; statehood in 1811–1812; and the British invasion of 1814–1815.

Former Vice-President Aaron Burr, whose political career ended when he killed Alexander Hamilton in a duel in 1804, allegedly conspired with General James Wilkinson and others to wrest Louisiana and Western states away from the United States or a part of Mexico from Spain to set up his own country. In the summer of 1805 Burr was in New Orleans to meet with Edward Livingston, Daniel Clark, and members of the Mexican Association, a group of traders

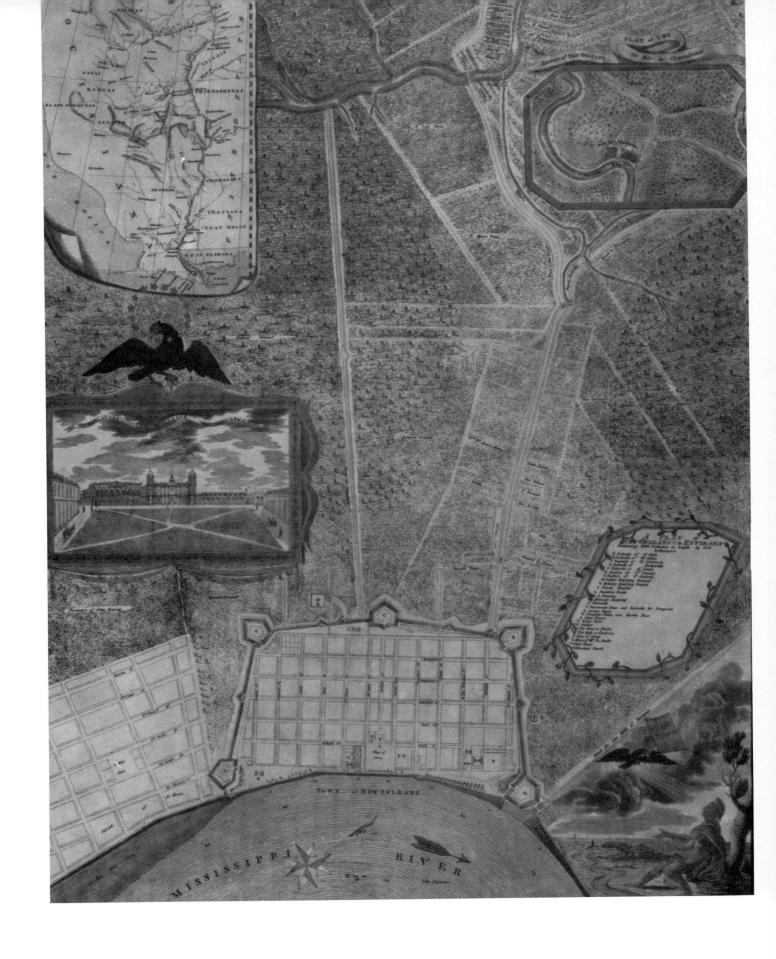

and adventurers that wanted to invade Mexico. To New Orleans Burr carried a letter of introduction from Wilkinson (then governor of the Louisiana Territory, not including the Territory of Orleans, but formerly a spy in the service of the Spanish). What Burr was really up to may never be fully known: Burr had previously told British, French, and Spanish ministers in Washington of his plans to separate the Western Territory and states from the Union; and told others he was going to settle property he owned along the Ouachita River area in the Territory of Orleans; to still others he told of his intention to invade Mexico.

In 1806 and 1807 New Orleans was alive with rumors of Burr's advancing army and every new arrival from upriver, especially Kentucky and Tennessee, was suspected. Many New Orleanians believed that the Spanish in neighboring West Florida were working with Burr to regain Louisiana. Governor Claiborne interviewed all newcomers in the city from upriver to satisfy himself that they were not vanguards of Burr's army. The cabal never fully materialized, however, and Burr was later arrested, tried, and acquitted.

While fears of the Burr invasion subsided in 1807 war was blazing on the Atlantic between Great Britain and France. Although the United States professed neutrality in the conflicts, hundreds of its ships were seized at sea by both

England and France. Repeated appeals by President Jefferson were ignored, so the President and Congress reacted by passing the Embargo Act of 1807, prohibiting all exportation of American goods to either of the warring powers.

This act had devastating effects on the American economy — particularly on port cities such as New Orleans. Smuggling became commonplace and American exports fell from $108 million in 1807 to $22 million the following year. In the same period imports dropped from $138 million to less than $57 million. Jefferson stuck by the act and his course of action, hoping to force the French and British to respect America's rights on the seas. In New Orleans, mercantile companies foundered and young men who came to the city with dreams of making their fortune became destitute. Such was the case of young Nathaniel Cox, who came to New Orleans in 1806 from Kentucky. Writing to his business associate back home on May 2, 1808, he described the effect of the Embargo Act on their business prospects:

. . . This infernal Embargo has so effectively stopped our Commercial career that the prospects once so flattering have become extremely gloomy — and the profits arising from the business we are now doing will not justify the step.

Lamenting his inability to build a home and settle down, Cox wrote on September 15, 1809:

If there had been no failures in New Orleans, no frays with the Chesapeake — no Embargo — no non-intercourse — no Burr — no Wilkinson, no proclamations — and in short, if the usual commertial [sic] arrangements had continued between the United States and Europe my calculations might in some measure [have] been realized.

By 1812 the depredations committed by the British upon the American nation, coupled with expansionist ideas, led the young nation into a war which up to that point had been a European affair.

While the attention of the rest of the nation

was directed to the growing menace of war with Great Britain during 1811 and well into the next year, New Orleanians were pressuring Congress for statehood. The 1810 census showed the population of the Territory of Orleans had risen to over 76,500 residents — 60,000 was the number required for statehood. In January 1811 the territory's delegate to Congress, Julien Poydras, proposed statehood in the House of Representatives and numerous petitions were sent from New Orleans to Congress in support of the move. The following month Congress authorized the territory to draw up a constitution. Delegates met in New Orleans at Tremoulet's Coffee House, and after long debates even on a name for the state (the name "Jefferson" was discussed and summarily dismissed), Congress ratified the document on April 8, 1812. At first the Florida Parishes, which had been annexed to the territory after the West Florida rebellion of 1810, were not included in the constitution. A few days later, however, they were added to the state by an amendment. Louisiana became the nation's 18th state on April 30, 1812. During the subsequent gubernatorial election, Claiborne — appointed governor six times by Jefferson — defeated Jacques Villere, a prominent Creole.

Many observers, including Jefferson and Claiborne, believed that many years would pass before New Orleanians would be ready to participate as full citizens in the Union. After all, the reasoning went, they had never known the democratic process and had always lived under one monarchy or another. But perhaps the population was better suited for its new status than most critics realized. In addition to the many Anglo-Americans already living in New Orleans before and shortly after the purchase, there were subtle differences between the French and Spanish Creoles and their counterparts in Europe. Louisianians during the colonial era did not receive hereditary titles as did the Europeans or even those in other colonies. Many were titled before coming or after returning to their homelands. The Louisiana colony also lacked the strict class delineation found in the mother countries. People — from all strata of society — most often came to Louisiana in quest of opportunity. To make their fortunes, which many did, they worked side by side. Such was the case of Louis Brasillier, called "Touranjeau," who came to Louisiana in 1717 as an illiterate valet to a military officer, and Captain Renault D'Hauterive, a member of the French gentry, who arrived in the colony in

1720. After three decades, Brasillier was a prosperous plantation owner on nearby Bayou St. John. The Brasilliers by the next generation owned a successful shipping concern. By this time D'Hauterive's son was signing his name Dauterive in the more egalitarian fashion. Both the Brasilliers and "Dauterives" married into the same New Orleans families.

Another major event in New Orleans—one that would shortly revolutionize commerce on the Mississippi and its thousands of miles of tributaries—took place the same year, although not everyone paid it the attention it deserved: On January 10, Nicholas Roosevelt arrived on the *New Orleans,* the first steamboat on the Western territorial waters.

Only slightly more than a month had passed since Louisiana gained statehood when Congress declared war against Great Britain. Since the end of the American Revolution, the young nation had endured repeated insults to its national sovereignty at the hands of the British. American ships were stopped at sea and their seamen impressed. British ships blockaded American ports. In violation of the treaty ending the Revolution, Great Britain maintained forts on American territory near the Great Lakes from which they encouraged Indians to attack westward-moving settlers. British harassment was not the only incitement for the War of 1812: "War Hawks" in Congress and Westerners believed that in the event of war, Canada and Spanish Florida would fall easily to the United States. Some Westerners also believed that war would solve their agricultural problems and enable them to ship their cotton, tobacco, and wheat to markets for higher prices. Despite opposition in the New England states, war came and the United States was hardly prepared to fight.

The steamboat New Orleans, *whose reconstructed plan is shown here, was the first steamboat to ply the western territorial waters of the Mississippi River. (THNOC)*

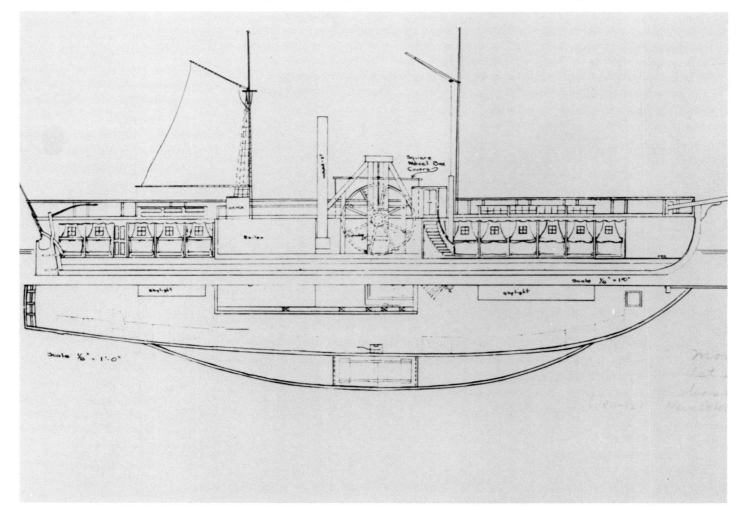

The Americans enjoyed some success early in the war, especially Oliver Hazard Perry's victory in the Battle of Lake Erie. The British successes, however, were more impressive. They defeated the Americans at Fort Dearborn (Chicago) and Detroit. They captured and burned Washington, D.C., and effectively blockaded American ports. America's dreams of capturing Canada vanished when several invasion forces were soundly defeated and turned back.

In Louisiana, Governor Claiborne was busy preparing for a defensive war while two British blockade ships sat at the mouth of the Mississippi. Not all Louisianians were enthusiastic in their support of the American war effort. Some French Creoles asked the French consul in New Orleans for protection, claiming they were French, not American, citizens. Other New Orleanians were ready to fight the British, while still others were suspected of supplying the enemy with important intelligence. In early 1814 General Andrew Jackson marched south from Tennessee to suppress the Creek Indians who, at the instigation of the British, had massacred white settlers along the Alabama River.

Meanwhile, Claiborne met with Caddo Indian chiefs at Natchitoches to make sure they did not follow the lead of the Creeks.

By the spring of 1814 word began reaching Louisiana that the British were planning an attack against New Orleans and the Gulf Coast area. Claiborne ran helter-skelter trying to prepare the city's defenses against a possible British attack. On August 24, Claiborne wrote to Jackson and complained about the lack of cooperation: "I have a difficult people to manage; native Americans, native Louisianians, Frenchmen, Spanish, with some English."

In September 1814 the British brig *Sophia* dropped anchor near Grande Terre, the stronghold of the celebrated pirate Jean Lafitte (also Laffite). Captain Nicholas Lockyer presented Lafitte with a letter from British Lieutenant Colonel Edward Nicholls, who had occupied Pensacola with an expeditionary force in July. Nicholls offered Lafitte the rank of captain in the British forces, and land and money in return for his help against the Americans. While Lafitte was passing this information along to state officials, Claiborne and the Committee of Defense sent a force of regular United States

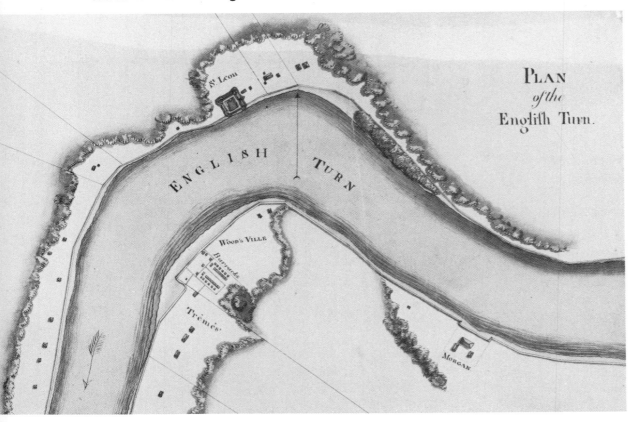

B. Lafon drew this plan of English Turn. Fort St. Leon on the Mississippi River below New Orleans was one of several forts, both active and abandoned, which defended the city and its approaches. Lafon was commissioned to make a survey of existing and projected military fortifications in the Gulf South. (THNOC)

soldiers and navy out to capture Lafitte and to break up his sanctuary. Although most of the Baratarians escaped, including the Lafitte brothers, others were taken as prisoners.

Nicholls soon left no doubt in the minds of Louisianians what the British intentions were when a proclamation began appearing all over the city:

> *Natives of Louisiana! On you the first call is made to assist in liberating from a faithless, imbecile government, your paternal soil: Spaniards, Frenchmen, Italians, and British . . . you also I call to aid me in this just cause. The American usurpation of this country must be abolished, and the lawful owners of the soil put in possession.*

In response, Jackson issued his own proclamation, which read in part:

> *Louisianians! The proud Briton, the natural and sworn enemies of all Frenchmen, has called upon you, by proclamation, to aid him in his tyranny, and to prostrate the holy temple of our liberty. Can Louisianians, can Frenchmen, can Americans, ever stoop to be the slaver or allies of Britain?*

Word also circulated throughout the city and state that the British planned to arm slaves and give them their freedom if they would rise up against their owners.

In September British forays against Mobile were driven off by Jackson and later the next month, Jackson moved successfully against Pensacola, sending Nicholls and his troops back to their ships. Claiborne flooded Jackson with dispatches describing the problems—both real and imagined—the governor was facing in preparing Louisiana to defend itself. Not enough troops, not enough money, spies, and trouble with the state legislature filled the governor's letters to the general. Jackson often lost his temper with Claiborne's seeming inability to take hold of the situation.

Meanwhile, reports continued to arrive in Washington describing the massive buildup of British troops and supplies in Jamaica in preparation for the invasion of Louisiana. With this information in hand, Jackson set out from Mobile to New Orleans on November 22, only days before the British set sail on their Gulf Coast expedition. Jackson arrived in the Crescent City on December 2.

Eight days later the British fleet of 50 ships dropped anchor off North Chandeleur Island near Lake Borgne. Aboard was an army of over 10,000 troops commanded by General Sir Edward Pakenham, the Duke of Wellington's brother-in-law. The fleet itself was under the command of Admiral Sir Alexander Cochrane. So confident were the British of victory that aboard their ships they brought civil officials to take over the Louisiana government as well as their wives and those of the military officers. Also aboard was a government printing press to promulgate the new government's policies and proclamations.

Lord Castlereagh, British foreign secretary, was so confident that the New Orleans campaign would be successful, that he wrote on his way to the Congress of Vienna in December 1815: "I expect at this moment that most of the large seaport towns of America are laid in ashes, that we are in possession of New Orleans, and have command of all the rivers of the Mississippi Valley and the lakes, and that the Americans are now little better than prisoners in their own country."

Upon his arrival in New Orleans, Jackson began immediately to prepare the city for war. He ordered Major Arsene Lacarriere Latour, an engineer sent to Louisiana by Napoleon in 1802, to rehabilitate and strengthen the city's

General Andrew Jackson was the commander of the American forces at the Battle of New Orleans. (THNOC)

defense lines. With the help of Mayor Nicholas Girod, every available person — both white and black, free and slave — worked furiously. Batteries and earthworks were thrown up at the Rigolets, Chef Menteur Road, and the two forts below the city on opposite banks of the river.

Jackson's dilemma was determining where the British would attack first. Would they come over land from Mobile and attack the city from the east or northeast or would they sail up the river in a head-on attack? Perhaps they would sail into Lake Borgne and attack by land from the south. Jackson had to prepare for all possibilities. He ordered troops standing by in Baton Rouge, Mobile, Natchez, and in other sections to march to New Orleans as soon as possible. He also sent Captain Henry Miller Shreve, and his steamboat *Enterprise,* who had just arrived downriver from Pittsburgh, back upriver to pick up supplies. Everyone who could carry a weapon was needed. Jackson took a bold step for the times — despite considerable local opposition — and accepted the help of free black military units of Louisiana which had distinguished themselves during the French and Spanish colonial periods. Earlier Jackson had sent a letter to Claiborne making known his wish to use the free blacks:

The free men of color in your city are inured to the southern climate and would make excellent soldiers. They will not remain quiet spectators of the contest. They must be either for or against us. Distrust them and you make them your enemies. Place confidence in them, and you engage them by every dear and honorable tie to the interest of the country by extending to them equal rights and privileges with white men.

These free-people-of-color again distinguished themselves on the battlefield as they had done under Galvez against the British almost four decades earlier.

Jackson made another bold move, again against Claiborne's advice, by inviting Lafitte and his Baratarians to fight the British. Lafitte and his men were given full pardons in return for their service. Lafitte offered Jackson badly needed flints, muskets, and other armaments along with his own skilled artillerists.

New Orleans was alive with activity as Latour so graphically noted:

The citizens were preparing for battle as cheerfully as if it had been a party of pleasure, each in his vernacular tongue singing songs of victory. The streets resounded with 'Yankee Doodle,' the 'Marseillaise,' the 'chant du Depart,' and other martial airs, while those who had been long unaccustomed to military duty were furbishing their arms and accoutrements.

Above
The Battle of New Orleans was truly a group effort on the part of the American forces. In addition to regular troops, free blacks and the band of "pirates" led by Jean Lafitte also fought. (THNOC)

Below left
Captain Henry Miller Shreve's innovations in steamboating made routes on the water to Northern Louisiana navigable. His accomplishments were instrumental in breaking the steamboat monopoly on territorial waters. (THNOC)

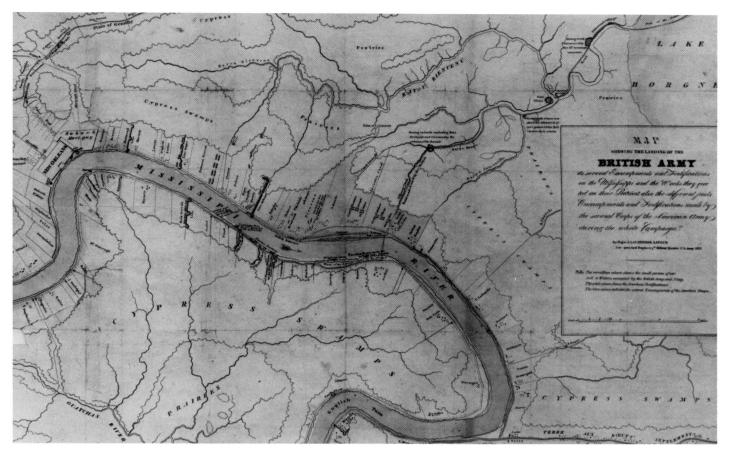

Jackson did not have to wait long to learn the direction of the British attack. On December 14 Admiral Cochrane sent troops from the south in oared barges to destroy the small American naval force in Lake Borgne which was under the command of Lieutenant Thomas ap Catesby Jones. The British concentrated their forces on Pea Island at the mouth of the Pearl River. On December 22 British forces began moving across Lake Borgne to Bayou Bienvenue and set up camp on the Villere Plantation on the banks of the Mississippi River. In a brilliant strategic move, Jackson decided to attack the British on the night of December 23. The weary British army was taken completely by surprise when they saw the American ship *Carolina* drifting on the river toward their position. They were even more surprised when the *Carolina* opened fire, inflicting havoc and carnage in their camp. Then Pierre Denis de la Ronde and John Coffee at the head of 600 mounted Tennessee volunteers, Hind's Dragoons, and John Beale's Rifles attacked the British right flank. Jackson led the advance against the left flank with the 7th and 44th Regulars, Plauche's Orleans Volunteers, Daquin's Battalion of Free Colored, and Jugeat's Choctaws. When the smoke had cleared and the utter confusion abated, 24 Americans were dead, 115 wounded, and 74 missing. The British suffered 46 killed, 167 wounded, and 64 missing.

For the rest of December the British continued to land troops and supplies and Jackson dug in along the Rodriguez Canal above the Chalmette Plantation. Behind hastily built fortifications of dirt mounds, cotton bales, and cypress logs, Jackson waited. On December 28 the British attacked the American line to determine its strength but retreated. The British right actually turned Jackson's left flank in the cypress swamp. They possibly could have driven the American main force from their lines had not Pakenham lost control of his reconnaissance. He sounded recall when victory was within his reach. The retreat severely wounded the morale of the proud British regiments, as was recounted by one of their officers:

The map showing the plan of attack at the Battle of New Orleans was drawn by Major Arsene Lacarriere Latour. Much of the territory traversed by the British on their way to attack the city was swampy, and this fact of geography hampered their efforts. The Americans were diligent in their attempts to defend all possible approaches to the city. (THNOC)

When the fog lifted on the morning of New Year's Day 1815, the British artillery brought in from the ships opened a barrage on the American line. The American artillery responded, and after almost five hours of bombardment in both camps, a considerable proportion of the British cannon had been silenced. A British soldier later wrote: "It was a sad day for men who, a year before, had marched through France from the Pyrenees to the sea."

During the following days, 2,000 Kentuckians and other militia units arrived to reinforce Jackson's army. He dispatched many of them above New Orleans to prevent a surprise attack from the north and sent over 800 troops along with General David Morgan to guard the west bank of the river. Jackson is estimated to have had about 3,000 troops at Chalmette with another 1,000 in reserve. Pakenham had between 5,000 and 6,000 men with which to attack Jackson with 1,200 in reserve. He sent another 1,200 across the river to attack Morgan. The Americans also had eight batteries of cannon fixed on the open stretch of field separating the two opposing armies.

As the day of the main attack neared, Pakenham expressed grave reservations against a frontal attack across such a wide open space. Sarcastically, Admiral Cochrane told Pakenham that the navy would take on the task if the army believed it too difficult: "The soldiers can then bring up the baggage," he said.

On January 7 the armies prepared behind their lines for what both sides knew would be the decisive battle. Shortly before daybreak, on January 8, two signal rockets were fired into the sky from the British lines. The battle and drama were about to unfold. When the low-lying fog lifted, the Americans, crouched behind their defenses, could see coming toward them three columns of brightly uniformed British soldiers. With drummers beating cadence and bagpipes wailing ancient regimental airs, the 93rd Highlanders dressed in their kilts and tartans, the 95th Rifles, the 44th Regiment, the Duchess of York's Light Dragoons, the King's

A cease-fire at New Orleans was called shortly after the death of General Sir Edward Pakenham (pictured here). It was a serious blow to the British troops. (THNOC)

Own, the 21st Royals, the West India regiments, and others marched forward with weapons and ladders to scale the breastworks. Cannon fire savagely ripped through their lines, but still they marched on. American riflemen joined in with the artillery to mow broad swaths through the British ranks. The few attackers who managed to reach the American line were soon felled by sharpshooters. Finally, the carnage was too much even for the disciplined British troops to endure. Their ranks broke and ran to the rear, discarding weapons along the way. Pakenham himself was killed when he rode forward to rally his troops. "Shame! Shame! Remember you're British! Forward, Gentlemen, Forward!" the general shouted before the fatal bullet struck.

A cease-fire was called to allow both sides to tend to their dead and wounded. A British officer later described the horrors he had witnessed in the British camp:

The scene now presented at de la Ronde's plantation was one I shall never forget; almost every room was crowded with the wounded and dying. . . . I was the unwilling spectator of numerous amputations; and on all sides, nothing was heard but the piteous cries of my poor countrymen, undergoing various operations . . . and I cannot describe the strange and ghastly feelings created by seeing a basket nearly full of legs.

Shallow graves were made for many of the fallen British troops on "the field of slaughter" and after a light rainfall, parts of bodies could be seen, making the field resemble a gruesome garden. Wounded British prisoners were taken to New Orleans for medical care. When space could not be found for them in the barracks and hospitals, New Orleanians opened their homes to them and nursed their wounds.

British forces lingered in the area for several more weeks before rejoining the fleet on January 27. The fleet had just returned from an unsuccessful attempt to bombard Fort St. Philip into submission. The British then moved on to Mobile Bay where they were met by fresh reinforcements from England. The battle for New Orleans had only begun. Fort Bowyer at the entrance of Mobile Bay fell to the British as they planned a new overland attack against New Orleans.

Jackson had returned to New Orleans in triumph. January 23 was declared an official day of celebration. the *Te Deum* was sung in the Cathedral and an arch of triumph was erected in the Place d'Armes (later renamed Jackson Square in the general's honor). Public opinion soon turned against Jackson for he was determined to maintain martial law as long as the British fleet remained near New Orleans. Reports had reached the city that the United States and Great Britain had signed a peace treaty at Ghent, Belgium, on December 24, two weeks before the battle of January 8. Jackson maintained that he would continue martial law and keep the local milita in service until he received official word of the treaty from Washington. One of the more interesting events occurring from the martial law edict was the arrest of New Orleans' Judge Dominic Hall and United States District Attorney John Dick. Jackson ordered Louis Louaillier arrested for publishing uncomplimentary statements about the general and Hall ordered Louaillier's release on a writ of habeas corpus. Jackson in turn had Hall and Dick arrested. Hall later fined the general $1,000, which he paid. Twenty-nine years later, Congress reimbursed Jackson the amount of the fine plus interest.

On March 13 Jackson received word from Washington that the treaty had been signed. The Battle of New Orleans was over. Martial law was suspended and the following month, Jackson returned to Nashville with his wife Rachel and adopted son. The British troops replenished their supplies and joined their countrymen in defeating Napoleon at Waterloo.

Reports differ slightly on the number of casualties suffered on both sides that fateful day in early January. One participant on the American side placed fatalities at 13, 39 wounded, and 19 missing. The British reported 858 dead, 2,468 wounded, and many others missing. The gargantuan accomplishment of American military arms in the British campaign against New Orleans has been recalled for generations. The Battle of New Orleans dispelled any fears held by other Americans that New Orleanians might not make good Americans. This people of diverse and unique ethnic background fought side by side courageously against a common enemy — an enemy of the United States.

This view entitled New Orleans from the Lower Cotton Press *looks upriver toward the Vieux Carre. By the mid-19th century New Orleans was a large, growing city extending both upriver and down from the original settlement.* (THNOC)

CHAPTER IV
THE MAGNIFICENT HALF-CENTURY

The nearly five decades preceding the Civil War are referred to as the golden years of New Orleans. New Orleans became synonymous with prosperity. It was a boom town, pulsating with energy—the energy of commerce, business, change, and expansion.

The city's Caribbean-flavor marketplaces teamed with the sights and smells of prosperity: produce, wild game, and seafood; spices, European wines, and hundreds of other commodities that eventually found their way into New Orleans' homes. People of every size, hue, and shape mingled among the stalls, either hawking their wares or purchasing food for their tables, candles to light their homes, or cloth for their garments.

The city and surrounding areas experienced commercial and population explosions. By 1840 the population of the state had reached 350,-000, almost half of whom were either slaves or free-people-of-color. New Orleans had become the fourth-largest city in the nation and vied with New York for the title of the country's leading port.

The great changes in New Orleans during those years were hastened by the arrival of the steamboat *New Orleans* in 1812. Behind the *New Orleans* venture were Robert Livingston, the American negotiator for the Louisiana Purchase, and steamboat pioneer Robert Fulton. Livingston and Fulton believed the economic future of the Western lands would be carried on the decks of steamboats. To ensure their own fortunes, the entrepreneur and the inventor secured from the territorial legislature a complete monopoly for steamboat commerce on territorial waters in the West.

All went well for a couple of years, until Captain Henry Miller Shreve arrived in New Orleans in December 1814 aboard his own steamer, the *Enterprise*. Acting in behalf of the Mississippi Steamboat Navigation Company, Edward Livingston, a kinsman of Robert Livingston, tried to seize the boat with a court order. General Jackson saved Shreve's day by sending him and the *Enterprise* upriver for needed supplies to fight the approaching British. After a series of legal maneuvers and counter-maneuvers, a New Orleans court broke up the Livingston-Fulton monopoly in April 1817. Shreve went on to improve steamboat construction, invent the "snag boat" and open the Red River to commerce by de-snagging the Red River Raft. The city of Shreveport bears his name today.

The Mississippi and Ohio rivers and their hundreds, even thousands of miles of tributaries, became highways for steamboats ladened with cotton, sugar, and other agricultural and manufactured goods en route to their point of export in New Orleans. The rivers also became the return highways for imported goods from Europe and South and Central America passing through Bienville's port city.

A traveler visiting the New Orleans docks in the early 1830s noted the vitality and vibrance

of the city's port:

With what astonishment did I, for the first time, view the magnificent levee, from one point or horn of the beauteous crescent to the other, covered with active human beings of all nations and colors, and boxes, bales, bags, hogsheads, pipes, barrels, kegs of goods, wares, and merchandise from all ends of the earth! Thousands of bales of cotton, tierces of sugar, molasses; quantities of flour, pork, lard, grain and other provisions; leads [and] furs . . . from the rich and extensive rivers above; and the wharves lined for miles with ships, steamers, flatboats, arks, and four deep! The business appearance of this city is not surpassed by any other in the wide world; it might be likened to a huge bee-hive, where no drones could find a resting place. I stepped on shore, and my first exclamation was, "This is the place for a business man!"

With the burgeoning commercial activity in the port came the cotton and sugar factories, importers and exporters, and banking houses and insurance companies. The first bank estab-

lished in New Orleans after the Louisiana Purchase was the Louisiana Bank in 1804. In 1811 the Bank of Orleans and the Louisiana Planters Bank appeared on the scene. The Louisiana Bank, located on Royal Street in the building currently occupied by the famous Brennen's Restaurant, closed in 1818, but reopened in 1824 as the state-supported Bank of Louisiana. By 1827 five banks were operating in New Orleans, including a branch of the United States Bank, and the Consolidated Association of Planters Bank.

Banks in New Orleans were mostly financed by banking institutions from the Northeast, and especially from England. Banking in antebellum New Orleans was based primarily on the returns of immediate profits rather than long-term meaningful investments. Banks took mortgages on land, slaves, and houses and sold bonds on these mortgages to foreign speculators. The money obtained from the sale of bonds was then passed on to borrowers, who in turn put up their future crops as collateral.

New Orleans grew and prospered despite severe economic depressions in 1820, 1837, and 1839, which were caused in part by shaky banking practices; the adverse financial impact

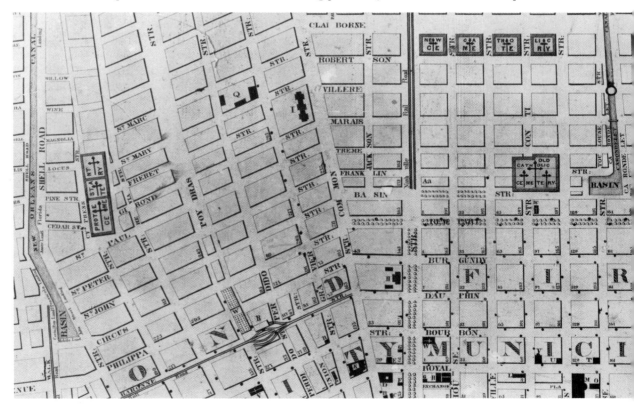

of the new canal system in the Northeast; and the constant fear of yellow-fever epidemics in the port city. As a result, increasing quantities of Western products were transported directly to Eastern ports along the new canals, including the Erie Canal, and along the emerging railroads.

The importance of canals and railroads to commerce was not lost on New Orleanians. In 1830–1831 local investors built the Pontchartrain Railroad from the lower end of the market out through Elysian Fields to Milneburg. They had hoped to develop a port on the lake that would benefit the development in Faubourg Marigny. Other investors above Canal Street, however, especially entrepreneur Samuel J. Peters, were not to be outdone. They formed the New Orleans Canal and Banking Company and, with a charter from the state legislature, built the New Basin Canal from the American Sector to Lake Pontchartrain. Although scores of immigrants lost their lives digging the canal

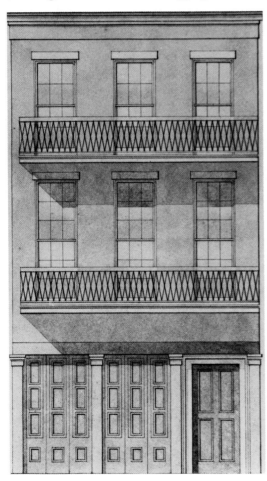

through the mosquito-infested terrain, the new waterway had a significant impact on the economy of the American Sector. In 1832 another group of investors planned to build a canal to link the city directly to Lake Borgne, but the project failed. Three years later, the Carrollton Railroad began service, connecting the village of Carrollton with New Orleans. The Carrollton Railroad contributed significantly to the development of the suburbs and communities above the city. Today, fashionable residential neighborhoods, universities, and parks line the track-bed of the old railroad, which is still in existence as the St. Charles Avenue Streetcar.

The decades before and after the depressions of 1837 and 1839 were a bustle of activity in New Orleans. Faubourg Ste. Marie above Canal Street was slowly transformed into neat and classically designed "Yankee-styled" red-brick row buildings. Americans and newly arriving immigrants moved upriver to the fashionable Coliseum Square area or to other communities along the river, like the town of Lafayette and the "Garden District," which were annexed by the city in 1852. In the Old Quarter Esplanade Avenue developed its opulence as wealthy Creoles strove to maintain their identity in a changing culture.

Competition was the spirit of the times from the 1830s through the 1850s. Rivalry thrived not only among commission merchants and others seeking their fortunes, but also between cultures.

Architect Benjamin Henry B. Latrobe, writing in his journal in late January 1819, reflected on the changes and cultural clashes taking place in New Orleans during this period:

The state of society at any time here is puzzling. There are in fact three societies here: 1. the French; 2. the American; and 3. the mixed. The French society is not exactly what it was at the change of government, and the American is not strictly what it is in the Atlantic cities. The opportunities of growing rich by more active, extensive and intelligent modes of agriculture and commerce diminished the hospitality, destroyed the leisure, and added more selfishness to the character of the Creoles. The Americans, coming hither to make money. . . . are in an eternal bustle. Their limbs, their heads, and

Below left
The architecture of the American Sector reflected a Northeastern style of construction and appearance quite different from that of the French and Spanish builders. (THNOC)

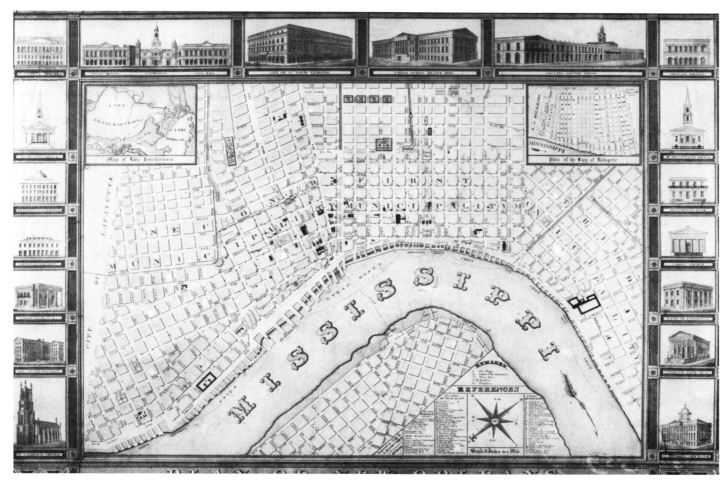

their hearts, move to that sole object, cotton and tobacco, buying and selling, and all the rest of the occupations of a money-making community.

In the early 1830s there existed three well-defined sections in the city: the American Sector above Canal Street, or the Faubourg Ste. Marie; the Vieux Carre; and Faubourg Marigny below Esplanade Avenue. As mentioned earlier, Faubourg Marigny was laid out by the colorful, if not prudent, Bernard Marigny, who gave the streets such interesting names as Desire, Frenchmen, Good Children, and Love.

The competition commercially, politically, and culturally had become so intense by 1836 that the state general assembly gave the city a new charter which divided the city into three separate municipalities. The First Municipality consisted of the Vieux Carre and its predominantly Creole population. The Second Municipality was the American Sector and the Third

Municipality was comprised of the remainder of the city below Esplanade Avenue, including the Faubourg Marigny. Although the three were united theoretically under a mayor and general council, each municipality had its own recorder and council. With minor exceptions, all actions taken by the general council had to be approved by the three individual councils before they could be put into effect. This system lasted until 1852 when the city again was given a new charter. This charter signaled the new political dominance of the American Sector in that the seat of government was moved from the Cabildo at the Place d'Armes to Gallier Hall facing Lafayette Square. This shift in political power away from the conservative sugar planters and French population to the burgeoning American faction was ultimately symbolized by the removal of the state capital from New Orleans to Donaldsville in 1830–1831, then back to New Orleans until 1849 when it was moved to Baton Rouge.

This 1840 Plan of New Orleans was drawn by L. Hirt. New Orleans was divided into distinct sections, each with its own character. The three municipalities were superseded by municipal districts. The Vieux Carre (Old First Municipality) became part of the Second Municipal District, and the American Sector (formerly called the Second Municipality) became part of the First Municipal District. (THNOC)

The emergence of political parties in the 1830s, matched with the cultural differences in the city, made politics a violent business in New Orleans. During the 1840s and 1850s many elections were marred by armed confrontations between Whigs and Democrats and later Native American Party "Know-Nothings" and Democrats. The most serious incidence of political violence was during the election of June 1858. The city became a battlefield between Know-Nothings and the Vigilance Committee which had vowed to "maintain the rights unviolable of every peaceful and law-abiding citizen, restore public order, abate crime, and expel or punish, as the law may determine, such notorious robbers and assassins as the arm of the law has, either from the infidelity of its public servants, or the inefficiency of the laws themselves, left unshipped of justice." The committee decreed that it was assuming police powers and pleaded with the people to join its cause. It seized the state arsenal, the courts, and the jail, and set up an armed camp in Jackson Square. Supported by confiscated artillery, the vigilantes held off Know-Nothing attackers. The group finally dispersed after the elections. The New Orleans *Bee* described politics during those years as "the despotism of faction."

Prosperity and the competitive spirit between sections of the city dramatically changed the landscape of New Orleans. Americans, wanting to emulate other prosperous cities on the East Coast, and Creoles, with their eyes to Europe and to their own architectural heritage, built antebellum New Orleans. Above Canal Street stood such splendors as the St. Charles Hotel, City Hall (Gallier Hall) on Lafayette Square, the University of Louisiana on Common Street, blocks of three-storied red-brick row houses, and the new Customs House at the foot of Canal Street. Below Canal, Creoles and residents of that area boasted of the splendors of the U.S. Mint at Esplanade Avenue and the levee, the newly rebuilt St. Louis Cathedral, and the magnificent Pontalba Buildings facing the Place d'Armes. The construction of these buildings, and the renovation of the Place d'Armes (not yet named Jackson Square) were directed and financed by the Baroness de Pontalba, who had fled to New Orleans with her family after the 1848 revolution in France. She was no stranger to the city, however, for she was the daughter of Don Andres Almonester y Roxas, who contributed considerable sums of money to build a hospital, the Cabildo, St. Louis Cathedral, and other public buildings in

Left
The Second Municipality Hall, as this building was originally named, became the seat of city government in 1852. The building is now known as both Old City Hall and Gallier Hall, after architect James Gallier. (THNOC)

Facing page, bottom
The First Presbyterian Church, Gallier Hall, the St. Charles Hotel (middle distance), and the low dome of the St. Louis Hotel may be seen in this city view looking toward the Vieux Carre. (THNOC)

colonial New Orleans after the fires of 1788 and 1794.

Landscape architect and diarist Frederick Law Olmsted, traveling through the Southern states in 1855–1856, had little good to say about the South except for New Orleans whose uniqueness intrigued him. But he disliked most of the public buildings he encountered in the South, and the city's antebellum St. Charles Hotel was no exception: "I was landed before the great Grecian portico of the stupendous, tasteless, ill-contrived and inconvenient St. Charles Hotel." Not all visitors to the city agreed with Olmsted's opinion of the St. Charles. L. Webb, a young North Carolinian, apparently was awed by the hotel. He noted in his diary on January 24, 1853:

. . . stopping some time to take a look at that most magnificent of hotels, the St. Charles, which was reopened today — two years and one week since it was burned down. It is by far the most elegant hotel I ever saw. The exterior appearance of the building is beautiful in style and architecture with the most perfect and harmonious proportions I ever beheld.

This second St. Charles Hotel burned to the ground years later and was replaced with a third hotel bearing the same name. But unfortunately, in recent years this New Orleans landmark fell victim to the wrecker's ball and an ill-conceived business venture. The site is now a parking lot.

Ironically, many of the urban reforms made in New Orleans during the early-19th century were initiated not by industrious Yankees but by French-born Joseph Roffignac, who served as the city's mayor from 1820 to 1828. During his administration, the city acquired its first waterworks, which was built by Benjamin Latrobe. Curbs and gutters of the city's main thoroughfares were paved with stone. In 1822 the city sold bonds to pave major streets in the French Quarter and American Sector with cobblestones covered with a layer of fine gravel. Actually, the street-paving began in 1817 with the cobblestoning of a block of Gravier Street between Magazine and Tchoupitoulas streets, but the project proceeded no further. Despite Roffignac's efforts, most of the city's streets went unpaved for several more decades. Roffignac could boast of many more accomplishments during his term in office. Thousands of trees were planted along streets, the levee, and in public squares, many sidewalks — or *banquettes* — were paved with bricks, new drainage canals were dug, two new markets were opened, gutters were flushed with river water, and a clock was placed in the tower of the cathedral.

The St. Charles Hotel, located two blocks from Canal Street, was one of the dominating landmarks in the American Sector of the city. (THNOC)

One of the most noteworthy events of the Roffignac years was the Marquis de Lafayette's visit to the city in 1825. His visit had a special meaning to New Orleans. Not only was he a famous Frenchman, which endeared him to Creoles, but he was a Revolutionary War hero and a personal friend to both George Washington and Thomas Jefferson. Lafayette arrived in the city on April 10, 1825, aboard the steamboat *Natchez* that had been dispatched to meet him in Mobile. He stepped ashore to a tumultuous fanfare complete with speeches and an arch of triumph erected in the Place d'Armes in his honor. The legislature appropriated $15,000 to prepare an apartment in the Cabildo for his use while visiting the city. From the gallery of the Cabildo, Lafayette overlooked the militia as they passed in review. Special receptions also were held in Caldwell's American Theatre and the Theatre d'Orleans. On April 15 he boarded the *Natchez* and departed for Baton Rouge and other points. Although his visit lasted only four days, it was an event talked about for many years.

Amusement and the arts were always important elements in New Orleans. In the antebellum period town folk and visiting planters with their families frequently enjoyed the many entertainments the city had to offer. The American Theater and others provided plays and concerts by traveling troupes or visiting impresarios. P. T. Barnum and Jenny Lind, the "Swedish Nightingale," were smashing hits in 1851, as was Adelina Patti, the 18-year-old soprano opera singer, a few years later.

Prosperity brought the artists and their studios flourished. Many of the works of both native and visiting artists, such as Adrien Persac, Jules Lion, Vaudechamp, G.P.A. Healy, and John Wesley Jarvis have survived to this day.

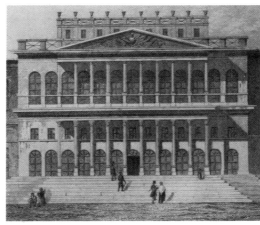

Then there was the opera, where blacks and whites, rich and poor — sitting in separate sections, of course — could hear a Bellini, a Meyerbeer, or a Donizetti opera at one of the several opera houses in the city. There was the St. Charles Theater in the American Sector and the Theatre d'Orleans in the French Quarter, and later the new French Opera House on fashionable Bourbon Street.

A gentleman could take fencing lessons from one of the several fencing masters in the Quarter on Exchange Alley; or perhaps an evening could be spent at one of the several gentlemen's clubs, be it the Boston Club on Canal Street, named for the then-popular card game, the Pelican Club, the Pickwick Club, or even Odd Fellows Hall on Camp Street. It was not uncommon for some gentlemen to keep concubines, including mulattoes, quadroons, and octoroons of legendary beauty. Men of less means but of equal infidelity enjoyed the many brothels and "dance halls" for which the city was famous. During certain seasons, a gentleman and his lady could enjoy a cotillion at the St. Charles or equally popular St. Louis Hotel

in the Vieux Carre. Idle time could also be spent at gambling, for which the Creoles were noted, or one of the many sporting events popular during the era, including horse racing, sailing on the lake, rowing in the Mississippi, and boxing.

For a family outing, there was the city library or art gallery, or an afternoon in a public square watching children play a game of cricket. Evenings often were passed listening to a visiting lecturer speaking at one of the many public halls or taking in the sights of a traveling circus stopping over for a few weeks. A fine meal could be had at the St. Charles or St. Louis hotels or one of the many fine restaurants, such as Antoine's, Victor's, or Moreau's.

New Orleans also became famous during these years for its international intrigues. The city abounded with young men looking for adventure, as well as merchants and other financiers ready to stake a filibustering expedition against some small Latin American country with its promise of riches and profits in return. Perhaps the most famous of these New Orleans-based intrigues were the Texas Revolution in 1835; General Narcisco Lopez's abortive invasion of Cuba in 1851; and William Walker's unsuccessful campaign against Nicaragua in 1855. And without question, the city's most famous den of intrigue was the three-story Banks Arcade, on Magazine near Gravier Street, which was built by Thomas Banks in 1833. New Orleanians also thoroughly enjoyed General Zachary Taylor's de-

During antebellum times the St. Louis Exchange Hotel was an elegant place to stay or dine in the French Quarter. It was located at the corner of St. Louis and Royal Streets. The hotel, demolished in the early 20th century, was replaced by the Royal Orleans (THNOC)

parture for the Mexican War in 1845 and were beside themselves with excitement upon his victorious return in 1847.

Without question, however, the most famous of New Orleans' pastimes came once a year — Mardi Gras. Mardi Gras balls in New Orleans were as old as the city itself. But not until the late 1820s did Mardi Gras celebrations begin to take the form for which they have become so widely known.

The Mardi Gras parade reportedly began as early as the 1820s and continued for three dec-

ades as an unwieldly and diverse band of masquers winding through the streets throwing confetti and flour upon onlookers. The practice of throwing flour eventually was stopped when some mischievous masquers threw quick-lime into the faces of spectators. The first parade utilizing vehicles was in 1839 when an odd assortment of wagons and carriages paraded from the Orleans Theater on Orleans Street, up Royal Street to St. Charles, down Julia to Camp Street, Chartres, Conde, Esplanade, and back up Royal to the Orleans Theater. That

In 1857 the Mystick Krewe of Comus began parading. With rare exception, the parade has rolled every Mardi Gras since then. (THNOC)

night a ball was held at the theater for the more affluent participants. This type of procession continued off and on for the next five or six years. Ironically, the first carnival organization in New Orleans was not formed by the Creoles of the city, but by the Anglo-American community. Taking their lead from the Cowbellions of Mobile, who held their first parade on New Year's Eve 1831, 12 prominent Americans founded the Mistick Krewe of Comus and the

Pickwick Club in 1857. Comus held its first parade that year with Milton's *Paradise Lost* as its theme. Mardi Gras, which at one time had been almost exclusively a Creole event, was by the end of the era celebrated by all segments of the community — whites, blacks, Americans, Creoles, newly arriving immigrants, Catholics, and Protestants.

Not everyone, however, was enamored by the annual festivities, including the young

North Carolinian Webb, who described a Mardi Gras parade in 1853:

The street was full of men, women and children of the lower classes on foot and the higher in carriages —
As I walked down the street, I was met by a crowd of boys and men fantastically dressed and masked running with a crowd at their heels who were hollering and yelling and filling the air with flour, eggs, and mud which they were throwing at the maskers who in turn filled the eyes of all with whom they came in contact with flour — I got out of the way, least they should give me some of their favors in the liberal distribution.
These had hardly passed when I heard not far distant the yelling of the boys which betokened another crowd of maskers coming — I went towards them and saw coming down the street a large cart filled with men in masks and fantastic dresses. Just as I approached, they stopped the cart and sprang out with horrid rath and accused someone in the crowd of spectators of throwing stones at them. They were all armed with short heavy clubs and soon got into a row in which several of the maskers and spectators got bloody noses — One great ruffanly [sic] fellow pounced upon a small boy and beat him badly — arousing my indignation and contempt which I could have given him positive proof of had I been able. . . . After several fights in which neither party gained anything, they mounted their cart and proceeded on followed by a crowd of yelling boys.
There were maskers on horseback and on foot — male and female followed by crowds. The whole street was alive with spectators and the scene to me was certainly strange and as a hideous or foolish looking masker would pass me and the horrid oaths and noises fell upon my ears, I could not help exclaim — Is this festival recognized by the Church of Rome. Can any Christian Church countenance much less allow such a profanation of its ceremonies.

New Orleans was indeed a place in which one could make his fortune or enjoy the many pleasures of life. But there was also poverty, squalor, and disease. The almost annual visitation of yellow fever took thousands of lives and sent wealthier residents fleeing to summer cottages in Mandeville, north of Lake Pontchartrain, or to the Mississippi Gulf Coast to avoid the misery. Cholera, typhus, and other plagues took their tolls as well. New Orleans, famed for its port, also gained recognition as being one of the unhealthiest cities in the world.

In 1856 the Louisiana Board of Health attributed 2,760 deaths in a one-year period to yellow fever, 1,029 deaths to cholera, and 652 deaths to tuberculosis. By far the most serious yellow-fever epidemic hit the city in the summer of 1853. Not knowing the cause of the dreaded disease, city officials tried a multitude of tactics to stop the disease from spreading: cannons were fired into the air in the belief that yellow fever lingered in the clouds, ships entering the port were quarantined, and a day of prayer was offered; mass graves were dug for the dead victims of the pestilence. New Orleanians died in such staggering numbers that open wagons made the rounds through the city to pick up heat-swollen, rotting bodies. In stacks of 50 or more they were carted to the cemetery where they were buried in shallow graves. A reporter for the New Orleans *Crescent* described one mass grave as nothing more than a ditch 14-inches deep. The coffins, he wrote, were placed side by side in the trench with their tops clearly above the ground level. About a foot of dirt was placed over the tops of the coffins. After a rainstorm, the caskets and their grotesque occupants clearly could be seen.

New Orleans businessman Zac Robertson, writing in 1853 to his business associate in Massachusetts, described some of the horrors he saw almost daily in the city:

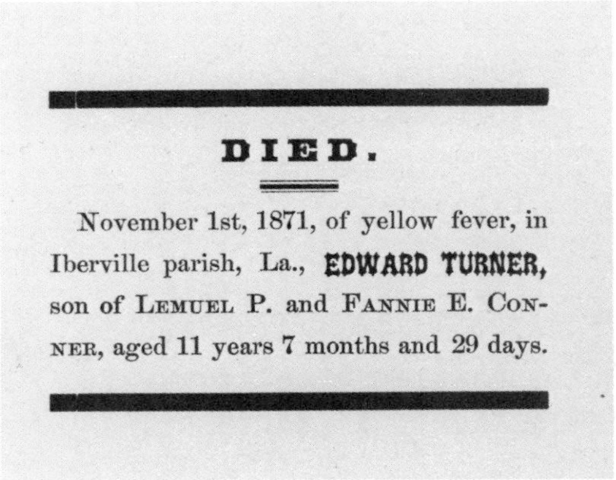

DIED.

November 1st, 1871, of yellow fever, in Iberville parish, La., **EDWARD TURNER,** son of LEMUEL P. and FANNIE E. CONNER, aged 11 years 7 months and 29 days.

The scourge of yellow fever hit New Orleans and the southern part of Louisiana nearly every summer for many years. Epidemics varied in severity and continued until the early 20th century when improved drainage helped eliminate mosquito breeding grounds. (THNOC)

Despite the heroic work of the city's physicians, nurses, and the benevolent Howard Association, over 8,000 men, women, and children lost their lives that summer. Hardest struck among the city's population were the immigrants arriving in America with hope for a new life. Writing in his diary on June 11, 1853, just before the worst of the epidemic was to strike, Webb reflected on a shipload of German immigrants entering the port:

The Battle of New Orleans, yellow fever, commerce, and steamboats were all major factors in shaping the history of antebellum New Orleans, but perhaps the most interesting aspect of that era was the people themselves. As the visiting Frederick Olmsted graphically described:

This is how New Orleans looked to the thousands of European immigrants who arrived in the city during the two decades before the Civil War. (THNOC)

During the two decades preceding the Civil War, immigrants from Europe arrived in the city by the thousands. Most shipped from the ports of Liverpool, Havre, Bremen, and Hamburg for voyages lasting up to six weeks. Packed into steerage many did not survive the crossing. By far the two largest groups of immigrants were the Irish and Germans, who left the problems of their homelands for the promise of the New World. By 1860 almost 25,000 Irish resided in the city. Many of the Germans who arrived in New Orleans did not remain but moved in farther upriver. Prospects of cheaper land elsewhere, yellow-fever epidemics in the city, and competing slave labor discouraged most immigrants from remaining in New Orleans. Those who did stay became merchants, tradesmen, and laborers. They generally settled along with the Irish below Esplanade Avenue, or in Lafayette, or along the New Basin Canal. Some also settled on small farms in the village of Carrollton above the city. Many Irish and Germans crowded into tenement houses in the "Irish Channel" between Magazine Street and the river.

Two segments of the New Orleans population unique to pre-Civil War America were the Creoles and the free-people-of-color. Historians as well as travelers to the city in the antebellum era often differed widely in their views and descriptions of the Creoles. Even the word Creole, itself, and as it applies to New Orleans, has never been defined adequately. In colonial times, it generally meant native born, but of European ancestry including Irish, German, English, French, and Spanish. To early-19th century Americans, the word was usually used to differentiate the descendants of old colonial families of Louisiana from the new arrivals. During both periods, French-speaking blacks and free-people-of-color also were called Creoles to distinguish them from their English-speaking counterparts from other parts of the nation.

Creoles, as did their American counterparts, occupied all levels of society from laborer, shopkeeper, and merchant to the local aristocracy. By the 1850s the upper classes of all three sections of the city's population — Creole, Anglo-American, and immigrant — were intermarrying, forming not only familial bonds but economic ones. The sons of the wealthier classes of Creoles often enjoyed a Paris education while their daughters were sent to the nuns at the Ursuline Convent for training.

The physical beauty of Creole women is legendary and has been retold by generations. Describing female society in New Orleans in 1819, Benjamin Latrobe wrote:

This French drawing is entitled La Creole. *The charms of Creole women in New Orleans have been a topic of conversation—and disagreement—from earliest times. (THNOC)*

My impression then, as to the surface of female society is, that there are . . . more correct and beautiful features, more faces and figures for the sculptor, than I ever recollect to have seen together in the same number. A few of them are perfect and a great majority are far above the mere agreeable.

The Duke of Saxe-Weimar, visiting the city in the 1820s, praised the Creoles, but Karl Anton Postl, of Germany, noted that Creole women were poorly educated and unable to carry on an intelligent literary conversation. A comparable view came from L. Webb who wrote in April 1853:

The walks in Jackson Square were crowded with gentlemen and ladies. . . . The dark complexion, black hair and black eyes would have proclaimed their descent had not their gaiety, excessive politeness and language told me they were all French.

I had heard much said of the beauty of the Creole or French population of this city. . . .

After an hour's scrutiny, I unhesitatingly declare I never saw in so large a crowd so much ugliness. The female faces were positively the worst looking as a general thing I ever before saw among so many.

There was a degenerated unintellectual cast of countenance and expression that at once engaged my attention and I saw scarcely a single exception.

Eyes black as night but without those charms that led Byron to sing of "the dark eye in woman" for they had a lack lustre, vacant expression and presented so many cases of shortsightedness and obliquity of vision that I could not divest myself of the idea that they were sadly degenerated from some cause. . . .

Much has been written about blacks and slavery in the antebellum South. The horrors of the system in the "land of the free" have been condemned and rationalized by generations of historians and polemics. By 1860 there were approximately 25,000 blacks living in the city of which almost 11,000 were slaves owned either by local whites and free blacks or just arriving in the city and awaiting sale on the auction block. New Orleans, one of the major slave markets in the South, had a number of auction places in the city, including the Cabildo; the St. Charles, and St. Louis hotels; and Maspero's on Chartres Street.

As suggested by this drawing entitled A Slave Pen at New Orleans-Before the Auction, *New Orleans was a major center of slave trade in the South. (THNOC)*

Although slaves in the border and northernmost slave states shuddered at the thought of being sent "downriver," some historians apparently believe that slaves in New Orleans may have had a better lot than those in other areas. University of North Carolina historian Loren Schweniger wrote that:

> *. . . many blacks, slave and free, considered the slave trading capital of the south . . . as a place of enjoyment, excitement, and delectation, even, ironically, as a refuge from the brutalities of the South's 'peculiar institution.' They rejoiced at the city's heterogeneous mixture of peoples, its thriving river front, its delightful shops, cafes, restaurants, and hotels, its numerous theatres, amusements and sporting events.*

Slaves in the city were generally used in domestic work or were leased out to local shops, companies, the city, and on the docks. The majority of slave owners in New Orleans owned less than three slaves; few owned more than that number, including the approximately 700 free blacks who owned slaves.

A slave could gain his freedom through one of several ways. Freedom could be purchased, which was not an uncommon event, or the slave owner could simply free his slave through legal action or in a will. The legislature could manumit a slave or slaves for some particular service. Almost 300 slaves in the city gained their freedom through the local office of the American Colonization Society. One of the society's founders was New Orleans philanthropist, John McDonogh.

As the abolitionist rhetoric increased in the South in the late 1850s, freedom for a slave

New Orleans community were the free-people-of-color. Free blacks occupied all levels of enterprise in the city from draymen to journalists: there were shopkeepers, cabinetmakers, barbers, plantation owners, artists, writers, publishers, and investors. There were some very wealthy free-people-of-color who owned millions of dollars in real estate in the city. Free blacks also manned the sea-going ships and steamers constantly moving in and out of the port. The life-styles of the free blacks paralleled their counterparts, and often relatives, in the white community.

The *gens de couleur libres,* free-people-of-color, community produced many gifted artists, composers, and writers, many of whom were educated in European universities. Unfortunately, social conditions in New Orleans at the time drove many of these talented people to take refuge in Southern European cities where race was not a barrier to creative expression.

Despite the artificial handicaps of race in New Orleans, the talented *gens de couleur libres* produced. Their contributions in the arts and letters ranged from pedestrian to excellent. The list of writers and poets is a long one and includes Armand Lanusse (1812–1867), editor of *Les Cenelles* (1845), the first anthology of poetry by free-men-of-color in America; Camille Thierry (1814–1875); Pierre Dalcour; and, Victor Sejour. Sejour enjoyed considerable literary success in Paris, including work with the Comedie-Francaise.

Free-people-of-color excelled in the visual arts, and in some cases, gained international reputations. Jules Lion was one of the city's earliest lithographers and daguerreotypists. Without question two of the city's most talented sculptors during this era were the Warburg brothers, Eugene and Joseph Daniel. They were the sons of Daniel Warburg, a member of the important Jewish family of Hamburg, Germany, and his slave-mistress, Marie-Rose, a native of Santiago, Cuba. Warburg freed her and she bore him five children. Eugene moved to Paris where he gained considerable fame while his brother, Joseph Daniel, remained in New Orleans practicing his art. Perhaps Eugene's most famous work is the bust of United States Minister to France, John Young Mason, which was executed in 1855. Joseph Daniel's son, Daniel, carried on the art.

became almost impossible to secure. City and state officials, fearful of outside agitators stirring up trouble among the slaves and free blacks, passed strict regulations governing the personal liberties of both free blacks and slaves.

Perhaps the most fascinating segment of the

The best example of the younger "Daniel" Warburg's work is the carved column of the Holcome-Aiken monument in Metairie Cemetery.

Like their free-black counterparts, many gifted white New Orleanians also traveled to Europe to find success. Such was the case of Paul Morphy, the international chess champion, Louis Moreau Gottschalk, and Ernest Guiraud. Gottschalk was born in New Orleans in 1829 and at the age of 13 traveled to Paris to study music. Before his death while on tour in Rio de Janeiro in 1869, Gottschalk had gained considerable fame and acclaim in Europe and America for his musical compositions, many of which were based on the music and dances he had heard and seen slaves perform in Congo Square. His best-known composition was *La Bamboula*, based on a popular dance among the city's early French-speaking slaves. Guiraud, born in the city in 1837, also went to Paris to study music. During his career in Europe, which spanned several decades, Guiraud gained distinction for his operatic compositions, won the Prix de Rome, and became a teacher at the Paris Conservatory. Perhaps Guiraud's most long-lasting accomplishments were the music he wrote for portions of the famed opera, *Carmen*, after the death of its composer, Georges Bizet, and completion of the unfinished *Tales of Hoffmann*, when Jacques Offenbach died.

The people, architecture, climate, and its history indeed made New Orleans a unique city in antebellum America. Despite highs and lows in its economy, the Crescent City was riding high on a wave of economic prosperity by the end of the 1850s, the golden era of the antebellum years. The banks were strong and the cotton crops were setting new records. European textile mills were buying all the cotton they could get. Sugar prices were kept high by protective tariffs and the city's port was in constant activity. A considerable amount of the commerce of the Midwest passed across the city's wharves each day.

The nation, however, was racing toward civil war. New Orleans joined the political struggle with as much fervor as it did the acquisition of commercial wealth. The city's adherence to the Southern cause was understandable yet confusing. The city had prospered under the economic protection of the United States, and its commercial and familial connections with the North and Midwest were greater than any other Southern city. The Civil War would bring economic ruin and stagnation to a city that had looked ahead only to prosperity.

William Mure, the British consul in New Orleans caught the despair and ruinous impact of secession agitation in the city just after the election of Abraham Lincoln. In a letter to Foreign Secretary Lord John Russell in December 1860 Mure wrote:

Your Lordship is aware that this city, from its geographical position, is the great entrepot of the agricultural produce of the Valley of the Mississippi, and of the great Western States, the value of which received during the last year, reached the enormous sum of 185 millions of dollars. It did not seem probable, therefore, that such vast interests would be imperiled without due and deliberate consideration. And yet, within three weeks after the (Presidential) election, and before any overt act of hostility could be committed by the President-elect, the agitation of the question of dissolution of the Union has been so widespread as entirely to destroy confidence — obstruct the usual channels of trade and depreciate the value of property of all kinds to a runious state.

Before a shot was fired and even before secession and the formation of the Confederacy, New Orleans was feeling the effects of the coming storm.

WASHINGTON ARTILLERY

OF

NEW ORLEANS.

RECRUITS WANTED.

Officers of this Battalion are now in the South to enlist such Young Men, citizens of Louisiana, as are within conscript ages, who may come forward and offer themselves for service.

By special authority of the Secretary of War, any person liable to conscription may be enlisted, and conscripts enrolled may be assigned to fill up this organization.

A bounty of FIFTY DOLLARS will be paid to all liable to conscription, who come properly recommended.

The recruiting stations will be Mobile, Ala.; Jackson, Miss.; and other points on the N. O. J. & G. N. R. Road, nearer New Orleans.

Captain M. B. MILLER, 3d Company, will be stationed at Mobile, as Recruiting Officer; and Captain SQUIRES, 1st Company; Captain RICHARDSON, 2d Company, and Lieut. NORCOM, 4th Company, at Jackson, and vicinity, to whom or to the undersigned, at Mobile, applications may be addressed.

J. B. WALTON,
Col. Com'g and Chief of Artillery, 1st Army Corps, Dep. Nor. Va.

I have established my Recruiting Office at Room No. 82, Bowman House, Jackson, Miss.

C. W. SQUIRES,
Captain and Recruiting Officer, Battalion Washington Artillery.

CHAPTER V
"THE UNION MUST AND SHALL BE PRESERVED"

On January 26, 1861, Louisiana somewhat reluctantly seceded from the Union, a decision that would result in death, destruction, financial chaos, and social upheaval. The years of debate on the constitutionality of secession were soon followed by years of war, occupation, Reconstruction, and economic stagnation.

Not all New Orleanians favored breaking off from the Union, although most agreed in principle that a state had the right to secede. Ties to the North, both economic and social, were especially strong in New Orleans. According to historian Charles Roland, "Much of the population of the Deep South's chief metropolis, New Orleans," was against secession. This was especially true among the "merchants and bankers because of their economic ties with the North, and the European immigrants because of their newly kindled American patriotism . . . and their opposition to slavery." The European immigrants, who comprised some 40 percent of New Orleans' white population, also had lingering class resentment they had brought with them from Europe. Even among the sugar planters, who would seem to have had a vested interest in preserving slavery, "there was an important element with exceptionally firm ties to the Union."

Some observers realized that New Orleans and the rest of the South lacked the resources to win a protracted war with the industrially more advanced Northern states. In an 1858 speech to a commercial convention in Montgomery, Alabama, Louisiana newspaper editor J.D.B. DeBow wryly emphasized the South's dependency on Northern industry by describing his journey to Montgomery:

They will start in some stage or railroad coach made in the North; and an engine of Northern manufacture will take their train or boat along; at every meal they will sit down in Yankee chairs, to a Yankee table, spread with a Yankee cloth. With a Yankee spoon they will take from Yankee dishes sugar, salt, and coffee which have paid tribute to Yankee trade, and with Yankee knives and forks they will put into their mouths the only thing Southern they will get on the trip.

After Lincoln's election the voices for moderation gave way to those of the firebrands and the demands in the city press for secession. On December 14 the New Orleans *Bee* claimed: "The North and South are heterogeneous and better apart. . . . We are doomed if we proclaim not our political Independence." Louisiana's representatives in the U.S. Senate, Judah P. Benjamin and John Slidell (a native New Yorker), joined forces to declare: "We must be blind indeed if we entertain the re-

motest hope that widespread ruin, degradation and dishonor will not inevitably result from tame submission to the rule which our enemies propose to inaugurate." Their prediction came true, of course, but directly as a result of the course they steered.

Public reaction to secession was generally enthusiastic. The New Orleans *Picayune* proclaimed: "The deed has been done. We breathe deeper and freer for it. The Union is dead. . . . No government ever rose as she did — none has ever so perished." But some Louisiana residents were deeply sorrowed by the growing schism in the nation. Superintendent William Tecumseh Sherman of the State Seminary of Learning in Alexandria (forerunner of Loui-

siana State University) resigned his post. He wrote to Governor Thomas O. Moore, stating that, "if Louisiana withdraws from the Federal Union, I prefer to maintain my allegiance to the Constitution as long as a fragment of it survives."

Louisiana was an independent nation between January 26, the date of secession, and March 21, when it joined the Confederacy. The governor served as president, the legislature as a congress. At first the state flag was used as the national emblem, but in February the convention adopted a new flag, consisting of 13 stripes — six white, four blue, and three red — and a yellow star on a field of red in the upper left corner. The stripes represented the original 13 American colonies; the three colors, the tricolor French flag; and the yellow star, the state's Spanish heritage. The "new nation" began immediately to mobilize for war. Governor Moore appointed a military board to coordinate the establishment of training camps and the issuing of arms to volunteers. Moore also ordered the seizure of U.S. government installations in Louisiana, including armories, barracks, and the U.S. Mint.

The extraordinarily diverse strains of Louisiana's ethnic makeup were brought together in the initial enthusiasm surrounding the anticipation of war. Nowhere was the strange, colorful mixture of national uniforms and weaponry more apparent than in New Orleans. Foreign papers sent correspondents to the city to report on the activities of their former nationals. An English reporter wrote that the streets of New Orleans "were full of Turcos, Zouaves, Chasseurs . . . there are Pickwick rifles, LaFayette rifles, Beauregard guards, Macmahon guards, and Irish, German, Italian, Spanish, and native volunteers." Gangs of Irishmen reportedly roamed the streets, exhorting the city's Spanish residents to join them in the war effort, saying: "For the love of the Virgin and your own soul's sake, Fernandy, get up and cum along wid us to fight the Yankees."

Their chance to "fight the Yankees" would soon come. On April 12, 1861, (less than a month after Louisiana formally joined the Confederacy), Southern troops under Louisiana General Pierre Gustave Toutant Beauregard opened fire on Fort Sumter in Charleston Harbor and the war was on. Louisiana, during the next year of fighting, supplied men and mate-

Left
General P.G.T. Beauregard was one of the South's military leaders during the Civil War. After the war he remained active in public affairs in New Orleans.
(THNOC)

Below
This Panorama of the Seat of War by John Bachmann was published in 1861. In addition to showing the geographic relationships of key cities and forts, it shows how dependent the South was on maritime commerce, and consequently, how much it was affected by the Union blockade.
(THNOC)

rials to the Confederate forces in Virginia, while also preparing in case the clouds of war should descend within its own boundaries. By the spring of 1862, it had become increasingly clear that those clouds would first descend on New Orleans. Possession of the city and the lower Mississippi River was strategically essential to either side's control of the West. But, despite pleas from Major General Mansfield Lovell — Confederate commander of the city and son of former U.S. Surgeon General Dr. Joseph Lovell — the Confederate government which

considered the war in the East more important, ignored New Orleans and the rest of the state. Troops and materiel essential to the defense of the Crescent City were sent elsewhere. Lovell was ordered to send most of his trained soldiers to Corinth, Mississippi, to join General Albert Sidney Johnston and General Beauregard. This left the defense of New Orleans to "ninety-day" troops, most of whom were untrained and undisciplined. Moreover, the economy of the port city had been in chaos since the Federal blockade of the Mississippi began on May 26, 1861. Prices soared as imported goods, medicines, manufactured products, and other essential items became scarce. The city opened a free market to feed and clothe hundreds of poor families. The cost of a 40-pound box of soap rose from $5 to $19 and flour brought up to $20 a barrel when available. New Orleanians learned to do without or to rely on their own ingenuity. When coffee, a long-time favorite beverage, became in short supply, newspapers suggested such additives as milled okra, rye seeds, or toasted and ground sweet potatoes. When paper grew scarce, newspapers put out smaller editions or used wallpaper or anything else they could get.

By the end of February 1862, a U.S. Naval fleet, under the command of Flag Officer David G. Farragut, had begun to concentrate near Ship Island off the Mississippi Gulf Coast. On Ship Island was Major General Benjamin F. Butler with a large force of Federal troops.

Union Captain David G. Farragut, who had moved to New Orleans from Tennessee as a child, captured the city on April 24, 1862. Three months later he was promoted to rear admiral. From Cirker, Dictionary of American Portraits, Dover, 1967.

On April 18 Federal gunboats began to bombard Fort Jackson and Fort St. Philip, which protected the lower river and the approach to New Orleans. For the next six days skirmishes continued between the U.S. Navy and the Confederate batteries. Then, in the pre-dawn of April 24, the Federal fleet piped all hands to deck and made a bold run by the forts, which had been considered impassable since the days of the Battle of New Orleans in 1815. Spectators reported that the battle was furious and magnificent.

Confederate Captain William B. Robertson, viewing the action from the batteries of Fort Jackson, described the splendor of the pyrotechnics:

The mortar-shells shot upward from the mortar boats, rushed to the apexes of their flight, flashing the lights of their fuses as they revolved, paused an instant, and then descended upon our works like hundreds of meteors, or burst in mid-air, hurling their jagged fragments in every direction. The guns on both sides kept up a continual roar for nearly an hour, without a moment's intermission, and produced a shimmering illumination, which, though beautiful and grand was illusive in its effect upon the eye, and made it impossible to judge accurately the distance of the moving vessels from us.

A Union army officer, observing the battle from a distance, wrote that one could "combine all that you have heard of thunder, add to it all that you have ever seen of lightning, and you have, perhaps a conception of the scene." From aboard the Union flag ship *Hartford*, an officer likened the battle scene to "the breaking up of the universe with the moon and all the stars bursting in our midst." The grandeur of the spectacle was not lost on Farragut himself, who later said "it was as if the artillery of heaven were playing upon the earth."

Despite over four hours of almost constant fire from both the Union and Confederate forces, the casualties were surprisingly low. On the Union side, 37 were killed and 147 wounded. Fort Jackson had 9 killed and 33 wounded, while Fort St. Philip had two killed and four wounded. Fifty-seven Confederates were killed aboard the vessel the *Governor*

This depiction of the bombardment of forts Jackson and St. Philip appeared in a French newspaper of the time. These forts, located on the Mississippi River some miles below New Orleans, were virtually the only barriers between Farragut's fleet and New Orleans. (THNOC)

A ferocious battle took place between the Union fleet and the forces manning the forts below the city. (THNOC)

Moore and 16 more fatalities were recorded aboard other Confederate naval craft. Union Commander David Porter later denounced Commander Mitchell of the Confederate ironclad *Louisiana* in his journal: "Had her commander possessed the soul of a flea, he could have driven us all out of the river."

After the Federal ships passed the forts, 250 mutineers manning Fort Jackson rose in revolt, spiked the cannons, and ran away. Many of them were later picked up by Federal patrol boats. In desperation, Lovell considered attacking the Federal fleet, boarding the ships and driving the invaders off in hand-to-hand combat: but he later gave up the idea when he could not find enough volunteers.

Defeated, Lovell reported the reasons for the city's loss to his superiors. In addition to untrained troops and insufficient weaponry the "unprecedented" high water in the river had washed away shipping obstructions, contractors had failed to complete the construction of the ironclads *Louisiana* and *Mississippi* on schedule, and two naval officers had disobeyed orders by not placing the *Louisiana* in a battery position near the forts and by not dispatching the fire rafts downriver against the Federal fleet.

"The river-defense fleet," he wrote, "proved a failure . . . unable to govern themselves, and unwilling to be governed by others, their almost total want of system, vigilance and discipline

DIMENSIONS:

4000 Tons,
4 Engines,
2 Wheels,
2 Propellers.

Left
The ironclad Louisiana *was among the ships with which the Confederacy hoped, in vain, to break the Union blockade. (THNOC)*

Below left
John T. Monroe was mayor of New Orleans when Admiral Farragut's fleet anchored at the city and demanded that the residents surrender. (THNOC)

rendered them nearly useless and helpless when the enemy finally dashed upon them suddenly on a dark night."

Panic seized New Orleans residents when word reached the city that Farragut had passed the forts. People began destroying their Confederate money and officials ordered the destruction of anything that could be used by the Yankees. Warehouses of cotton, sugar, molasses, tobacco, and lumber were put to the torch. Ships lying idle along the wharves were sunk. Amid the blaze, smoke, and confusion, the Confederate army withdrew from the city, making its way to the Florida Parishes across Lake Pontchartrain. Angry mobs roamed the streets, looting stores, and hanging a man because he looked like a stranger.

Mayor John T. Monroe, however, refused to surrender the city and for the next week there was a standoff between the mayor and Farragut. Farragut, at one point, threatened to bombard the defenseless city unless it surrendered. Monroe wrote defiantly to the admiral, stating: "We will stand your bombardment, unarmed and undefended as we are. The civilized world will consign to indelible infamy the heart that will conceive the deed and the band that will dare to consummate it." Foreign consuls residing in the city met with Farragut to dissuade him from such a course and the captain of a French warship in port reportedly told Farragut that he would have to account to the French nation if he bombarded the city.

On April 29 word reached the city that the two forts below the city had surrendered. Farragut ordered Mayor Monroe to lower all Louisiana and Confederate flags in the city. He sent a naval squad ashore to remove the Louisiana state flag from atop the City Hall. Monroe was permitted to remain in office until the Union Army arrived. New Orleans was now an occupied city.

NEW ORLEANS.

Mayoralty of New Orleans,
CITY HALL, April 25th, 1862.

After an obstinate and heroic defence by our troops on the river, there appears to be imminent danger that the insolent enemy will succeed in capturing your city. The forts have not fallen; they have not succumbed even beneath the terrors of a bombardment unparalleled in the history of warfare. Their defenders have done all that becomes men fighting for their homes, their country and their liberty; but in spite of their efforts, the ships of the enemy have been able to avoid them, and now threaten the city. In view of this contingency, I call on you to be calm, to meet the enemy, not with submissiveness nor with indecent alacrity; but if the military authorities are unable longer to defend you, to await with hope and confidence the inevitable moment when the valor of your sons and of your fellow-countrymen will achieve your deliverance. I shall remain among you, to protect you and your property, so far as my power or authority as Chief Magistrate can avail.

Right
This proclamation by Mayor Monroe warns the people of New Orleans of the imminent capture of the city and informs them of the battle that had occurred downstream. (THNOC)

Far right
A small boat carrying Federal troops landed at the New Orleans levee to demand the surrender of the city. (THNOC)

Below right
Major General Benjamin Butler was military commander of New Orleans for part of the city's occupation. In spite of a strict and sometimes corrupt rule, he did bring improvements and needed aid to the beleaguered city. One of the enduring legacies of his administration is the inscription he ordered for the base of Andrew Jackson's statue in Jackson Square: "The Union must and shall be preserved." (THNOC)

Although fighting continued in the rest of the state until well into 1865 — even after Lee's surrender at Appomattox — the loss of New Orleans had grave consequences for the Confederacy's war effort. According to historian Charles Dufour, the city's occupation gave the Federal forces a base of operations that would eventually allow them to divide the Confederacy in half at the Mississippi River. The flow of supplies from Rebels in Texas to the Southeast would be severely hampered, and the South had lost New Orleans' essential machine shops and foundries. Lost, too, were the ironclads *Louisiana* and *Mississippi* that the Confederacy had hoped to use to break the Union blockade of Southern ports. Beyond these practical considerations, the capture of New Orleans dealt a severe blow to Southern morale.

On May 1, 1862, Major General Butler, a Massachusetts politician turned warrior, arrived in New Orleans and took formal possession of it. He ordered Mayor Monroe and former U.S. Senator Pierre Soule arrested. In Monroe's place, Butler named General George F. Sheply as the military commandant of the city. He established a military provost court to try civil and criminal cases. A month after entering the city, Butler ordered the hanging of William Mumford from the flagpole of the U.S. Mint, where he had cut down the American flag in protest of the occupation of the city. He monitored local newspapers carefully to make sure they did not instigate defiance among the populace against the Federal troops and government. He even admonished several Episcopal clergymen for not offering prayers for President Lincoln.

Five months after taking possession of the city, Butler implemented the Federal Confiscation Act, which the government had enacted on July 17 and which called for the seizure of the private property of all "unreconstructed" Rebels in the Southern states who would not swear allegiance to the United States. By the end of October, almost 70,000 New Orleanians had taken the oath. Because of its early capture, New Orleans would have the dubious distinction of enduring Reconstruction, a term yet to be coined, for a longer period than any other city of the South — nearly 15 years, from May 1, 1862, to April 24, 1877.

Butler's administration has been viewed by

generations of New Orleanians as thoroughly corrupt. His subordinate officers, including his brother, Andrew Jackson Butler, reportedly made fortunes by acquiring confiscated goods at public auction, purchasing items, in many cases for 10 percent of their value. General Butler, whether or not he personally profited from this practice, acquired the nicknames "Silver Spoon" (sometimes just "Spoons") and "Beast Butler." The verb to "Butlerize" became synonymous with "to steal."

But the general's most notorious act was the issuance of General Order No. 28, which was denounced in Europe and even in some quarters in the North. Order No. 28 was designed to counteract "insults" directed against Federal officers and their soldiers, which were often the only way New Orleanians dissatisfied with occupation could fight back. The city's women were reputed to be especially insulting, so Butler devised the following solution:

As the officers and soldiers of the United States have been subject to repeated insults from the women (calling themselves ladies) of New Orleans in return for the most scrupulous noninterference and courtesy on our part, it is ordered that hereafter when any female shall, by word, gesture, or movement, insult or show contempt for any officer of the United States, she shall be regarded and held liable to be treated as a woman of the town plying her avocation.

Modern historians, removed in time from Butler's occasionally outrageous behavior, have been kinder in evaluating his administration. Credit has been given Butler for the improvements and reforms he made in the city. Upon capturing New Orleans, he had quickly restored order to a city he described as "seven miles long by two to four wide, of a hundred and fifty thousand inhabitants, all hostile, bitter, defiant, explosive." He kept his troops under tight discipline, hanging four of them for plundering homes. He fixed prices to prevent unscrupulous profit-taking. Butler instituted special taxes to feed the poor and support orphanages; at one point, 10,000 families were reported to be receiving support. The public school system was reorganized under Butler, and it remained, at least in concept, little changed into modern times. He enforced fumigation laws and quarantine regulations, and put to work thousands of unemployed

C.S. REINHART

whites and blacks—almost 10,000 of whom
flocked to the city from nearby plantations—
cleaning streets, enlarging drainage canals, and
rebuilding wharves and levees. Blacks not
working on city improvements joined the army
or were sent back to the plantations to work
the fields as wage earners. Unfortunately, many
of them fell victim to unscrupulous Federal bu-
reaucrats who stole their wages. After 1865 the
Freedman's Bureau was created by Congress
to care for the former slaves and to find land for
them among the abandoned and confiscated
plantations, an effort which was ultimately unsuccessful. To restore the economy of the city,
Butler lifted the Federal blockade into the interior of the state, but Confederates embargoed
all goods to New Orleans. The items which
managed to get through Confederate lines
found a ready market in the city.

On December 12, 1862, Butler was replaced
by General Nathaniel P. Banks, a former governor of Massachusetts and speaker of the U.S.
House of Representatives. Butler left New Orleans quietly and without fanfare, but not forgotten. Banks perhaps is best known in
Louisiana history for his military exploits rather
than his reorganization of the "Free State" of
Louisiana, which meant that portion of the
state occupied by Federal troops.

Banks' troops were long remembered for
their expeditions into the Bayou Lafourche and
Bayou Teche areas, where they confiscated
plantations, cattle, sugar, cotton, and household furnishings, and destroyed salt and sulphur mines so vital to the Confederate cause.
Between May and July 1863, Banks with about
50,000 Federal troops, including former slaves
and free blacks from New Orleans, defeated
the Confederates at the river town of Port Hudson north of Baton Rouge after weeks of siege,
bombardment, and bloody skirmishes. Port
Hudson, the Confederate's last stronghold on
the Mississippi, fell on July 9, five days after the
surrender of Vicksburg. It was a battle in which
white Confederate New Orleanians fought,
killed, and were killed by black New Orleanians
wearing the Union blue. Many of their ancestors on both sides had fought together in the
1815 Battle of New Orleans, with Galvez, and
even earlier with Bienville against the Chickasaws. When the war first broke out, many
free-men-of-color formed their own units, like
the Louisiana Regiment of Native Guards, and
asked the Louisiana state government to let
them fight for the state and the Confederacy.
But they were not trusted and therefore not
used until the Union came. It must have been a
pathetic scene to see the funeral processions
for both sides winding through the streets of
New Orleans to bury their dead. Where Banks
had succeeded at Port Hudson, he failed the
following year to defeat Louisiana's Major General Richard Taylor in the Red River Campaign.
Taylor—who was President Zachary Taylor's
son, as well as Jeff Davis' brother-in-law—performed brilliantly as commander of the District
of Western Louisiana. In fast-moving strikes
against Union forces, Taylor was able to drive
Federal soldiers temporarily from portions of
south Louisiana. He even made feints against
New Orleans though he never carried through
with an attack on the city. The war in Louisiana
was one of attrition, that is, to deny supplies to
the Confederates and to slowly envelop them.
By the end of the war Confederate lines had
drawn close to the Confederate state capital in
Shreveport.

Banks had his hands full in reorganizing the
"Free State" government and trying to make
New Orleanians loyal Unionists. When Banks
took over the job from Butler, he tried to relax
many of Butler's tough restrictions, but doing

so only caused him problems. Incidents like the "Battle of the Handkerchiefs" in 1863 made the general's job even more difficult. On an early morning in February, thousands of women gathered at the levee in front of the city, waving handkerchiefs to cheer Confederate prisoners being shipped out for a prisoner exchange. The women, caught up in the passion of the moment, shouted insults at Union soldiers. Fearing an attack by the parasol-waving Southern belles, the Union commander called for reinforcements.

After that incident Banks began tightening up on New Orleanians. On May 1, 1863, he ordered all registered enemies of the United States out of the city within two weeks. He clamped down on all anti-Union public demonstrations. In 1864 provost judge and future governor of Louisiana Henry Clay Warmoth ordered two "respectable" women to spend 60 days in jail for cheering Jefferson Davis.

In December of 1863 President Lincoln announced his formal plans for "reconstructing" the South. Lincoln and Radical Republican members of Congress disagreed vehemently on Reconstruction. Lincoln argued that the South had never really left the Union and that the President, not Congress, was to administer Reconstruction. Lincoln tried to make it as easy as possible for the 11 Confederate states to resume their positions in the Union. Southerners, with certain exceptions, had to swear an oath of allegiance. The President could recognize a state government once 10 percent of its 1860 electorate had taken the oath and slavery in that state was abolished. These steps were taken by Louisiana and Arkansas in 1864, but Congress refused to seat their representatives. The Radical arm of Congress wanted to treat Rebels as traitors and the South as a conquered territory.

In January of 1864, in accordance with the President's plan, General Banks called for an election to be held the following month to choose a civilian governor, lieutenant governor, secretary of state, treasurer, and other officials. After a heated campaign of "Negro baiting" by all factions, Bavarian-born and long-time New Orleans resident Michael Hahn was elected governor of the "Free State" of Louisiana. The Confederate portion of the state, of course, had its own civil government. On another call from General Banks, a constitutional convention con-

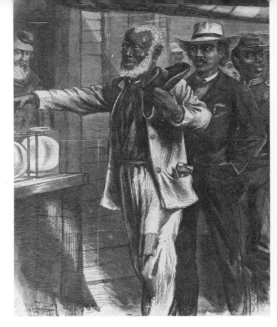

vened in New Orleans to write a new state constitution. Slavery was abolished and a free public school system was set up for all children regardless of race. This was the first time in Louisiana that a constitution provided for the education of blacks.

The real battle of rhetoric came with the debates on whether to grant suffrage to blacks. Many delegates at the convention vowed not to give blacks the vote, but they later changed their minds at the urging of Hahn and Banks. Initially Banks ignored politically the former free-people-of-color. In January 1864 they formed the Union Radical Association and sent a delegate to meet with Lincoln. The meeting was successful. Before the constitutional convention opened, Lincoln wrote to Hahn, asking that the franchise be given to some blacks, especially those who were literate, owned taxable property, and, most importantly, had fought with the Union army against the Confederacy. The black political leaders in New Orleans during Reconstruction were mostly French-speaking and had been free-people-of-color before the war.

Voters living in the occupied section of the state ratified the constitution by a vote of 6,836 to 1,566. The first meeting of the "Free State" legislature ratified the 13th amendment, abolishing slavery, but refused to act on the Negro suffrage issue.

Governor Hahn, who resigned his office in February 1865 to go to the U.S. Senate, where he was refused a seat, was succeeded by Louisiana-born Lieutenant Governor James Madison Wells, who had opposed secession. Wells, who was governor at the time of Lincoln's as-

sassination, was at first popular among Democrats for his open-armed welcome to returning Confederate veterans. But because of this, he gained the displeasure of Radical Republicans.

The Radicals would not recognize Wells's administration nor the state's Congressional delegation. Instead they held their own convention and later elected 23-year-old Illinois native, Henry Clay Warmoth, to Congress. This was the first election in the state in which blacks voted. Warmoth, who would become governor in 1868 and one of the most colorful characters during the state's Reconstruction era, shared the same fate as the state's other Congressional delegation — Congress refused to seat him.

After the inception of the 1864 constitution, blacks became an important force in Louisiana politics. Increasingly, Negro suffrage became a rallying cry for Radical Republicans who needed them as a balance of power against Democrats and Independents. Later, when they got the vote, blacks would be courted by the Democrats as well.

The growing conflict between Republicans and Democrats over the role of blacks in politics caused the bloody Mechanic's Institute riot on Canal Street in July 1866. Radical Republicans convened in the Institute on that date for the purpose of rewriting the 1864 constitution to enfranchise all blacks. Acting on the advice of his Democratic advisers, Mayor John T. Monroe, who was returned to office by voters in 1865, declared the meeting illegal and prepared to use the police force to disband it. However, General Absalom Baird (temporarily in command of Federal forces in General Philip Sheridan's absence) told Monroe "the convention, meeting peaceably, could not be interfered with by the officers of the law." Baird promised to send troops to keep order, but he thought the convention opened at 6 p.m. instead of at noon. By the time his troops got there, the bloody riot was over.

On the day of the convention, Monroe had issued a proclamation asking people to stay home and not to gather near the convention hall. Despite this request crowds of both blacks and whites crowded on Canal Street and around the Institute. A brief disturbance broke out when blacks marched from Burgundy Street down Canal Street to the Institute. The chief of police, hearing about the disturbance, dispatched a detachment to Canal Street and sent word to outlying stations to send reinforcements. Shots rang out on Canal and some of the side streets. Blacks retreated to the entrance of the Mechanic's Institute where they fired on the mob of whites and police. Police reinforcements were sent in and returned fire on the building. The white mob joined the police in the shooting. Both were prepared to rush the entrances when a white flag appeared in an upper window. Thinking this was a flag of surrender, the police advanced only to be met by volleys of fire. The police again returned the fire and the fighting intensified. Blacks trying to escape the building were shot or stoned as they dropped from the windows. Many of the prisoners taken were either shot or beaten to death

by the angry mob.

Monroe reported to President Johnson that 42 policemen and several citizens were either killed or wounded. A U.S. Army officer investigating the riot estimated that 38 people were killed and 146 wounded on both sides. Thirty-four blacks and two whites were killed in the Institute. On July 31 Baird appointed an investigative committee to delve into the cause of the riot. The commission concluded the attack was a result of hostility against the renewal of the constitutional convention.

Above
W. L. Sheppard made this sketch of Electioneering in the South *in 1868. After ratification of the 1864 constitution, blacks became a political force to be reckoned with in Louisiana politics. Their votes were eagerly sought by all major political parties. (THNOC)*

Left
A meeting of the Radical Republicans in the Mechanic's Institute was held in July of 1866 with the purpose of rewriting the 1864 constitution. Rioting, which began in the street, had its bloody finish in the chambers of the Institute. (THNOC)

General Sheridan returned to New Orleans on August 1 and also made an investigation. In a telegram to General Grant, Sheridan characterized the promoters of the reconvened convention as "political agitators and revolutionary men." He threatened to arrest the leaders if they tried to meet again. Sheridan's letter to Grant accused Mayor Monroe of suppressing "the convention by the use of police force" so brutally that Sheridan considered it murder. "It was an absolute massacre by police. . . . A murder which the mayor and the chief of police perpetrated without the shadow of necessity," the letter stated. On August 2 Sheridan recommended that Monroe, "this bad man," be removed from office. Monroe, however, continued as mayor under the watchful eye of General A.V. Kautz, commander of the city. Kautz did not interfere in civil matters and martial law was ended on August 2.

In December a Congressional committee investigating the riot placed all blame on Monroe and the "rebels." A minority report, however, blamed the riot on "the incendiary speeches, revolutionary acts and threatened violence of the conventionists." The incident in New Orleans gave impetus to the Radical Republicans' Reconstruction bill which was passed over President Johnson's veto in early 1867.

The Reconstruction Acts of 1867 grouped Louisiana with Texas into the Fifth Military District under the command of the U.S. Army. The act enabled General Sheridan to suspend municipal elections in New Orleans, remove Monroe from office, appoint Edward Heath as mayor, and remove the attorney general, the judge of the First District Court, and other officials from office.

At the end of August 1867, President Johnson relieved Sheridan of his duties in the Fifth Military District, naming him commander of the Department of Missouri. The new commander of the district, General W.S. Hancock, pursued a more conciliatory policy toward Louisianians.

The Louisiana constitutional convention of 1867–1868 called for new city elections. After a tense campaign and election, John R. Conway, a Democrat, defeated Republican Seth W. Lewis. Mayor Heath, refusing to recognize the results of the election, had to be forcibly removed from the mayor's office in city hall by the military and city police.

Military control of New Orleans came to an end during Conway's administration, when Congress readmitted Louisiana into the Union in June 1868. At first glance an observer might think Home Rule had been returned to Louisiana, but the opposite was true. Fresh from the victory of obtaining the liberal state constitution of 1868, which guaranteed civil rights, including suffrage, to blacks, Republicans sought to reinforce their strength by more direct means. One such means was the creation of the predominantly black Metropolitan Police Force — considered by many, including historians, to be Governor Henry Clay Warmoth's most despotic action. The Metropolitans were formed because the army refused to use troops in Louisiana to serve Republican ends. In effect the governor had a small army at his call.

Warmoth, realizing that white Republicans were few in number and freed slaves had little chance of protecting themselves, sought to have Congress repeal its law prohibiting the former Confederate states from forming a militia. While Congress eventually cooperated with Warmoth, the governor sought a different solution to obtain a military force in Louisiana that would be even more loyal to him than a statewide militia. In September 1868 the legislature combined Orleans, Jefferson, and St. Bernard parishes into the Metropolitan Police District. Using the remnants of the old New Orleans Police Department as a core, Warmoth built his Metropolitan Police as a military extension of the Radical Republican regime in Louisiana.

Below left
General Winfield Scott Hancock succeeded General Sheridan as commander of the Fifth Military District in 1867. Unlike his predecessor, however, Hancock allowed the government of Louisiana to function somewhat autonomously. From Cirker, Dictionary of American Portraits, Dover, *1967.*

Facing page
The Reconstructed Constitution of 1868 guaranteed the civil rights of black citizens. Black members of the constitutional convention and assembly of 1868 are shown here. (THNOC)

Democrat John McEnery (below) was claimant governor of Louisiana in 1872. In an incident related to the Warmoth impeachment, the governorship of Louisiana was claimed by both McEnery and Radical Republican William Pitt Kellogg (below right). In the bloody episode that followed the election, President Grant finally recognized Kellogg as the legal governor of Louisiana, and ordered all citizens to accept him as such. (THNOC)

Well-armed but poorly trained, the Metropolitan Police force served as the triparish law enforcement agency from 1869 until the end of Reconstruction in 1877.

The force was administered by a board of five commissioners, three of whom were black, appointed by the governor. The board had authority to levy taxes upon the people of the triparish area to pay for the force. In addition the statute stripped the New Orleans city government, including the mayor, of all police powers. In retaliation the city council and Mayor Conway created a city police force and placed it under the control of the city administration and not the governor.

Despite the popular belief, which persists to the present day, the state-operated metropolitan police force was not a new idea or even a creation of Governor Warmoth. It had been around a long time, going back to Sir Robert Peel's Police Act of London, which created a Metropolitan Police District in 1829. In the United States it was considered to be one of the major progressive reform ideas in the last half of the 19th century. Many major cities in the nation already had such a force or were urging its adoption, including New York (1857); Baltimore (1860); St. Louis, Kansas City, and Chicago (1861); and Detroit (1865). The idea persisted to the end of the century as Cleveland and San Francisco adopted it in 1877; Indianapolis (1883); Boston (1885); Omaha (1887); and Charleston, South Carolina (1896).

Aside from its policing function in the state, the Metropolitans were used extensively to ensure Republican victories at polling places by preventing Democrats from gaining control of the ballot boxes, either physically or through

voter intimidation with the help of their secret organizations like the Knights of the White Camelia and the Ku Klux Klan.

Warmoth effectively used the Metropolitans in January and February of 1872, to thwart his opponents' attempts to gain control of the legislature. One of the more amusing results of this tense political struggle was a duel with rifles between George Carter, leader of the anti-Warmoth legislators, and General A.S. Badger of the Metropolitans. Neither man, however, was injured.

Warmoth's administration and the legislature were riddled with controversy and corruption. One New Orleans newspaper declared: "If we were to sum up in one accusation the crimes of which Governor Warmoth has been guilty, we would say that it consists in his having stabbed public virtue to the heart and trampled it under his feet." The state's printing cost rose from a high of $60,000 in the pre-Warmoth days to over $1.5 million in a three-year period. Practically every bill initiated during the 1870 legislature had a bit of corruption tacked on to it. During the Warmoth era the state debt rose from $17.5 million to over $25 million by the end of 1872. One of the primary instruments of corruption was the Louisiana Lottery Company. The company was chartered by the state legislature in 1868 and given a monopoly for the entire state. It reaped millions of dollars in profits each year, out of which it gave the state $40,000 a year for the support of charitable institutions. Bribes (which were not illegal at the time), theft of school funds, land swindles, sale of commissions, and graft in state-backed projects were but just a sampling of the corruption of Louisiana politicians and entrepreneurs during the era. Corruption, however, was not unique to Reconstruction politics in Louisiana and it was as rampant among Republicans as it was among Democrats. Corruption existed before, during, and after Reconstruction. Warmoth was most perceptive in describing these conditions:

These much abused members of the Louisiana legislature are at all events as good as the people they represent. Why, damn it, everybody is demoralized down here. Corruption is the fashion.

Although Warmoth was hated by reformers, Democrats, Liberals, and Republicans alike during his term in office, they flocked to the Warmoth Republicans during the 1872 elections to stop the Custom House Gang and Radical Republicans from getting their candidates for governor and lieutenant governor elected. The Warmoth fusion supported Democrat John McEnery for governor and named D.B. Penn, a member of the Liberal Republicans, as McEnery's running mate for lieutenant governor. The Radical Republicans dubbed William Pitt Kellogg their gubernatorial candidate; for lieutenant governor, they chose C.C. Antoine, a prominent black Louisianian.

When the voting returns came in, both McEnery and Kellogg claimed victory. Supporters on both sides were guilty of massive voting frauds. Warmoth's Returning Board declared

Left
When Governor Henry Clay Warmoth was impeached in 1872, the House of Representatives named the black president of the Senate, P.B.S. Pinchback, to serve the remainder of Warmoth's term. The appointment was approved by President Ulysses S. Grant. (THNOC)

Below
Acting on orders of "Governor" McEnery, Brigadier General Fred Ogden and his troops attacked the Metropolitan Police placed in the Cabildo on Jackson Square. Federal troops eventually dispersed Ogden's forces. (THNOC)

McEnery the winner and the rival Radical Returning Board decided in favor of its candidate, Kellogg. Governor Warmoth called a special session of the legislature to meet on December 9, 1872, to settle the matter. But on December 5 Federal Judge E.H. Durell ordered the U. S. Marshal Samuel Packard to seize the Mechanic's Institute, where the legislature was to meet, and to issue a call for Federal troops if necessary. The next day Packard occupied the "State House" and refused entry to Warmoth legislators.

The House of Representatives impeached Warmoth and named P.B.S. Pinchback, a black and the president of the state senate to serve out the remaining month of Warmoth's term. Despite pleas from Warmoth and McEnery for a fair hearing, President Grant approved the Pinchback appointment. With the power of Presidential recognition, Federal troops, and the Radical state government behind him, Kellogg was inaugurated on January 13.

McEnery, refusing to step aside, was also sworn in the same day in Lafayette Square, then convened his own state legislature in Odd Fellows Hall in Camp Street. Encouraged by the support of the Democratic press, and perhaps a majority of the state's white population, "Governor" McEnery issued a proclamation in February forbidding all citizens to pay taxes to the Kellogg government. Moreover he called for all able-bodied young men to join his state militia under the command of McEnery-appointed Brigadier General Fred N. Ogden.

On March 5 McEnery ordered Ogden and the militia to attack and seize the police stations in the city. The first attack was on the Metropolitan station in Jefferson City, then a suburb of New Orleans. McEnery's troops were successful at first, but were later driven away by Federal troops. The McEnery militia then launched an assault against the Metropolitans stationed in the Cabildo on Jackson Square. An intense battle took place and the Metropolitans, fleeing bullets, took refuge around the walls of St. Louis Cathedral. Approximately an hour

In the disputed governor's election of 1872, Federal troops intervened to oust members of the losing faction. (THNOC)

Facing page
Left
James Longstreet, who attended West Point with Sherman and Grant, led the Metropolitans in the occupation of Odd Fellows Hall, which took place one day after the "Battle of the Cabildo." From Cirker, Dictionary of American Portraits, Dover, 1967.

after the battle began, Metropolitan reinforcements arrived and drove Ogden's militia back to St. Peter Street. With the arrival of Federal troops a short time later, Ogden's force dispersed. After the smoke cleared, three men were dead and eight wounded.

"The Battle of the Cabildo," as the engagement was later called, was a major defeat for McEnery. The next day Metropolitans, under the command of former Confederate General James Longstreet, occupied Odd Fellows Hall and jailed members of the McEnery legislature. The confrontation between followers of McEnery and Kellogg erupted in bloody riots and battles in other parts of the state, such as the bloody race riot in Colfax, in Grant Parish, on Easter Sunday, April 13, 1873.

The gubernatorial election of 1872 eventually ended up in a Congressional investigation. The majority report declared that McEnery ought to have been named governor or new elections should have been held. Congress, however, doubted whether it had the Constitutional authority to set aside state elections. President Grant finally made the decision in a proclamation issued on May 22, 1873. He recognized Kellogg as the legal governor of the state and ordered all citizens to submit to Kellogg and the state government.

The war, Reconstruction, and the political corruption and squabbling had a devastating impact on the economy and cost of government. The state debt escalated to previously unheard-of heights and New Orleans property owners were paying almost 50 mills in state and city taxes, or about $5 on each $100 of assessed property value. Commerce and business, the life blood of New Orleans, had become so stagnated by 1873 that a small group of community business leaders, both black and white and led by the popular P.G.T. Beauregard, tried unsuccessfully to end the strife through what historians now call the Unification Movement of 1873.

Prominent white New Orleanians drew up a far-sighted proclamation calling for the unifica-

General Philip Henry Sheridan and Congressional Committee member W.W. Phelps discuss the situation of the Louisiana governorship. A congressional investigation into the 1872 governor's election was eventually ordered. The majority decision was to either recognize McEnery as governor, or hold an election. President Grant decided to recognize W.P. Kellogg as legal governor. (THNOC)

tion of "our people," which it defined as "all men, of whatever race, color or religion who are citizens of Louisiana, who are willing to work for her prosperity." It advocated recognition of the 14th and 15th amendments of the United States Constitution. In addition, it recognized the civil and political rights of every citizen—whether black or white—under the Constitution. Its resolutions called for the integration of public schools and all public places and conveyances. "We shall maintain and advocate the right of every citizen of Louisiana and of every citizen of the United States," the proclamation further stated, "to frequent at will all places of public resort, and to travel at will on all vehicles of public conveyance, upon terms of perfect equality with any and every other citizen." This was a remarkable document, drawn up by Southerners almost a century before the Civil Rights Act of 1964. The movement enjoyed considerable support in New Orleans, but it was vehemently denounced by white conservatives in the rural parishes of the state and by white and black Radical Republicans, who decried it as an attempt by white Democrats to subvert the Republican Party.

But subversion was hardly necessary; the Republicans were doomed. Resistance to Kellogg's administration continued through his term. Despite his successes and the ill-fated attempts at political, economic, and social reforms, Kellogg was loathed by conservative whites because he represented the party that blocked their return to power. "Kellogg was far more hated than Warmoth had ever been," wrote historian Joe Gray Taylor. Midway through Kellogg's term, the city erupted into open rebellion. The "Battle of September 14,

1874," also known as the Battle of Liberty Place, between Metropolitans and Democrats, sent ominous shockwaves through the nation's political power structure.

In June 1874 Democrats and their allies formed the White League in New Orleans as a military organization to drive the Republicans from office. The League, under the command of Fred N. Ogden, formed regiments, battalions, and companies, including a cavalry unit. Kellogg, aware that the Leaguers were secretly training, ordered the Metropolitans to be on the lookout for arms shipments. The Metropolitans also began to stockpile weapons, including two Napoleon guns and Gatling guns.

On the morning of September 14, word reached the city that the Metropolitans would attempt to prevent the landing of the steamer *Mississippi,* which had an arms shipment aboard destined for the League. Democratic leaders called for a mass meeting at the Clay Statue (then in the center of the Canal Street neutral ground, with Royal Street on one side and St. Charles on the other) to demand Kellogg's resignation. While speeches were being made to a crowd of over 5,000 spectators, Ogden and his commanders planned the at-

tack. President Grant, however, had gotten wind of the expected events and dispatched Federal troops to the city from their quarters in Brookhaven, Mississippi, but they got there too late.

General Longstreet prepared his defenses to stop the Leaguers from unloading the *Mississippi.* His force consisted of about 600 Metropolitans, including approximately 30 mounted policemen called "Uhlans," and about 3,000 black militiamen. The League had more than 8,000 armed men. Longstreet's defense line extended from Jackson Square to Canal Street, and from the Custom House to the river.

In the afternoon Ogden's force advanced toward Canal Street from Poydras and, amidst rebel yells, artillery fire, and rifle volleys, attacked the Metropolitans, sending them into chaotic retreat. Kellogg's militia fell back on Jackson Square. After the brief but fierce fighting, 11 of the Metropolitans were killed — five black and six white, including a former Confederate officer — and 60 were wounded. Twenty-one White Leaguers were killed and nineteen were wounded.

The Leaguers replaced city and state offi-

The White League was made up of Democrats and their allies for the purpose of forcefully removing the Republicans from state offices. On September 14, 1874, the White League clashed with the Metropolitans in what was termed the Battle of Liberty Place. The White League succeeded in loosening the Republican hold in state politics. From Frank Leslie's Illustrated Newspaper. (THNOC)

cials with those elected with McEnery in 1872. Penn was sworn in as lieutenant governor and McEnery was summoned back to Louisiana to become governor. Leaguers, reveling in their victory, roamed the streets while Kellogg's government fell apart throughout the state. President Grant, however, came to the rescue of his fellow Republicans once again. He demanded that the Leaguers submit to Kellogg's government. To make sure they did, he sent in additional Federal troops and three warships.

But by the end of 1874 Radical Republicans, who for years had been propped up by the army and a Republican administration in Washington, began losing control. On January 4, 1875, Democrats tried to topple the Kellogg legislature. The next day General Philip Sheridan, who had been sent by Grant to study conditions in the South, wrote to Secretary of War W.W. Belknap (who was later forced from office himself for questionable business deals in

the Indian Territory), describing the Democrats as "terrorists" and urging the President to declare them to be "banditti." He said they should be arrested, tried, and punished.

In 1876, while the nation was celebrating its centennial, two elections took place which would set into motion the end of Reconstruction in Louisiana. The first was the gubernatorial race between Maine-born Radical Republican Stephen B. Packard and Liberal Democrat Francis T. Nicholls. On the national scene was the hard-fought Presidential campaign between Republican Rutherford B. Hayes and Democrat Samuel J. Tilden.

When the popular votes were counted in the Presidential election, Tilden clearly defeated Hayes. The Republicans, however, refused to concede defeat and charged that the returns from Louisiana, Florida, South Carolina, and Oregon were fraudulent. The election was eventually thrown into a specially created Elec-

A group of commissioners met with New Orleans residents on November 16, 1876, at the St. Charles Hotel to discuss the Presidential election that had just taken place. The election was fraught with intrigue and corruption. Eventually, the commission selected Rutherford B. Hayes as President. To win support from Southern states, many concessions were made. This dealing eventually led to the end of Reconstruction in Louisiana. (THNOC)

toral Commission, which through complex machinations finally selected Hayes as President. To silence and win support from Southern Democrats, Hayes and the more conservative national Republicans made them several attractive promises, including a pledge to withdraw support from Radical Republican governments still controlling "Reconstruction" states in the South, such as Louisiana. The South was promised a railroad to connect east Texas to the Pacific and Federal appropriations for internal improvements. In addition, at least one Southerner would receive a Cabinet appointment and, most importantly, Federal troops would be withdrawn from the South.

Meanwhile Louisianians back home were participating in their own fraud-ridden gubernatorial election. When the votes were tallied, Nicholls emerged with a majority. The Republican Returning Board, which had been appointed by Kellogg, threw out several thousand Nicholls votes and declared Packard the winner. At least one board member — former Governor James Madison Wells — reportedly sold his vote to the highest bidder. When the Democrats could not meet his price, Wells voted for Packard.

President Grant, remembering the Republican Party's promises, declared that all appointments to state offices had to be approved by both Nicholls and Packard until the legitimacy of one or the other could be established. Packard, unsure of his party's support, permitted Nicholls to gain the upper hand by making appointments. Nicholls appointed Ogden's troops as the state militia, who moved quickly to seize the state arsenal, police stations, and the courts. Grant and then Hayes, after his inauguration in March, took no action against Nicholls in support of fellow Republicans. On March 24, 1877, Nicholls declared his government to be complete and in control. A month later, on April 24, Hayes kept another promise — Federal troops were withdrawn from New Orleans and the South. More than 15 years of violent, bloody, corrupt, and financially devastating Reconstruction in Louisiana was over and Home Rule and Redemption were about to begin.

Horror stories about Reconstruction have been handed down by New Orleanians from generation to generation. Historians delving into diaries and the personal papers of those who lived in the city during those years, however, have found quite another story. For the most part and after the initial shock of the war and occupation, the daily lives of New Orleanians changed but little from the prewar days. Despite the political upheavals during the era, most people, white and black, were more concerned with the activities of their daily lives.

A gray pall did not hang over the city during the Reconstruction years. Canal Street and Esplanade Avenue at times were alive with the gay color of promenaders. The French Opera House and the St. Charles Theater played to large audiences, while the schedule of parties, balls, and picnics at all levels of society kept even the shiest lass busy. The St. Charles and St. Louis hotels, both of which enjoyed national reputations even before the war, had full guest registers. For the more pedestrian tastes, gam-

The inauguration of Governor Francis T. Nicholls took place on the balcony of St. Patrick's Hall. (THNOC)

Francis T. Nicholls (above) initially shared the office of governor with Stephen Packard due to the disputed 1876 election. He was able to make certain key appointments however. By appointing Ogden state militia commander, he was able to seize the state arsenal, police stations, and the courts (facing page). When President Hayes took no action against him, Nicholls declared that the state government was under his control. (THNOC)

by 1869 and enjoyed by both blacks and whites. New Orleans boasted of several ball teams with such names as Southerns and Robert E. Lees. Baton Rouge had the Red Sticks. Boxing had also become popular by that same year. New Orleanians always enjoyed a good race, especially a horse race. The city enjoyed several good tracks, but lost the popular Metairie course when its owners converted it into the Metairie Cemetery in 1872. When viewed from the air, the oblong design of the original race track is still visible. Also popular among racing fans and the population in general were the steamboat races that have become legend. The most notable of these was, of course, the famous July 1870 race between the *Natchez* and the *Robert E. Lee* from New Orleans to St. Louis. The *Robert E. Lee* was declared the winner when it arrived in St. Louis 3 days, 18 hours, and 14 minutes after departing the Crescent City. The 1870s was the beginning of the great era of steamboats, many of which became floating palaces and their staterooms, so-called because they bore the names of the states in the Union, boasted the finest trappings.

Reconstruction, however, did bring changes. The war and occupation brought a large influx of Northerners to the city. The migration of Northerners to New Orleans was commonplace before the war, but the attitudes toward the newer arrivals changed during Reconstruction. Many unscrupulous Northerners followed the army into the city, and the South in general, to profit from the chaos. They were referred to as "carpetbaggers." But then there were those Northerners, who like their antecedents before the war, simply came because there were good and honest business opportunities to be had for the industrious. There was another class of opportunists during this time whose name sent shivers through diehard Southerners—the "scalawags." These were Southerners who collaborated with and took part in the Reconstruction government. These so-called scalawags saw themselves as realists, trying to adapt to a new order and a new South.

Perhaps the greatest changes were for black New Orleanians and the thousands of former slaves who flocked to the city during and after the war. They came from plantations and contraband camps from upriver and neighboring

bling halls and saloons abounded, while temperance societies continued their prewar struggle against demon rum. Mardi Gras' annual visitation provided its usual merriment, as did the many circus troupes visiting the city. A popular Sunday outing for many New Orleanians was an excursion to Lake Pontchartrain on the Pontchartrain Railroad, or perhaps an overnighter to Mandeville on the north shore of the lake or to the Mississippi Gulf Coast by steamboat. By the end of 1864, the Mississippi River was open to traffic to all points north and ships arrived regularly from the East Coast.

During Reconstruction new sources of entertainment were added to the list of pastime activities. Baseball was on the New Orleans scene

Mississippi. Coming in search of a new life, they met only hostility from whites and many blacks. They glutted the labor market thereby depriving many whites and local blacks of their much-needed jobs. Violence was often the result. Despite various civil rights legislation, the constitution of 1868 and the Federal Civil Rights Act of 1875, the age-old practices of segregation continued. Except for a few Radical Republicans, few whites advocated social equality between whites and blacks.

Blacks in New Orleans, however, did benefit from Reconstruction, especially in educational opportunities. Before the war, state law prohibited the education of slaves, except in areas absolutely necessary to the economy of their white owners. During Reconstruction and under Federal orders, the New Orleans public schools were integrated. Moreover, three institutions of higher learning were established in the city for blacks during the postwar era. In 1869 Union Normal in New Orleans was opened to provide training for black teachers. That same year the Congregationalist American Missionary Association founded Straight University and two years later the American Baptist Home Missionary Society (Northern) opened the doors to Leland University. Whites also attended Straight University's law school to prepare for the state bar. In later years Straight and Union Normal were merged to form Dillard University, which is in operation to the present day.

With the withdrawal of Federal troops in April 1877, one of the most romanticized periods in the city's history was over. Generations of New Orleanians and moviegoers have seen and heard tales about the horrors of Reconstruction and the unequaled political corruption it brought to the city. Corruption did exist, but it was not exclusive to this era. Corruption existed on a large scale during the colonial period and during the magnolia-scented antebellum years, of which much has been written. It continued through Reconstruction — and not just among "carpetbagger" Republicans — and on into the years of Home Rule. Reconstruction was an era when the American principle asserting the equal protection of all citizen's human rights was reinforced and then callously abandoned. But, most of all, it was an era like nearly all eras, where most people went about facing the problems of everyday living.

In the Gilded Age New Orleanians recaptured some of the gaiety they had lived without during Reconstruction. This carnival picture was drawn shortly before the practice of holding daytime Mardi Gras parades was initiated. (THNOC)

CHAPTER VI
NEW ORLEANS IN THE GILDED AGE

New Orleans nearing the turn of the century was still the South's largest city, boasting a population of more than 216,000 inhabitants. In transition from the antebellum and strife-ridden Reconstruction periods to the 20th century, New Orleans benefited from a resurgent economy and a conscious air of boosterism. Palatial mansions began springing up along the major avenues, while the old American Sector began taking the form of the new modern American city.

For the well-to-do there were Sunday excursions to the popular Spanish Fort on Lake Pontchartrain, or the enjoyments of the new sporting rage — bicycling out to West End, Milneburg, Audubon Park, or the Gentilly Road. It was also during this period that Mardi Gras began to take the form we know today, with daytime parades led by Rex — a practice instituted by a fraternal organization founded in 1872 to honor the visit of Grand Duke Alexis of Russia — followed by the Independent Order of the Moon and Phunny Phorty Phellows. Nighttime parades and balls were offered by Comus, Momus, and Proteus. During the next two decades, new carnival organizations came and went each year.

But the 20-year period between 1880 and 1900 was also an era of severe economic depressions, racial retrenchment, corruption and reform, and labor unrest. Violent riots and scandals came with almost as much frequency as the summer's heat and mosquitoes. It was an era during which personal honor still compelled newspaper editors, politicians, and businessmen to take to the streets and alleys to solve their differences, with pistols or by flailing their walking sticks. But these years, most of all, served as an economic, social, and psychological bridge to the new century.

The 1880s in New Orleans were extraordinarily busy, even hectic years. During this decade, the South began to regain some of the momentum and energy—economic, political, and cultural—that the Civil War and Reconstruction had depleted. The South, and New Orleans, joined in full force the industrial revolution that had already begun the transformation of the North. The decade was ushered in on an ironic note, when former President Ulysses S. Grant, nemesis of the city's Democrats, visited New Orleans in 1880. Four years later

this irony was balanced somewhat with the erection of a statue of Confederate General Robert E. Lee that was dedicated at Lee's Circle. In 1884, too, the University of Louisiana became more clearly the city's own when it was renamed Tulane University after Paul Tulane, a New Orleans merchant and benefactor of the university.

But the highlight of public events in New Orleans during the 1880s was the World's Industrial and Cotton Centennial Exposition of 1884–1885. The 1880s and 1890s were an era when Southerners heralded the "New South" of industrial progress. Southern cities tried to outdo each other with bigger and better industrial expositions. Atlanta was the first, with its International Cotton Exposition in 1881 followed by Louisville's Southern Exposition in 1883. New Orleans' exposition opened a year later, but Atlanta was not to be outstripped by New Orleans. In 1887 Atlanta held the Pied-

As the South's largest city in the 1880s, New Orleans' future was promising. (THNOC)

mont Exposition. Again, eight years later, in 1895, Atlanta boosters opened the even bigger Cotton States and International Exposition. Two years later Nashville hosted its Centennial Exposition.

In 1884 New Orleans' businessmen and boosters were putting other cities on notice that they were ready to compete. The 1884 (which supposedly marked the 100-year anniversary of America's first export shipment of cotton) exposition was designed to be the Crescent City's calling card to the world, demonstrating its commercial and industrial potential.

The exposition was organized by state treasurer and New South booster, Major Edward A. Burke. Burke, an affable Confederate veteran, epitomized the Gilded Age entrepreneur. He was a railroad executive, a prime mover in state politics, and publisher and editor of the New Orleans *Times-Democrat,* one of the South's leading newspapers. Moreover, Burke was among the first to envision the great potential wealth the South and Central American trade and investments could have for New Or-

leans and other Gulf Coast ports.

To raise the huge amount of money needed to finance the exposition, Burke convinced Congress to grant a $1-million loan, plus a $300,000 gift to build government exhibits. The New Orleans city government donated $100,000 and private stock sales provided the rest.

The grounds of the World's Industrial and Cotton Centennial Exposition were located on 249 acres of Upper City Park—now Audubon

Left
This monument standing 106 feet, 8 inches tall with a 42-square-foot base, honors Confederate hero Robert E. Lee. It was dedicated in 1884 in a circle at the intersection of St. Charles and Howard avenues. (THNOC)

Below
The University of Louisiana was renamed for benefactor Paul Tulane in 1884. Several years later the campus was moved from its downtown location to its present site on St. Charles Avenue across from Audubon Park. (THNOC)

The opening ceremonies of the World's Industrial and Cotton Centennial Exposition included a reading of a speech by President Chester A. Arthur. President Arthur officially opened the exposition from the White House by pressing a button that turned on the electric lights at the fair. (THNOC)

Below
The exposition, which had the character of a World's Fair, was held on the grounds now occupied by Audubon Park. (THNOC)

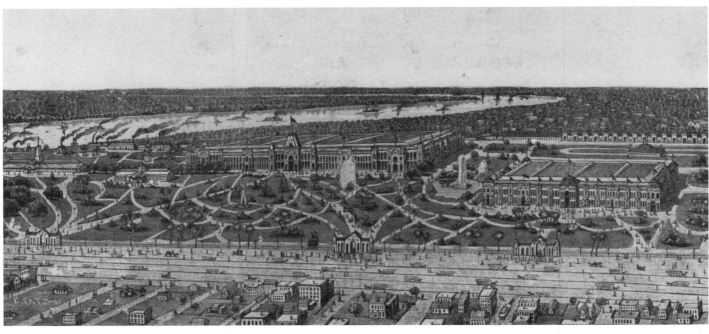

Park—that had once been part of the plantations of Pierre Foucher and Etienne Bore. Construction was far from completed, however, on December 17, when President Chester A. Arthur pressed a button in the White House which rang a bell at the fairground as a prearranged signal to start up the generators and the festivities. New Orleans was enjoying one of its famed carnival events. In the tradition of Mardi Gras, the exposition began with a grand parade, complete with steamboat processions, the Mexican army band and military units, and welcoming artillery.

Despite the carnival atmosphere of opening day ceremonies, the exposition was plagued with problems from the start. Besides poor management, the initial difficulties in obtaining financing, and the building delays, many of the exhibits failed to show up on time. Often when they did arrive, the exhibits sat around on loading docks in unpacked crates. Foreign exhibits were tied up in bureaucratic wrangles. Although Congress had exempted them from import duties, this was not communicated to local customs officials in time to prevent further delays of weeks or months. The popular Belgian exhibit did not get completely unpacked until late February, 1885.

The items that were in place at the exposition grounds must have been a great disappointment to the approximately 14,000 people who flocked to the opening day. They certainly did not get the promised "unrivaled" and "unparalleled" sights and scenes. The 31-acre Main Building, which had been built of wood under the direction of Swedish-born architect G. M. Torgerson, was almost empty. New Orleans' historian and archivist D. Clive Hardy described its architecture as "typical nineteenth-century eclecticism," but a contemporary account called it an "eyesore." A trade journal of the day further declared: "The result calls to mind the effect of looking behind the scenes at a theater when all the beautiful solidity of masonry disappears, and is replaced by dirty canvas and very small scantlings."

Attached to the Main Building was the Factories and Mills Building which contained 67,500 square feet of floor space, and the United States Building which covered over a half-million square feet but lacked flooring. Other major buildings included Horticultural Hall, which housed only a few plants provided

by local gardeners at the last moment, the Art Gallery, the Grand Rapids Furniture Pavilion, and the Mexican National Headquarters. Numerous smaller buildings scattered around the grounds were connected by walkways, actually muddy mires that made it nearly impossible for people to walk from building to building.

By most contemporary accounts, the buildings and the exhibits themselves were lackluster. One foreign consul described the exhibits built by various American manufacturers as not "representative" of the "perfection" American enterprise had obtained. British manufacturers also were poorly represented, but apparently only Belgium made any real effort to send a quality exhibit. Conspicuously absent were the industrial manufacturers of leading European powers. France sent among other things artificial flowers and perfumes, while Germany and Russia displayed textile samples. Japan, China, Siam, Turkey, Jamaica, Hawaii, Honduras, Venezuela, Brazil, Guatemala, Colombia, Nicaragua, Costa Rica, San Salvador, and Asia Minor also sent exhibits of their industries, natural resources, and folk crafts. Of the non-European nations, Japan and Mexico sent the most elaborate exhibits. Moreover, Mexico constructed two buildings on the exhibition grounds. The Mexican Pavilion was built in a Moorish design and the other was a barracks for the Mexican band and cavalry.

Despite the city's efforts to promote the exposition, newspaper reports chronicled its increasing problems. Sightseers expected from all over the world did not materialize in the expected numbers. The "conservative estimate" of four million visitors eventually amounted to little more than a million. A month after the World's Industrial and Cotton Centennial Exposition opened its gates, it was $250,000 in debt. In February the deficit had increased to $360,000. Congress appropriated an additional $335,000 in federal funds, but the

exposition was forced to close on June 1, 1885. An attempt to reopen was made — under the title "North, Central, and South American Exposition" — but the exhibits were closed down for good in April of 1886. The assets eventually hit the auctioneer's block to help offset debts which reached a final tabulation of $470,000.

Almost nothing of the exposition's buildings and vast halls remain today. A large chunk of iron ore from the Alabama exhibit (which local legend holds to be a meteorite) is the only survivor of the grounds themselves. Exposition Boulevard — then little more than a walkway — still exists, lined by beautiful residences facing Audubon Park. Not far from the boulevard on Hurst Street is a small, attractive house that served as a railway ticket office. Another survival, and all but forgotten is the small statue of the goddess Ceres, which stands atop a grossly oversized terra cotta base in Gayarre Place on Esplanade Avenue near Broad Street.

Historian Joy Jackson has ventured several possible reasons for the failure of the exposition. Besides gross mismanagement by exposition officials, the opening festivities, held in the dead of winter, were less well attended than they might have been in the summer months, when transportation from the North would have been easier. The distance of New Orleans from the major population centers of the East and Midwest was also a factor in the poor attendance, especially since land routes to the city were still few and badly kept up. Although James B. Eads had completed his system of

jetties at the mouth of the Mississippi River in 1879, deepening the ship channel and greatly aiding traffic, the first railroad linkup to the West Coast had not been finished until 1882 and had yet to become a familiar route of access to New Orleans. Most important in keeping people away, however, was probably the city's reputation for yellow fever epidemics. The memory of the last major epidemic, in 1878, was still fairly fresh.

Although the exposition, at least financially, was virtually an unqualified disaster, it did help spread the word that progress had been made in New Orleans and further improvements were underway. The 1880s had witnessed an economic revival that would be solidified and increased in the coming years. The city was slowly working its way out of the financial morass of Reconstruction. In 1880 it had had 11 state and national banks with total capital and surplus of just over $5 million. By 1895 New Orleans would boast 19 state and national and 4 savings banks, which came into being during this era, with capital and surplus exceeding $8 million and deposits of more than $26 million. In addition, 24 homestead associations were formed between 1880 and 1896.

Manufacturing concerns also improved their return with new investments and greater productivity. The value of goods manufactured in the city rose from a little more than $18 million in 1880 to almost $64 million by 1895, while the number of manufacturing establishments went from about 900 in 1880 to nearly 2,000 in 1890, when they actually began to drop again. By 1900 there would be only about 1,500 manufacturing concerns in New Orleans.

This dropoff did not indicate a slowdown in economic growth, however, only the tendency of smaller companies to be absorbed into larger corporations. The rise of the corporation, which had begun in the North after the Civil War, was a nationwide phenomenon of the period, and not just a local trend. It was an era of mergers, consolidations, associations, and organizations of all sorts. John A. Garraty explored some of the reasons for this development in his *The New Commonwealth: 1877–1890*. "Industrialization," he writes, "with its accompanying effects — speedy transportation and communication, specialization, urbanization — compelled men to depend far more than in earlier times on organizations in managing

their affairs, to deal with problems collectively rather than as individuals." New Orleans was no exception to this: merchants and businessmen organized, as did the work force into labor unions.

Before the war, most business dealings in local commodities were conducted on street corners or on levees. According to Louisiana historian Joy Jackson, a commercial revolution took place in New Orleans during the 1870s. Moving from the street corners, saloons, and levees, merchants formed commodity exchanges to transact their business. Factors dealing in cotton futures formed the Cotton Exchange in 1871 to boost cotton business, to draw up regulations for the cotton trade, to exact standards, and to provide cotton men meeting rooms where they could discuss business. Bankers organized into the New Orleans Clearing House Association in 1872, in order to stabilize finances and business dealings between banks. The Produce Exchange, in which produce merchants came together to represent their interests, was begun in 1880. The following year the Mechanics, Dealers, and Lumbermen's Association was organized. The Sugar Exchange came into being in 1883, to publish information about the sugar industry and to provide meeting rooms. And, in 1889, members of the Produce Exchange, the Chamber of Commerce, and the Merchants and Manufacturers' Association formed the Board of Trade to expand their influence. They were later joined by representatives of the Cotton Exchange and Maritime Association.

In the area of city government, the Board of Liquidation was formed in 1880 to oversee the city debt. By the end of the century, management of the Port of New Orleans became a controversial issue. Toward the end of Mayor John Fitzpatrick's administration, the city council, with the support of the city's commercial establishment, enacted an ordinance placing the wharves under the control and management of a public body. The ordinance later was repealed by the council during Mayor Walter C. Flower's term. Businessmen then formed a special committee and, with Flower's nod, drew up special state legislation to create the Board of Commissioners of the Port of New Orleans, popularly known as the Dock Board. The legislature created the board in 1896 and four years later gave the Dock Board control of the

The commodities of sugar and cotton were important to the economy of New Orleans. The buying and selling of these, and other items, were carried out in the exchange buildings built for those purposes. The exterior (right) and interior (below right) of the Cotton Exchange building are shown here. (THNOC)

wharves.

In the political arena, the Democratic political machines, which had directed their affairs with organizations of their own, such as the Crescent Democratic Club and its successor, the Choctaw Club (1897), also encountered organized opposition. City reformers joined together to form the Committee of One Hundred in 1885, the Law and Order League in 1886, the Young Men's Democratic Association in 1887, and the Citizen's League in 1896.

The rise of the corporation and its need for large numbers of skilled workers also brought the rise of organized labor. The Central Trades and Labor Assembly, numbering over 30 member unions, was created in 1881 to coordinate and support the goals of both black and white labor unions in the city. National labor unions, especially the American Federation of Labor (AFL) established in 1886, also made inroads. Scores of other local unions also started up in the 1880s and 1890s. "Trade unionism had become so popular by this time that even shoeshiners and horseshoers organized," historian Joy Jackson wrote.

As in many other American cities during this period, however, the demands of laborers for better pay and working conditions often met with resistance. The ensuing conflicts between striking workers and business and government officials sometimes resulted in violence.

A nine-day strike by New Orleans streetcar drivers in May of 1892 was followed by a general walkout by teamsters, screwmen, packers, longshoremen, pressmen, and gas and utility workers in November. The city's 42 AFL unions issued the strike call in support of the Triple Alliance of teamster, screwmen, and packer's unions which were demanding a 10-hour workday, overtime pay, and closed shops. When negotiations broke down between the unions and the Board of Trade, almost 20,000 laborers walked off their jobs. The city was dark at night, activity on the wharves ceased, and drays went unharnessed. The workers returned to their jobs only after Louisiana Governor Murphy J. Foster threatened to send in the state militia to break up the strike. The strike had been only partly successful: the Triple Alliance got its 10-hour work day and overtime pay, but not its demand for closed shops.

The militia was actually called out again three years later for a more serious labor upheaval on the city wharves, with considerably graver consequences. The Panic of 1893 had left some segments of the New Orleans economy depressed and built up frustrations among merchants and workers alike. These frustrations erupted into violence that revealed the ugly underbelly of racial resentment that had changed little since Reconstruction. During times of economic prosperity, black and white unions cooperated with each other. They divided up the work between the two and often struck together as in the general strike of 1892. But during hard times, such as the Panics of

1873 and 1893, racial tensions increased as employers generally tended to hire lower-paid black workers. Competition for jobs often became bloody. When a British ship attempted to replace white screwmen, the high-paid aristocracy of all dock workers, with lesser-paid black screwmen in October 1894, the white screwmen rioted. They raided the ships hiring their black counterparts, and several blacks drowned when they jumped overboard to escape the angry mob. Fights, beatings, burnings, shootings, and killings continued well into March of 1895. Governor Foster called in the militia to protect blacks returning to work, and the violence was finally quelled.

Another violent incident — the assassination of Police Chief David Hennessy — resulted in strained relations with another of New Orleans' ethnic communities, the Italians and Sicilians, and eventually attracted international attention.

By 1890 the city's Sicilian and Italian population had grown to 25,000 or 30,000. As modern-day historian-journalist John Wild recently wrote: they were "strangers in a not-too-friendly land, scrounging for an existence, they were ripe for exploitation by leaders who came from an environment in which terrorist gangs and secret societies flourished."

While a detective on the New Orleans police force, Hennessy had gained a national reputation in 1881 by capturing the infamous Sicilian bandit, Esposito. Facing numerous charges in his homeland, including murder and kidnapping, Esposito had fled to the United States. Eventually landing in New Orleans, he opened up a fruit and vegetable business and went by the name of Randazzo. He named his boat *Leone* after his Sicilian mountain band.

When Hennessy and his brother, Mike, received word that Esposito was in the city, they tracked him down and informed the New York City police of his whereabouts. The Hennessys and two New York marshals captured him in Jackson Square on July 5, 1881, and he was quietly slipped aboard the steamer *New Orleans* bound for New York. Esposito was extradited to Italy, where he was indicted for 18 murders and scores of kidnappings, but a death sentence was later commuted. Vendettas were waged against people thought to have informed on Esposito and blood flowed in certain segments of the New Orleans Italian community.

David Hennessy in 1889 was named chief of police as part of Mayor Joseph A. Shakspeare's reform campaign to rid the city of the criminal underworld. In 1890 Shakspeare publicly denounced the secret Sicilian criminal gangs as "horrid associations: No community can exist with murder associations in their midst. These societies must perish, or the community itself must perish." Esposito's betrayal had not been forgotten, but the continuing war between the Provenzano and Matranga families was primarily over control of the produce business on the city's wharves. Chief Hennessy met with the warring families and demanded the violence be stopped, stating, "The Mafia cannot flourish while I am chief of police." Despite Hennessy's warning, the blood feud continued. On May 1, 1890, members of the Matranga family were attacked and one was severely wounded. Several Provenzano gang members were later convicted and jailed for the assault. Hennessy, considered to be a friend of the Provenzanos, managed to secure a new trial for them.

Then at 11 p.m., on October 15, 1890, Chief Hennessy was shot down while walking home along Girod Street. "Oh, Billy, Billy. They have given it to me and I gave it back to them as best I could," Hennessy reportedly whispered to a friend, who had rushed to his side shortly after the shooting. His friend told newspaper report-

The rail link to the West Coast from New Orleans was opened in 1882. This provided still another method for goods to reach the Port of New Orleans. (THNOC)

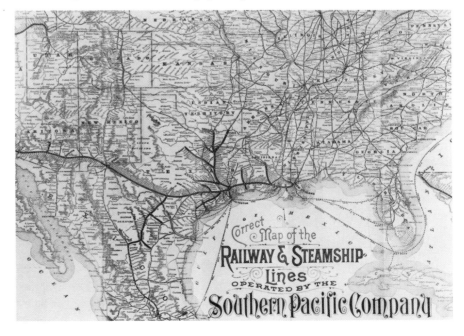

The severe indictment of New Orleans' Italian population because of the Hennessy incident overshadowed the many contributions the Italians made to the city. The Italian Union Hall on Esplanade Avenue is only one symbol of the positive contribution by New Orleanians of Italian heritage. (THNOC)

ers that Hennessy had been shot by "Dagoes." The police chief died the next morning.

On the night Hennessy was shot, Mayor Shakspeare ordered the arrest of every Italian found in the streets. Nineteen Sicilians and Italians were later indicted for the shooting, but only ten were actually charged. Nine others were also indicted as accessories before the fact.

The trial began on Feburary 16, 1891, and after 11 days a jury was finally selected. During the next two weeks a parade of witnesses took the stand for both the defense and prosecution. Eyewitnesses, both reliable and questionable, placed several defendants at the scene of the shooting, while several leading citizens, testifying for the defense, provided alibis for others on trial. On March 13 the jury acquitted seven of the defendants and declared a mistrial for the remaining three.

The next morning, the *Daily States* prepared an extra edition with a front-page appeal to the people of New Orleans to turn out in force to take justice into their own hands:

Awake. Arise. Rise in your might, People of New Orleans.
Rise, citizens of New Orleans. When murder overrides Law and Justice, when Juries are bribed, and suborners go undetected and unwhipped, it is time to resort to your own natural indefensible right of self-preservation.

Local newspapers carried notices exhorting the people to turn out for a mass meeting at the Henry Clay statue on Canal and Royal streets. They were told to come prepared for action. After inflammatory speeches were made by several prominent civic leaders, the armed mob moved on to the parish prison located near Treme and Basin streets.

After being denied entry to the prison by officials, the mob battered down the door to the Treme Street entrance. Meanwhile prison guards had released the Italians to let them hide wherever they could. Two of those who had been tried for the Hennessy murder were shot to death in a locked cell. A third one was shot in the back of the head as he tried to leave the cell. A member of the mob put a shotgun to the chest of the wounded man, blowing off the Italian's hand when he grabbed for the barrel. Trying to shield his face with the remaining stub of his arm, a second load of buckshot was emptied into his chest. Six other Italians ran into the prison yard and begged for mercy, but they were shot on the spot. Two of the defendants were dragged into the streets and hanged. When one of them grabbed for the rope with his hands, he was lowered, his hands bound, and raised again. Shots ripped through his body and bystanders took pieces of his shirt as souvenirs.

New Orleans newspapers generally praised the mob's work. The reaction around the nation was mixed. Some large metropolitan newspapers condemned the mob action, but others, especially those in cities with large Italian populations, tempered their censure, referring to similar "secret societies" in their own cities. The United States eventually had to pay the Italian government about $24,330 in reparations to soothe its feelings and to put an end to the growing international reaction. On May 5, 1891, an Orleans Parish grand jury concluded that the Mafia existed in New Orleans and that Hennessy had been murdered by its members. It further stated that the lynchings had been justified.

The incident resulted in an unjust indictment of the entire Italian community. Perhaps no other segment of the city's population was held with so much suspicion during those years as the Italians.

New Orleanians in the Gilded Age continued their zestful pursuit of factional politics, as the Democratic and Republican parties struggled for dominance, and sometimes even survival. New, more complicated scandals were added to the problems of Reconstruction, although there was one controversial holdover from that especially corrupt era — the Louisiana State Lottery Company.

Founded in 1868 by Baltimore-born Charles T. Howard, the Lottery Company's tentacles reached into every segment of the New Orleans community and even into the national power structure. It had gained its 25-year charter from the state legislature through bribery and it always kept powerful city, state, and national politicians on its payroll. To maintain a beneficent image, the company donated miniscule amounts of its huge profits to various charitable, educational, and cultural institutions, such as the Charity Hospital and the French Opera House. The Lottery Company was also always ready with a helping hand to victims of floods, hurricanes, and other disasters.

New Orleanians from all walks of life, with an affinity for lotteries since colonial times, were ever ready to pour their money into the Lottery Company's coffers, purchasing 25-cent, 50-cent, and $1 tickets. If someone really felt lucky, he could buy a $20 ticket for the $300,000 prize or the $40 ticket for the big prize of $600,000. The company had more than 200 shops in New Orleans with branch offices in New York, Kansas City, Chicago, Washington, and other major cities.

The New Orleans *Democrat* estimated that a ticket holder had one in 76,076 chances to win, stating further:

The man who buys a ticket every day at every drawing will have only one chance in 84 years to draw even the $243.35 prize. Old Methusaleh himself had he bucked up against the lottery from his earliest childhood to the day of his death and bought a ticket every day, would have found himself winner of $2678.85 after about $250,000 having been spent on the lottery.

To give an air of respectability to the drawings, the Lottery Company hired two former Confederate generals — the "Hero of Fort Sumter," P.G.T. Beauregard, and the crusty old Jubal Early. Both worked for the company for 16 years with reported annual salaries ranging from $10,000 to $30,000. The drawings were gala events: huge crowds turned out, each person with his dreams on a single ticket clutched tightly in his hand. When the wrong number came up, there was always tomorrow and a new ticket.

The Lottery participated heavily in politics simply to ensure its own survival. It supported and was supported by many Republicans and Democrats. During the post-Reconstruction period it was able to retain its monopoly and survived several attempts to revoke its 25-year charter, which was due to expire on January 1, 1894.

The Louisiana State Lottery was formed in 1868 with a 25-year charter. It was an institution fraught with scandal and, despite the advertisements to the contrary, only small portions of the profits went to help needy institutions. (THNOC)

DRAWING TAKES PLACE AT THE ACADEMY OF MUSIC, NEW ORLEANS.

Right
The drawing of the winning lottery numbers, held at the Academy of Music, was a big event. Civil War hero General P.G.T. Beauregard worked for the Louisiana Lottery Company for 16 years. The company assumed that Beauregard's association would give its operation a semblance of legitimacy. (THNOC)

The Lottery issue was continually at the forefront of political debates during the era, especially in the 1892 elections. In the gubernatorial election of that year, Democrat and anti-Lottery candidate Murphy J. Foster narrowly defeated fellow Democrat and pro-Lottery candidate Samuel D. McEnery. The Republicans also fielded their pro- and anti-Lottery candidates for governor. The Republican party was split between two former governors of Reconstruction fame — P.B.S. Pinchback and Henry Clay Warmoth. Pinchback supported the company, while Warmoth had opposed the Lottery from its inception. With the Populist candidate in the field, there were five candidates for governor. Foster, however, carried the day.

In New Orleans in 1892, John Fitzpatrick and his pro-Lottery forces defeated incumbent Mayor Joseph A. Shakspeare and the Anti-Lottery League. Fitzpatrick and the Crescent Democratic Club (Regular Democrats) would face a tough four years in office with Foster, an avowed political opponent, in the governor's office.

By election day, however, the future existence of the Lottery Company was already a dead issue; but neither side would admit it. The resentment and hostilities were too deep-seated. The U.S. Supreme Court had struck the Lottery's death knell when it upheld a lower court's decision affirming the right of Congress to prohibit the Lottery's use of the mail in its advertising. The Lottery Company continued in the state until its charter expired in 1894. It then moved to Honduras, but operated illegally in New Orleans until its complete suppression in 1907. With the Louisiana State Lottery Company crushed, one more remnant of Reconstruction came to an end. The state was gradually being "redeemed."

After the long and hard-fought mayoral campaign, Mayor Fitzpatrick's problems were far from over. In addition to the national financial panic of 1893 and the labor troubles mentioned earlier, Fitzpatrick's administration was thoroughly discredited by the "Boodle Scandals."

In 1894 the Citizens Protective Association of New Orleans, while investigating graft and corruption in city government, uncovered a major scandal in the construction of the courthouse and jail on Tulane Avenue and Saratoga Street. The investigation and scandal went all the way to the city council and mayor's office. The contract to build the courthouse had been awarded during Shakspeare's reform administration, but the actual construction was completed during Fitzpatrick's term. Even though no evidence could be found against the mayor, the citizens' group and the district attorney filed suit in civil court, asking for the impeachment of Fitzpatrick for "nonfeasance, malfeasance, favoritism, corruption, and gross misconduct." Fitzpatrick won the suit. The investigation eventually led to the indictments of 10 councilmen, the city engineer, and a former tax assessor. Three of the twelve were later convicted of misconduct in office.

By the end of Fitzpatrick's administration in 1896, the Crescent Democratic Club (CDC), riddled with scandal, began to fall apart. There were mass defections to the newly formed Citizens' League. During the 1896 municipal elections, Governor Foster refused to support the League's candidate for mayor — New Orleans businessman Walter C. Flower. Foster backed instead the CDC's candidate, Congressman Charles F. Buck. Fitzpatrick was refused the machine's nomination because of the scandals during his term and because of Foster's deep resentment toward Fitzpatrick dating back to the 1892 Lottery fight. After a bitter campaign, Flower defeated Buck. The CDC disintegrated after the election, but out of its ruins the Choctaw Club of Louisiana was formed the following year. This political organization would in three years take control of city government and hold it for over three decades, until the ascendency of a powerful political force from Winn Parish — Huey Long.

Mayor Flower, although he lasted only one term in office, provided the city with an efficient and progressive administration. Many of the municipal improvements begun during his tenure would not be completed until well into the next century. Among the accomplishments listed by his administration were reduction of city employee salaries to a level comparable to

private industry, the regaining of control of municipal services that had been franchised to private companies, and the beginning of construction of sewerage and water systems that were still in use by the 1980s. The Flower administration also reorganized the city government under a new charter, which provided for a councilmanic form of government and civil service. Perhaps the most well-known "reform" during his time in office was the creation of Storyville—the infamous red-light district which gave the city such colorful characters and places as Lulu White, Tom Anderson, Josie Arlington, the Countess Willie Piazza, Mahogany Hall, and Basin Street.

Popular legend, both in print and in the movies, has credited Storyville with being the birthplace of jazz. But jazz historian Al Rose considers Milneburg, Old Spanish Fort, Little Woods, Bucktown, and West End as the "hallowed" grounds of the birth of jazz. "To a limited and lesser extent Storyville . . . served as a forge in which some of the pure gold jazz was smelted," Rose said. Rose also traces the origins of jazz to Canal Street, South Rampart Street, Bourbon Street, Perdido Street, the legion of small dance halls on both sides of the Mississippi River, and to the Tango Belt, "an almost unbroken line of cabarets, dance halls, and honky-tonks" surrounding Storyville.

The purpose for creating Storyville was not to legalize prostitution but to confine it to one section of the city. This was not the first attempt to regulate "the world's second oldest profession," that had existed in Louisiana since colonial days. Only 14 years after the Louisiana Purchase, the city fathers had passed an ordinance that fined a prostitute if she "shall occasion scandals or disturb the tranquility of the neighborhood." In 1837 another ordinance was added to the books that enabled the mayor to evict a harlot from any premises upon the signature of three respectable citizens. Two years later prostitutes were forbidden to occupy and ply their trade in the ground-floor buildings in the Vieux Carre. In 1845 ladies of ill-repute were prohibited from visiting or drinking in coffee houses and cabarets. During the 1850s Know-Nothing businessmen initiated two reform drives to rid the city of harlots; and in 1857 the city made its first attempt at licensing the trade and restricting it to certain types of structures. The harlot paid annually a $100

license fee and the keeper of a house of prostitution paid $250 annually. Although the ordinance prohibited them from one-story edifices, they could live and conduct business in any multistory building in the city. The ordinance was an attempt to placate both anti-prostitution crusaders and powerful factions in the city that supported the practice.

Throughout the century prostitution was a lucrative source of income for corrupt politicians, government officials, policemen, lawyers, and landlords. The well-known philanthropist John McDonogh, who had extensive landholdings all over the city, was often berated in the newspapers for renting property to harlots.

After the 1896 municipal elections, Mayor Flower and the Citizens' League were ready to deal with the problem. On January 29, 1897, the city designated a certain "restricted district" to which prostitutes must confine their business. The district shortly gained the name Storyville, much to the displeasure of City Councilman Sidney Story, author of the ordinance creating it. Story's measure, called Municipal Ordinance 13,032 CS, read in part:

From the first of October, 1897, it shall be unlawful for any public prostitute or woman notoriously abandoned to lewdness to occupy, inhabit, live or sleep in any house, room or closet situated without the following limits: Southside of Customhouse (Iberville) from Basin to Robertson Street, east side of Robertson Street from Customhouse to St. Louis Street, south side of St. Louis Street, from Robertson to Basin Street.

The city government believed that restricting prostitution to a certain area was the best way to deal with the situation, since attempts to outlaw it had proven futile. The ordinance did not legalize harlotry, but simply made the practice of it outside the district illegal. Even

Left
Joseph Shakspeare and his anti-Lottery forces were defeated in the 1892 municipal elections. The Lottery operated in Louisiana until 1894, when its charter expired. It continued to operate clandestinely from Honduras until 1907. (THNOC)

Below
Storyville was a district of the city set aside for the houses of prostitution, which flourished at the time. Blue Books contained directions to the brothels, saloons, and clubs in the district named after the city councilman Sidney Story. (THNOC)

though Storyville was created by a reform administration, it would soon come under the attack of more zealous reformers until its eventual "elimination" during World War I.

The Citizens' League itself lasted only one term. In the 1900 municipal elections the League's successors, the Jacksonian Democrats, were handily defeated by the resurgent Regular Democratic Organization. The Regular Democrats rallied to the new Choctaw Club.

The same year that Flower and the Citizens' League began their campaign to ready New Orleans for the 20th century, the U.S. Supreme Court handed down the *Plessy v. Ferguson* decision which would have a devastating impact on race relations throughout the nation. The high court upheld Louisiana's 1890 separate railroad coach law and fostered the "separate but equal" standard in the nation (until it reversed itself in the 1954 *Brown v. Board of Education of Topeka* decision).

Homer Adolph Plessy, who brought the suit, described himself as "seven-eighths Caucasian and one-eighth African blood." He bought a ticket on June 7, 1892, aboard a train bound from New Orleans to Covington, north of Lake Pontchartrain. Plessy sat in the "white only" coach despite a clearly marked Jim Crow car. Plessy had resolved to test the constitutionality of the state law, which stated that "all railway companies carrying passengers in their coaches . . . shall provide equal but separate accommodations for the white and colored races." The law also required blacks and whites to ride in the coaches designated for their races. Criminal Court Judge John H. Ferguson was the original trial judge in the case.

In handing down the majority decision for the U.S. Supreme Court, Justice Henry Billings Brown declared that state legislatures can pass laws "with reference to the established usages, customs, and traditions of the people, and with a view to the promotion of their comfort, and the preservation of the public peace and good order." Delivering the minority opinion, Justice John Marshall Harlan said that separation was but a mere "badge of servitude."

While the "separate but equal" ruling had a damaging effect on black civil rights, an even more severe blow was struck two years later when the writers of the state constitution of 1898 disfranchised the vast majority of black voters through an ingenious exception to the literacy qualifications clause. During the 1890s Southern states rewrote their constitutions to disfranchise Negro voters. States such as Louisiana adopted the literacy test, property qualifications, and poll taxes in their new constitutions to achieve that end. These consitutions, however, included certain "escape" clauses to enable whites, who could not meet the literacy and property qualifications, to register to vote.

The states tried various means and wordings to accomplish this, and Louisiana's 1898 constitution included a "grandfather clause" as an exception to these two requirements. The grandfather clause stated in part that no male could be denied the right to register to vote if he, his father, or grandfather, had been eligible to do so on January 1, 1867, or before. The year 1867 was important because it was not until the Louisiana "Black Reconstruction" constitution of 1868 that blacks in general were extended full "civil, political, and public rights." The new constitution achieved its aim. In 1896 there were 126,822 Negroes registered to vote. By 1900 the number had dropped to 5,320. Other states copied Louisiana's grandfather clause until the U.S. Supreme Court declared it unconstitutional in 1915. The 1921 Louisiana constitutional convention adopted Mississippi's "understanding clause," that required a potential registrant to be able to read parts of the state constitution, or be able to give a reasonable interpretation of it when read to him.

The 1898 constitution came as a hard blow to many black Louisianians who realized that progress — both social and economic — was in direct proportion to their political strength and having the right to vote. One of the last major advancements of Radical Reconstruction was gone.

During the 1800s the Crescent City had risen from a relatively insignificant colonial outpost to one of the major cities and ports in the nation. Like the progress of the nation itself, the growth and changes were phenomenal. Men and events like Thomas Jefferson, the Louisiana Purchase, the Battle of New Orleans and Andrew Jackson, the Mexican War, yellow fever, Ben Butler, the Civil War and Reconstruction, and the Louisiana State Lottery Company had been important in shaping chapters in the city's history. A new chapter and century with new names and events was about to commence.

The 1896 municipal elections caused the breakup of the Crescent Democratic Club. Other organizations were formed from the disintegration of the CDC: the Citizens' League, whose candidate Walter Flower was elected mayor; and the Choctaw Club, which was to become the organ of the Regular Democratic Organization and would dominate local politics for three decades. (THNOC)

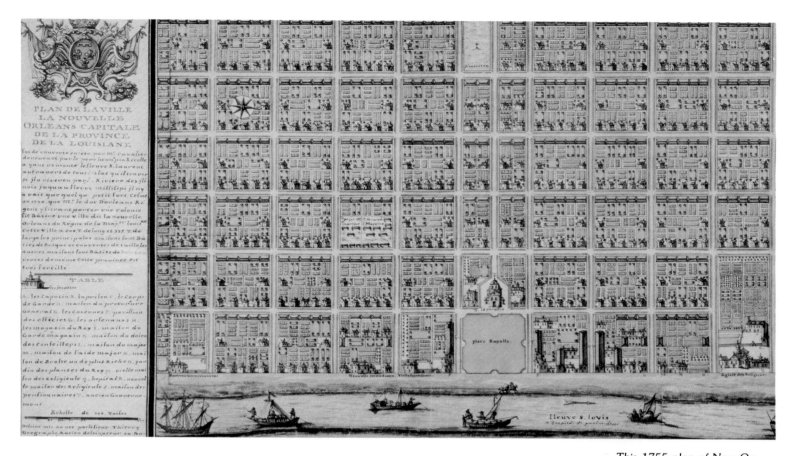

This 1755 plan of New Orleans by Thierry seems a bit fanciful in its depiction of neat houses and parterre gardens, but accounts by inhabitants of the city at that period attested to the physical charm of New Orleans. (THNOC)

137

Facing page
*With his success against the
British at Pensacola, Galvez
received recognition for his
exploits from the king of
Spain. The monarch allowed
him to add to his coat of arms
the words "Yo solo" (I alone)
for his heroism against the
British. The addition appears
in a scroll above the ship in
the lower right quadrant of the
shield. (THNOC)*

Above
*The Battle of Lake Borgne,
depicted in this oil painting,
was a naval skirmish which
preceded the final Battle of
New Orleans early in 1815.
(THNOC)*

A motley group of troops that included regulars, recruits, and volunteers commanded by General Andrew Jackson achieved a victory over British forces in January 1815. The Battle of New Orleans was painted by Dennis M. Carter. (THNOC)

These lithographs from the 1870s depict the New Orleans establishments of George Merz, proprietor of the Old Canal Brewery, and C. Cavaroc, wholesale liquor dealer. The end of Reconstruction government in Louisiana marked the beginning of a new era of prosperity in New Orleans business. (THNOC)

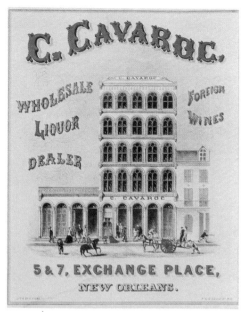

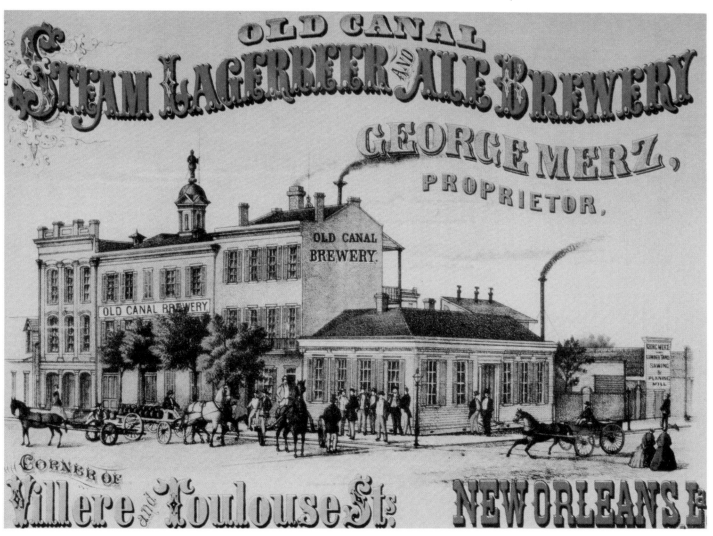

Steamboats were important movers of commercial goods, passengers, and mail throughout the Mississippi Valley, and New Orleans was the most important port on the route. This painting is by Hippolyte Sebron. (THNOC)

Entitled New Orleans: Die Canal Strasse, *this view depicts
Canal Street circa 1850–1860.
The street has always been a
fashionable and important one
to New Orleans. Despite many
changes in its appearance
throughout the years, the
street has retained the essence
of its former character.
(THNOC)*

143

*Lafayette Square was the
main public square of the
American Sector and a popular place for people to congre-
gate for an afternoon of relaxation. This drawing is from an
1850s edition of* Ballou's Pictorial Drawing-Room Com-
panion. *(THNOC)*

This oil painting depicts the destruction that occurred when the Federal fleet passed the forts below New Orleans. (THNOC)

Importing, roasting, and packaging coffee has been an important industry in New Orleans since the early 1800s. These colorful, decorative labels are only a part of the lore associated with the coffee trade. (THNOC)

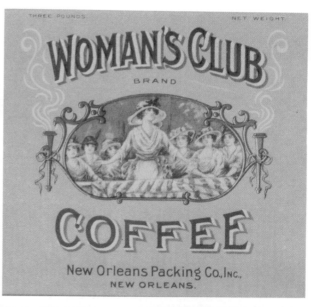

147

Construction and installation of the buildings and exhibitions at the World's Industrial and Cotton Centennial Exposition experienced many delays, and the exposition had to be opened in a partially completed state. Pictured here are some of the workers at the site. (THNOC)

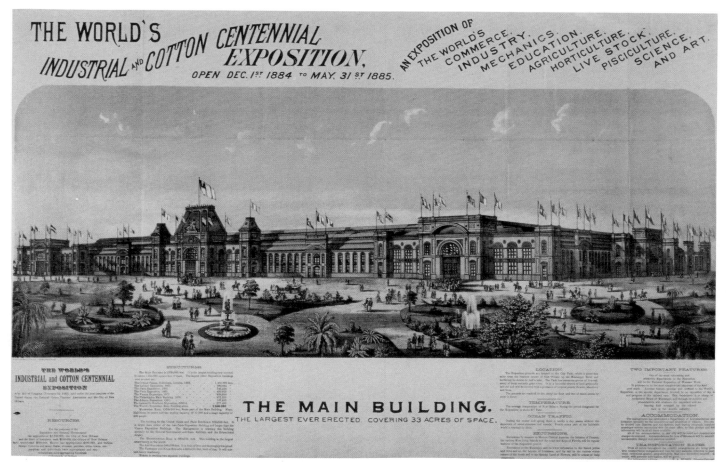

As shown in this brightly colored poster announcing the opening of the W.I.C.C.E., several large buildings were constructed to house the event's many exhibits. Audubon Park was the site of the exposition. The Main Building at the W.I.C.C.E. (right) covered 33 acres. (THNOC)

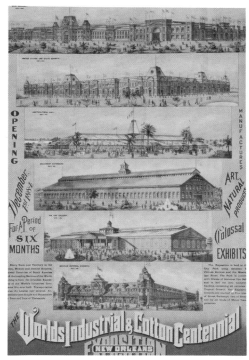

Mardi Gras invitations and posters during the "golden age" were often very elaborate, being intricately colored and/or die-cut into complicated and unusual shapes. Themes for the parades and balls that followed were often drawn from ancient history or mythology. (THNOC)

CHAPTER VII
A MODERN CITY EMERGES

New Orleans entered the 20th century with great optimism. The nation had just emerged victorious in its war with Spain and at home in Louisiana, the Democrats had become by far the dominant political party, while New Orleans boosters were busily trying to sell the city's attributes to the nation's business community.

During the first three decades of the new century, the face of the city began to change. Uptown New Orleans continued to grow and new and more lavish mansions joined their predecessors on the prestigious St. Charles Avenue. New and higher skyscrapers jutted through the skyline of the Central Business District, dwarfing the 19th-century structures of the old American Sector. It was a period of dramatic building activity, especially multistoried commercial edifices.

Three Presidents — William McKinley, Theodore Roosevelt, and William Howard Taft — visited the city during the first decade. McKinley was the first President ever to come to the Crescent City while in office.

During these early decades, New Orleans jazz moved north and eventually to the hearts of jazz enthusiasts around the world. The famous Galatoire's Restaurant first opened its doors in 1905 and four years later an automobile speed record was set in the city by Ralph de Palma, traveling 50 miles at an average speed of 60 m.p.h. These were the

beginning years for many of the city's cultural, entertainment, and educational institutions. The New Orleans Symphony Society was founded in 1906, as was the Louisiana State Museum (located in the Presbytere and Cabildo). In 1910 the first motion-picture house opened its doors and in the years following "movies" would join vaudeville marquees in the city's major theaters. A year later Loyola University was established and the Isaac Delgado Museum of Art opened in City Park. Another center of higher learning came into being in 1916 with the founding of Xavier University. Another French Quarter institution, Le Petit Theatre du Vieux Carre, began its long career of delighting New Orleans audiences. During the 1920s the French Quarter became a popular place for young artists and writers to meet and to create. In 1921 the short-lived *Double Dealer* began publishing the early works of the

then little-known William Faulkner and others who would gain fame.

In this period many of the city's antiquated and inadequate public utilities were replaced. New drainage and sewerage systems were built and a modern water purification plant took the place of individual rainwater cisterns. Perhaps the most important achievement during the first decade of the new century was the elimination of the city's dreaded perennial visitor — yellow fever.

By the turn of the century, however, New Orleans still did not show many of the signs of growth exhibited by other American cities. While Atlanta, Memphis, Cleveland, and Baltimore almost doubled in population, New Orleans increased by only 25 percent. Its national standing according to population dropped from ninth to twelfth in 1900 and to sixteenth by 1918. New Orleans' greatest business asset,

its port, had fallen into decay and disrepair during Reconstruction and the decades following it. But with the activities of the Dock Board (formed in 1898) and the building of the Public Belt Railroad in 1908 the annual revenue from the port increased from approximately $215,000 in 1902 to $430,000 in 1912.

The city's economic growth during these years was sporadic. From 1899 to 1904 the city rolled on a tide of national prosperity, as was reflected in the increase of its capital assets. But good fortune was short-lived. New Orleans, as well as the rest of the nation, suffered from a general economic depression in 1907. From that year until 1913 the city's economy steadily deteriorated; capital assets fell by almost 5 percent and the market value of its products fell by 12 percent. With 1914 and the war in Europe, New Orleans and the nation once again began to prosper. By 1920 the city's

Above
In the early 20th century, jazz became quite popular. It was played in clubs and aboard luxury steamboats. This band aboard the steamer Sydney *was led by Fate Marable. (THNOC)*

capital had more than doubled and the total market value of products tripled 1914 figures.

New Orleanians looked to the new century with almost childlike optimism, but of course events did not always justify it. The first year of the century, three major events took place that would have a profound impact on political and social matters for several decades. It was the year that the Regular Democratic Organization, usually referred to as the Choctaw Club or Regular Democrats (later Old Regulars), took the reins of city government and would hold them for almost three decades. It was also the year of the streetcar employees riot and the Charles riot — one of the most violent race riots in the city's history.

Robert Charles, a black native of Columbus, Mississippi, came to New Orleans as a member of a movement to encourage blacks to return to Africa. He and a cousin rented rooms near Washington Avenue and Dryades Street where they resided and worked toward their cause. White neighbors became suspicious and reported the two black men to police. When police officers came to their apartment on July 23, 1900, Charles and his cousin opened fire, seriously wounding one officer. The cousin was captured, but Charles escaped. The next day Charles shot and killed a police captain and corporal as they approached an abandoned house where he had taken refuge.

News of the policemen's deaths spread rapidly through the city. Mobs of young white men roamed the streets randomly beating

blacks. Mayor Paul Capdevielle, the last of the Creole mayors, cut short his vacation and returned to the city. He immediately ordered the mobs off the streets and sent out a call for 1,500 volunteers, whom he deputized as special police. Seven blacks, who were overheard to praise Charles' "war on the whites" were jailed.

Charles was later trapped in a house on Saratoga Street. A policeman or one of the hundreds of volunteers surrounding the house set fire to the structure to force the fugitive into the open. As Charles tried to escape the smoke and flames, he was shot to death. The resulting riot lasted four days, causing the deaths of three policemen and approximately ten private citizens (white and black).

Three months after the Charles riot, labor

Right
*During the streetcar workers'
riot of 1901, Mayor Paul Capdevielle tried to mediate between management and labor,
but was unsuccessful. The
state militia eventually intervened, and the strike ended.
Capdevielle was replaced as
mayor by Martin Behrman in
the 1904 election. (THNOC)*

Far right
*Citizens erect a barricade of
streetcars and billboards on
Canal Street during the 1901
riot. Courtesy, Louisiana State
Museum.*

troubles began among the city's streetcar workers. In October the carmen went out on a two-
day strike, but their grievances were quickly
resolved. The following September 27, however, they called a general strike and effectively
stopped every streetcar in the city for over a
month. The workers demanded an eight-hour
workday at 25 cents an hour. The strikers had
the support of the populace and several trade
unions. Canal Street businessmen and merchants and Mayor Capdevielle tried to arbitrate
the dispute. An offer of a 10-hour workday and
23 cents an hour was made, but turned down.
On October 8 violence broke out when the
company tried to operate four cars on Canal
Street with strikebreakers from St. Louis. Despite police protection, the strikers attacked
and stopped cars at Galvez and Canal streets.
Three strikers were arrested.

Having little confidence in the emergency
capabilities of the police department, Capdevielle called for volunteers to act as special
police, but few responded. So at the mayor's
request, Governor Heard ordered out the militia. But before they could arrive, violence
erupted between strikers and police on Canal
and Dorgenois streets. Two policemen and ten
civilians, including striking carmen, were injured. A police wagon hurrying reinforcements
to the scene was overturned by strikers, also
causing a number of injuries. On October 9
Heard arrived in the city with 700 militiamen
and forced the strikers to accept 20 cents an
hour for a 10-hour workday. The strike lasted
about 14 days and ended with considerable loss
of life and injury on both sides.

After the settlement of the streetcar strike,
New Orleanians turned to a game they were
more familiar with — politics. The municipal
elections of 1904 and the victory of Mayor Martin Behrman, the Regular Democratic Organization's candidate, was the beginning of 16
years of uninterrupted Tammany Hall-styled
machine politics in New Orleans. The reform-
minded New Orleans *Times-Democrat* (which
became the *Times-Picayune* in 1914) strongly
opposed Behrman's candidacy:

*A man of pleasant personality and popularity
. . . Mr. Behrman does not rise to the
standards but represents the very elements
that would assure misgovernment of the city
and seriously hinder and check its
prosperity. . . . When New Orleans falls into
the hands of the ring, when the arch masters
of the politicians, the bosses, get possession of
its government and administer it in the
interest of the ward workers, hangers on and
all of the others of the great army of
janissaries who make up the machine, it
suffers in every department, in every branch
of government and in its business as well.*

The Regular Democratic Organization
(RDO) — also known in New Orleans as the
Choctaw Club, the Ring, machine, Regulars,
and after 1922, as the Old Regulars — represented all walks of life in the city: workers,
businessmen, attorneys, physicians, bankers,
gamblers, clerks, and professional politicians.
According to a study of the organization in the
early 1930s by a Columbia University graduate

Left
The Times-Democrat, *a New Orleans newspaper, was opposed to Martin Behrman's candidacy for mayor, seeing him as a typical "boss" type. (THNOC)*

Below
The key to Behrman's controlling city politics was a system of patronage and kickbacks to the political machine. The machine was the Regular Democratic Organization. Behrman is shown here with some of the members who made the system work. (THNOC)

complete charge of his organization. He chose his precinct captains and dispersed all patronage in his territory. Behrman once claimed that the success of a ward boss was due to "personal traits, hard work, uneven distribution of patronage, and luck."

The nucleus of the organization was in the precinct clubs. The machine's success was in direct proportion to the efficiency of the precinct captain and his workers in getting out the vote on election day. Precinct leaders had to possess an encyclopedic knowledge of the people in his area: their problems, jobs, hobbies, likes and dislikes, and ambitions provided clues to getting their votes.

Running the RDO and winning elections was expensive. Club members paid a dollar a month in dues and everyone on the city payroll was required to belong. During a political campaign, city department heads had to collect "contributions" from the employees in their sections. A political candidate, seeking the RDO's endorsement, had to pledge to kickback 10 percent of his salary to the organization, and in some cases, depending on the candidate and the office, larger percentages would be levied. Corporations and small businesses, as well as gambling dens and bordellos, had to contribute to the "war chest."

student, the success of the organization was due to the simplicity of its structure and to patronage. The RDO was divided into the caucus and the club. The caucus — the ruling body of the machine — was composed of the ward leaders from the city's 17 wards. All policy decisions were made by the "Council of Seventeen" and it decided who would run for office with the Regular's endorsement. Anyone in the organization who did not go along with its decisions could have his patronage cut off.

The machine was, in effect, a federation of ward organizations in which the ward boss had

The RDO's success was also partly attributable to its good relationship with the business community, which it considered "normal, necessary and in the interest of the city." Behrman's own motto was that "nothing would be done to hurt business and business was to be judge." He worked closely when he could with such booster organizations as the Progressive Union (formed in 1902) and its successor, the New Orleans Association of Commerce (formed in 1913).

Behrman's relationship with business was not uncommon. Historian Harold Zink concluded in his 1930 work, *City Bosses in the United States,* that most city bosses of the late-19th and early-20th centuries had some form of business connections. For examples, "Colonel" Ed Butler of St. Louis, "Honorable" William Tweed of New York, and Abraham Reuf of San Francisco were either presidents or directors of numerous corporations, while "Old Boy" George Cox of Cincinnati, Christopher Magee of Pittsburgh, and Roger Sullivan of Chicago controlled banks, street railways, and gas companies.

Businessmen, like any other group of people, could not always agree among themselves and often Behrman was caught in the middle. One such occasion occurred in the 1915 session of the state legislature. The Louisiana sugarcane growers introduced a number of "anti-corporation" bills hoping to free themselves of the sugar trusts. The American Sugar Refining Company, the New Orleans Association of Commerce, the New Orleans Clearing House Association (banks), the Sugar Exchange, and

labor groups employed in the refineries (yielding to the corporations) led the opposition to these measures. The Association of Commerce warned that these bills were the first step on a path toward "socialism." As mayor and leader of the strongest faction in the state legislature, Behrman was in a difficult position for he had to decide whether to back the sugar growers or the business interests within his own city. Aware of the growing tendencies in the state and country toward regulations of monopolies, Behrman backed the growers.

This was just one of the highlights of Behrman's first 16 years in office (1904–1920). Others included the 1905 confrontation with the colorful Dominick O'Malley—publisher of the New Orleans *Item*—over control of the police department; the city's last yellow-fever epidemic the same year; and, the creation of the Public Belt Railroad in 1908. The city tried unsuccessfully to get the 1915 Panama-Pacific Exposition; and a police superintendent was assassinated in 1917. Although Behrman wore the badge of political boss, many important improvements were made in the city during his tenure, such as extensive street-paving, a modern sewerage system, new schools and playgrounds, and increased fire and police protection.

Throughout his mayorality, Behrman faced constant opposition from such "reform" groups as the Home Rulers (1904), Independents (1908), Good Government League (1912), and Governor John M. Parker and his Orleans Democratic Organization (1920). Cries for government reform in New Orleans usually took the form of progressive democracy—abstract *versus* practical politics. The reformers were middle class and generally lawyers, businessmen, social uplifters, and editors; there were as many Catholics as Protestants, and included Jews. A look at those who supported Behrman revealed they were also middle class, with the same religious and ethnic diversity. Behrman characterized the reformers as a disgruntled combination of discontented Regulars, idealists, opportunists, and "uptown silk stockings." The silk-stocking reformer, the mayor claimed, was one "who knew all about municipal government because he read magazines and books . . . and did not know where to file his complaint if the garbage man did not come early enough to suit him." This perennial op-

position, he said, was nothing more than "the outs wanting in." Only the professional politician, Behrman declared, "knew how to get the job done."

The most successful attack against Behrman and the RDO was made during the 1920 mayoral elections. Reform Governor John M. Parker and his New Orleans-based Orleans Democratic Association (ODA)—a political offspring of the RDO—succeeded in getting Andrew McShane elected mayor. The contest between the Behrman-RDO faction and the Parker-ODA-McShane alliance had been the most heated mayoral election in decades.

In an attack on Behrman's administration on August 7, 1920, Governor Parker appointed a committee led by prominent businessmen and labor leaders to investigate the city's municipal government. The ODA worked diligently for months compiling incriminating evidence against Behrman. Behrman, in a countermove, obtained a court injunction to postpone the investigation until after the election. The ODA, stunned, pointed to the injunction as an admission of guilt to the charges. Esmond Phelps, chairman of the McShane campaign, claimed that Behrman had pleaded guilty to "inefficiency, extravagances, and poor business methods . . . by enjoining an examination of the city's affairs." Behrman told the ODA that he did not oppose an investigation of his administration, but asked that it be held after the election. When the ODA refused, Behrman ac-

cused the organization of using the investigation to create political jobs.

McShane campaigned on a ticket calling for "public decency, free politics and civil progress," while accusing Behrman of being "irreconcilably for public vice, political bossdom and social and civil stagnation."

The *Times-Picayune* kept up a constant and unrelenting attack on Behrman. From August 25 to September 14, 1920, it carried daily front page spreads attacking Behrman's record, especially concerning vice, poor street conditions, and the city debt. Damaging articles and photographs appeared daily on the front pages showing neglect in street-paving, drainage, and garbage collection: "Anywhere off the 'show streets' there is the same dreary picture of neglect." In defense Behrman asked, "Why don't these damnable, slimy, unfair newspapers print pictures of the avenues and pretty places?"

The *Times-Picayune* also charged that policemen were stationed in the city's "dives" to protect gamblers and underworld characters. In a series of articles entitled "Under the Shadow of Vultures' Wings," *Picayune* reporters exposed saloons, gambling parlors, and houses of prostitution allegedly permitted to exist by the police and Behrman. In his memoirs Behrman denied the *Picayune's* charges. After the passage of the National Prohibition Enforcement Act, or the "Volstead Act," in 1919, there were no saloons in New Orleans or illegal liquor, he claimed. Any liquor that may have been on hand was purchased legally before the law. "Besides," he said, "I didn't have time to go around investigating such foolishness." Alcoholic beverages could be gotten with little difficulty in the city that boasted of its unique history, sophistication, and cosmopolitan attitudes toward good living. As historian Joy Jackson wrote: "Although bars, restaurants, groceries, and fruit stands were highly likely spots to purchase alcoholic beverages, it could be bought in poolrooms, from bellhops, taxi drivers, and the neighbor down the street who operated a still or winery in the drop-shed adjacent to his house. Making home brew became almost a universal practice among Orleanians."

During the campaign Parker and the ODA accused Behrman of using the infamous Storyville as a source of political power. Behrman reminded Parker that Storyville was already in existence when the Choctaws had gained power in 1900. He also reminded Parker that Storyville had been created in 1897, during Flower's administration, by the Citizen's League of which Parker had been a member. The ODA characterized Behrman as the "King of the Tenderloin" (another name for Storyville) in that he fought to keep the district open during World War I, an accusation that Behrman denied, saying he had done all he could to close Storyville during the war.

A Liberty Bond parade takes place on Canal Street in 1917. That year Storyville was ordered closed as a threat to military men. Quite a number of military personnel were billeted in and near New Orleans during World War I, and the presence of a red-light district was seen as too much of a problem. (THNOC)

The Iberville Federal Housing Project occupies the site where Storyville once stood. Storyville had been "closed" for nearly 20 years before it was demolished. (THNOC)

Just after the war mobilization had begun, both public and governmental attention focused on the prevention of social diseases among servicemen. Behrman, after discussing the matter with the military commanders of army camps surrounding the city, decided to place Storyville off limits to soldiers, and military commanders were requested to place a ring of guards around the district to keep out uniformed personnel. Behrman thought that this would take care of the problem. However, in 1917, Raymond Fosdick arrived in New Orleans and ordered the district closed. Fosdick, a member of the Navy Department's special Federal Commission on Training Camp Activities, was sent to the city to investigate and

eliminate places of vice near military bases. Behrman told Fosdick that he did not intend to close Storyville until he had heard from Secretary of War Newton D. Baker. Fosdick demanded that the Tenderloin District be closed, but Behrman again refused to comply with Fosdick's order until he could confer with Baker.

Before traveling to Washington, Behrman called a special meeting at City Hall. Present at the meeting were John M. Parker and the editors of the *Item, Times-Picayune,* and *States.* Behrman told them of the situation and his intentions and they all agreed that the district would remain open until after Behrman's conference with Baker.

In his meeting with the secretary, Behrman

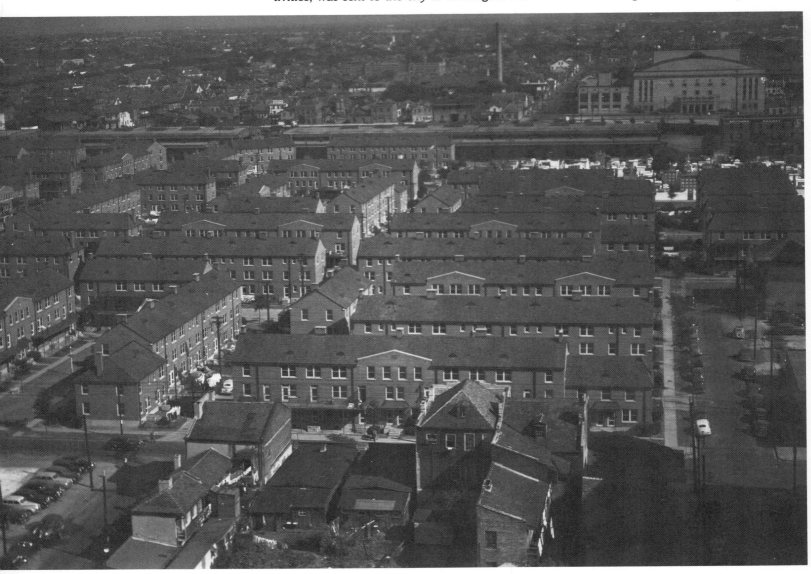

argued that closing the district would cause prostitution and vice to spread throughout the entire city. But Baker, a former mayor of Cleveland, Ohio, drawing from his own experience in cleaning up that city's "red-light district," disagreed with the idea that restricting prostitution to a specified district was the best way to handle such a "difficult situation." Baker, however, instructed the "king" to maintain the "status quo" until further word. Behrman assured the secretary that he would abide by any decision the government made.

A short time later Behrman received an order to close Storyville from the Secretary of the Navy "Tea Totaling" Josephus Daniels. Behrman offered no more resistance: "I had gone as far as I thought I ought to go in impressing my opinions on one member of the Cabinet and I did not care to go further." In compliance with Daniels' instructions, Behrman introduced a bill to the city council directing the closing of the district. The bill passed and Storyville was "officially" closed; however, it continued to operate illegally until the 1940s when it was razed to make way for a federal housing project.

Toward the end of the campaign, the *Times-Picayune* made an appeal to Behrman's supporters to defect and join the ODA. It warned that Behrman and his machine were on the way out:

On the road to ODA: The plaint of the Long-Suffering "Regular"
In the City Hall, while idling, thinking anxiously the while,
There's a Regular a-gazing at his fading salary pile,
And the wind above the rafters seems to whisper, soft and low:
"The Behrman ship is sinking; don't you think it's time to go?"
Hurdle to the ODA
Where you'll get an even play.
Can't you feel the ring a-slippin'
As it totters on its way?
On the road to ODA
You can keep your monthly pay,
With no Choctaw Club a-waitin' for it's just across the way.

The relentless attacks by Governor Parker, the ODA, and the *Times-Picayune* were suc-

cessful; McShane defeated Behrman 22,986 votes to 21,536. The ring was smashed, at least temporarily, and the ODA captured four of the five seats on the city council. The fifth, the only seat won by a Choctaw, went to Paul Maloney. Obviously pleased with the results, Parker reminded the victors that it was not the time for "crowing" but to get busy and make the most of the opportunity.

In searching for the causes of his defeat in 1920, Behrman looked to World War I and its effects on the nation's attitudes:

It happened that the people were in the frame of mind of being against everything. They seemed to be against the war itself, in their hearts. . . . My defeat in 1920 was due to many causes. The very fact that I had been mayor for so long means that I had accumulated enemies. No matter what you do in office, you still make enemies. Sixteen years of enemies is a lot of them.

Behrman, however, failed to admit that the majority of the voters were convinced that vice and corruption in the city were being tolerated by his administration.

The combined efforts of Governor Parker and the Orleans Democratic Association defeated Martin Behrman and the Choctaw Club in 1920. But the ODA had been a loosely knit organization composed of many different factions with the common goal of defeating Behrman. Once this objective had been achieved the coalition degenerated into petty factionalism and quickly returned the Old Regulars to power. Behrman did not retire from New Orleans politics after his rejection in 1920. He stepped aside, rebuilt his machine, and planned his comeback. The Old Choctaw's first step back into public life was his election to the 1921 state constitutional convention.

During the 1919 gubernatorial campaign, both Parker and his opponent, Colonel Frank Stubbs called for a new constitution. Parker referred to the 1913 constitution as a "patchwork" document containing more amendments than all of the other 47 state constitutions combined. With an eye on the 1920 New Orleans municipal elections, Parker thought that it would be a mistake to convene the convention until after the city elections. Otherwise

he said, "It would be a political convention." He believed that only through the machine could society in general prosper. Business was an essential part in the scheme but subordinate to the machine. During the constitutional convention of 1921, the ex-mayor was content, as mentioned earlier, to be merely a part of the proceedings, rather than a leader. The most important result of the convention, for Behrman at least, was that it gave him a new aura of victory which he desperately needed after his defeat in 1920.

The Old Regulars' comeback was temporarily halted on Wednesday, October 4, 1922, when Behrman announced that he was retiring from politics because of poor health. The Choctaws then dubbed as their new leader Paul Maloney, commissioner of public utilities. Actually Behrman's announced reasons for retiring were not quite the whole truth. Behrman resigned at the urging of the Choctaw Caucus

because of his defeat in 1920, failing health, and rising ambitions of younger members. The war bonnet was passed to Maloney because of the Choctaw's custom of naming as its leader the official holding the highest office. In the 1920 municipal elections, he was the only Old Regular not to go down with Behrman. Reporters asked Maloney if his selection meant that he would be the 1925 Old Regular candidate for mayor. Maloney, coyly refusing to commit himself, told them that the election was too far in the future to comment, although he undoubtedly believed that he would be the Old Regulars' candidate. (Maloney's life was a traditional success story. He began his career in 1892 as a $15-a-month office boy for the Crescent Transfer and Shipping Company; by 1917 he was the full owner.)

But Behrman would not be content with retirement after so many years of wielding power. Though illness forced Behrman into retirement, his ego and love of a campaign could not keep him there. He helped elect judges to two New Orleans benches in 1922, assisted in the 1923–1924 gubernatorial campaign, and made another bid for mayor in 1925, all of which attest to his political nature.

The 1923–1924 gubernatorial race was probably the most controversial campaign for that office in 20th-century Louisiana history. By the end of the summer of 1923, three main candidates and their supporters had committed themselves. They were Henry L. Fuqua, a Protestant from southern Louisiana; Hewitt Bouanchaud, a French-Catholic from the southern parish of Pointe Coupee; and Huey Long, chairman of the Public Service Commission and a Protestant from northern rural Louisiana. The main issues during the campaign, regardless of efforts to avoid them, were religion and the Ku Klux Klan (KKK), which had become an ever-increasing power in state and national politics.

Fuqua, the general manager of the state penitentiary at Angola, had the endorsement of former governors Sanders and Pleasant. Although Fuqua had been an important member of Governor Parker's administration, he did not receive the governor's support. Parker endorsed Hewitt Bouanchaud, his lieutenant governor and a Catholic. Catholics, at that time at least, had practically no chance of being elected in statewide contests because of northern Loui-

siana's predominantly Protestant population coupled with Protestant voters in the southern part of the state.

Most political observers found it difficult to understand why Parker would back an almost certain loser. Historian T. Harry Williams, writing in his Pulitzer prize-winning *Huey Long*, ventured several possible reasons for Parker's commitment. First, he may have felt a sense of personal loyalty to his fellow "good government" reformer. Secondly, he wished to demonstrate that he could elect his own hand-picked successor over the opposition of Sanders, Pleasant, and the Old Regulars of New Orleans. Thirdly, the reform governor, believing that both Fuqua and Long were afraid of alienating the Klan vote, felt that at least one candidate had to stand staunchly against the hooded order. Actually Parker had little choice.

He could hardly back Long because of his attacks against Parker's pro-Standard Oil stand during the constitutional convention of 1921. Nor could he back Fuqua who had received the enthusiastic support of Behrman.

Behrman and the Old Regulars were impressed with Fuqua's strength in the country parishes. Fuqua was Protestant and anti-Klan, but not as vigorously as Bouanchaud. Behrman could not support Long because he believed Long to be a "radical opponent of business," and he could not join forces with Parker and back Bouanchaud. Besides, he did not think the lieutenant governor had a chance to win. The Old Regulars put their entire organization to work for Fuqua and formed "Fuqua clubs" in each of the city's 17 wards. Although a Catholic himself, the Old Choctaw chief realized that a Protestant from southern Louisiana had a far

Canal and Rampart streets in the 1920s, with the turrets of some of the Storyville brothels in the distance on the right. The transitions apparent in the city at the time are clearly seen in this photograph. Visible are many types of vehicles: electric streetcars, gasoline-powered automobiles, and horsedrawn wagons. The Southern Railway terminal is at the center of the photograph and just to the right is the Saenger Theatre. (THNOC)

greater chance than a Catholic. Furthermore, Fuqua's moderation toward the Klan did not alienate its members or sympathizers as did Bouanchaud's vehement attacks.

Long attacked everything and everyone. The *Item,* he said, was owned by Wall Street and the *Times-Picayune* by New York bankers; Fuqua and Bouanchaud were both Parker's men; Behrman and Colonel John Sullivan, both agents of Wall Street, were actually working together. "If Behrman took a dose of laudanum," he charged, "Sullivan would get sleepy in ten minutes." But regardless of how hard he tried, Long could not evade the real issue of the campaign — the Klan.

In the beginning of the campaign each candidate expressed his position on the hooded order. Bouanchaud said that he stood for law and order and was opposed to the "Invisible Empire of the Ku Klux Klan." If elected governor, he promised, he would go to the limits of the federal and state constitutions to protect the people from the Klan. Fuqua stated that masked and secret societies bred violence and mistrust. If elected, he promised to push for an anti-masking law, one that would require all secret societies to file at regular intervals with the secretary of state lists of their memberships. Long, on the other hand, attempted to evade the issue. The campaign, he said, should be free from religious agitation. He gave a long discourse on the principle of separation of church from state, saying he hoped everyone would live by the "Golden Rule." Later, when pressured for a clearer statement of his views on the Klan, the Winn Parish candidate evasively said that he was "against any unlawful practices by the Klan or anyone else." He doubted that Fuqua's plan for an anti-masking law would work. He pointed out that there was already an anti-masking law in the statutes: "We don't need two, just enforce the first." Bouanchaud challenged his opponents to come out against the Klan "as an un-American organization that cannot exist because it is opposed to constitutional forms of government." Fuqua accused the lieutenant governor of trying to make the Invisible Empire an issue in the campaign in order to distract attention from the "real issues." The real issues for New Orleans, Long asserted, were natural gas, free textbooks for *all* school children, improved workmen's compensation laws, paving Claiborne Avenue,

reduction of taxes, and elimination of governmental extravagances. Long accused Bouanchaud and Fuqua of having no issue but the Klan. The only difference between the two, he remarked, was "that Bouanchaud wanted to hang them before the election and Fuqua wanted them to vote for him first then hang them."

According to most predictions in New Orleans, at least among Bouanchaud supporters, Long did not have a chance. Both the *Item* and the *Times-Picayune* predicted that the lieutenant governor would win, Fuqua would finish second, and Long, a miserable third. The results, however, proved them only partially correct: Bouanchaud received 82,910 votes; Fuqua, 82,177; and Long, a surprising 73,275. The most dramatic results were in New Orleans: Bouanchaud, the Catholic, received 23,232; Fuqua, the Protestant, 32,999; and Long, 12,303. Behrman and the Old Regulars delivered 15 out of the 17 wards to Fuqua. In the second primary Long's supporters swung over to Fuqua giving him the final victory and the governorship.

The most ominous results of the 1924 gubernatorial campaign in New Orleans were the rise of Huey Long in the city's politics and the return of Behrman. The Public Commissioner from Winn Parish realized that great inroads would have to be made in New Orleans if he was to have any future success in the state or national political arenas. This strategy set the pact and drew new political lines in New Orleans politics for the next two decades.

In his campaign for governor in 1924, Huey Long from Winn Parish ran a nonstop race. Although he drew the fewest votes of the three major candidates, fewer than 10,000 votes separated him from Hewitt Bouanchaud, the winner of the primary. (THNOC)

Behrman's next step in his comeback was at the 1924 state Democratic convention which followed the gubernatorial election of that year. The party met in June to select delegates for the national convention. The state convention was merely a formality as it had been the practice for many years in Louisiana that the governor would meet with other state leaders and New Orleans bosses to select the delegates. Fuqua and Behrman saw no reason why 1924 should be any different. In a secret meeting 20 delegates were chosen, 16 on a geographical basis and 4 at-large. After a bit of political manipulation the delegates-at-large were decided upon: Fuqua, Behrman, former Governor J.Y. Sanders, and Lee E. Thomas, mayor of Shreveport. Huey Long denounced the secret agreements as a fraud, stating that Sanders and Behrman had both been rejected by the voters in their last attempts at political office. The Winn Parish upstart vowed that he would go to the convention and help select a new slate.

Actually, Long did not get a chance to change anything. From the moment the convention was called to order, Behrman and Sanders assumed complete control of the proceedings. Behrman was chosen permanent chairman of the convention and in turn appointed Sanders head of the resolutions committee. They ruled the meeting with as heavy a hand as any South or Central American dictator. They tabled and allowed to be shouted down all proposals with which they did not agree, such as the resolution denouncing the KKK. One delegate advocating support for the 18th amendment was physically thrown off the stage by Behrman. Huey Long jumped on the stand and proposed that the number of delegates-at-large be increased from four to eight. That way, he said, the "has beens," referring to Behrman and Sanders, could keep their seats while four more reflecting the "will of the voters" could be chosen. Huey's resolution was tabled by a voice vote. He had been beaten and New Orleans newspapers gleefully wrote the obituaries: "Huey Long is finished."

As the 1924–1925 New Orleans mayorality election approached, Behrman was ready to take advantage of his startling series of political successes since 1920. In a special meeting of the Choctaw Caucus, Behrman was selected to head the Old Regular ticket. The caucus was not unanimous, however; Paul Maloney re-fused to step aside. He walked out, taking many supporters with him. Behrman dubbed those Old Regulars who backed Maloney as deserters and called Maloney a champion of "mediocrity." On January 4, 1925, Maloney announced his ticket and platform.

On the same day Maloney announced his platform, Huey Long was seen meeting with the Williams brothers, John Sullivan, and Colonel Ewing, owner of the New Orleans *States*. Long was taking advantage of the unprecedented division in the Old Regular organization to gain a foothold in New Orleans' politics. Shortly after their conferences they announced that they were supporting Maloney. The *Times-Picayune* asked why, with so much against him, would Behrman run again for mayor. Francis Williams declared that the Old Choctaw was politically sick and would be "politically dead within 30 days." He charged that Behrman, while telling labor of what a good friend he was, had his "loyalists" in the state legislature killing labor bills. Behrman, Williams said, took the working men and women of New Orleans to be a "bunch of boobs."

The two main issues of the campaign were "bossism and labor." On bossism, Behrman's two main opponents were Miss Jean Gordon, a nationally known New Orleans reformer, and the *Times-Picayune*. Miss Gordon supported Maloney. "This was not the time," she said, "to take chances and be sorry afterwards." She reminded voters of Behrman's trip to Washington in 1917 to save Storyville and of his efforts to suppress enforcement of the Sunday closing laws.

The *Times-Picayune* said that Behrman could no more change than the "Ethiopian can change his skin." His methods, it continued, and attitudes were fixed by a lifelong practice of "autocratic" leadership. He was too old and opinionated to change his views. "Behrmanism," wrote the *Picayune*, was the nearest thing to despotism remaining in the United States and was the common enemy of all those who believed "in independent political thought and in public administration which serves primarily and above all else the common will of the whole community." A surprise announcement by Governor Fuqua hit Behrman hard. Fuqua stated that he was going to stay out of the New Orleans campaign and not give state patronage in the city to anyone until

Facing page
Mayor Martin Behrman controlled almost every aspect of political life in New Orleans in the years he held office. He also had considerable influence in state politics. (THNOC)

after the election. Fuqua warned that any promises made by either faction were without foundation.

Organized labor leaders were divided between Behrman and Maloney. David Marcusy, president of the Central Trades and Labor Council, gave his full support to the incumbent McShane. John F. Bowen, chairman of the state legislative board of the Brotherhood of Railroad Trainmen, who had made the opening speech in Behrman's 1920 campaign, backed Maloney. Bowen accused Behrman of not being loyal to the Choctaws. If he had been loyal, Bowen claimed, he would have worked to keep the organization together and not left that job to the rank-and-file. Fuqua's election in 1924, he said, was due to their efforts and not Behrman's. The Choctaws were strong again, he continued, because they had backed Fuqua and now they could win the local election by backing the "logical candidate" — Maloney.

Behrman, borrowing a stratagem from Huey Long's 1923–1924 campaign, used the radio to broadcast his political rallies. Before a crowd at the Folly Theater in Algiers and a radio audience, Behrman made his opening address. "Let's get together," was the keynote of the speech. He pleaded with the voters to give the "battle scarred veteran of many political campaigns" the chance to move New Orleans ahead.

In the same broadcast, Behrman commented on the two newspapers opposing him. He said that he knew Colonel Ewing, of the *States,* about as well as any man in the community. At times, he continued, there had been cordial relations between them, but only when "Behrmanism . . . (was) in full accord with Ewingism." But when they did not agree, Behrmanism was "as wicked a thing as the works of Satan himself." The only comment he had for the *Times-Picayune* was that it was "the prime example of consistency." The former mayor expressed the hope that the campaign would be conducted with more dignity than in 1920. "The reckless display of unjust and untruthful publicity," he asserted, "served (no other) purpose but to injure the standing of the city."

During the campaign an editorial feud developed between the *Item* and the *Times-Picayune.* The *Picayune* accused the *Item* of "lending itself . . . to the baldest and oldest strategy of despots and bossdom." "For

years," said the *Picayune,* "the *Item* did not have a kind word to say about Behrman and during the 1920 campaign called him King of the Tenderloin and an undesirable citizen as well as public official." But during the 1925 campaign, continued the indictment, it was Behrman's strongest supporter and defender. The *Item* denounced the *Picayune* and other Maloney supporters for using smear and character-assassination tactics against Behrman.

The *Picayune* said that it did not have anything against Behrman personally but that he was too old and "broken under the strains of ambition." "For the safety of the city," it pleaded, "his desire to come back must be denied." His type of government, it argued, was based on patronage: "An employee has two masters, the city, who pays his salary, and the boss who gives the jobs." Loyalty to the ring superseded the welfare of the city and it was this type of situation that caused his downfall in 1920. The *Picayune* claimed that Behrman was at his "peak" in 1912, for then he had "vision and drew about him alert and competent men." But as time progressed Behrman turned to machine politics to protect his power: "Behrman the mayor talked about playgrounds and schools while Behrman the boss facilitated the marriage of the lowest strata of the 'ring' with the darkest elements of the underworld of corruption and commercial vice, that poison youth and taint all society." From 1916 on, continued the denunciation, Behrman had been in a state of visible decay and had fallen victim to the strain of high office.

As the campaign neared its conclusion the *Picayune* became more vehement: "Out of the slough of degrading bossdom New Orleans clambered four years ago. Much of the mud of it, the slime of it, still clings to our governmental garments. . . . But we have climbed out." In the same edition it pleaded with voters in an editorial, entitled "Think It Over," to consider their votes. Behrmanism and ring government, it wrote, were a thing of the past. Behrman, in rebuttal, said he believed the people wanted "an administration with party obligations and party responsibilities — for it is only through party government . . . that true progress has ever been made in government." The *Picayune* said what Behrman really meant was that he believed in government by faction and that had to be completely under his control. "Papa," it

continued, believed that he was the "anointed, indispensable and infallible shaper of human desires. . . . Behrman's ethics were ethics of gangdom."

Many voters apparently disagreed with these accusations and denunciations. Behrman received 35,731 votes to Maloney's 33,631. Since "Papa" did not receive a clear majority, a second primary would have been in order, but Maloney withdrew.

Behrman's reelection in 1925 was accomplished over almost insurmountable odds. His opponents thought him politically dead and wondered why he had run at all. Though his reelection was due in part to the lack of coordination among his rivals, his own energies and the effectiveness of the Choctaw's organization were the decisive factors. Behrman's reelection marked the climax of his political career and he immediately began working to fulfill his campaign promises as if inwardly he knew what fate awaited him. On January 12, 1926, one year after his reelection, Martin Behrman died. He died of *chronic myocarditis*, "which was a degeneration of heart muscles due to over work," his physician claimed. Governor Fuqua in a tribute to Behrman said he "pushed himself to become mayor and it killed him." "He died in harness," continued Fuqua, "as he would have liked to die." Governor Alfred E. Smith of New York said he had lost a personal friend.

The *Picayune* in a special editorial ironically stated that Behrman's death would be regretted by all. He was a politician, it said, who liked a good fight, and had fewer personal enemies than one with a lesser public life. His critics, continued the editorial, could never question his sincerity in wanting to do what was good for New Orleans: "His growth in vision and understanding, his broadening concepts of public service and duty, proved something better than the ordinary type of successful politician." It continued its laudatory but hypocritical tribute to Behrman in describing him as "a kindly citizen, a forceful leader and a municipal servant who made the most of his opportunities for service to the city he loved." Behrman's death marked the end of a lengthy political career of over 40 years. It also left a void in New Orleans politics that would soon be filled by Huey Long, who was elected to the governor's office in 1928.

New Orleanians awoke Friday morning October 25, 1929, to read about tremors in the stock market the day before. Black Thursday would affect their lives for the next decade, for the Great Depression had begun. Beside "Stock Exchange Panic," were headlines stating that President Harding's Secretary of the Interior Albert B. Fall had been convicted of bribery, and a report from the YWCA's National Council of Business Girls that "a painted face" was not a woman's guarantee of a good job. Also in the news that morning was Governor Huey P. Long, who had just reorganized the New Orleans Dock Board, eliminating his opposition.

Huey Long, often called the 'Kingfish,' was a force in Louisiana that affected the lives of New

Left
Huey Pierce Long was elected governor of Louisiana in 1928. He was a dominant force in state politics for many years afterwards, with his influence being felt even after his assassination. (THNOC)

Facing page
A street in the French Quarter as it appeared in the early years of the Depression. (THNOC)

Though the Depression had begun, Canal Street looks as busy as ever in this photograph. (THNOC)

Orleanians to a greater extent than even the Depression. On Black Thursday 1929 former Governor John M. Parker warned a gathering of the Young Men's Business Association in New Orleans, that we should not "permit ourselves to be the toy and the plaything of the greatest Mussolini the United States has ever seen."

Huey Pierce Long's election to the governor's office in 1928 marked a break in the political history of Louisiana. Until that time governors were products of the old Bourbon and "aristocratic" class of planter-merchants that had ruled the state since antebellum days (with the exception of Reconstruction). Long in fact campaigned for the office on the promise that he would sweep the Bourbons out. When elected Long set about destroying his opposition — particularly the machine in New Orleans that had so vigorously fought his candidacy — through tight control of the state legislature and by acquiring complete power over state patronage in New Orleans.

Political power in New Orleans up to and during the 1930s was synonymous with patronage — the ability to provide jobs to rank-and-file voters was the lifeblood of the Old Regulars, and this is what Long immediately set out to seize and use for his ends. (Long, however,

believed that his purposes were in the best interest of the poor of Louisiana, and his campaign program — featuring pledges of better roads, better schools, free textbooks for children, and a better court system — was at least partially the reason for the success of his campaign.)

In his first year as governor Huey Long was able to shift patronage for state jobs in New Orleans to his direct control. But in doing so, he met stiff resistance in the state legislature. He reorganized the Orleans Levee Board and the state Board of Health. Opposition in the legislature, however, blocked his attempts to reorganize Charity Hospital in New Orleans and the Orleans Courthouse Commission, as well as his attempt to replace the elected assessors in Orleans Parish with his own appointee.

In the spring of 1929, Long's opponents made a frontal assault, attempting to destroy him politically through impeachment. Nineteen charges were filed against him ranging from misuse of appointive powers and attempted bribery of legislators, to illegally using the state militia to raid New Orleans gambling houses and engaging in immoral behavior in a New Orleans night club.

"The reason for this is that he [Long] is temporarily and otherwise unfit to hold the office,"

said the *Times-Picayune*. "His tactics and methods reveal him to be a cruel political tyrant, willing to resort to almost any expediency to carry out his own wishes and purposes. Long cleverly defeated a conviction in the state senate by having 15 senators sign the infamous "Round Robin," saying they would refuse to convict Long no matter what evidence was presented.

In his successful 1930 bid for the U.S. Senate, Long formed his own political organization, the Louisiana Democratic Association, to counteract the Choctaws in New Orleans. In January 1932 Long took the oath of office for the U.S. Senate. His successor to the governor's office was his hand-picked candidate, Oscar K. Allen. Robert Maestri, later mayor of New Orleans, was appointed head of the Louisiana Democratic Association in the city. Before assuming his Senate seat, Long finally achieved an uncomfortable peace with the Choctaws: in exchange for their support in the legislature for several of his pet bills, Long promised New Orleans state money to pave and repair city streets, pay the debt of the Port of New Orleans, and build a free bridge across the Mississippi River at New Orleans.

While Huey Long's reign was detested by liberals across the country, at home his campaign on a platform of helping the "little man" seemed to work well as the Depression was hitting New Orleans very hard. Five New Orleans banks collapsed in 1933 as did many homestead, or building and loan, associations. Unemployment lines grew longer as the ability of the city to provide jobs became increasingly difficult. In 1934 11 percent of the people of Louisiana were on federal relief. By 1939 federal spending on relief agencies in New Orleans totaled more than $50 million.

Employment opportunities were so hard to acquire that riots erupted at several places in New Orleans when hundreds of job seekers showed up answering job announcements in the classified sections of newspapers. In 1930 Mayor T. Semmes Walmsley, who served from 1930–1936, announced a new job program for the city's unemployed: selling oranges. The needy bought boxes of Louisiana oranges and peddled them on the streets at two for a nickel. According to Louisiana historian Roman Heleniak, local newspapers urged people to buy "Louisiana's golden oranges," with the slogan "Health for you—Help for the Needy." New Orleans even had its pathetic variation of the apple vendor standing in the snow to make a few nickels. Bertha McMahon, a 27-year-old orange peddler, although gravely ill continued to sell oranges during bad weather because her family needed the money. She later died of influenza.

To deal with the Depression as it was affecting New Orleans in 1931, Mayor Walmsley took a bold new step. He formed the New Orleans Welfare Committee to find jobs for the unemployed and relief for the destitute. At

first, funds were collected from private individuals and businesses. But in 1932 New Orleans voters approved a $750,000 bond issue to support the Walmsley program. This project would be a preview of President Roosevelt's New Deal programs and especially the Works Progress Administration.

Walmsley's Welfare Committee also marked a transition in New Orleans' political and economic history. Except for a brief period during the Civil War, it was the first time New Orleans city government got into the business of relief. City government here had always provided jobs, but for different reasons. Now it was doing so for the survival of the people and the political system. But according to historian Roman Heleniak of Southeastern Louisiana University in Hammond, Walmsley's committee could not begin to solve the problem.

More help came for beleaguered New Orleanians and Louisianians that same year when Huey Long formed the State Unemployment Relief Committee to provide part-time work programs for the unemployed with funds from the federal Reconstruction Finance Corporation. But because of the on-and-off-again antagonisms between Long and the Old Regulars, New Orleans usually took a back seat to the rest of the state in getting the relief programs.

By mid-1933 the cooperation between Long and the Choctaws began to break down, especially when Long attacked President Franklin D. Roosevelt's New Deal programs pending in the Senate. Long had vigorously supported Roosevelt in the 1932 Presidential election but that was short-lived. The following year Long launched his national campaign of "Share-The-Wealth" in what many believed would be his bid for the Presidency in 1936 or 1940. Roosevelt, meanwhile, awarded all federal patronage in Louisiana to Long's opponents and in 1935 the President sent the Internal Revenue Service to investigate the senator's past income tax returns.

The enmity between Long and the Old Regulars erupted into bitter warfare between August 1934 and September 1935, when Long personally orchestrated a drive in the legislature to strip New Orleans of its autonomy. Open hostilities between Long and the Old Regulars broke out in the 1934 elections. Long ordered an investigation of vice and corruption in the city on the eve of the election in an effort to embarrass the city administration. Fearing that the Old Regulars might use the city police force to falsify the election returns, Long ordered Governor O.K. Allen to send the National Guard to New Orleans, where the guardsmen seized the city's voter registration offices. Long also warned the city that if one policeman was seen at a polling place, he would send in a squad of troops. Mayor T. Semmes Walmsley, enraged, denounced Long: "I warn you, Huey Long, you cringing coward, that if a life is spent in defense of this city and its right of self-government, you shall pay the penalty as others have done before you."

By the time of his assassination in September 1935, the Old Regulars had been soundly defeated. After his death, Huey Long's influence was felt in New Orleans politics for another decade. Particularly during the Depression, New Orleans' economic stability depended upon its relations with the state

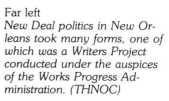

administration. At the time of Long's death in 1935, the Old Regulars were ready to surrender. They had been thoroughly defeated, according to historian Edward F. Haas of New Orleans.

Governor-elect Richard Leche, the Kingfish's political heir, accepted their surrender with the understanding that Walmsley and the Old Regulars would have to step down. Walmsley reluctantly agreed to leave office only if the legislature restored to the city some of the powers it had lost to Long in 1935.

At a secret meeting in Hot Springs, Arkansas, Leche named Robert Maestri, one of Huey Long's financial backers, to be mayor of the city in August 1936. Maestri, described by Haas as "earthy" and a "financial wizard," is probably best known for his famous question to a visiting President Roosevelt: "How ya like dem ersters?" and for a city wide open to corruption, prostitution, and gambling. Historians,

however, have been kinder to Maestri. According to Haas, Maestri reorganized the city's financial structure and made it more efficient. In addition his administration took an active interest in bolstering the city's cultural and recreational programs.

For the duration of the Great Depression, Maestri and Leche worked closely together, Haas said, to create jobs for the city's work force. They were also able to get millions of dollars from the federal Works Progress Administration to employ many New Orleans writers, artists, musicians, laborers, and craftsmen.

Maestri and his "ersters" remained in office until 1946 when he was defeated by a young veteran returning from World War II who preached reform and promised to turn out the rascals. De Lesseps Story "Chep" Morrison symbolized a new era of politics and prosperity and a break with the old order of New Orleans political history.

CHAPTER VIII
THE POSTWAR CHALLENGE

World War II brought a prosperity to New Orleans and other Southern cities that they had not seen in almost a century. "World War II activated another cycle of change in the South. To a greater degree than the previous war it put people on the move: to shipyards, war plants, training camps, and far-flung battlefields," according to historian George B. Tindall. "It intensified established trends: in economic development, race relations, and politics."

As the war effort cranked up, the South began to receive a great percentage of the war-production contracts, especially in shipbuilding and assembly plants. By the end of the war the South's 17 major shipyards had received 23 percent of federal expenditures for shipbuilding. Shipyards like Ingalls in Pascagoula and Higgins in New Orleans provided jobs for the residents, dollars for the community, and naval vessels for the war effort. New Orleans—like other Southern cities—also got a share of the aircraft assembly and components plants.

Although the war boom was only temporary, "still [it] created permanent assets," wrote Tindall. "If the South later slid back from the wartime peaks, it remained on a plateau higher than ever before." New Orleans used the war years to launch its quest for commercial and industrial prosperity. For example, in 1943 a group of businessmen in the city formed a trade club to encourage foreign nations, especially in Latin

America, to use the port of New Orleans. Two years later, the International House opened its doors in the downtown area. Today the International Trade Mart is a cornerstone of the city's foreign commerce. In the years following the war, New Orleans would also assume a leading role in the petrochemical industry. Many of the major oil companies established large offices in the city to be close to the on- and offshore oil fields and refineries. New Orleans also became one of the important centers for the nation's efforts to explore outer space during the 1960s. The Michoud Assembly Facility, which built the Saturn S-1 booster rockets for the Apollo program, was responsible for the development of eastern New Orleans and the nearby community of Slidell in neighboring St. Tammany Parish. Thousands of acres of marshland in eastern New Orleans gave way to residential subdivisions, shopping centers, motels, gas stations, and restaurants.

After the war New Orleanians, fresh from cheering the downfall of dictators in Nazi Germany and Facist Italy, were ready for a change in local politics. The city's national reputation for political corruption, wide-open gambling, and prostitution had become an embarrassment. Reminiscent of the voting after World War I, a wave of civic morality dictated a change in city government. Mayor Maestri had given the city a good and efficient administration during his early years in office; but in later years, the mayor's office became a friendly ally to the *demi-monde*. Reformers demanded a change and they turned to a 34-year-old returning veteran, Colonel de Lesseps Story "Chep" Morrison, to lead the crusade in the 1946 mayoral campaign.

Morrison was able to unite behind his candidacy all of those people who had grown complacent under 46 years of machine politics. During Morrison's campaign, the "new broom sweeps clean" became the rallying slogan to rid the city of corruption. When the votes were counted, Chep had narrowly defeated Maestri. Commissioner Fred A. Earhart was one of the few members of the old order to survive Morrison's "clean sweep."

According to Morrison's biographer, Edward Haas, the new mayor had the rare ability of being many things to different people. To the national press, and most New Orleanians, Chep was an efficient and capable young politician who was delivering New Orleans from corruption. To New Orleans, Chep Morrison

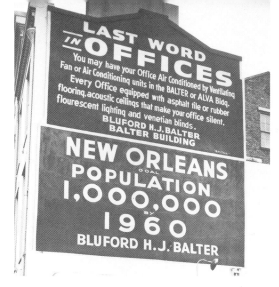

brought new industry; a Union Passenger Terminal; a network of overpasses in the city; the nationally acclaimed New Orleans Recreation Department (NORD); the Civic Center; an expressway system to connect the city with its suburbs; and, national attention. On the other side of the ledger, Morrison's building and streets programs threw the city's bonded debt into chaos; the expressways facilitated white flight to the suburbs during the 1960s; and, the national attention was not always good. Morrison and some members of his political organization — the Crescent City Democratic Association — allied themselves with the old machine politicians and gambling and vice interests in the city, Haas wrote.

Although Morrison allegedly had some political ties with gambling interests in the city, he played an important part in the federal government's nationwide campaign against organized crime. In 1949 and 1950 Morrison, who was then president of the American Municipal Association, called for a concerted local, state, and federal investigation of organized crime and later for passage of the Kefauver bill to investigate interstate gambling.

Meanwhile in New Orleans public clamor against wide-open gambling and vice had reached such a point that a grand jury inquiry was arranged in July 1949. Two days before the grand jury met, Superintendent of Police Joseph Scheuering, in a transparent move, ordered handbook operations to close down. After the jury completed its task, the gamblers were permitted to resume their trade. The jury later recessed with no indictments or any plans for future actions.

New Orleans hosted a national spectacle in January 1951, when Senator Estes Kefauver held nationally televised public hearings on the

Far left
This advertisement for the Balter Building embodies the spirit of general optimism ushered in by the "Chep" Morrison administration. Post-World War II New Orleans was characterized by a flurry of building activity. (THNOC)

Above
The Michoud Assembly Facility in eastern New Orleans had a great impact on the area and was one of the major factors that spurred development there. (THNOC)

Below left
The young "Chep" Morrison was a reform-minded candidate who was a different type of politician than his predecessors. (THNOC)

corruption in the city police department and city government. The wife of a former chief of detectives claimed that her husband as a patrolman had received $150,000 from gambling and prostitution figures during a six-month period. The hearings also revealed that an association of pinball machine operators had one of the city attorneys on its staff as a legal adviser. Testimony also connected some members of Morrison's Crescent City Democratic Association with gambling operations in the city.

Between September 1952 and February 1953, the city administration was embarrassed once again when the state police, under the direction of Colonel Francis Grevemberg, conducted a number of raids on New Orleans gambling and prostitution houses operating under the eyes of the police department. In March 1953 Morrison came to the defense of the city police and his administration, claiming the city "has in seven short years achieved the greatest degree of law enforcement we have ever had." But the city's commission council was not convinced by Morrison's claims. It appropriated $50,000 and called for a special investigation of the police force by a three-man team, representing the Bureau of Governmental Research, the Metropolitan Crime Commission (formed in 1952), and the Society of Former FBI Agents. Morrison publicly supported this team called the Special Citizens Investigating Committee (SCIC), but privately he opposed it.

In June SCIC hired Aaron Kohn to manage the police probe. Kohn, a lawyer and former FBI agent, previously had conducted a similar investigation of the Chicago police force. Despite obstructions placed in his way by police and city officials, Kohn energetically and tenaciously went about exposing corruption at all levels of the department. Between November and the following January, public hearings on police corruption were held once again. During the hearings the Orleans Parish grand jury went to work and indicted the police superintendent and chief of detectives for malfeasance. But a month later a criminal district court judge dismissed the indictment and returned the men to office. On January 7 a court injunction reportedly initiated by top police officials ended the hearings. Three months later SCIC published the results of its investigation which included nine pages of recommendations for reorganizing the police force and for curbing vice in the city.

Haas wrote that Morrison was caught in the middle between the "reform morality and the human nature of the average man":

The Union Passenger Terminal, located near the Civic Center, was the starting and ending point for over a dozen passenger trains that served New Orleans in the 1950s. (THNOC)

Morrison . . . could not overlook those New Orleanians who held different hopes. Over the years gambling, prostitution, and various forms of vice had become pleasurable aspects of Crescent City life that many residents enjoyed and wanted to preserve. . . . This dichotomy in urban mores and local ideals found the new mayor in the middle. Caught between reform morality and the human nature of the average man, Morrison had to find a suitable approach to law enforcement that would not alienate any segments of New Orleans society, even those who were less than respectable.

Morrison's most disappointing political defeats came in the 1956, 1960, and 1964 gubernatorial elections. In the first campaign (1955–1956), Morrison met his old political nemesis, Governor Earl K. Long, Huey's younger brother. The younger Long was backed by the Old Regulars in New Orleans and by the rural supporters who had been instrumental in electing Huey. "Uncle Earl" carried out a comical but successful attack on Morrison. "I'd rather beat Morrison than eat any blackberry huckleberry pie my mama ever made. Oh, how I'm praying for that old stump-wormer [Morrison] to get in there," Long said before the campaign got under full way. "I want him to roll up them cuffs and get out that little old tuppy [toupee], and pull down them shades, and make himself up." While "Uncle Earl" was mocking "de Lasoups" and the mayor's toupee, Morrison attacked the governor's record in office between 1948 and 1952.

After his victory Earl Long turned to wooing New Orleans with the honey of the state treasury. He gave the city Louisiana State University in New Orleans (now the University of New Orleans); Southern University in New Orleans; and, expanded the Delgado Trade School. In addition, the Long-controlled legislature approved large appropriations to the Orleans Parish Teachers' Retirement Fund; Charity Hospital; Ochsner Foundation; and Touro Infirmary.

In the 1959–1960 gubernatorial campaign Morrison lost to former "Singing" Governor ("You Are My Sunshine") Jimmie H. Davis, who capitalized on New Orleans' integration problems and the mayor's associations with movie-star Zsa Zsa Gabor and Senator John Kennedy. Davis also had the invaluable assistance of Judge Leander Perez of Plaquemines Parish and William Rainach of Claiborne Parish. Perez and Rainach, who were leaders of the White Citizens' Council, traveled the state feeding racial hatred in support of Davis' candidacy. Davis' workers claimed Morrison was an integrationist working hard to end segregation in New Orleans. Morrison was a segregationist, but not a rabid racist. When ordered by the federal courts to desegregate public transportation in the mid-1950s, he did so.

Morrison's greatest political crisis came with the school desegregation order of 1960. For almost a decade school integration was litigated in the nation's courts. Then came the order from federal Judge J. Skelly Wright to integrate public schools in New Orleans by November 1960. City officials had given little thought or preparation to handling this problem. Governor Davis and the state legislature jumped in and passed 47 acts and 17 resolutions in an attempt to circumvent the court order. But one by one, the federal courts struck down the legislature's feeble attempts. Then on November 4, 1960, six-year-old Ruby Bridges, led by her mother and U.S. marshals, entered the previously all-white William Frantz School amid the shouts, threats, and torments of white

hecklers. Three other black children attended McDonogh No. 19 that same day. The swift action by the New Orleans Police Department spared the city a bloody racial confrontation. Some rioting took place during the daylight hours by white students and after dark by blacks, but these were minor considering the impact of integration on the entire social order. Integration had arrived and even threats by the New Orleans White Citizens' Council, men like Leander Perez, and the state-supported white private "segregation" schools, could not stop it. "During the desegregation crisis, Mayor Morrison received criticism from all sides," Haas wrote. "Civil Rights advocates blasted the mayor for his reluctance to take a firm stand on school integration, and segregationists argued

that he favored racial mixing."

In the spring of 1961 Morrison took a middle-of-the-road course on the racial issue. He ordered the arrest of civil-rights workers staging sit-ins in downtown lunch counters; as well as a busload of George Lincoln Rockwell's American Nazi Party "stormtroopers" when they caused a disturbance in front of a downtown theater. One of the city's primary industries—tourism—suffered as a result of the bad publicity the city got in the national news media. People were hesitant to visit New Orleans for fear of racial violence. The Citizens' Council's most vocal members were constantly on the nation's stage. Not until the city's business community finally spoke up for an end to violence and for open schools, did the precariously tense situation begin to ease.

But Morrison's political future looked bleak after he failed to have the city charter amended to enable him to have another term as mayor. However an old acquaintance, then President John F. Kennedy, came to his rescue. In July 1961 Morrison resigned to become the U.S. ambassador to the Organization of American States. Morrison ran for governor a third time against "Won't you please help me!" John McKeithen and lost again. A year later, the former mayor and his younger son died in an airplane crash.

Morrison's successor at city hall was the short, balding, but bouncy and affable Victor Schiro, whose favorite slogan was, "If it's good for New Orleans, I'm for it." Schiro unlike Morrison took a firmer stand on the school integration issue. The court had ordered it and Schiro, through the police department, enforced it with proper planning. Among his many accomplishments, Schiro and police Superintendent Joseph I. Giarusso restored public confidence in the police force. Schiro also has been given little credit for the business revitalization in the Central Business District. Over much criticism, Schiro widened and beautified Poydras Street,

Far left
John J. McKeithen took over the Louisiana governor's office in 1964 after defeating "Chep" Morrison, former New Orleans mayor. Courtesy, New Orleans Public Library, Louisiana Division.

Left
Victor H. Schiro succeeded "Chep" Morrison as mayor of New Orleans and served the city at a time of considerable social strife. Courtesy, City of New Orleans, Public Information Office.

VOTE
JOHN McKEITHEN
INDEPENDENT CANDIDATE
FOR GOVERNOR

GOVERNOR
John McKEITHEN   No. 6 ☒
COMPTROLLER
Roy R. THERIOT   No. 30 ☒
COMM. OF INSURANCE
Dudley A. Guglielmo   No. 43 ☒
HOUSE OF REPRESENTATIVES
Clyde F. BEL, Jr.   No. 111 ☒

ENDORSED BY
13th Ward Independent Committee
Thomas J. Heath, Chairman

which is rapidly becoming the business center of the city. Many New Orleanians will never forget the television program that appeared only days before the 1965 mayoral election in which Schiro, recovering from an appendectomy, announced plans for a domed stadium in the city. Many say the announcement won him the election.

Schiro was able to hold together a declining political coalition that kept him in office until 1970. During the 1960s, New Orleans had experienced dramatic demographic changes. The lure of suburban subdivisions with colorful names, coupled with real and imagined fears of racial integration, caused many whites to flee to the predominantly white suburbs surround-

ing the city. The Brooklyn and New Jersey-style accent of the old Third and Ninth Wards, with their "choiches" (churches) and "zinks" (sinks), moved to nearby "Metry" (Metairie), Chalmette, and Slidell. One was more likely to hear the familiar greeting "Where y'at!" in the suburbs than in the Irish Channel or St. Claude Avenue, which are populated now mostly by blacks, Vietnamese, and Cuban refugees.

These suburban expatriates built their own style of New Orleans living. Restaurants and bars abound along the major suburban thoroughfares separated only by residential subdivisions, apartment complexes, and vast shopping centers. In neighboring Jefferson Parish, local entrepreneurs built Fat City—a Bourbon

Street-style assemblage of saloons and night spots. One can even participate in one of the many new Mardi Gras parades now rolling in the outlying areas. Left behind in the city were decaying neighborhoods, poverty, and spiraling crime rates.

While thousands of blue-collar and some middle-class whites were fleeing to the suburbs, many of the more affluent middle to upper-middle class whites began buying and renovating the gingerbread-draped Victorian cottages in the Uptown and University areas. Entire neighborhoods, which had been populated by blue-collar whites and then blacks, have given way to the restoration craze. The restored cypress cottages, which once sold for a few thousand dollars, have fetched prices in the six figures. The almost pioneer spirit of the renovation movement has given older sections of the city new life.

Even in the Central Business District (CBD)—the old American Sector of the early-19th century, where many architectural treasures have been lost to fires or "progress"—the restoration of commercial buildings has been economically feasible. Individual preservationists and preservation groups in the city had a difficult struggle during the 1960s and 1970s convincing property owners and the municipal government of the importance of preservation to the economic health of the Canal Street area. Widespread destruction of the 19th-century buildings in the CBD was occurring so rapidly in these decades that preserva-

tionists were able to get Mayor Landrieu and the city council to declare a moratorium on further destruction. Convincing city government to take such a bold step did not come easily. Preservationists waged a long but stubborn campaign to win over city officials who at first were less than enthusiastic. Despite the great losses in the old Faubourg St. Mary, many 19th-century edifices, which have been restored with internal modifications, mingle quietly but magnificently among their 20th-century neighbors.

Since World War II, New Orleans has continued to slip in rank as compared to other Southern cities. Between 1940 and 1950 the city's population increased from 494,537 to 570,445. But despite this almost 20-percent increase, it dropped in rank from the South's largest city to the second largest, falling behind Houston. By 1970 New Orleans would be only the fifth largest and the 1980 census showed the city falling even further behind other Southern cities. Preliminary census figures for 1980 placed the city's population at 556,913. When these "startling" numbers were released city officials protested vigorously, insisting the population was actually closer to 643,000. City officials issued a press release in September 1980, declaring that "since about 1977, people have been moving into New Orleans after nearly 10 years of migration out of the city." Another important change surfaced in the 1980 census: more than 55 percent of the city's population was black.

Reflecting on the white flight to the suburbs, Mayor "Moon" Landrieu (1970–1978) said New Orleans "lost 125,000 people — mostly white and affluent — moving out to the suburbs, and in their place, 90,000, mostly poor and black, moved in."

The rapidly changing demography brought increased tensions between the races. The upwardly spiraling crime rate in the black communities spilled over into the white communities. Many middle-class whites have become so afraid of the violence, they have formed neighborhood vigilance committees and hired off-duty policemen and private security guards to protect themselves. In September and November 1970 bloody battles took place between the police and an arm of the Black Panthers in the vicinity of the Desire Street Housing Project. On January 7, 1973, Mark Essex — a young,

demented black sniper from Kansas — paralyzed the city as he ran about the downtown Howard Johnson Motel with his high-powered rifle, randomly killing and wounding. Before police machine-gun fire finally brought him down, Essex managed to kill nine people and wound almost a score of others.

The changing demography in the city coupled with the 1965 Voting Rights Act and the voter registration drives of the 1970s also drew new political lines in the city. For the first time since Reconstruction, blacks were a political force, if not the dominant force in the city's political arena. Blacks have gained new economic opportunities that have reinforced and expanded the black middle class. Like their white counterparts, many of the affluent young black families have fled to the suburbs of eastern New Orleans.

In 1970 the able and politically astute "Moon" Landrieu formed his own political organization and actively solicited the help of the influential black political groups in his bid for the mayor's office. Blacks held high-level jobs during Landrieu's administration. While in office Mayor Landrieu gained national attention because of his leadership role in the U.S. Conference of Mayors. After relinquishing his mayoral seat he was appointed by President Jimmy Carter to head the federal Office of Housing and Urban Development.

In the 1977–1978 mayoral campaign, New Orleans made a major break with the city's political past. Blacks, with sizable support from whites, elected the city's first black mayor, Ernest N. "Dutch" Morial. Morial, who had been one of the leaders of the civil rights movement of the 1950s and 1960s, inherited a city plagued with financial and social problems, and labor unrest among city employees (for example, the 1979 police strike crippled the city and caused the cancellation of most Mardi Gras Parades that year).

Even with the economic uncertainties and the growth of violent crime during the 1970s and early 1980s, New Orleans has shown remarkable resiliency. Since 1970 the skyline changed dramatically as new skyscrapers rose above the foundations of the 19th-century old American Sector. The awe-inspiring $180 million Louisiana Superdome — despite the controversy that surrounded its construction — launched a building boom and economic revitalization in the Central Business District, while the French Quarter took on the trappings of a tourist-oriented economy. The oil industries have invested millions of dollars in CBD construction and towering hotels have risen from the ruins of run-down tenements and warehouses. In 1980 city officials announced the development of the Almonester-Michoud Industrial District in eastern New Orleans as a new source of prosperity for the city.

In late 1980 Mayor Morial expressed intensive optimism for the city's future. Waving a hand toward the CBD, he claimed there had been more commercial construction in that area since 1978 than in the previous 20 years. Large corporations were moving to New Orleans, he said, because they were convinced the city had a new-found vitality. The city has charm, the mayor said, but "it is more than a Bourbon Street or Fun City U.S.A." To attract more businesses to the Crescent City, Morial formed a committee of 100 businessmen to wage an intensive public-relations drive to sell the city.

It required a great deal of persuasive skill to convince the Bureau of International Expositions in Paris that permitting New Orleans to host the 1984 World's Exposition was a good idea; but it was done. The exposition was organized by a group of private corporations under the title the Louisiana World Exposition, Inc., which raised over $40 million in pledges from the business community to make the fair possible.

The site for the exposition, which took for its theme, "The World of Rivers: Fresh Water as a Source of Life," is an 80-acre stretch of land in the old riverfront warehouse district in the CBD. At the center of the exposition grounds, the taxpayers financed a 820,000-square-foot exhibition hall at a cost of over $88 million. An economic study projected the exposition would draw 11 million visitors and generate $2 billion in business activity, not to mention 39,000 temporary jobs and 14,000 new permanent jobs once the fair is closed.

That the 1984 World's Exposition is to be held in New Orleans epitomizes New Orleanians' determination that their city will remain prosperous and vibrant into the 21st century and beyond. But the future is not their sole concern. New Orleanians are working as never before to preserve their heritage, as Mary Lou Christovich explains in the following chapter. So while the towering structures of the Central Business District may seemingly dwarf the remaining edifices of the 18th and 19th centuries, an appreciation of both can ensure that the Crescent City's future will be no less remarkable than its past.

CHAPTER IX
A NEW CUSTOM IN NEW ORLEANS: PRESERVING THE PAST

BY MARY LOU CHRISTOVICH

As a 20th-century concept, historic preservation in New Orleans did not commence until almost 200 years after the city's founding. Although there were isolated instances of vocal concern — objections to demolition and alteration of place — serious appreciation of the city's cultural and physical environment began only at the end of the 19th century.

Perhaps the first locally documented objection to city planning is to be found in the September 5, 1722, journal entry of Jean Baptiste-Martin d'Artaguiette d'Iron. At that time Adrien de Pauger, a French military engineer, laid out the original city according to the plan of his superior, Pierre Le Blond de La Tour, in the French, fortified manner with an enclosed grid-street pattern.

A few years earlier a Monsieur Traverse had built a residence not in alignment with the newly planned streets; he was ordered to move his house or tear it down. Private motivation prompted him to seek preservation or restitution for his home. Infuriated by Traverse's stubborn appeal to the French Superior Council, Pauger attacked him with a stick, administered a thorough thrashing, and summoned the *gendarmes* to cast him into jail. The house was summarily expropriated and demolished to complete what may have been preservation's most one-sided setback.

Writing about New Orleans in 1722, Jesuit Father Charlevoix said:

Overleaf
The elegant interior of the Longue Vue Gardens house provides a glimpse of New Orleans' rich architectural heritage. Photo by Robin Boylan.

These creole cottages may be found in the Faubourg Marigny District, one of New Orleans' first suburbs. Photo by Robin Boylan.

"The eight hundred fine houses and the five Parish Churches that Le Mercure [a French newspaper] gave it two years ago is today reduced to about a hundred huts placed without much order, a large warehouse built of wood, two or three houses that would not grace a French village and half a wretched warehouse that they had been good enough to lend to the Lord."

There is some concern for the validity of the *Le Mercure* description of the early settlement. Glowing and romantic tales that had little relationship to actuality often encouraged emigration. In reality life in the colony was a constant struggle against the elements. A flood in 1717 was followed by hurricanes in 1719, 1722, and 1723; the settlers' hold on property was at best a precarious one.

The dramatic vicissitudes of the semitropical New Orleans climate were not expected by early French architects and builders and their plans did not take them into account. Unstable, spongy land caused massive foundation problems; only after the structural failure of the original soldier's barracks designed by architect Ignace Broutin were the problems of soil conditions solved. Armed with experience in 1745, Broutin designed the Ursuline Convent, which survives as one of the earliest French colonial buildings in the Mississippi Valley.

Although soirees, banquets, and even balls

occurred during the governorship of Pierre Rigaud de Vaudreuil in the 1740s, New Orleans essentially remained the river town and trading post founded by French-Canadian Jean Baptiste Le Moyne, Sieur de Bienville in 1718. New Orleans' fate was sealed and her direction altered when the French king, Louis XV, gave the entire Louisiana territory to his Spanish cousin, Charles III in 1762. Four years later Spanish officials arrived to claim the colony thus beginning a Spanish domination that lasted until 1803.

Numerous tile-terraced houses, employing the creole-cottage floor plan of the four square rooms, were constructed along the planked *banquettes* of the French town; patios were integrated into important outdoor activity areas in the Spanish style. Evidence of most of these buildings remains only in notarial property descriptions because fires — one in 1788 and another in 1794 — destroyed 856 and 215 buildings, respectively. Although fewer buildings were lost in 1794, the value of the property lost was far greater. These disasters removed permanently most of the tangible evidence of New Orleans' 18th-century architecture and prevented the possibility of effort toward its preservation.

New Orleanians built and rebuilt without a conscious concern for the past. They replaced the houses lost in the 1788 fire with similar frame ones in the amalgamated French and Spanish styles. Salvaged materials — bricks, iron, flooring, and structural timbers — were reworked into the fabric of the new buildings. There is evidence that, after the 1788 fire, structurally sound surviving walls and floors often were incorporated in new construction. Despite these conservations, many of the new buildings were lost to fire just six years later.

After the 1794 fire the Illustrious Cabildo (the Spanish governing body of the city) prohibited frame construction and ruled that all buildings from then on would be of brick or brick-between-posts and plastered over with at least a one-inch layer of cement stucco. Frugality prompted Don Andres Almonester y Roxas to use the demolished brick walls from around the old St. Peter Street cemetery for rebuilding of the St. Louis Parish Church and the Cabildo building which were destroyed in the fire of 1788. The new Cabildo structure of 1795 utilized the walls and brick floor of the 1750 French *corps de garde* which can be viewed

Courtyards and patios have provided quiet, privacy, and a degree of coolness to Vieux Carre residents almost from the beginning. Many, such as this one at Brennan's, are lavishly landscaped, containing trees and fountains. Photo by Robin Boylan.

Built in 1795–1799, the Cabildo, perhaps New Orleans' most historically significant building, served as city hall from 1803 to 1853, as the Louisiana Supreme Court building from 1853 to 1911, and as part of the Louisiana State Museum since 1911. Within its walls the formal transfer of Louisiana from France to the United States took place in 1803. Photo by Robin Boylan.

today in that building.

Further tolls on New Orleans' early architecture were taken by hurricanes, such as the one that struck in 1811, destroying the new French Market. The river was always a potential threat; a break in the levee system in 1816 caused the inundation of the entire city from eight miles upriver to the Marigny section below the Vieux Carre. One wonders, however, why the city didn't develop an effective fire-control system very early. In the fall of 1816 another large block of buildings in the Vieux Carre was lost; this time 60 buildings turned to ashes.

With the destruction of these buildings and the advent of the American period following the Louisiana Purchase in 1803, the architectural character of the Vieux Carre became a mixture of retardate French and Spanish colonial styles and the newer Eastern Seaboard English townhouse.

The city expanded beyond the Old Quarter both up- and downriver and back-of-town as the population in the early 19th century reached almost 15,000. Bernard de Marigny had his downriver plantation subdivided in 1805, and Claude Treme sold his land behind the city for the first municipally planned suburb in 1810. With the development of Canal Street and the American Sector (known as Faubourg Ste. Marie or St. Mary), the French Quarter began to lose business and residents, and many of the buildings became rentals.

Other changes were occurring in the French Quarter; an 1823 appeal from the Widow Carrick vividly illustrates the advent of a destructive practice. Mistress Carrick inherited 90 feet of property on Levee (now Decatur) Street between St. Philip and Ursulines from her late husband who, she declared, had purchased the property and buildings from Elie Beauregard in 1800. She claimed that the property was ac-

quired with privileged frontage to the river, including all other servitudes and advantages incidental thereto, such as a free, direct, and uninterrupted view of and intercourse with the river. These rights in the past had been considered in conformity with the title deeds and sanctioned by the Spanish government. The city, however, had just erected a vegetable market on the vacant ground, thus depriving Mistress Carrick of all her rights and diminishing the value of her property. She publicly protested against the mayor and aldermen and sought financial redress. The city denied her claim.

A few years later in 1830, no fewer than 25 leading residents and property owners in Faubourg Ste. Marie wrote to the mayor and city council:

The experience has taught them, that the erection of cotton steam presses in the faubourg St. Mary, is a nuisance of the worst description, at once interfering with the comfort of the inhabitants and tending greatly to lessen the value of their property. The contiguity of a steam press to the dwelling of individuals, not only increases the rate of Insurance, but greatly jeopardizes those dwellings by means of the vast masses of cotton constantly on hand and liable to conflagration, both from the nature of the article, and from external causes. To those grievances may be added, the disagreeable and unremitted noise of the machinery, and the constant emission of smoke, which penetrates every aperture of our dwellings, and soils and destroys every article of furniture within them. We are aware of the great importance of the cotton trade to the City of New Orleans; but they do not admit it as a right of any individual, community or even, government itself, to take, injure, destroy or deteriorate the property of individuals without their consent, or at least without giving them an equivalent for such taking, injuring, destroying, or deterioration.

On the fringe of the French Quarter in 1832, the homeowners facing North Rampart Street petitioned the city council in objection to a railroad in the center of their street. They claimed that they had purchased their lots with the as-

surance that they would peacefully enjoy the advantages of a public walk. Theirs, too, was another citizens' battle lost; the St. Claude "Railroad" ran down to the parish line terminating at the Jackson Barracks.

It was not the loss or alteration of any part of their physical setting that stirred the founders of the Louisiana Historical Society to organize in 1836. It was the expressed desire of these learned men to record over 100 years of events, providing posterity with a documented history of their city and state. To this end, they searched the archives of France and Spain returning with much of the information that still affords present-day historians with the basis for historical recollection.

The society's third president, Charles Gayarre, elected in 1860, served the next 28 years giving numerous lectures and papers on both the colonial periods. These were later bound into two of a four-volume series entitled *Louisiana History*. In 1850 when the wardens of the St. Louis Cathedral planned the demolition of Almonester's Cathedral, it was Gayarre who publicly objected to the plans and outspokenly condemned the designs by Jacques N.B. de Pouilly. With injured dignity Gayarre proclaimed: "This venerable relic of the ancient past was demolished in mere wantoness of vandalism and replaced by this upstart production of bad taste."

Rampart Street, pictured here from Canal to Esplanade Avenue, marked the extreme western boundary of New Orleans as originally laid out. The land approaches to the city were defended by two forts from which Rampart Street takes its name. Though homeowners along North Rampart fought to keep a railroad from running down the center of their street in 1832, they lost the battle and tracks (pictured here on the far left) were laid for the St. Claude "Railroad."

Owned by the State of Louisiana, the red-brick lower Pontalba Building is one of two block-long structures built by the Baroness Micaela Almonester de Pontalba in 1848–1849. The cast-iron cartouche, designed by the baroness, incorporates the initials "AP," which stand for Almonester and Pontalba. Architects James Gallier, Sr., and Henry Howard designed the Pontalba Buildings. Photo by Robin Boylan.

Below
In addition to constructing the symmetrical Pontalba Buildings, the baroness relandscaped Jackson Square, giving it the appearance of an elaborate French garden. This 1855 lithograph of the square is by Pessou and Simon. (THNOC)

The Baroness Micaela Almonester de Pontalba and city officials concerned themselves with a rejuvenation of the Place d'Armes as early as the 1830s. Actual alteration began at the same time as the new cathedral, when mansard roofs were added to the Cabildo and Presbytere overlooking the Place d'Armes (which was renamed Jackson Square in honor of General Andrew Jackson, hero of the Battle of New Orleans). There may have been some displeasure when the Baroness Pontalba tore down her parents' buildings flanking Jackson Square in order to replace them with the symmetrical rows of the Pontalba Buildings; if so, it was not recorded. But when she turned Jackson Square into a baroque garden, destroying the old sycamore trees placed in rows of three on both sides of the square, there was an uproar; un-

daunted, she continued her improvements.

The Civil War cut deeply into the psyche of New Orleans. Occupied from 1862 until 1877 — when Federal excesses were ended — the citizens suffered survival without the luxury of future planning. The saga of the St. Louis Hotel in the French Quarter demonstrated essential elements of these political events and the citizens' position.

For many years social and political conflict grew between the Creole (meaning native born) community and that of the new Americans. Financial differences in banking, real-estate expansion, commodity futures — almost everything — reached an apex of antagonism in the early 1830s. When French architect Jacques N.B. de Pouilly came to New Orleans from Paris freshly inspired by its latest influences, he was engaged to design a commercial exchange in the French Quarter. The Americans immediately hired Irish architect James Gallier, Sr., (ne Gallagher) who planned the St. Charles Exchange Hotel to house business transactions in the American Sector.

De Pouilly's plan encompassed an Exchange Passage beginning at Iberville Street and continuing down to and through the St. Louis Hotel to the Citizen's Bank on Toulouse Street. A rhythmic harmony of arched facades was arranged to reach a crescendo at the entrance of the hotel. Completed in 1836, the hotel burned but was immediately rebuilt in 1841. Sweeping stairways, domed ceilings, and crystal chandeliers were the opulent setting for the Creole *creme de la creme*.

The St. Louis, like its rival the St. Charles Exchange Hotel in the American Sector, was

occupied by Federal troops during the war. In 1877 Louisiana overthrew the Reconstruction government and reclaimed the state politically. It purchased the old St. Louis Hotel and there established the capital; but in 1882 the capital was finally moved to Baton Rouge. An architectural and social renaissance was attempted for this building when it opened two years later as the Hotel Royal. The venture failed, and again the New Orleans climate whirred a destructive fate, critically damaging the structure in the hurricane of 1915. The remnants were demolished in 1916 despite the plaintive appeals and objections of N. Courtland Curtis, Dean of the Tulane School of Architecture. The site ironically became the home of Kross Lumber and Wrecking Yard. Classic marble columns and some of the granite sections were salvaged, redressed, and "utilized for architectural beauty and traditional interest for excellent effect" on the Railway Passenger Terminal at South Rampart and Girod streets.

The demolition had been preceded by a poorly conceived attempt at beautifying the French Quarter. The entire square directly in front of the old St. Louis-Hotel Royal was destroyed. Private homes were replaced with a giant Civil Courts Building. The design — in grandiose white marble and terra cotta, rendered in the popular eclectic style of the period — disregarded all consideration of scale. The *Journal of the American Institute of Architects,* referring to the white elephant, carried an editorial entitled "Speaking of Ugliness." Nevertheless today the building is valued as a bona fide architectural expression, constructed with fine materials and with excellent execution of detail; these mark it as a building worthy of preservation. (Interior spaces are commodious and the Louisiana Supreme Court justices desire to return, having grown crowded and discontented with their new quarters.)

The "American" style of architecture was ushered in by architects like James Gallier, Sr., and his son, James Gallier, Jr., and the firms with which they were associated. This elevation of a building on Camp Street, which Gallier and Turpin designed, dates from about 1835. Photo by John Lawrence.

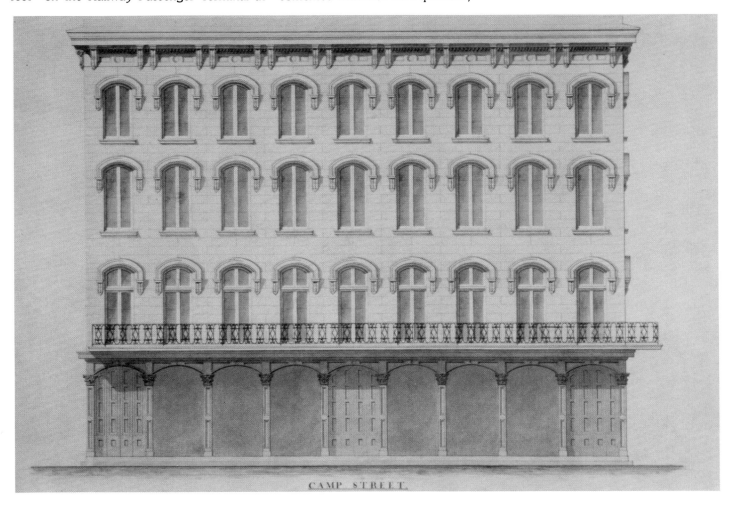

CAMP STREET

New Orleans historian Grace King had not only lamented the demolition of the square but also had photographed the buildings. The glass negatives produced a positive treatise to the superiority of the original buildings *in situ*. Her enlightened appreciation of scale, texture, and design inherent in the Vieux Carre may have been sparked by New Orleans' 1885 World's Cotton Exposition.

Formally known as the World's Industrial and Cotton Centennial Exposition, the fair is treated more kindly by history than it was by contemporary observers. Grace King wisely demurred, saying that the exhibit in the Women's Department ". . . was incredible, astounding. Indeed, it was the opening of the past history of the city, not only to strangers, but to the citizens themselves." D. Clive Hardy in his monograph on the exposition claimed that what the local citizens "had taken for granted was in fact their own unique and rich culture. Ultimately, this awareness would be the most important legacy of the exposition."

It was at this time that the embryonic notion of New Orleans preservation was conceived. Nourishment was obtained through an art movement fostered by the Woodward brothers, William and Ellsworth, at Newcomb College Art School, and was further developed by the superb writings of Lafcadio Hearn, Lyle Saxon, Sherwood Anderson, and scores of others who became literary greats. Arnold Genthe in 1926 produced a magnificent photographic essay that won praises for his talent and for the French Quarter.

Historians joined the movement with the formation of the Louisiana Historical Association in 1889; its purposes paralleled those of the earlier-formed Louisiana Historical Society. The latter organization received a boost from the St. Louis Exposition of 1904. When the exposition ended, all the artifacts gathered for Louisiana's participation were placed in the Cabildo and Presbytere, forming the nucleus of the Louisiana State Museum collection. The need for a museum building was fortuitous because members of the city council had actually proposed the demolition of the Cabildo. Fortunately, members of the society and association were ready to defend the continued existence of the historically significant building.

The growing appreciation of architecture as an element deserving preservation was allied with visual images, letters, and later, the theater. The Arts and Crafts Club, organized in 1921 and located in the old Broulatour Court (Seignoret House on Royal Street), continued in community service until its dissolution in 1957. It provided a forum for young architects as well as artists. Charles B. Hosmer, Jr., in his book *Preservation Comes of Age* (1981), lists short-lived organizations that were certainly forerunners of Vieux Carre preservation groups; among them was *La Renaissance du Vieux Carre,* chaired in 1930 by historian and author Stanley C. Arthur. It saved sections of the French Market from demolition thus scoring its lone victory.

There was no unevenness about what is now understood to be a continuum of the preservation movement. It was certainly a straight-line activity and commitment by the feminine element of New Orleans. If the ladies did not act directly in promoting events connected with preservation, they inspired the male community to do so. This was true in the Arts and Crafts Club, *Le Petit Theatre du Vieux Carre, Le Petit Salon,* and particularly in the attainment of a state constitutional amendment enabling the city council to establish the Vieux Carre Commission.

The organization, *Le Petit Theatre,* hired architects Armstrong and Koch in 1922 to adapt a building near Jackson Square for their theater. They purchased buildings on St. Peter Street, and Koch conceived one of the first buildings consciously designed to blend with the surrounding Vieux Carre buildings. *Le Petit Salon,* a literary group of socially prominent ladies led by Mrs. Elizabeth M. Gilmer (who wrote a syndicated column as Dorothy Dix), Mrs. Charles F. Buck, and its first president, Grace King, bought the Victor David House next to the Little Theater. This renovation was an extremely brave venture for the Old Quarter's slum conditions made their act socially daring. When the same architectural firm adapted the Wogan House at 711 Bourbon Street into apartments, still another milestone in architectural preservation and reuse was reached.

Despite her busy writing schedule, Grace King founded the Society for the Preservation of Ancient Tombs in the early 1920s. By 1923 a newspaper article revealed that the organization had the support of the Louisiana Historical

Society and listed luminaries from throughout the city among its members. Its stated purpose was to save for future generations the historic tombs that were crumbling away. Sixty years later, this battle continues under Save Our Cemeteries despite the disappearance of many tombs and family histories once etched on marble tablets. The intent of this modern preservation group reiterates that of the earlier one.

Ironically, two of New Orleans' most active early 20th-century proponents of preservation came from outside their adopted city. Elizebeth Thomas of Bay City, Michigan, had studied voice in England and France for four years before making her first visit to New Orleans in

Intricate wrought-iron balconies still adorn Vieux Carre buildings, although many have been lost since the early 1900s, when Elizebeth Werlein began cataloging them. Photos by John Lawrence (below left) and Robin Boylan (below right).

1908. She met and married Philip Werlein six weeks later, thus continuing a dual love affair with her new family and city. Her first home was the historic Flowers-Morrison House in the Lower Garden District. Through her European exposure, she recognized the charm and ambiance of the Vieux Carre, and until recently was the only person who attempted a catalog of rare and exquisite wrought-iron balconies in the Vieux Carre, many of which vanished even before her monograph could be published.

Mrs. Werlein's enthusiasm over the architecture and atmosphere of the Old Quarter was encouraged as the city began to teem with experts gathering data about the past. The American Institute of Architects had participated in the sponsorship of the Historic American Buildings Survey, a nationwide architectural survey that by 1941 had yielded thousands of drawings and negatives. However, this rich strike of researched materials remained hidden like a rare ore itself; its availability was limited and impact on local preservation nonexistent.

The ambitious Mrs. Werlein interpreted the importance of the Historic American Buildings Survey study and strove for implementation through preservation. She won a victory for the city and the nation when in 1936 she convinced the Louisiana legislature to pass a constitutional amendment authorizing the city to create the Vieux Carre Commission. The mayor was empowered to appoint members to this commission with some selected from the Louisiana Historical Society and the Louisiana State Museum board, and three qualified architects. Among its powers, encompassing signs and alterations to all exterior elevations, the Commission could cite and fine violators and even levy taxes.

Through the decade of the 1930s, Elizebeth Werlein was to battle not only bars and brothels but often the Vieux Carre commissioners who were not always entirely scrupulous and dedicated to the law. By this time she was living on St. Ann Street, and had helped to organize the Vieux Carre Property Owners, becoming its president in 1938. The American Institute of Architects, recognizing her invaluable tenacity, fortitude, and leadership in the preservation of the Vieux Carre *tout ensemble,* made her an

The Hermann-Grima House, located at 820 St. Louis Street, was built in 1831 by merchant Samuel Hermann, who sold it to attorney Felix Grima in 1844. Today it houses the Christian Woman's Exchange, which has preserved the house and its old furnishings. The entry hall, courtyard, and one of the bedrooms are pictured here. Courtesy, the Hermann-Grima Historic House. Photos by Robin Boylan.

honorary member. Mayor Robert S. Maestri, trading humor and support for the prestige of her association, crowned her Mayor of the French Quarter.

Mrs. Werlein—and consequently the city—lost several skirmishes against businessmen whose encroachment caused gerrymandering of the French Quarter to exclude their projects

from Vieux Carre Commission controls. The Monteleone Hotel, the river side of Decatur Street, and the lake side of North Rampart were excluded from its jurisdiction. After years of litigation and demolitions, the Vieux Carre Property Owners with Jake Morrison's leadership, carried the case to the state supreme court. It was held that the exclusion of these properties was unconstitutional. But by that time there was little left to save on either Decatur or Rampart streets.

William Ratcliff Irby adopted New Orleans over his home state of Virginia. He was a pioneer preservationist and philanthropist who purchased Vieux Carre properties and bequeathed them to educational institutions. To the Louisiana State Museum in 1927 went the lower Pontalba Building and the Jackson and Creole houses; to Tulane University, the Bank of Louisiana and the Old French Opera House. The upper Pontalba Buildings were purchased in 1921 by other financiers who sold them to the Pontalba Building Museum Association in 1930, who in turn donated the buildings to the city.

New Orleanians of prominence and prestige began to interest themselves, not only in buying Vieux Carre properties, but also in actually liv-

The Historic New Orleans Collection occupies buildings on Royal and Toulouse streets purchased in the 1940s by General and Mrs. L. Kemper Williams. The structures include the Merieult House (built in 1792 by Jean Francois Merieult and one of the few buildings to survive the 1794 fire) and the very fine 1889 house known as the Williams Residence, adopted by the Williamses as one of the Quarter's "hidden houses" and now maintained as it was when they lived there. General and Mrs. Williams established the Collection in 1966. It was opened to the public in 1974. This view of the courtyard and Williams Residence is from the Merieult House. Photo by Robin Boylan.

ing there. Matilda Geddings Gray bought the magnificent Gauche House on Esplanade and Royal streets, as well as surrounding properties. General and Mrs. L. Kemper Williams purchased the Royal Street Merieult House and three connecting Toulouse Street buildings. Many years later the Williams' buildings would house the Historic New Orleans Collection, one of the city's small elegant museums and finest research centers. The *Vieux Carre Survey,* 130 volumes of 108 squares within the area, is available to the public in the Historic New Orleans Collection library. The accumulation of this material was the result of a collaboration between Tulane University, the Schleider Foundation, and the Collection beginning in 1961; research continues with a special grant from architect Collins Diboll and assistance from the Historic Preservation Seminar of Tulane University.

Architectural historian Samuel Wilson, Jr., began teaching a class in Louisiana architecture at Tulane University in 1949. Shortly thereafter, the Olivier House, an early-19th century raised, galleried house was threatened with demolition by the New Orleans Roman Catholic Archdiocese. Mr. Wilson and most of his class — including Angela Gregory, Mrs. S. Walter Stern, Clem Binnings, and author T. Harnett Kane — along with Martha Gilmore Robinson and J. Raymond Samuel, organized the Louisiana Landmarks Society in 1950 to save that plantation. They did not succeed, but other victories would provide the group with the strength to prevent many demolitions and to become a statewide organization. As its first president, Mr. Wilson continued to guide preservation through principles established on sound architectural and archaeological

research.

The Louisiana Landmarks Society's first lady, Martha Robinson — lovingly known as "Miss Martha" and "the Senator" by friends and foes — carried the banner of preservation New Orleans-style to Washington, D.C., when she, with hundreds of concerned citizens, defeated the Riverfront Expressway in the 1960s. A tireless, lovely lady, she won by charm, astute judgment of human nature, excellent preparation, and timing. She knew and loved her city; her contributions to preservation are exhibited in structures and environment saved and in the inspired spirits of thousands.

This major preservation-versus-city planning conflict in New Orleans had its inception with New Yorker Robert Moses' Transportation Plan. Limited-access super highways with elevated sections were the rage in engineering and city planning immediately after World War II. To get America on the road was an at-any-cost ambition. In New Orleans a Riverfront Expressway was first proposed in the 1950s. Members of the Vieux Carre Property Owners were probably the first preservationists alerted to the planned roadway cutting the Vieux Carre off from the Mississippi River and permanently damaging the historic area with an elevated

Above
These stately homes are located on Esplanade Avenue. Known as the "Promenade Publique" in the 1830s, Esplanade Avenue became the fashionable place to live for New Orleans' socially prominent residents in the late 1800s. In this century, it became the scene of many restorations undertaken by concerned residents. Photos by Robin Boylan.

Below left
The French Market is highlighted in this view down Decatur Street. Though originally built in 1791, the market was rebuilt in 1813 and modernized in 1937–1938. The structure's basic Spanish Colonial characteristics have been preserved. Photo by Robin Boylan.

roadway.

The Louisiana Council for the Vieux Carre was formed in 1960. Its first president was Harnett Kane; he was succeeded shortly after by Martha Robinson. The organization soon became a vehicle to oppose the Riverfront Expressway. More than 35 organizations joined, creating one of the first preservation conglomerates in the country. Armed with a cause, they put a stop to the expressway in 1969 when Secretary of the Interior John A. Volpe withdrew federal funding. This issue polarized the city as no other; its victorious conclusion remains to be written as further studies and plans for city development continue to include a Riverfront Roadway.

The expressway was one of many Vieux Carre issues that siphoned time and energy from Mary and Jake Morrison after their move to New Orleans in 1937. Together they worked toward its physical improvement by actively organizing the Vieux Carre Property Owners, whose corporation purposes were synonymous with the Morrisons: ". . . the awakening, fostering and cultivating of a feeling of civic pride around the residents and property owners of that section of New Orleans, bound by the Mississippi River, Rampart, Esplanade, and Iberville — known as the Vieux Carre — and to encourage and assist in the preservation, restoration, beautification and general betterment of said section."

Combining his roles as attorney and preservationist, in 1957 Mr. Morrison wrote *Historic Preservation Law,* a comprehensive nationwide study on the subject. In 1974 the Morrisons received the Crowninshield Award from the National Trust for their activism and devotion to preservation. The Friends of the Cabildo, honoring Mr. Morrison for his past presidency and constant contributions to the organization, dedicated the fifth volume of the *New Orleans Architecture* series to him in 1977. The always-vigilant Mary Morrison serves on the Vieux Carre Commission, alert to the recurring topic of the Riverfront Roadway and infractions against the law in her beloved Quarter.

The Friends of the Cabildo, formed in 1954, was organized to assist the Louisiana State Museum in the maintenance and preservation of its buildings and collections. As a membership auxiliary, it is "a catalytic organization, with its exhibitions, lectures, guide programs, and books serving as effective instruments of education and even propaganda for preservation. By relating the past to its present, the Friends hopes to remove history from institutional isolation and encourage citizen awareness of our historic environment." This quotation from the first of six volumes entitled *New Orleans Architecture,* introduced the sponsoring Friends of the Cabildo to city leaders as well as to individuals desiring information. The organization

Wealthy New Orleans residents of yesterday spared no expense in constructing their beautiful St. Charles Avenue homes which are still a source of delight today. Photos by Robin Boylan.

has become a powerful and respected voice for preservation. The series is the most influential publication on the architecture of New Orleans neighborhoods and has been directly responsible for many allied studies and monographs. As a result of the mammoth, all-volunteer Friends effort, the following organizations were formed for the protection of individual neighborhoods: the Coliseum Square Association (1972), the Central Business District Improvement Association (1973), Save Our Cemeteries (1974), Save Our Riverfront (1975), Faubourg Marigny Association (1976), the Esplanade Improvement Association (1977), Historic Faubourg St. Mary Corporation (1976), the Improvement Association of the Irish Channel (1974), Mid-City Improvement Association (1975), City Park Mid-City Improvement (1971), the Canal Area Service Association (1978), and many small neighborhood groups, all of which belong to the Preservation Resource Center (1974).

Sixty preservation and neighborhood organizations belong to the Preservation Resource Center. The potential wisdom and effectiveness of a consolidated preservation organization are obvious. In addition to sponsoring meetings, programs, tours, mailings, and publications, its successes include the proposed and partial restoration of Julia Row, an 1830s set of 13 rowhouses; the publication of a monthly newspaper carrying citywide preservation news from Algiers Point to New Orleans East; and its combined efforts to save the "Warehouse District" in the Central Business District. Such accomplishments promise the transposition of preservation from "pioneer defender" to "promoting planner."

Often when New Orleanians are found to plead for preservation, they apologetically eschew many of their true ideals such as historicity, human scale, patina, and texture; it is defended, as in the case of the Vieux Carre, as being only economically important. Economics alone will never be an effective preservation motive. Apartments were once hailed in the Vieux Carre as a viable economic solution to preservation, but time-sharing condominiums and their evils may well sound the final doom of many structures.

John Kenneth Galbraith, Harvard University professor emeritus of economics, in his essay in *Preservation: Toward an Ethic in the 1980s* wrote:

Above left
This shotgun house—so called because its long, narrow design would allow one to stand at the front end of the house and shoot a bullet straight through the back door—is located in the Irish Channel. Photo by Robin Boylan.

Above
Along Bayou St. John stand many charming older homes such as the one pictured here. Photo by Robin Boylan.

When Dr. Margaret Mead, anthropologist, psychologist, and one of the world's most respected intellectuals, was interviewed in 1978 by *American Preservation* magazine, she was asked, "How do you see the preservation movement today?" Her response, after stating that she thought the bicentennial celebration in 1976 had been a great stimulus for preservation, was: "I think it's another of the many ways we're beginning to compensate for ruthlessness towards the past, this country's past. We're ruthless towards the past, we're ruthless towards the old, we're ruthless towards the environment. . . . Tearing down, destroying—it does have an effect. . . . The destruction of things that are familiar and important causes great anxiety in people."

Preservation in New Orleans, to be effective, can not be a piecemeal process. New Orleans needs not only the Vieux Carre and Garden District, but it also requires the contrast of low-scale buildings to high-rises within the Central Business District. The city needs all of its 19th-century neighborhoods, those along the river's edge, as well as those that lead back toward Bayou St. John and Lake Pontchartrain.

The appreciation of the past had a slow beginning in New Orleans, but it has arrived. Today its forces fortunately include the talents of the entire spectrum of the community. The fields are less those of battle, more those of computed probabilities, preferably liberally combined with the esthetics of man and his relation to his environment. New Orleans' spirit is enriched by its living past; its body is enhanced in a humane urban setting; its wealth is invested in its perception of both.

The U.S. Mint, now restored, was built in 1835 on the site where Fort St. Charles once stood. Photo by Robin Boylan.

One of the dominant subjects of this book is the way in which New Orleans has been seen, by its residents and visitors, in succeeding periods in the past. This section, however, divided into seven groups, is devoted exclusively to the look of the city today, with an emphasis on some of the enduring landmarks and institutions that give New Orleans its special character.

These pages and overleaf *Some of the older homes that line many of New Orleans' streets, avenues, and boulevards. Fascinating in the variety of their settings, design, and details, it is hardly surprising that so many of them have been beautifully maintained. Photos by Robin Boylan.*

New Orleans is, in the American imagination, almost synonymous with unrestrained gaiety and the celebration of being alive—and for good reason. Shown here and on the following pages, festivities associated with music, pageantry, or both. Facing page (top) and this page (below and far right), scenes from the New Orleans Jazz and Heritage Festival; facing page (below) Preservation Hall; right, street entertainers in the French Quarter. Photo at right by John Lawrence. Rest by Robin Boylan.

213

Mardi Gras is on Shrove Tuesday, the day before Ash Wednesday (the beginning of Lent). The peak of the period of celebration that begins soon after New Year, Mardi Gras is the day thousands of residents and visitors make merry in the streets of the city.

Photos on facing page, bottom right, and this page, left, by Robin Boylan. Rest by John Lawrence.

The form New Orleans' early tombs took was the result of two factors: the Catholic prohibition against cremation and the water-soaked ground residents encountered. After 1800 it became mandatory to build tombs above ground, which also marked the point at which the city's cemeteries became famous. Like the early houses, the early tombs were usually built of brick and plaster. The small white buildings and the narrow passageways that divide them create a strange, melancholy beauty that reminds us of the attitude toward death of the earlier residents: while death was mourned, it was also idealized in these cities of the dead. Photos by Robin Boylan.

This TOMB of
LAFAYETTE HOOK & LADDAR
VOLUNTEER FIRE CO #1
being restored by
FIREFIGHTING
HISTORICAL SOCIETY
in cooperation with
SAVE OUR CEMETERIES INC.

New Orleans has a deep fondness for its heroes, as is reflected in the many monuments that grace the city. Far left, the remarkable statue of Andrew Jackson in Jackson Square by Clark Mills. Left, a view of the monument to Robert E. Lee. Below, the participants in the Battle of New Orleans are honored at Chalmette. The 110-foot-high structure marks Andrew Jackson's position during the battle.

218 • NEW ORLEANS

Parks make an important contribution to the quality of life in New Orleans. Pictured here are (above) the entrance to Audubon Park, named for ornithologist and artist John James Audubon; a scene of the Louisiana Nature Center (above and right); and New Orleans Museum of Art in City Park (right). Photos (both pages) by Robin Boylan.

The churches of New Orleans have tended to the spiritual needs of residents from the city's founding. Facing page, St. Louis Cathedral is the fourth structure to bear the name. The first two were destroyed by a hurricane and a fire, respectively, and the third, constructed by Don Almonester y Roxas in 1794, had to be rebuilt in the mid-19th century.

On this page, the breathtaking interiors of St. Patrick's Church (above), designed in the 1830s by James Dakin and completed by James Gallier, Sr.; and St. Louis Cathedral. At right, an exterior view of St. Mary's Assumption. Photos by Robin Boylan.

Facing page, Bottom
The first attempt to establish an institution of higher learning was made in 1811, with the short-lived College of Orleans. But it was not until 1835 that the Medical College of Louisiana began educating students. It started with only 16 students and grew slowly until it became part of the University of Louisiana thanks to the state legislature in 1847. In 1883 a large bequest by Paul Tulane caused the university to further expand. It was then that the name was changed to honor him. A significant part of Tulane is Newcomb College, founded by Josephine Le Monnier Newcomb for women, with an extremely generous endowment in 1886.

Top
Loyola University of the South began its existence as Loyola Academy in 1904. In 1910 the academy, now known as Loyola College, merged with the College of the Immaculate Conception and in 1912 the college was incorporated as a university. Photos by Robin Boylan.

Right
The cargoes, look, and techniques of importing and exporting goods at the Port of New Orleans have changed somewhat over the last two centuries, but this is still very much a port city, whose location on the Mississippi is still of great importance. At bottom right, the New Orleans skyline and the Mississippi River Bridge from the west bank of the river. Photos by Robin Boylan.

As this 19th-century view emphasizes, New Orleans has always owed its prosperity to the port. And yet, the business community that has evolved since this illustration was done is diversified to an extent that hardly could have been foreseen then. (THNOC)

CHAPTER X
PARTNERS IN PROGRESS

BY JOHN CHASE AND JOHN WILDS

In 1881, it has been reported, New Orleans had 915 factories employing 8,404 persons. That's a hundred years before this writing, and New Orleans was just stumbling out of the harassing years of Reconstruction that followed the Civil War, when one governor amassed a fortune of a million dollars on his $8,000 per year salary. But New Orleans can remain rich while being robbed, as attested by so many of the business biographies in this chapter that had their beginnings around 1881.

This city can bounce back from adversity because of its number one natural resource—the Mississippi River. Folklore tells us that 75 cents of each dollar in an Orleanian's pocket is attributable to the riches of the river, and this folklore dates back before inflation.

Back in 1718, France planted New Orleans on the river because she thought it was good business. But it wasn't for France. Nor was it good business for Spain, who inherited the colony. Nor for France's Napoleon either, after he took the province back from Spain. Yet, present-day New Orleans is deeply indebted to all three of these.

Later, in the 1760s, when Spanish rule began, trade upriver became New Orleans's best business. Annually, a fleet of bateaux left the city for the Illinois Country, across the river from Laclede's Village.

Then came Napoleon. At first he tried to make Louisiana his business. Failing this, and badly in need of cash, he sold it all—more land than he had ever conquered—to the United States for 2½ cents an acre, and provided New Orleans with an incredibly rich hinterland, populated by then from America's greatest folk movement that settled the Ohio Valley and reached the Pacific in a single generation.

Soon New Orleans was the greatest export port in the world, serving its great valley. The early money crop of furs soon was joined by flour and tobacco as well as cotton, sugar, rice, lumber, leather, whiskey, meats—the list becomes endless. Suddenly there were more steamboats trading on the river than all the tonnage of the British navy that ruled the seas.

Louisiana began the 20th century with the discovery of oil. Soon the treasure trove of the offshore resulted in the petrochemical industry, which has marshaled a fleet of nearly 28,000 river barges pushing petroleum products upriver to return laden with mid-western grain and Ohio Valley coal, all for Europe. Today the port of New Orleans is the second largest in the United States.

Although much turmoil has beset New Orleans—from the rule of France and Spain to Reconstruction, from ambitious politicians and merchants to the failures of Napoleon—the business community has remained strong and concerned about the quality of life in this colorful city. Side by side, old river-based companies share new futures with diversified businesses in the fields of real estate, banking, medical facilities, and an ever-growing tourism industry, just to mention a few.

Today New Orleans boasts a business community committed to growth and love for their city as expressed in the following histories, biographies, and success stories. Through the purchase of these pages in "Partners in Progress," this book was made possible, and attests to a warm civic pride. The companies you may be employed by, services that you may patronize, the familiar places that you may see in your travels all contribute to the rich historical charm and forward-looking ideals of New Orleans.

ABRY BROTHERS, INC.

Along with his wife and infant son, John G. Abry arrived in New Orleans from his native Frankfort, Germany, to establish this business in 1840. Already an experienced shorer, his guardian angel must have directed John G. to this city where the uncertain soil conditions of its delta land were to provide a great need for his services.

So, much like his doctor friends, he was soon making house calls all over town. By 1981, 141 years later, doctors seldom made house calls any more. But Herman Joseph Abry, who became the fifth-generation president of Abry Brothers, Inc., in 1976, and his associates were still making house calls. Because, you see, this firm is in the business of fixing sick houses. Besides shoring—the word is of Old English origin and means to "prop

George J. Abry, third-generation president of Abry Brothers, managed the company for more than 40 years.

up"—the Abry company also levels houses, raises and lowers them, even moves them. Obviously, the possibility of such "sick" houses making office visits is ridiculous.

Ten years before his death in 1885, John G. Abry bought a small house on a large lot at 816-18 North Johnson Street. Soon after, property was acquired for the yards to stable the mules and house the wagons and shoring equipment a few blocks down St. Ann Street. This was still the Abry address in 1903, when the *Daily States* carried a long article about the company. It identified Emile Abry, son of John G., as "senior member of the firm." Emile was born the year his father founded the business. The *States* further identified George J. Abry, his son, as junior partner and active manager, and went on to say, "He is thoroughly up-to-date in all business matters, and stands very high in business and social circles." The *States* article continued, saying George was a member of the board of directors of a homestead, a member of benevolent societies, as well as a member of the Mechanics, Dealers and Lumbermen's Exchange, where Abry Brothers had an office. In these days before telephones, it was necessary for active businessmen to have a centrally located office. As partner, George managed the company for more than 40 years. It was during his tenure that Abry Brothers acquired property on Orleans Avenue at Bayou St. John, which is still the company's headquarters in 1981. His two brothers, John and Emile Herman, were long associated with him as superintendents. In 1930 Emile Herman succeeded him, at age 51, becoming the company's third-generation head.

It was during these years that Morris (Ferdinand) Lewis, a remarkable black man who had come to work for the company in 1900 at age 13, rose to become an Abry superintendent. Following in his footsteps, his grandson Livingstone (Rudy) Lewis, is playing an important role in the Abry organization in 1981.

Herman Joseph Abry, great-nephew of George J. Abry, is the company's fifth-generation president.

The fourth-generation president, Herman Andrew Abry, son of Emile Herman, did not assume office until 1948, when he was 41 years old. As an energetic young man, Herman Andrew decided there were too many Abrys around, so he left to become a successful certified public accountant. He had advanced to comptroller and then secretary of a large manufacturing firm when his mother called him. His father had died. Would he return and head up Abry Brothers? How could he refuse? It was in his blood. He returned and gave 28 years of service before retiring in favor of his son, Herman Joseph Abry, who had been company-trained since 1959. So once again this venerable old company that "doctors" houses was placed in expert young hands.

His father, a veteran calculator, can certify to that. And besides, there's the new president's younger brother, John Paul Abry. Since 1840, Abry Brothers, Inc., never seems to run out of brothers.

COLEMAN E. ADLER & SONS, INC.

On Royal Street in New Orleans's historic French Quarter, Coleman E. Adler hung the shingle of his family's jewelry business in 1898. In establishing Coleman E. Adler and Sons, Inc., he came also to establish a reputation for excellence in the sale of fine jewels, a reputation that would persist for several generations. As a result, Adler's is one of the few remaining family-owned jewelers of its size in America today.

With his sons, Milton and Walter, Adler worked tirelessly to mold a family tradition based on individualized service. Personal attention to every detail and the assurance of trusted advice were ingredients of the Adler ilk, hallmarks that were recognized throughout the South. No job was ever too small. Family members still travel extensively within the region, hand-delivering selections to customers who cannot visit one of their two fine stores.

At the turn of the century, Adler's moved to a new location at 722 Canal Street. Their ornate street clock became a landmark of New Orleans's financial district and a dependable timepiece for New Orleans residents.

Adler's is to New Orleans what Tiffany's is to New York. Open the glass doors and step inside a New Orleans institution of elegance and fashion. In the long double-aisle salon, showcases display a cache of diamonds, emeralds, rubies, sapphires, and natural pearls atop raw ribbed silk; trays of rings, coils of studded bracelets, glittering necklaces, and rows of watches reflect light as customers pause, sighing and pointing at the glass.

For eight decades, debutantes, the betrothed, and other fortunate recipients have anticipated the arrival of a treasure from Adler's—a gift of taste and distinction from specialists in fine silver, porcelain, crystal, and bone china. Objets d'art and Steuben glass sculpture were recent additions to the oeuvre. In 1965, when the store underwent a major renovation, the original rosewood cabinets, used since 1908, were presented to the Louisiana State Museum from the Adler family.

Today, three stories above Canal

In 1898, Coleman E. Adler founded the firm that bears his name.

Street, Coleman E. Adler II administrates from behind a large executive desk, a mounted mallard posed on the corner, its head tucked inside one wing. Mr. Adler, groomed by his father and uncle, was traveling with them on buying trips by the age of 10, inspecting and grading fine gems. This was the beginning of a professional competence he now employs in the service of the serious collector as well as those who invest in gemstones.

President of the firm since 1974, the handsome, earnest 37-year-old attends meticulously to his customers— many of whom he acquired as a teenager and who still prefer his regal touch. From the purchase of a $50,000 bracelet to the restringing of a strand of pearls, the young Adler's attentions and air of congeniality are in constant demand. And the tradition of family leadership continues; Tiffany Adler, the first member of generation number four, entered the family business in 1975.

In the jewelry business, reputation is everything. Coleman Adler is mindful to carry on in the style characteristic of his antecedents; however, he exerts an influence all his own. He has catalyzed a new amalgam—a coming together of the classic, traditional profile of Adler's with the sleek, modern image of the 1980s.

Coleman E. Adler & Sons' jewelry store had ceiling fans when this photograph was taken in 1913.

ARNAUD'S RESTAURANT

Leon Bertrand Arnaud Cazenave appeared a happy man to friends dining in his restaurant in 1940, when he made his nightly entrance. Affectionately titled "the Count" by his New Orleans friends, Cazenave, never without a carnation in his lapel, epitomized courtly demeanor and sartorial elegance.

The count had reason to appear happy in 1940. In 20 years his restaurant had grown from 811 Bienville to 813-19 on that French Quarter street, and its reputation as a fine eating place had spread worldwide. He resided in a magnificent, 22-room mansion on Esplanade, happily married and the father of an attractive daughter. Perhaps he would have been even happier had he known then that after operating the restaurant for 31 years, that daughter—then Mrs. Germaine Cazenave Wells—would continue its operation another 30 years. And for 26 of these years Mrs. Wells has also presided over an Easter parade in horse-drawn buggies. In addition to its route through the French Quarter, the parade stops for Mass at St. Louis Cathedral, ending up at Arnaud's Restaurant. In 1948, when her father died and she took over, Mrs. Wells became the first female proprietor of a major U.S. restaurant.

It was just accidently that Arnaud Cazenave was to end up the distinguished restauranteur he became. On June 27, 1878, he was born in southern France, near the Spanish border. At age 17, in 1895, he was sent to Paris to continue his education. Primarily what Arnaud acquired in Paris was a deep devotion to France that lasted all his life. But he wanted to be a doctor, and accepted the invitation of relatives in the United States to come here and study. Records seem to indicate that he landed in New Orleans, because he was sent to St. Stanislaus College in nearby Bay St.

Louis to learn enough English to study medicine at Tulane. What he also learned there was that he didn't have enough money to finance a medical education, and he turned to selling wines. His knowledge of French vineyards particularly qualified him for this. Altogether young Cazenave would spend 14 years selling wines, which he didn't enjoy, and dabbling in the restaurant business, which he grew to enjoy very much. Before he acquired sufficient capital to purchase the Bienville Street property, he appears to have rented the Old Absinthe House building, and for some time conducted a successful cafe. A novel idea of providing each customer with a small bottle of red wine, gratis, appeared to have been a successful promotion.

In the carriage of one of the 26 Easter parades she sponsored is Germaine Cazenave Wells, Count Arnaud's daughter. Riding with her (at right) is her daughter, Arnaud Elizabeth Milner. Before her untimely death in 1977, she bore a son who is also named Arnaud.

Although never a cook, Arnaud quickly learned the restaurant business that his future success indicated. Just as he knew good wine, Arnaud came to know good food. Also he learned to work with his chefs, the first of whom was Madame Pierre, whose knowledge of French and Creole cuisine was considerable. Arnaud, the epicure, was constantly making suggestions to Marie and the chefs who would follow her. The results are the long list of famous Arnaud's Restaurant creations in New Orleans cuisine. Arnaud was more than one of the finest restauranteurs in the country, more than an artist with foods. He was a rare phenomenon, an artist in living.

In December 1979, after running the restaurant for as many years her father had, Germaine Cazenave Wells leased the business. So, once again, the New Orleans institution Count Arnaud founded so long ago has achieved continuity—Orleanians hope Arnaud's Restaurant will continue to serve their community for many years to come.

Count Arnaud.

BAUERLEIN, INC.

G. (for George) Wallace (Wally) Bauerlein was a fun-loving gourmet, and he didn't like snow. He fell in love with New Orleans on a visit, went back to his home in Kansas City, Missouri, sold his small ad agency, and took a train for the Crescent City.

That was in the early spring of 1922. By mid-May of that year "Wally" Bauerlein had opened an office in the then-new Hibernia Bank Building—the tallest commercial building in the South. Within a matter of months he and his advertising agency, Bauerlein, Inc., had gained quick recognition. After all, Wally Bauerlein was the only adman in New Orleans to carry a gold-headed cane, wear spats, and sport a vest with piping.

From a modest beginning Bauerlein, with an account executive named Harry McGehee and a secretary, grew and prospered through the years until it now is one of the largest agencies in the region. Bauerlein's first client was New Orleans Public Service, then known as the New Orleans Street Railway Company. It was still with Bauerlein going into the 1980s.

The agency was the second tenant in the Hibernia Building. The first was the Illinois-Central Railroad, at the time another of Bauerlein's clients. After 56 years at that location, the company moved to 615 Baronne Street, where it is presently headquartered.

After Wally Bauerlein died of smoke inhalation in his apartment, Clarke Salmon, a former editor of *The Item* and *The Item-Tribune*, took over the agency in 1942. Upon his death in 1959, Salmon was succeeded by Kenneth (Ken) Gormin, who had been a columnist and an editor of *The Item*, *The Tribune*, and a reporter on *The Times-Picayune*.

Gormin and Pierre Villere ran the agency as a team until Pierre's death in 1967. Under their direction Bauerlein promoted major area projects such as

the Lake Pontchartrain Causeway and the Rivergate. More recently Bauerlein has promoted the Mississippi River Gulf Outlet and the Louisiana Superport.

Eugene (Gene) Barnes succeeded Gormin as president in 1979, Gormin becoming chairman of the board at that time. Today Bauerlein handles clients along the Gulf Coast from Mobile to Lake Charles, as well as regional advertising for national accounts, with recognized expertise in the energy, real estate, and financial fields.

Bauerlein's offices in the Hibernia Bank Building (background, with dome visible) rise over Carondelet Street in this Charles Franck photograph of the city's financial district taken in 1924, just two years after the agency was founded. Wally Bauerlein's small advertising agency was the second tenant in the building, where the agency remained until 1979, when it moved to new quarters at 615 Baronne Street.

BISSO TOWBOAT COMPANY, INC.

Grenoble, in the southeastern corner of France, was the ancient capital of the former province of Dauphine, tucked between the Rhone River and the Italian border. Despite the region's alpine beauty and its opportunities for employment in the glove factories there, 10-year-old Joseph Bissot ran away from home in 1853 to go to sea.

Young Joseph has never explained, and no historian knows, how he managed to get down the 100-plus miles of the Rhone River to the Mediterranean where he signed on as a cabin boy, most likely at the port of Marseilles. But resourceful Joseph Bissot traveled light. By the time his vessel reached New Orleans in 1862, he had even dropped the extra "t" off his name. "Everybody called me Bisso," he has explained. "I didn't need the extra 't'."

Unfortunately for Bisso's ship, it reached New Orleans at the same time Farragut's Union fleet arrived to capture Confederate New Orleans and blockade the river in April 1862. A blockaded ship needs no crew, so Bisso was forced ashore to find work. We know for a time a blacksmith, in Iberville Parish, hired him to shoe horses. One historian tells us he joined the Confederate navy on the river. But

From his portrait on the wall of the company's executive office, the legendary Captain "Billy" Bisso, son of the founder, looks down on his daughter and her son—Mrs. Cecilia Bisso Slatten and Captain W.A. Slatten—1981 managers of the Bisso family towboat operations.

teenaged Bisso did sign up as water tender for the Union gunboat *Albatross*. A French sailor, stranded ashore, had no side in the American Civil War. He needed a job, and work was scarce. Little is known what action, if any, 19-year-old Bisso saw before the war, and his job, ended in 1865. Suffice it to say, a gunboat in those days was any boat with a gun

(cannon) mounted aboard. Mostly the *Albatross* probably did patrol duty south of Vicksburg. So there was much time for Bisso to watch the river, study it, and learn about it.

Following his discharge from the navy, he settled at Walnut Street on the river, which has remained Bisso headquarters to this day. At first he worked for the Fischer Lumber Company, and within five years he was in the lumber business for himself and married to Mary D. Damonte. There were a number of children, five of whom grew to adulthood. It was Ol' Man River caving in the levee at Walnut Street that forced him out of the lumber business. A new levee, farther back, had to be built. Thus, in 1890, circumstance brought Bisso into the towboat and ferry business. That year he bought *The Leo*, and the Bisso Towboat Company, Inc., had its beginning.

Before his death on Christmas Day in 1907, the first Captain Bisso had sailed the river first with the U.S. Navy, then on flatboats of logs from Natchez downriver to his Walnut Street lumber mill, and before the turn of the century on *The Leo*, plus four other Bisso tugs and a river steamer. W.A. Bisso, who had been educated at McDonogh 14 on Peters (now Jefferson) Avenue and Soule Business College on Jackson Avenue, took over the business. Almost immediately he also founded the New Orleans Coal Com-

Units of the Bisso fleet of towboats range up and down the 250 miles of the New Orleans river-seaport. Between assignments they await further orders at any one of the 25 Bisso mooring stations along the river.

pany.

Captain Billy, as W.A. Bisso was soon generally known, was to spend 56 years piloting the company through two world wars and a Great Depression without serious mishap. However, his coal company—which had become number one in the port—could not survive the transfer of steamships and tugs to diesel power. It was shut down in 1954. At this same time, to effect the conversion of the entire Bisso fleet from steam to diesel power was a continuing capital investment for some time to come.

On shore leave, Captain Bisso appears to have found relaxation from nautical nuisances by steering a course in New Orleans city politics, with its cross currents and undertows but little less hazardous than Ol' Man River's. Nevertheless, the captain found safe harbor in election to both the city council and state legislature, as well as seeing candidates he backed successfully stowed aboard. All in all, Captain W.A. (Billy) Bisso's enterprise and accomplishments won for him respect throughout the maritime community, and for years, he was happily married to Cecilia E. LeBreton, member of an old French family. The couple had one son and one daughter.

Upon his death at age 88 in 1963, both the third and fourth generations took charge in the persons of his daughter, Mrs. Cecilia Bisso Slatten, and his grandson, Captain William A. (Billy) Slatten. A thoroughly reorganized and modernized family company entered the 1980s, a short decade before its 100th anniversary, with Captain Slatten its general manager and the other major owner, his mother, functioning as its chairman of the board. Like his grandfather and great-grandfather before him, this second Captain Billy began learning the river's secrets at an early age, completing an education at Tulane University qualifying him for leadership.

Unlike any other business is that of operating a towboat service in the country's largest seaport day and night along 250 miles of the Mississippi from Head of Passes to Baton Rouge. Besides its historic Fleet Landing Office on 800 feet of the riverfront at Walnut Street, there is a branch landing office 65 miles upriver near the Sunshine Bridge in St. James Parish, which Bisso dispatchers refer to as "St. James." Then, strung along the river from Buras to Baton Rouge are 25 Bisso anchorages, where tugs tie up momentarily awaiting reassignment. It

is unlikely one can view the river at New Orleans very long without having a familiar red and white Bisso tug, with the yellow band on its black stack, move into sight.

The dispatchers at Walnut Street and St. James know exactly each tug's schedule, as they do every unit of the Bisso fleet of some 20 units. In addition to towing, the company is organized to provide fresh water, slop, derrick, lineman, barge rental, and salvage services.

All steamship lines have contracts with its towboat services in major seaports and in the Port of New Orleans; Bisso has its share. So when a Bisso-contracted vessel enters the harbor, a Bisso towboat is there to meet it at an appointed place. Such contracts can be arranged beforehand directly with Bisso's New Orleans or New York offices, but most likely by the steamship's agency in the port.

It has been said of the Bisso company that since 1890 it has always been ready with services most needed. First there was the lumber business of the founding Bisso, then ferry service, coal service, and towboat service. And now, as the Mid-East OPEC oil cartel continues unreliable, the whole Western World is turning to coal readily available for its energy needs. In 1981, the Port of New Orleans was gearing up to export 120 million tons of U.S. coal by 1990. It is already exporting over 12 million tons. It looks like the Bisso Towboat Company, Inc., is going to be back in the coal business—towboat-wise, that is.

BOH BROS. CONSTRUCTION CO., INC.

Contributions made by Boh Bros. Construction Co., Inc., and its predecessors to the face-lifting that has transformed greater New Orleans in the 20th century lie more than skin deep.

Above the surface, such landmarks as the Louisiana Superdome, the Greater New Orleans Mississippi River Bridge, One Shell Square, and the overpasses and traffic exchanges that mark the Interstate 10 and 610 highway systems and the Union Passenger Terminal grade separation program all are projects in which the Boh people were involved.

On the surface, hundreds of miles of streets were paved and sidewalks laid by Boh crews. And underground, a maze of literally thousands of miles of waterlines, sewerage and drainage pipes—many installed by Boh Bros.—allowed home builders to shatter the

One of the major projects undertaken by Boh Bros. was the construction of the approaches to the Greater New Orleans Mississippi River Bridge. Note the Louisiana Superdome on the right of the roadway.

The Judge Seeber Bridge over the Industrial Canal at Claiborne Avenue is a Boh Bros. project.

bonds that formerly limited the habitable areas of the metropolis. No matter where he goes, a motorist cannot drive for many blocks on a New Orleans street without passing over subsurface conduits placed there by Boh workers.

In 1979, 70 years after Arthur P. Boh ventured out on his own as a residential contractor, the firm that he founded went over the billion-dollar mark in the accumulation of projects completed in the city and elsewhere in the South. At today's prices the total would be several billion dollars, since much of the work was finished in early years when a job could be done for a fraction of present winning bids.

Arthur Boh's first contract was for the construction for $16,500 of four double residences on Hagan Avenue (now Jeff Davis Parkway). The houses still are occupied.

In 1913 Henry Boh joined his older brother in the A.P. Boh Construction Company. They formed a partnership in 1937 under the name Boh Bros. Construction Company, and in 1960 incorporated as Boh Bros. Construc-

tion Co., Inc., bringing key employees into the ownership. The firm still is owned by the Boh family and employees.

By 1917, when the city government began a major extension of sewerage and water systems beyond the restricted area where New Orleanians had been huddled together for many years, the Bohs were ready to graduate from home building to public works.

Paving Tulane Avenue near the central business district was undertaken by Boh Bros. during the 1960s.

Their company developed a special skill for subsurface installations in the soggy soil. Later, they would drive the piling on which rest the Superdome, One Shell Square, and the Marriott Hotel.

They had a significant part in filling the Carondelet (Old Basin), New Basin, and Orleans canals. They did much of the work in the mammoth drainage complex that keeps New Orleans dry even though much of the city is below sea level and the annual rainfall approaches 60 inches.

Works Progress Administration projects helped the brothers to survive the Great Depression, and they were ready to meet the wartime construction demands of the 1940s. Their company built most of the overpasses and underpasses for Mayor deLesseps S. Morrison's grade separation program of the '50s and '60s. The extension of the interstate highway system through New Orleans in the '60s and '70s kept Boh crews busy. The towering I-10 Bridge over the Industrial Canal is a Boh structure, as is the Judge Seeber Bridge. The approaches to the Greater New Orleans Bridge were built by Boh, which has a contract for construction of three piers for the new twin bridge that will be erected alongside it. The Nashville Avenue Wharf and other Port of New Orleans facilities are Boh products.

In the early 1980s there was no slowing of momentum. Boh was busy in the construction of the area's first nuclear power plant at Taft, and in the onshore storage facilities for the Louisiana offshore superport.

The company long ago extended its operations beyond the New Orleans area. Boh had a hand in the construction of dozens of the industrial plants that line the banks of the Mississippi from Baton Rouge almost to the river's mouth. The yellow and black signs that identify Boh Bros. projects are almost as familiar in Baton Rouge as they are in New Orleans. The firm has completed work in Mississippi, Arkansas, and other southern states as well.

Arthur Boh, who was born in 1884,

became chairman of the company in the 1960 reorganization. He continued in this position until 1967, and then served on the board until his death in 1973. Henry Boh was president from 1960 until 1967, when he became chairman, clearing the way for the election of his son, Robert H. Boh, as president. The younger Boh joined the company in 1951. A member of the third generation, Robert S. Boh, son of the president, prepared for his participation in the family business by obtaining civil engineering and graduate business administration degrees at Tulane University. His grandfather and great-uncle learned their engineering on the job. Neither was a college graduate.

Below
Boh Bros. Construction Co., Inc., built the towering I-10 Bridge over the Industrial Canal in the late '60s.

Above
Bridging bayous and streams in the south Louisiana coastal country is a specialty of Boh Bros. Construction Co., Inc.

CANAL BARGE COMPANY, INC.

From Brownsville to Pittsburgh, from Port St. Joe to Minneapolis, up the Illinois River to Chicago, along the Mississippi, the Missouri, the Tennessee, the Cumberland, the Arkansas, and the Tombigbee rivers, towboats emblazoned with a red Old English "C" shove their cargoes to the boundaries of the mid-continental inland waterway system.

They belong to a New Orleans enterprise, the Canal Barge Company, Inc., pioneer in a new era of transportation on waters once traversed by stately steamboats. The cry "mark twain" no longer is heard; electronic depth finders have taken the place of crewmen sounding with knotted ropes to warn of sandbars ahead.

Samuel Clemens, prophet of the packets, would grope for words to describe the innovations—1,000-foot-long strings of barges propelled by towboats having the power of 5,600 horses, cargoes of molten sulphur kept at 270 degrees Fahrenheit, or refrigerated anhydrous ammonia at 28 degrees below zero.

What would the author have thought of boats with pilothouses that are raised high to afford clear views for entering locks, or hydraulically lowered to permit passage under bridges? or of engine rooms with spotless white machinery? or of a robot bow steering boat, controlled via radio by the pilot on the towboat far to the rear, which rides at the front end of a tow and is used to maneuver the barges around tortuous bends?

The new day in cargo carrying in inland waters was hastened by the incorporation on December 6, 1933, of the Canal Barge Company. The name was chosen because the firm was organized to serve small petroleum terminals on the Harvey Canal. Incorporators were Joseph Merrick Jones, attorney; Thomas Jordan, cotton trader and Wall Street investor; and Harry B. Jordan, oil company marketing executive.

The company started with a 1,000-barrel, all-welded steel tank barge complete with a pumping unit, the first vessel of its kind in the Mississippi River-Intracoastal Canal system. It was moved from terminal to terminal by chartered tugs.

In 1939 the firm built the M/V *Bull Calf*, whose motive power was the prototype of the power train for the LST. She was powered by a high-speed diesel engine with a revolutionary clutch and reversing gear that enabled

One of the founders of the Canal Barge Company was attorney Joseph Merrick Jones. He was succeeded as president in 1963 by his son, Joseph M. Jones, Jr.

the vessel to change from full-speed ahead to full-speed astern in eight seconds. The maneuverability impressed U.S. Navy observers, and the M/V *Bull Calf* became the model for the landing craft that helped the Allies win World War II. In 1940 Canal ordered ten 9,000-barrel steel tank barges that were delivered in time for the company to assist in the movement of gasoline to fuel the war effort.

As the years passed, Canal pioneered in the development of integrated tows. Formerly, a tow consisted of barges of different sizes and drafts. The result was increased resistance as the string was pushed through the water and forward progress was slowed. An integrated tow includes two or more barges and a towboat designed to travel as a unit. The lead barge has a long, tapering bow end that glides through the water with a minimum of drag. The trailing barge also has a tapering stern end. Additional barges placed between these two are shaped like boxes, the ends of which are identical in size. When assembled as a unit the tow presents a uniform, smooth underwater configuration creating minimum resistance. Towboats of the M/V *Bull Calf*'s generation could push a 5,000-ton tow upstream in the Mississippi at only four miles per hour. A new Canal towboat can take an integrated tow of 24,000 tons over the same course at six miles per hour.

In 1957 the M/V *Hamilton* pushed the first fully integrated pure chemical tow on the inland waterways, and now Canal has become a specialty carrier of chemicals produced in Texas and Louisiana plants. Chemicals transported in corrosion-resistant barges include alkylates, alcohol, and lubricating oil. Special barges can keep molten sulphur from cooling into a solid en route, or anhydrous ammonia from boiling. The company also carries coal for Commonwealth Edison's Chicago generating plants up the Illinois River from Havana, Illinois.

Canal's fleet in 1980 included 16 towboats, 100 tank barges, and 112 coal barges. Its affiliate, Central Marine Service, Inc., had more than 200 flush-deck barges used in the inland system and also in the world's oceans to service oil exploration and production activities.

Joseph M. Jones, who at the time of his death was president of the board of administrators of Tulane University, bought out the interests of the Jordans and became president of Canal in succession to Thomas Jordan. Mr. Jones in turn was succeeded in 1963 by

In 1939 the company built the M/V Bull Calf, which became the model for the landing craft that helped the Allies win World War II.

Joseph Merrick Jones, Jr., the third president. The company is wholly owned by the Jones family.

Canal's spruce towboats lack the gingerbread and chandeliers of Mark Twain's floating palaces, but it is doubtful that modern crewmen would trade their immaculate, air-conditioned quarters for the frills of 19th-century staterooms. The food is renowned, so much so that Elaine Douglass Jones, wife of the president, collected recipes from captains, cooks, and crewmen and published them in a book entitled "Galley Ho!" By 1980, the daily food allowance for everyone on board had risen to 10 dollars each, enough to destroy the budget of a family eating at home.

Canal, which has approximately 300 employees, has trained more towboat captains than any other line operating on inland waters. A deckhand can rise to pilot in a matter of five years.

The fleet with the red Old English "C" as its symbol is carrying on New Orleans's historic involvement with the river, which supplies much of the city's lifeblood. The storied race of the *Robert E. Lee* and *Natchez* started at Canal Street. Nowadays, a Canal towboat, unencumbered by a tow, would easily beat either to St. Louis.

The M/V Joseph M. Jones *is a 4,300-horsepower towboat with a pushing unit tow of 72,000 barrels of oil.*

C.F. BEAN CORPORATION

Mr. C.F. Bean began moving Louisiana's soil in 1929. It's a unique environment here—an environment that is constantly changing. What is water today becomes an island, and shorelines are continually being eroded by the encroaching waters.

It was in those early days that the need arose to develop new petroleum reserves. To do this, access to oil fields had to be provided by canals dredged by specialized equipment. Mr. Bean helped develop this equipment, and thereby established a reputation for innovation—the sort of innovation that helped his company grow to become one of the largest dredging concerns in the United States.

From its beginnings in 1953 in the town of Plaquemine, Louisiana, C.F. Bean Corporation expanded its operations throughout the United States and the world. Mr. Bean designed and personally supervised the construction of what was to become the most modern fleet of dredging equipment in the United States. It became a fleet large enough to provide everything needed to dredge the waters of the Gulf Coast and anywhere else in the world.

The company found itself expanding as naturally as its home geography constantly evolved. In 1971, Mr. Bean's son, J.W. Bean, became the president of the corporation. His father gives him full credit for guiding the firm's growth to new markets and for establishing its present position of leadership in the industry. Under Jim's guidance, Bean acquired a major U.S. dredging contractor in 1974, nearly doubling the size of C.F. Bean Corporation.

The following year, Bean established a relationship with a Dutch firm. Together they completed a $300-million project in Jubail, Saudi Arabia. Other international projects have been accepted and completed by Bean in Central and South America, the Middle East, Africa, and Asia.

The company's reputation for innovation led it to construct a "dustpan" dredge, the "Lenel Bean," named for Jim's sister. This was the first dredge of its kind built in more than fifty years, and it created an entirely new market of river maintenance dredging for this continually growing corporation.

And the spirit of innovation continues. In 1981 Bean commissioned the 6,300-cubic-yard-capacity "Eagle I," the most technologically advanced split-hull hopper dredge in the world. Few others like it have been built so large, but Bean has consistently taken leadership positions to cope with the expanding markets in its industry.

C.F. Bean Corporation and its 600 employees have also developed capabilities for engineering, design, and shipbuilding, and the search is continuing to provide additional means to help solve tomorrow's marine contracting problems to support shipping and energy development.

The watchword at Bean is "innovation." Bean has never been satisfied with existing technology; rather, it has sought new technology, equipment of advanced design, and dedicated and loyal people to challenge the soil anywhere in the world.

"Eagle I," world's largest trailing-suction, split-hull hopper dredge.

CANAL PLACE

Someone has said that if Bienville had built the International Trade Mart when he founded New Orleans in 1718, he would have had to build it in the middle of the river. Probably so. And had he also built Canal Place then, its address would have been a block out in the river.

We know for certain that when Jacques Tanesse subdivided the Commons 98 years later in 1816, his map showed Canal Street ending at Decatur. It was called Levee Street until 1870, because Decatur is where the

Canal Place, with the Custom House at left.

levee was in 1718. Since then Ol' Man River has been depositing a batture of new land from St. Louis Street uptown to Felicity. Today this deposit of alluvial land is more than the 258.5 acres that comprise Bienville's original city—the Vieux Carre.

Historically, new lands the river deposits always caused more controversy than the equal amounts it caved in on the opposite bank. Joseph C. Canizaro, premier New Orleans developer, found this out in the 1970s when he began assembling land for his Canal Place project—the monumental grouping pictured here. He had just completed his Lykes Center which initiated the development of Poydras

Street. Now he was ready with a $500-million-plus project at the foot of Canal Street, which would reunite the city and people of New Orleans with the Mississippi River in a series of office buildings, shopping areas, a hotel, and luxury living units—all offering magnificent views of the city's romantic river.

But the lands to accommodate Canal Place were adjacent to the French Quarter. Some of it even trespassed into the official precincts of the Quarter. In 1936, by authority of the state constitution, the New Orleans City Council created the Vieux Carre Commission. Since then it has made the Quarter a national model of historic preservation, after first saving it from the wanton neglect and willful destruction which threatened Bienville's city at the turn of the century. It is its function to view with suspicion anything different or new in it, or even near it.

Canizaro and his staff came to know this and appreciate it. The project proceeded open and above board. Because land costs in the area were so great, buildings had to be of sufficient size to justify the investment. At the same time Canal Place also needed the proximity of the Quarter to further its acceptability, along with the nearby river. Canizaro also suggested what he planned on the Quarter's fringe would enhance its inherent value to all Orleanians.

Agreement was reached, and Phase I of the project was built. Next to it, Phase II, with the shopping center on Canal Street and the hotel behind it with entrance on Iberville Street, is scheduled for construction to start at the time of this book's publication, with Phase III to follow.

The developers of this project ask only that the Vieux Carre Commission, based upon historic precedent, judge Canal Place by those same protective standards, as it takes shape on the new grounds Ol' Man River has inserted between himself and colonial New Orleans since Bienville founded his city in 1718.

JOSEPH C. CANIZARO INTERESTS

Born in Maryland, Joseph C. Canizaro grew up in the New Orleans-Mississippi Gulf Coast neighborhood. He was educated at Mobile's Spring Hill College and at Mississippi State University. He is a man of average height, and that's about the only thing that is average about Joseph C. Canizaro.

New Orleans first became aware of this man of many interests in the mid-1970s. Then, construction on Poydras of One Shell Square was beginning, and further out Poydras at Claiborne, land was being acquired for a Superdome. Suddenly, the Lykes Company building appeared, already constructed on Poydras at Tchoupitoulas. It was Canizaro's first building in New Orleans. It anchored Poydras at the river. Before long the name Canizaro was as well known in downtown New Orleans as Canal Street, as Canal Place One, a 32-story office tower, opened in 1979. This was to be the first phase of one of the largest mixed-use complexes in the South, incorporating high-fashion retail, hotel, and 1.6 million square feet of office space under one roof. Saks Fifth Avenue will be opening its first New Orleans store in the fall of 1983.

Pictured here are Joseph C. Canizaro and one of his major interests, the American Tower in Shreveport.

But Joe Canizaro's interests are far-ranging. Almost coincidental with Canal Place, the American Tower opened in Shreveport. Another such tower is on the Canizaro drawing board, with a low-rise connecting building between the twins. Also on Poydras, construction of a 33-story granite office tower and a 450-room hotel will commence shortly.

Of the four divisions of Canizaro Interests, such urban developments are first, with plans for projects in St. Louis, Memphis, and Birmingham under study. An industrial division, which concentrates on manufacturing, distribution, and warehousing projects, is second of the four. The Plantation Business Campus at Destrehan is in this category. One of Louisiana's first completely master-planned industrial and office parks, it will surround the stately antebellum plantation house built in 1787 and later enlarged by Jean Noel d'Estrehan to house his 14 sons and daughters. The new Luling River bridge opens up this 880-acre project, with adjacent projects planned for the West Bank.

A third JCCI project is already under construction in Lafayette, where local interest has doubled the initial size of a low-rise office building in a parklike suburban area. This is the office parks division. It is impossible to list the scope and range of Joseph C. Canizaro Interests in this space. When asked of his objectives in his many-sided activities, perhaps Mr. Canizaro summed it up best when he said: "I have an ambition of having one of the most successful, completely diversified, fully integrated, high-quality real estate companies in the country. We would acquire land, construct the buildings, and rent them on long-term leases, because our object is to develop long-term cash flow for such properties."

Then he added: "We're a big company, and we're going to get bigger." What JCCI has already accomplished would indicate what Mr. Canizaro predicts for the future merits respect.

CHART HOUSE INC.

From the evening it opened in October 1974, this restaurant has been a success in a city of long-established famous restaurants. But Chart House, shown here, on the French Quarter corner of Chartres and St. Ann streets, with its entrance facing New Orleans's famous Jackson Square, is more than just another good place to eat. It is an establishment that demonstrates the know-how of a long-established Louisiana-based company which has become nationally successful by providing Americans who want to eat out with a selection of restaurants and with prices to accommodate a variety of family budgets.

New Orleans's Chart House, which opens only evenings for dinner, is one of 43 enterprises of Chart House Inc., the parent company based in Lafayette, Louisiana. Beginning far west in Hawaii, Chart House restaurants are spread across the United States in cities where patrons expect to find restaurants that provide quality food in handsome decor quietly served by well-trained staffs. The most easterly Chart House is a new one in the tourist-oriented Virgin Islands.

Like the New Orleans restaurant in the French Quarter, all Chart Houses are painstakingly built on equally expensive sites. The restoration architecture of a number of New England Chart Houses has won architectural awards. The Louisiana-based parent company, which generated sufficient capital to acquire the Chart House chain when there were only 17 restaurants, was then known as Self-Service Restaurants Inc. This was in 1969, six years after William E. Trotter II, now chairman of the board of the company, and his brother James M. Trotter, now retired, bought a Burger King hamburger outlet at 3735

On Jackson Square in the French Quarter, Chart House has the most historic address in New Orleans, and has itself become historic by association.

Airline Highway in Metairie, Louisiana. It was after Trotter and his associates increased their Burger King outlets to 25 that the company went public, that is, offered stock to investors in something better than a gold mine. After all, you can't eat a gold mine.

When Trotter acquired his first Burger King outlet, the corporation was still owned by its founders, two young restaurateurs in Miami who were operating 274 stores, as these food outlets are termed. In 1967 the two founders sold out to the Pillsbury flour company for $18 million. Then, in the winter of 1970, Self Service learned five franchises, who had 66 stores and a 99-year lease in Illinois territory that included Chicago, wanted to sell. Rather dramatically, Trotter arrived in Chicago during a snow storm and bought it all for $8 million. Equally interested in the Illinois properties, the Pillsbury Burger King Corporation arrived next day to learn there was a faster fast food company in Louisiana.

It was along about this time that Self-Service Restaurants Inc. bought two steak house chains—Chart House and Cork 'n Cleaver—and changed its corporate name to the more identifiable Chart House Inc. As by far the largest Burger King franchise, Chart House Inc. offered $100 million for the whole corporation, which the Pillsbury owners declined.

The number increases every year, but in 1980 Chart House Inc. was operating nationally 277 Burger King outlets, 67 Cork 'n Cleaver steakhouses, and 43 Chart House restaurants. More recently the company has announced the acquisition of several Luther Barbecue Restaurants in Houston, and the conversion of a number of Cork 'n Cleaver restaurants into another new dish on the menu— Cisco's Mexican Food.

More and more this Louisiana-based company is offering Americans a wide variety of good things to eat—and at prices to fit any purse.

CHEVRON U.S.A. INC.

Commencing some 70 million years ago, the Mississippi River began dumping its effluents and sediment over what was to become Louisiana and the Gulf offshore continental shelf, thus creating geological formations which were to make Louisiana one of the most prolific producers of oil and gas in the 20th century.

As the United States emerged from the post-World War I era and the Great Depression of the 1930s, one branch of a company that was to become known as Chevron expanded its search for hydrocarbons from Montana through the western states, to west Texas, then to east Texas and Louisiana, eventually establishing headquarters in New Orleans in June 1941.

The New Orleans-based company was first known as The California Company, a wholly owned subsidiary of Standard Oil Company of California, one of the world's recognized leaders in oil and gas exploration and production and the pioneering that made it possible. When its headquarters was established in New Orleans in 1941, The California Company had a manpower count of 146 employees. By 1981 the company—then known as Chevron U.S.A. Inc., Eastern Region—had grown to 2,041 employees.

The Gulf Coast headquarters branch of Chevron has certainly been symbolic of the well-publicized commercial which in 1980 began expounding the claim that "Chevron was born on the frontier. And we're still there." The company, which enjoyed modest success in its early years as it worked its way to Louisiana, was to make a significant impact as it drew oil and gas from the Mississippi's deposits of eons ago and grew into a leader in the industry in the Gulf South.

In the early 1940s, Chevron developed the Delta Farms Field, west of Barataria, after another company had given up on its potential. The firm then moved into development of shallow inland fields, discovering the Lake St. John Field in Tensas and Concordia parishes, Louisiana, in 1942, followed by the Cranfield discovery in 1943 in Adams County, Mississippi, only a few miles away.

As the industry moved into the Gulf of Mexico, first into the shallow, protected bays and marshes and the challenges of water depths of 30 feet, Chevron was there—designing platforms, developing drilling methods, and solving transportation problems.

Among the company's early offshore successes were the discovery of Main Pass 69 Field near the mouth of the Mississippi River in 1948 and the Bay Marchand Field 70 miles to the west in 1949. These fields continued to produce into the 1980s. When the shallow inland fields and the close-in offshore fields commenced declining, Chevron continued to search in the deeper water offshore areas for oil and gas in the 1970s and 1980s.

In 1975 Chevron made the initial discovery in the deep Tuscaloosa sands of central Louisiana. Its discovery and production of gas from depths of nearly four miles initiated intense industry activity in this attractive onshore frontier. (See below.)

Chevron Place, opened in the summer of 1981, is a 21-floor office tower in the heart of New Orleans's central business district.

Chevron was also moving aggressively offshore and in 1979 placed a historic structure 140 miles off the coast of Louisiana in 685 feet of water, farther offshore than any domestic structure.

Chevron, because of its expertise in the offshore Gulf of Mexico, was providing the savvy and much of the initial manpower for development of some of the important deposits in the treacherous North Sea as this publication went to press.

Left
This schematic map shows today's mineral-rich Louisiana offshore, and the Tuscaloosa Trend, the equally mineral-rich Louisiana offshore 70,000 years ago.

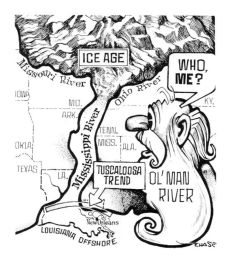

CHILDREN'S HOSPITAL

Had it not been for the determination of one woman, Children's Hospital of New Orleans, Louisiana's only full-service medical center exclusively for youngsters, would never have opened its doors in 1955.

Children's Hospital, today a 100-bed, not-for-profit teaching hospital serving thousands of inpatients and outpatients each year, sprang from the dreams and efforts of Elizabeth Miller Robin, daughter of a prominent New Orleans physician.

In the years following World War II, polio struck and cripped children in Louisiana as it did throughout the country. Mrs. Robin, herself a polio victim who had walked only on crutches, saw the need for a hospital to treat and rehabilitate these children close to home. She dreamed of a place designed just for children, where the newest developments in medicine would be practiced in an atmosphere of love and concern—a hospital where the child would be nurtured while being treated.

Determined that her idea would be more than a dream, Mrs. Robin enlisted the aid of doctors, the Louisiana Health Department, and social, business, and civic leaders in a citywide campaign to establish a hospital. In 1949 the Crippled Children's Hospital Corporation was chartered by the state as a nonprofit organization. One of its first actions was launching a capital funds drive.

Within a year of the charter, Mrs. Robin and the others who joined her as the hospital's founders saw the fruits of their labors. In 1950 they bought five acres at Henry Clay and Tchoupitoulas—a site which showed that the founders were thinking wisely of future growth.

In 1952 came the news that enabled construction to begin—a grant of $315,000 was awarded to the hospital. Another $600,000 was borrowed. A 5-year-old polio victim was guest of

Elizabeth Miller Robin, "fairy godmother" of all New Orleans children in need of medical care, died in 1967.

honor at groundbreaking ceremonies in 1953. Mrs. Robin's dream became a reality in 1955. The hospital she envisioned began giving the finest medical care to children needing to be rehabilitated from illness or injury.

The story of Children's Hospital since then is one of phenomenal growth and loving support from the statewide community. In the mid-1970s, Children's became a medical-surgical hospital as well as a rehabilitation center, which by that time was renowned. It doubled in size from the original 50 beds.

Today at Children's Hospital, a medical staff of nearly 300 pediatric specialists treat 3,000 inpatients and 16,000 outpatients each year. The therapy programs are acclaimed. A pediatric intensive care unit and skilled surgeons handle the most complicated illnesses and injuries. Children's pneumography service, the

only one of its kind in the region, helps detect babies prone to Sudden Infant Death Syndrome. A new unit to treat spinal injuries opened in 1981.

As a teaching hospital, Children's is the site of important research in pediatric medicine. Orthopedic techniques developed at Children's are used successfully to treat children throughout the world.

All of Children's growth has been achieved with Mrs. Robin's original idea in mind—commitment to the total child's needs. This growth would not have been possible without statewide community support. Children's remains a not-for-profit hospital governed by a board of trustees. Each year hundreds of volunteers give their gifts and their time.

Although Mrs. Robin died in the late 1960s, her dream thrives. As one of Louisiana's most beloved institutions, Children's Hospital is fast becoming a national leader in child health care.

Since Children's Hospital was founded in 1955, it has grown from a 50-bed rehabilitation center for handicapped children to a modern medical-surgical hospital of over 100 beds.

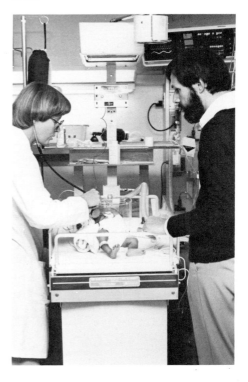

COOPER STEVEDORING COMPANY, INC.

Ervin S. Cooper, chairman of the executive committee.

In the 1920s Louisiana cattlemen were importing Brahman bulls to breed better traits into and inferior characteristics out of their herds. In 1925 one of these shipments of bulls broke loose at the Robin Street Wharf, stampeding all along the riverfront uptown and down.

It was a story that gained in the telling, and for a while everybody in the port, as well as affected nearby residents, were telling the story. One account reported a bull 70 blocks uptown in Audubon Park, which was possible. But another story has a Brahman trying to break into Antoine's Restaurant in the French Quarter, and being personally discouraged by the president and founder of the Cooper Stevedoring Company, Inc. This story is unlikely. Everybody in New Orleans knows you can't get into Antoine's Restaurant without a reservation, or

standing in line. But the bulls did break loose and run here and there, a fact that Angus R. Cooper, Sr., spent the rest of his life trying to forget.

He started stevedoring in 1908, and spent some years serving as gulf superintendent of stevedoring for the Munson Steamship Line, then headquartered in New Orleans. Later, his two sons, Robert and Ervin, joined him. Ervin, jointly with his two sons, Angus II and David, are now sole stockholders in the corporation, which has expanded to 19 Gulf, Pacific, and Atlantic seaports.

Ervin S. Cooper, whose picture is shown here along with his father's, was chairman of the company's executive committee at this writing, with corporate headquarters in Mobile, Alabama. Some say Mr. Cooper thoughtfully moved his headquarters to Mobile because Mrs. Cooper was a Mobile girl, although he, himself, is a high school graduate from Warren Easton in New Orleans, picked up a business administration degree from Tulane, and then worked six years on the riverfront for Munson and Alcoa before entering the family stevedoring business.

Representing the third generation, Angus R. Cooper II, his son, is now chairman and maintains his executive offices in the International Trade Mart on the Mississippi River.

In the company's early history, its founder's experience in stevedoring was wide and varied, handling on a regular basis such cargoes as sugar, sisal, hemp, bagged goods, packing house products, farm implements, machinery, lumber, cotton, pineapples, poles, piling, and livestock—although after 1925 Brahman bulls were viewed with some suspicion. With such a mass of break-bulk cargoes, it is understandable how he became the first to introduce the use of lift trucks in stevedoring. These first were platform-type lifts, forerunner of the more efficient fork lifts widely used in 1981. It is interesting, too, that when the first Angus started the business, longshoremen received 24 cents

an hour, as compared with the 1981 pay of $11.60 an hour.

Cooper Stevedoring Company, Inc., still handles its share of a variety of break-bulk cargoes, even more than it did three generations ago. But it has also been organized to handle the more modern bulk containerized and LASH shipments, involving the use of barges, cranes, and all the other modernized stevedoring techniques.

Angus R. Cooper, founder of Cooper Stevedoring.

DALTON STEAMSHIP CORPORATION

Just as antebellum cotton factors took care of all the requirements and needs of their client planters on remote plantations, so nowadays do steamship agencies act as branch offices for the steamship lines—mostly foreign-based—they are contracted to serve. Since its founding August 1, 1956, such a role has been that of Dalton at the Port of New Orleans.

But, in many ways, this firm has grown since John H. Dalton, who had been working for steamship companies since he graduated from high school, decided to do it alone, all by himself. It all began in a modest Queen & Crescent building office with six employees and an owner who assumed responsibility for an annual payroll of approximately $75,000.

Obviously, John H. Dalton didn't just sit around that office waiting for his ship to come in. Almost 25 years'

This 19th-century New Orleans office building, on Union Street in the heart of the financial district, was purchased by the Dalton company in 1970. It has been completely renovated, inside and out, to serve as the firm's headquarter offices. Dalton's preservation efforts seem to have inspired others in the neighborhood into renovating their old buildings, too.

accomplishments include corporate headquarters in his own New Orleans building, with supporting offices in the cities of Mobile, Baton Rouge, Port Arthur, Beaumont, Galveston, Houston, Dallas, and Memphis. Those six original employees had grown to well over 100 by 1980, with a combined payroll of all divisions of several million dollars.

Dalton Steamship is currently in the second generation with John H. Dalton, Jr., as president. The founder is now chairman of the board, but still keeps a watchful eye on the entire operation. After 50 years, the steamship blood is still present in the senior Mr. Dalton.

It was early in the history of this family-owned and -operated company that stevedoring facilities were added through two affiliates. Texas Stevedores, Inc., would handle the four Texas ports, with Louisiana Stevedores, Inc., to serve the ports of New Orleans, Mobile, and Baton Rouge. For its principals—clients are so termed in steamship parlance— Dalton is organized to handle all manner of cargoes, with equipment to provide all services required of modern stevedoring operations. In addition, in years past, Dalton stevedoring operations have provided many tractors to pull parading Mardi Gras floats.

Numbered among Dalton's current principals are the prestigious Japanese-owned N.Y.K. Line; Yugoslavia's Jugolinija Line; the Medafrica fleet; Polish Ocean Line; Turkish Cargo Line; Frota Amazonica of Brazil; and the Span-Chile service. In the late '60s and early '70s, thousands of tons of newsprint were handled by Dalton for the Finnlines providing paper to the *Times-Picayune*. This relationship resulted in John Dalton, Sr., being appointed the Honorary Consul of Finland at New Orleans.

The Port of New Orleans is the city's leading industry, and for the past 25 years Dalton Steamship has been an integral part of this industry.

DAMERON-PIERSON COMPANY, LTD.

In 1904 this company opened its first store at 317 Camp Street, and advertised it had for sale "everything for the office." It's hard to believe that Frank Dameron and J. Ogden Pierson thought they had picked the very best neighborhood in New Orleans to do just that.

Seemingly they had. Six years later a 6-story building was constructed to suit their needs and future growth, and the company moved into 400 Camp Street, corner of Natchez, which they subsequently bought—along with four smaller buildings directly behind it on Natchez Street. A 100,000-square-foot storage warehouse back of town on South Broad Street completes present-day Dameron-Pierson's facilities as the largest office furnishings and commercial stationery company in Louisiana.

For good reason, in 1978, the Central Business District Historic Landmarks Commission marked for preservation this neighborhood bounded by Camp and Tchoupitoulas from Common to Poydras, naming it "Picayune Place Historic District." It was the first area in the city settled by Americans. In the 1930s, when its riverfront was booming with record-breaking steamboat trade from up the Mississippi River Valley that was mak-

ing New Orleans rich, James H. Caldwell owned most of this area. In 1833 he cut the street named Natchez through his property, enabling Thomas Banks to build his "Ar-

Then as now, stationery was a large part of the company's business. Photograph circa 1919.

cade"—the city's first office building—on Magazine Street between Gravier and Natchez.

Later Caldwell opened a second street between Gravier and Natchez which was first called Banks for Thomas, then Bank when it became the rear entrances of two banks facing Magazine Street. Dameron-Pierson was already founded when the street's name was changed to Picayune Place, because it was the back door of the *Daily Picayune,* first newspaper on "Newspaper Row." Here, Camp Street was so called for a long time.

In its beginning, Dameron-Pierson was one of the first businesses on Camp between Gravier and Poydras that wasn't a newspaper. But it has survived to see them all either go away or go broke. Indeed, one of the company's smaller buildings on Natchez was formerly the home of the *Daily Item* one year after its founding in 1877 at the other end of Picayune Place in a barroom on Gravier Street.

Jack L. Becker, 36-year veteran in office furnishings, is the sixth president of Dameron-Pierson at this writing. Along with vice-presidents Carl J. Lavie, Lester J. Bourgeois, and Jack L. Becker, Jr., he heads a management

that directs a staff of 95, which includes 14 general-line outside salesmen, one contract salesman, and five full-time interior designers.

Compared with its ancient delivery truck pictured here, today the company maintains a fleet of 14 vehicles including six trucks to handle Dameron-Pierson's still important stationery business. Important, too, are the services it maintains in printing, engraving, lithography, and book binding. As for its office furnishings, over the years Dameron-Pierson had continually remodeled and increased its display area which now totals considerably over 9,000 square feet.

And should anyone suspect the neighborhood of its founding has not remained good for the company's business, Pan-American Life should remove all doubt. In 1980 this longtime good customer moved back into the neighborhood, building a handsome 28-story skyscraper across the street and engaging Dameron-Pierson to provide "everything for the office" on the seven floors the insurance company reserved for its own use. President Becker has indicated he wouldn't be surprised if this wasn't the largest such order in New Orleans history.

The upper floors of the Dameron-Pierson building are devoted to printing, lithography, and embossing departments and furnishings display areas.

DRUMM AND ASSOCIATES, INC.

In 1967, Streuby L. Drumm, Jr., formed Drumm and Associates to service a growing interest in apartment rental properties as major real estate investments. In 1968, he interested a group of Orleanians as investors in the purchase of a 300-unit apartment complex in Metairie, with an option for adjacent acreage. From this beginning Drumm and Associates has grown steadily in importance as buyer and manager of garden apartment complexes in the New Orleans area, as well as in Houma, Lafayette, Baton Rouge, Lake Charles, and Shreveport. Additional interests in the state of Mississippi include locations in the cities of Jackson, Vicksburg, and Greenville. Dorothy M. Elliot, a vice-president of the firm Drumm and Associates, supervises all management activities of these properties. The firm's most remarkable and ambitious project is Poydras Plaza. Drumm and Associates is responsible for the leasing, with vice-president R. Stephen Hogan designated as director of marketing and leasing.

Towering, gleaming Poydras Plaza is all the more remarkable because, before the Civil War, this corner marked the entrance into the city's more disreputable neighborhood which Orleanians called the "City of

With obvious satisfaction, president Streuby L. Drumm and two of his vice-presidents, Dorothy M. Elliot and R. Stephen Hogan, view a scale model of Poydras Plaza.

the Damned." But a few entered the low and swampy forbidding place, infested with alligators and overgrown with dismal willows wailing their plaintive sounds with every gust of wind. The community looked upon the place as unhallowed ground, so often the scene of foul deeds. It was long shunned for residential purposes. Before it became a street, Poydras was a canal that drained the city into this swamp—or tried to.

But time passes, things change. Soon Charity Hospital was built in the area, along with medical schools and two universities. The City Hall and Civic Center followed. Then the Illinois Central Railroad sold the state most of a 60-acre tract it had long

An example of the thousands of apartment units this company manages and owns in part. In 1981, one such complex was converted into condominiums. Sales were so brisk other conversions are planned.

owned for construction of the Louisiana Superdome. Drumm and Associates learned that 10 acres on Loyola, between Poydras and Girod, weren't sold and were available. No time was lost interesting the Ayrshire Corporation of Houston, as well as the Prudential Insurance Company of America and the owners of the Hyatt Hotels in the site.

These three national concerns began with the 1,200-room Hyatt Regency Hotel, which opened in 1976, followed by the 400,000-square-foot Amoco Building in 1977, with the oil company and Travelers Insurance Company leasing 70 percent of its space. Two years later a 24-story, 500,000-square-foot building called "1250 Poydras" appeared next to Amoco to become the New Orleans headquarters for the Mobil Oil Corporation. In the spring of 1981 a third major office building of 28 stories and a 5-story, 800-car parking garage were announced for the site to be called "No. 1 Poydras Plaza."

The year 1981 marked the 14th anniversary of this firm, during which Drumm and Associates has set records in marketing and leasing new building office space in downtown New Orleans and in significant areas of real estate activity—large-scale garden apartment ownership and management and condominium conversions. Drumm and Associates, Inc., is well organized to continue a worthwhile contribution to the real estate economy in the areas of its operation.

DELTA STEAMSHIP LINES

Steamship Lines invited its 80 employees to the first-ever coffee break, now nationally observed. Delta had just imported the idea from Brazil.

At the time, the Delta Line was only 11 years old. It was chartered March 24, 1919, as the Mississippi Shipping Company by some New Orleans businessmen interested in more regular importation of green coffee from Brazil. They were tired of depending upon tramp steamers. By 1980, Delta's fleet of 24 modern U.S.-flag vessels was providing regular service from the United States to all of South and Central America, and to the Caribbean and West Africa as well—in all, 100 ports of call in 50 different countries. Delta had come a long way since the S.S. *Bound Brook,* the company's first ship, cleared port at New Orleans on August 12, 1919, bound for Rio.

Strangely, back in 1914, the hiring of a Republican in Iowa to manage the New Orleans Joint Traffic Bureau was to prove useful for the founding fathers of Delta. When civic-minded Theodore Brent arrived from Iowa, he lost no time registering to become a voter in the new community that would be his home. But to the amusement of his new friends he registered as a Repub-

With a payload of passengers as well as cargo aboard (note the containerized cargo neatly tucked on deck aft), a Delta ship (above) of the Del Sud *class heads south. The map, at right, shows the dramatic growth of Delta sealanes from one coffee route in 1919 to hemispheric coverage by 1981. At bottom is the pioneering* Bound Brook, *first ship of Delta's fleet back in 1919.*

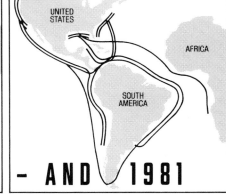

Free lunch was invented in New Orleans in 1837 by Philippe Alvarez, manager of the St. Louis Hotel Bar. It went on to become an institution of considerable national importance. However, after the repeal of Prohibition, bars reopened, but the free lunch counters didn't. The Depression in 1933 made it economically out of the question to provide a free lunch to every purchaser of a 15-cent drink. Besides, in 1933, even 15-cent drinks cost two bits.

But the coffee break—also invented in New Orleans—has fared better. At 3:30 p.m. on March 17, 1930, Delta

lican, as all Iowa voters did. In the then-solid South no Republicans ran for office; indeed, no Republican candidate for president had ever carried the South.

Then World War I broke out in Europe. Soon German U-boats were sinking Allied ships indiscriminately. Fortunately, early in 1917, the American Merchant Marine had no ships to sink. But by January 1917, the newly created United States Shipping Board was ready to meet. By law, it had to consist of three Democrats and two Republicans, all geographically located. Quickly, the Atlantic and Pacific posts were grabbed by the three Democrats and one Republican. President Wilson's McAdoo had to find a capable Republican for the Gulf Coast. Fortunately for the war effort, highly qualified Theodore Brent also qualified politically.

The shipping board performed miracles. At war's end the United States had a surplus of 700 ships, and it became the board's job to encourage the formation of responsible shipping companies at various U.S. ports—companies that could use a few ships.

Although Brent had resigned from the board sometime earlier, he still had contacts. So he joined a group of founding fathers for a New Orleans shipping company, requesting a trade route to Brazil. Later, Brent would become Mississippi Shipping Company's president, and it was he who proposed the company's name be changed to Delta. In 1962 Delta became its corporate name.

On May 1, 1919, the newly chartered company started business with offices in the old Queen & Crescent Building on Camp Street, paying $55 a month rent. Its VIP businessmen board of directors included M.J. Sanders, T.F. Cunningham, R.S. Hecht, George W. Westfeldt, William B. Burkenroad, William P. Ross, and Theodore Brent. Due to a conflict of interest, Sanders resigned almost immediately. So it was Cunningham as president who toured the company's South American ports of call with

general manager P.O. Pedrick in 1921.

With such enterprising leadership, a steady increase in trade and the beginning of passenger service marked the company's early years. During World War II, Delta established a distinguished record, manning and operating 58 ships, losing two vessels and 81 lives to enemy action.

The postwar years witnessed further expansion. Three sleek passenger-cargo vessels—the S.S. *Del Norte, Del Sud,* and *Del Mar*—went into service. They won fame for luxurious travel in South America. In 1947 the first U.S.-flag liner service from Gulf ports to West Africa was instituted. It brought raw-material wealth to American markets and helped develop emerging African nations, providing reliable transportation for American-made industrial products.

Delta was also first to offer LASH service to South America. As its name implies—Lighters-Aboard-SHip—cargo-laden lighters and barges are lifted directly aboard motherships. Much heavy machinery and equipment cargoes for Brazil, Uruguay, Argentina, and Venezuela have been carried by Delta's ships over the years.

Symbolic of the Mississippi River Delta, where this story had its beginning, is Delta's proud insignia on the stacks of all its ships at sea.

In 1969 Delta was acquired by Holiday Inns, Inc. As a consolidated subsidiary, Delta was provided with a larger base for more growth, such as the acquisition in 1978 of certain assets of Prudential Lines, Inc., operators of the famous Grace Line routes to South America. With passenger service along the Pacific Coast serviced by four Santa Magdalena-class ships with accommodations for upward of 100 passengers, all first-class, with 18,500-mile-cruises circumnavigating South America, Delta's operations were increased dramatically.

While Delta corporate headquarters and Gulf Division operations remain in New Orleans, they have been joined by Atlantic and Pacific divisions, headquartered in New York and San Francisco.

With all this activity going on, it's time for another coffee break—but not one attended by the 80 employees who turned out in 1930. At the time of this book's publication, 1,900 Delta personnel were on hand to cater to the client's every wish.

Southward, ho!

CARLO DITTA, INC.

Carlo Ditta's family came to America from Sicily in the 1890s, ambitious, determined, and anxious for opportunity.

Carlo Ditta was a young man when he met and married Felicia Trupiano. He was working on his father's farm at the time. His wife provided encouragement for him to start his own business; he began selling stone coal in 1934. Soon he sold sand, gravel, and bag cement, followed by Sheetrock, pipe, paint, and bricks. In 1941 Ditta bought his first concrete mixer, a 2-yarder. Until 1942, when the Gretna plant was built, he operated out of a yard next to his home. In 1972 the company's present location was established.

A manufacturing plant on New Orleans's West Bank was expanding its local facilities in 1946. Carlo Ditta supplied the concrete and began a long history of continued growth for his company. When World War II ended, the ensuing construction boom resulted in increased growth and development of the West Bank. The territory Carlo Ditta serviced was from Hahnville to Belle Chasse; and as the

Carlo Ditta is seated, left, with Felicia Ditta in center behind small daughter. Hubert Junca and Roland Ditta are seen at far right. Photo was taken before the Gretna plant was built in 1946.

West Bank grew, so did Carlo Ditta, Inc.

The dynamic force behind the firm was Carlo Ditta. Energy, honesty, hard work, efficiency, good judgment, and integrity were his attributes. He became a local business and community figure associated with the local bank and homestead. He used that position to help people accomplish their dream of owning a home. As the West Bank became a new boom area of New Orleans in the late 1950s, he helped entrepreneurs in their ventures through counseling or financing, or both.

Carlo Ditta's presidency of the company ended with his death in 1962. The present executive vice-president, Joseph "Jay" Carlo Ditta, was only 27 years old when he assumed that position. Actually, Jay's career began as a boy when his father apprenticed him at his side. In all his activities he offers tireless energy and shrewd business acumen. Under his management Carlo Ditta, Inc., has grown to its present status of 35 ready-mix delivery trucks and two complete batch plant locations. The many area jobs undertaken have included the Mississippi River Bridge, Zen-Noh Grain Elevator, West Jefferson Hospital, West Jefferson School, Gretna Sheraton Hotel, Continental Grain Elevator, LaPalco Bridge, Crown Point Bridge, Harvey Canal Bridge, John Ehret High School, various subdivisions, and street paving

including the recent Stonebridge Subdivision.

The company's original facility, built at Richard Street in Gretna, was the setting of its operations for 30 years. It was such an efficient structure that it was used as the prototype for the conception by Jay Ditta and John Uhl of the new plant built at 1445 MacArthur Avenue in Harvey. This new plant is considered by experts in the industry to be one of the finest of its kind. Based on efficiency and mechanization, it offers eight acres of modern facilities for producing more than 200 yards per hour of quality concrete. Through the latest in computerized batching, the plant performs the receiving and distribution of materials, raw ingredients which combine to form, in various quantities, the product called concrete. In addition, fuel is received and distributed into trucks through computer. With the push of a button, silos are filled from truck delivery into waiting concrete mixers. A 50-ton-capacity automatic ice plant has been installed recently to attain the temperature control required to ensure the high strength needed in concrete for such jobs as the Mississippi River Bridge.

It would be impossible to achieve the high-quality concrete produced by Carlo Ditta, Inc., without the talents of John Uhl, graduate of LSU with degrees in physics and chemistry, and ACI board member. His deals with the

This is the present-day, spacious Ditta concrete plant in Harvey, especially designed for operational requirements.

The family-owned company officers are (from left to right) Mrs. Rosalyn Weinstein, board member; Jay Ditta, executive vice-president; Mrs. Carlo Ditta, president; Mrs. Phyllis Woolfolk, treasurer; and Mrs. Lillian Uhl, secretary.

production and delivery of concrete, a field he keeps abreast of through continuing education. As general overseer of technical and maintenance functioning, John Uhl approaches the subject of concrete as a science and the customer has gained the benefits of his knowledge. He has achieved success in creating mix designs for the widest range of job specifications and continues to experiment with their endless possibilities.

The leadership of the company includes the president, Felicia Ditta, wife of the founder. Still active in policy making and diplomacy, she has played an active and vital role in the business from its founding until present. Her energy is boundless.

There are many important names who have had influential roles in the history of Carlo Ditta, Inc. The operational management includes an endless list of dedicated employees who have 30 to 40 years' service with the company. Among them are Roe Ditta, Carlo's brother, and Hubert Junca. Many of the drivers and yard employees began with Carlo in the

firm's beginning.

The oldest company member and most valued asset is its reputation, long established by Ditta. The most modern equipment available, the expertise of skilled employees, and a low-cost product backed by guaranteed quality all contribute to this company, which continues to look to the future.

Carlo Ditta II, representing the fourth generation has been active in

sales and management for the past four years. The namesake of the founder, the young man is the hope of the firm's future. Perhaps his brother, Joseph Carlo II, or one of the 13 other Ditta grandchildren will continue to provide leadership through ability and tradition.

The plant chemist is John Uhl (left), married to Lillian Ditta. Carlo Ditta II is at right.

EXXON COMPANY, U.S.A.

The year was 1901. Only eight months after Spindletop, an oil well near Jennings gushed in to establish coastal Louisiana's mineral potential. The following year, Standard Oil Company—a predecessor of what is now known as Exxon—brought in its first production in the area at Anse La Butte east of Lafayette.

Then and now, some three-quarters of a century later, the people of Louisiana and Exxon, as well as others mentioned in this last chapter, truly have been partners in progress.

Returning to the dawn of the 20th century, three years after production began at Anse La Butte, another Exxon predecessor participated in a major discovery in Caddo Parish. And for the next 40 years, Louisiana and Exxon continued their partnership in numerous major investments throughout southern Louisiana—investments that included finding and developing entire oil fields as well as constructing a huge refinery in Baton Rouge for turning oil and gas into products used every day.

The late 1940s brought Louisiana and Exxon to the frontier of offshore oil and gas exploration and production, a bonanza the state and the company continue to share ... in a number of ways.

Exxon people will tell you they feel fortunate to have the opportunity to operate in Louisiana. Likewise, Louisiana coffers are pleased to receive one-eighth of every barrel of oil taken from state lands. And other companies, too numerous to name, ranging from industry giants to family businesses, are a part of Louisiana's economy as a direct result of the state's oil production. These businesses lend support to companies like Exxon which, as of this writing, had drilled wells in more than 60 oil fields and outfitted more than 70 offshore platforms. And each of these "service" companies hires people, pays salaries, and pays taxes. And speaking of taxes, Exxon has paid close to a billion dollars to the state in taxes, alone.

So, the ripple effect from the development of Louisiana's oil

reserves by Exxon, the other oil-producing companies, and the many oilfield service companies that support the oil-finding and oil-producing efforts, is almost too pervasive to calculate. Suffice it to say that it would take a bigger book than this to try to cover it and its turn-of-the-century roots.

Louisiana and Exxon have come a long way since that early discovery opened their long and mutually beneficial partnership. A new 22-story building at 1555 Poydras in the shadow of New Orleans's Superdome attests to a confidence that the relationship is still going strong. The building, scheduled for completion in 1982, is the new home of Exxon's Southeastern Exploration and Production divisions, a committed partner in a state blessed with a treasure beneath its soil.

Across Poydras Street from the Superdome, this is Exxon's new building, scheduled for completion in 1982.

Exxon's first office building in New Orleans was located at St. Charles and Jackson avenues. Photograph circa 1919.

FAVROT AND SONS

The 15th of April, in 1718, has been fixed as the official day of New Orleans's founding by Bienville. In March 1721, the first census reported as many as 40 houses in addition to the company's warehouse. To Louisiana in 1728 came Claude Joseph Favrot, a cadet in the King of France's service. In New Orleans were found living quarters although family records do not mention where, and a family raised.

Claude's son Pierre Joseph Favrot, known as Don Pedro, was in Governor Galvez's army at the Battle of Baton Rouge in 1779 where he distinguished himself, and later built "Monte Vista," the Favrot plantation at Port Allen, dying there in 1824. Two generations later the Favrots returned to New Orleans when Charles A. Favrot established himself as architect, property owner, and civic leader. His sons, Clifford F. Favrot and Gervais F. Favrot, (see Gervais Favrot's biography in this chapter) represent a sixth generation of Louisiana Favrots.

Clifford's four sons, Clifford Jr., Thomas, Allen, and Blair, represent a seventh generation and, along with their progeny of 16, comprise the current generation for whom the Carondelet Realty Corporation was made possible with holdings that originated in the family as far back as the '30s.

The acquisition of properties began in 1936, when Clifford's wife, Agnes Guthrie Favrot, purchased the family's first apartment. By the mid-1940s she and Clifford had acquired four additional residential properties in uptown New Orleans. The first noteworthy acquisition, the Carondelet Building, a downtown office building, was purchased in 1950 and ended up in the original family corporation, which for a time was owned exclusively by Clifford F. Favrot and his eldest son.

Real estate was only a sideline at this time however, as Clifford and his

Captain Pedro Favrot was 45 years old and a veteran of over 23 years in the Louisiana Regiment when this portrait was painted.

younger sons were principals of the Asbestone Corporation, a roofing manufacturing operation. In late 1952 this firm was sold and the family entered the real estate market exclusively. Having a successful business career enabled Favrot Sr. to devote a great deal of time to beneficial civic projects for which his fellow citizens have made him recipient of many awards, including the *Times-Picayune* Loving Cup. Tulane University, his alma mater, conferred upon him the honorary degree of doctor of science.

The four brothers formed the Palmetto Realty Corporation in 1954, the Orleanian Corporation in 1956, and their children acquired the Carondelet Realty Corporation. The '50s and '60s marked a period of solid residential and commercial real estate expansion for the Favrot family business. The Carondelet Building was sold in 1969 and since then no additional acquisitions have been made by the corporations. Individual family members, however, continued to acquire other major real estate holdings in various locations throughout the greater New Orleans area. The family owns and operates a light industrial site, the Maritime Building (the city's first highrise) and 1,500 apartment units (spread between 10 apartment complexes), all of which represent living and working accommodations for more than 3,000 people.

Today, the four brothers and their wives continue in the tradition of their forefathers by being involved in a wide range of community activities. The younger brothers have served as chairmen and on the boards of many noted national and local organizations.

The family's civic activities represent years of dedication to the city of New Orleans. The family's real estate interests attest to their continued support of the city's business and financial development. The Favrots' current properties offer accommodations to more people than the entire city could offer the patriarch of this family in the 1700s, when he first came to New Orleans house hunting.

GERVAIS F. FAVROT COMPANY

Gervais F. Favrot's excellent reputation reflects its high standards of integrity. Over the recent past, as more expensive jobs have come into the New Orleans market, the company has had no difficulty in increasing its bonding capacity to meet the needs of growth. Bonding companies know that Favrot will get the job done.

Developers have also shown confidence in the company by negotiating many jobs based on a guaranteed maximum price, and now developers are showing increasing interest in Favrot's method of negotiating jobs on a team basis. In this system, architects, engineers, and major subcontractors cooperate with the owners and Gervais F. Favrot Company in the initial and continuing plans for a given project. This enables the owners to get advice from experts and thus obtain the utmost in efficient use of materials and the utmost in economy.

Integrity is one reason why many owners have returned to Gervais F. Favrot Company with repeat construction business. Whether a client's project costs $100,000 or $50 million, Gervais F. Favrot Company guarantees its work will be completed in accordance with plans and specifications. All employees take special pride in their work and know the quality standards they are expected to maintain.

In addition to direct client responsibility, the executives and employees are active in local community and trade organizations. The executives consistently hold positions of authority in the New Orleans AGC and this helps them assure high standards for the entire industry.

Gervais F. Favrot's reputation rests on skill, integrity, and responsibility. Whether a prospective client wants to build a bridge, a wharf, a shopping center, a hospital, New Orleans's tallest building, or a bomb shelter—chances are Gervais F. Favrot Company has built something like it before.

No developer's problems are new to Favrot, and no New Orleans construction company can top the experience Gervais F. Favrot Company has gained in over 60 years of building. No one can duplicate Favrot's expert management teams, and no one can duplicate the variety of projects and special jobs Favrot has successfully completed.

Shown here are Gervais F. Favrot and One Shell Square, largest of some 200 buildings constructed by Gervais F. Favrot Company.

FIRST HOMESTEAD FEDERAL SAVINGS & LOAN ASSOCIATION

sociations," "mutual loan associations," and "homesteads."

In England, in 1781, the first members of the movement were called "building societies," in spite of the fact that *homestead* is of Old English origin. The original word was *hamstede* and it meant "home-place." Obviously, *homestead* is the most apt derivation.

was named president. The antebellum building, shown here, has been First Homestead's main office since 1978. It is also proof of the homestead's abiding interest in preservation. As Marsiglia puts it, "It pencils out a display of our involvement in the renovation of our community."

Inside, the office decor is contemporary. Consumer readouts underscore

The historic marker on this building tells us that it was the site of the city's first Protestant church in 1811. After it burned in 1851, Judah Touro had this building erected. First Homestead has faithfully restored its antebellum facade for its main office.

Only in New Orleans are centers of 2-lane streets called "neutral grounds." Only in Louisiana are the state's counties called "parishes." And only in New Orleans and Louisiana was the first savings and loan association called "homestead."

First Homestead is *first* because it stems back to the People's Homestead founded September 14, 1882. This was the very time the homestead movement, which had begun in England 100 years earlier, hit its stride in America. The early U.S. ones were variously called "savings and loan as-

So it was on March 4, 1938, that the People's, Crescent City, and Acme Homesteads merged and changed the name to First Homestead. "Why did you join together?" Herman C. Steger, last president of Acme and first president of First, was asked. "I guess," he replied logically, "we thought together we would be bigger." Steger had spoken with more foresight than anyone dreamed back then.

There were 20 employees when the three homesteads became one. Today employees number in the hundreds. One office has grown to 12, with more planned. Still growing, too, are the company's assets, which amounted to $4 million in 1938. In 1981, they were approaching $.5 billion.

Steger, who has spent his life homesteading, was made chairman of the board in 1972, and John V. Marsiglia

the front-running leadership of Marsiglia. "Here," he points out, "it's the customer who is First." The 1981 addition of interest-paying checking accounts completes the basic philosophy of Marsiglia that "homesteads are for people, banks for businesses." Numerous services have been "first" at First Homestead: drive-up windows, 24-hour checking service, safety deposit boxes, free travel checks, and many other innovations, all topped by the posh Statesman's Club on the fourth floor. Membership is free to depositors who have $10,000 on deposit.

Indeed, Marsiglia's idea of being "more consumer-oriented" has made giant strides in "signing up" the community, and his new "savings and loan" philosophy—to use that Yankee term for "homestead."

FIRST NATIONAL BANK OF COMMERCE

The bank that ultimately became the First National Bank of Commerce has occupied the N.B.C. Building, a business district landmark, since 1927.

The stirring sounds of "Dixie" could serve as the theme song of a billion-dollar New Orleans institution, the First National Bank of Commerce, as well as a nostalgic paean to the antebellum South.

In fact, it was from the 10-dollar bill issued by a forebear bank of First National Bank of Commerce that the patriotic air of the Confederacy took its name. On the back of the bank note issued by Citizens Bank was printed in large letters the word *dix,* which meant "ten" to residents of New Orleans, where French still was the everyday language in the early decades of the 19th century.

The dix (outside of New Orleans, Americans did not know it properly was pronounced "dee") became the most popular form of currency along the Mississippi River. Boat crews were remunerated with the bills at the last stop before New Orleans, and "dixies" became a symbol for payday. "Dixieland" was the lower Mississippi, celebrated in the song written for New York music halls years before it was appropriated by the Rebels.

Another predecessor financial institution was the New Orleans Canal and Banking Company, which was chartered on March 5, 1831, the same year in which Citizens Bank was formed. The Canal and Banking Company's charter provided that it would construct a canal connecting Lake Pontchartrain with the business district. For years, until it was filled in during the 1940s, the busy New Basin canal had its terminus near the site where the Louisiana Superdome now stands.

By the 1920s, the Canal had become the nation's 19th largest bank. It absorbed Citizens Bank in 1924 after having acquired Provident Bank and Louisiana National Bank in 1905; German-American National Bank in 1914; and Commercial Trust and Savings Bank in 1919. In 1928, the Marine Bank and Trust Company was merged into the Canal.

The Canal did not reopen after the bank holiday in February 1933, although it was solvent. Depositors were paid, with interest, and shareholders formed several large and successful companies as lands foreclosed by the bank produced oil and sugar. On May 22, 1933, the National Bank of Commerce in New Orleans was founded, with shareholders, officers, directors, and quarters of the Canal, along with $17 million of the former bank's deposits.

In 1971, National Bank of Commerce was renamed First National Bank of Commerce, the property of a holding company, the First Commerce Corporation. On its way to becoming the second largest bank in Louisiana, First National Bank of Commerce constructed a business district landmark, the Commerce Building. By 1980 the bank had nearly 1,000 employees, and operated 16 branches.

Financing arranged by the bank made possible the construction of the Louisiana Superdome. Civic-minded First National Bank of Commerce officials plan to carry on the bank's 150 years of active involvement with the development of the New Orleans area.

Dixieland took its name from this 10-dollar bill issued by the predecessor of the First National Bank of Commerce. The French word for "ten" was dix, and "dixies" became the most popular form of currency along the Mississippi River.

FITZGERALD ADVERTISING, INC.

This agency was founded December 27, 1926, by Clifford L. Fitzgerald and Joseph L. Killeen, Sr., with an objective to provide southern manufacturers with the type of marketing and advertising skills then available only in the larger northern cities. More importantly, they were determined to establish a concept of inventiveness to guide their agency's marketing and creative strategy.

The agency was named for Fitzgerald, and he became its first president. However, within 10 years he left to join what is now the Dancer-Fitzgerald-Sample agency in New York, and Joseph L. Killeen, Sr., was named president—a position he held for 30 years.

Perhaps the progress of this longest-standing advertising agency in the mid-South is best told by recalling some of the strategies that established Fitzgerald's reputation over the years, such as its highly successful campaign for Alaga Syrup back in the 1940s and 1950s. Services of such black superstars as Willie Mays, Nat King Cole, and Hank Aaron were engaged. In a series of national ads, each was pictured saying, "I was raised on Alaga syrup." This early use of testimonial advertising made Alaga a household word.

Another account which prospered from its Fitzgerald association was a salad oil named Wesson. The agency invented the concept that the product could be promoted for frying. Soon "Wesson Oil liquid shortening" was showing up in supermarkets next to Crisco, whose sales it eventually succeeded.

Back in the 1950s full-color advertising was new to magazines, and a half page was the minimum space offered. This posed a problem for another Fitzgerald account, the McIlhenny Company's Tabasco pepper sauce, which required only a one-column color ad to picture the famous red bottle. The Fitzgerald agency was able to persuade *McCall's* and *Ladies Home Journal* to accommodate the Tabasco requirement, and eventually all major magazines were offering "Tabasco-size" space.

In 1961 Fitzgerald merged with the Knox-Reeves agency of Minneapolis, and Roy M. Schwarz—a longtime Fitzgerald executive—became president until 1966. At that time the merger was dissolved, and the company was reincorporated with all stock being held by the Fitzgerald Advertising, Inc., people in New Orleans. Soon after this Schwarz resigned to head another local agency, and Joseph L. Killeen, Jr., was named president, a position he still holds.

The agency's talent for new, enterprising marketing ideas has continued bold as ever, as evidenced by the solution of a problem when a batch of Dixie Beer had an off taste. The trouble was soon corrected, but Dixie sales suffered for weeks. Fitzgerald suggested 60,000 six-packs to be delivered to New Orleans homes. The unusual treatment worked, and normal sales of Dixie beer were resumed.

Louisiana Power & Light, Inc., which has been a Fitzgerald client since 1933, was still profiting from the association in 1981—winning the first place PUCA award for superior achievement in utility communications nationwide. That same year the agency was named to represent Bulmer, Ltd., the largest cider makers in the world, just after it had been assigned to promote the 1984 Louisiana World Exposition.

Seemingly, at Fitzgerald, the more things change, the more they remain the same.

Shown left to right are Joseph L. Killeen, Jr., who is president with vice-presidents Ronald J. Thompson and Gary D. Dickson. Together they comprise the executive committee of the Fitzgerald Agency.

GALLAGHER TRANSFER AND STORAGE COMPANY, INC.

Over the years, as its contribution to the Mardi Gras Carnival, Gallagher Transfer has provided two teams preceding and following most major parades. Called "property wagons," they carry men and materials to repair any float that breaks down. Pictured here is a 1939 parade. (Nowadays the property wagons are motorized.)

Not until 12 years after William Gallagher established his company to move household goods in New Orleans was the city made safe from yellow fever. For the first 187 years of its history this dreaded disease had literally plagued New Orleans. Every summer there were cases, and periodically cases in epidemic proportions. The worst of these outbreaks was in 1853, when half the population was stricken and 7,849 people died. Not until 1905 did medical science discover that the aedes agypti mosquito spread the disease. Clamping down on this mosquito's breeding ended the yellow fever menace.

In 1893, when Gallagher's organization of one wagon and two mules began business, there wasn't much moving during the warm summer, from mid-June to mid-September. That was the yellow fever season, and nobody moved until October. When it became the custom to lease rental property, all leases ended September 30, and everybody moved October 1. On that day Gallagher usually started at daybreak, and was often moving people after nine at night. This October 1 custom prevailed in New Orleans until after World War II.

Gallagher prospered over the years, and many days were firsts of October for the company. Along with moving, he had added storage facilities, and, after experimenting with GMC electric vans, by 1930 had settled on motorized vehicles. He was organized to dominate the moving and storage business in the city, and much of the time he did.

After 46 years of moving people, and two years before his death, Gallagher sold the company to Paul Maloney, Jr., in 1939. The new owner retained the company's name and its headquarters in the 400,000-cubic-foot storage building at Magazine Street and Howard Avenue. In 1981 this building was still used by Gallagher, along with others at 520 Howard Avenue and 940 Magazine Street.

Continuing Gallagher's success, Maloney regularly added to the fleet and kept it modern. At this writing, the company operates a fleet of six tractor-trailer units in long-distance moving, six more such units assigned to intrastate and local service, backed up by an additional eight single-axle trucks. Six more cars and station wagons for sales and personnel service complete the total of Gallagher's rolling stock. All vehicles are radio equipped for fast, efficient service.

Since 1928 Gallagher Transfer and Storage Company, Inc., has been a charter member of the huge fleets of Allied Van Lines. Six of Gallagher's tractor-trailer units are assigned to this service, along with the units of 1,000 other agents nationwide, all controlled by a dispatcher centrally located in Omaha. Allied International provides another phase of moving service for Gallagher customers.

Just in time for the publication of this book, Gallagher movers moved themselves to a vast new complex spanning almost 11 acres on Elysian Fields, alongside Interstate Highway 10, with I-610 nearby. The company headquarters was established in a huge 1,560,000-cubic-foot storage facility of 60,000 square feet. A 70-foot public truck scale, public diesel-fuel facilities, a shop building for vehicle maintenance and service, as well as living quarters for on-the-site security personnel were in phases of construction as this book went to press.

Paul Maloney, Jr., died in 1978. He had been chairman of the board since his son, Robert S. Maloney, assumed the presidency in 1964. And so, with a third generation of experience presiding over a company never better equipped to provide service, and wisely located away from the clutter of downtown city traffic, Gallagher management should have no fear of rush periods, such as October 1 used to be. Even if October 1 should come every other day.

Robert S. Maloney, company president since 1964.

GEORGE ENGINE COMPANY, INC.

From a one-room warehouse on Picayune Place to a 31-acre facility on the Harvey Canal, George Engine Company, Inc., has grown from a firm established with an investment of $7,500 to a business with annual sales amounting to more than $125 million.

George S. Frierson, Jr., lived to see George Engine Company, Inc., which he founded in 1945, grow into one of the world's most successful diesel engine distributorships and the largest marine engine distributor for the Detroit Diesel Allison Division of General Motors.

The company's complex at 1401 Destrehan Avenue in Harvey is the nerve center for a global operation. The sun never sets on the engines, generators, turbines, transmissions, and related equipment sold by George

Engine. At any hour, in some corner of the world, the company's machinery is powering oil field workboats, shrimp trawlers, oyster luggers, menhaden seiners, and military patrol boats. In the Egyptian desert an oil company uses dust-tight diesel electric generators that can operate in sand storms and under the blistering sun.

In Central America, Peru, Brazil, and Saudi Arabia, sets designed by GECO engineers furnish electricity for remote villages. In the Himalayan foothills of Asia, George Engine power units operate at advance radar sites. In the United States, hospitals and radio stations depend on standby George Engine generators to pick up the load in the event of failure of the regular power source.

The oil industry relies heavily on

George Engine Company's new main plant in Harvey, Louisiana, with the New Orleans Central Business District in the background.

GECO equipment to power workover rigs, elevating boats, marsh buggies, pumps in barges, storage tank farms, and refineries. Allison transmissions distributed by George Engine make life easier for the drivers of 18-wheel highway vehicles, school buses, garbage trucks, and tractors.

Huge engines manufactured by ALCO Power, Inc., distributed by George Engine, and ranging in size up to 4,500 horsepower, drive ferryboats, self-propelled drilling rigs, and some of the tugs that transport drilling equipment thousands of miles in the ceaseless search for oil and gas.

It all started as World War II was ending, when George Frierson, Jr., won a New Orleans distributorship for General Motors diesel engines that had established a reputation by powering landing craft for the armed services. He expected fishing-boat operators to be his best customers, but the development of offshore oil and gas exploration and production in the Gulf of Mexico brought undreamed-of demands, and his company was on its way. By the time of his death in 1976, George Engine was playing in the major leagues of American business.

The company now has a work force of about 500 persons. In the modern, efficient main plant—which has 1,350 feet of dock facilities along the Harvey Canal—George Engine maintains an inventory of parts and components valued in excess of $10 million, and representing 20,000 line items. The company uses computers to keep its stock current.

An engineering department designs complete power systems for customers. All new Detroit Diesel engines are modified at Harvey before being delivered. More than 2,500 units per year are tailored to customer specifications.

In 35 years, George Engine has designed and financed more than 1,500 complete boats for its fishing and industrial customers. The firm was a pioneer in the development of both all-steel and all-aluminum crew boats for oil companies.

GERTRUDE GARDNER, INC., REALTORS®

This is the story of a Tennessee violinist, whose family moved to Decatur, Alabama, soon after her graduation from the Harriman Conservatory. Although she had also completed a business course and was studying commercial law in Tennessee, teaching the violin became her first avocation in Decatur.

That was before she met Warren G. Gardner, whose business was banking. He took a position with the Federal Land Bank in New Orleans. It was in the midst of the Great Depression. Many banks were in trouble, and Gardner was a specialist in aiding ailing banks. For a time Gertrude was a model housewife, engaged in social affairs, doing volunteer civic work, and properly raising their only child.

By 1945, after his tour in the U.S. Navy, her son Glenn was attending Tulane University and also traveling in amateur tennis circles. Glenn was 9th-seeded in national singles. Money was needed, and Gardner's salary at the bank was frozen then, so Gertrude recalled one of her favorite civic activities, that of finding homes for couples newly arrived in town. Perhaps one of the real estate brokers in New Orleans would pay her for doing what she liked to do, she mused, and a prominent New Orleans real estate firm took a chance on Gertrude with the following results—she was soon a leader in sales, and she was soon filing her resignation. "What," the broker said, "you're going into business for yourself, opening an office uptown, and you a woman?" He added that things simply weren't done like that in the real estate business. Gertrude left anyway.

What happened soon proved that Gertrude could also make beautiful music selling real estate. Economically using her home for her first office, she

In 1943, Gertrude Gardner founded the real estate agency that bears her name.

persuaded two girl friends, similarly interested in finding people homes, to become the first associates of Gertrude Gardner, Inc., Realtors. Soon she needed a banker more than the Federal Land Bank did, so she made her husband an offer the bank couldn't match. He became an important associate.

Never a standoffish person, Mrs. Gardner is affectionately called "Gertrude" by everyone, even her grandchildren. By 1981 her one-home office had become 11 offices, in five Louisiana parishes. "That's where the business is," Gertrude explains, "we sell all types of real estate, fast." Those first two associates now number more than 500, and sales volume over the past several years has amounted to hundreds of millions of dollars. Gertrude Gardner, Inc., is among the largest and most influential agencies in the state. And it would be difficult to list all of her personal accomplishments, as well as the numerous honors and awards she has received over the

Glenn M. Gardner, Jr., Gertrude's grandson, is president of Gertrude Gardner, Inc., Realtors.

years.

In the 3-generation history of this firm, nearly all of the members of the Gardner family have sold real estate. Young Glenn, after his naval tour of duty, came into the firm and was active in all phases, especially commercial sales, until his accidental death in 1963. At Christmastime in 1979, Gertrude announced she was becoming chairperson of the board, naming her grandson as president. "Yes, I've had considerable experience," president Glenn Gardner, Jr., will tell you. "Not only have I been licensed in real estate since 1969, but I also understand I was along with my mother when she closed a big deal two months before I was born." The chairperson has made no comment about this, but it's understandable that she would expect agents to get an early start, especially if they expect to become president some day. Gertrude is still very active in the business, working out of the uptown office daily.

GILLIS, ELLIS & BAKER, INC.

The Great Depression that began with the Wall Street crash of 1929 lasted until the outbreak of World War II in 1939. In the opinion of the president of this insurance agency, nobody could have chosen a lower point in that Depression to go into business than Gary E. Gillis, Jr., picked in the summer of 1933.

But Gillis had no alternative. He quit a job with the largest insurance agency in town because he thought it was about to fail. There were no other jobs to be had. So he rented a small office in the Carondelet Building, and persuaded his wife Carlotta to join the agency at no salary. After three tough months, sufficient funds were generated to hire a girl for the office, and Mrs. Gillis was free to stay home and raise two daughters, who would later become the wives of two presidents of the firm.

No city boy, Gary Gillis had been raised on sugar plantations around New Orleans and was knowledgeable of the sugar industry's problems and processes. So he made a trip to the sugar country, with the result that several mills gave him their accounts. This actually launched his agency and was to prove a factor in attracting John I. Hulse and W. Ferguson Colcock to join in sharing the responsibilities of the rapidly growing business. Under the name of Gillis, Hulse and Colcock, Inc., the company was established in larger quarters at 839 Union Street, where it would continue to grow.

In September 1952, after completing his second term as an officer in the U.S. Navy, Richard Parke Ellis, Gillis's son-in-law, joined the firm. Six years later, he would be followed by a second son-in-law, William Anderson Baker, Jr.

In 1957 New Orleans was shocked by the untimely death of the agency's founder. During his later years, Gary Gillis spent much of his time in civic work, giving initial support to the formation of the Bureau of Governmental Research, the Metropolitan Crime Commission, and Ochsner Foundation Hospital. "There were times," Mrs. Gillis recalls, "when Gary was spending half his time with the hospital's promotion. Dr. Ochsner was our friend and neighbor on Lowerline Street."

For a time following Gillis's death, Hulse served as president, and upon his retirement, vice-president Ellis succeeded him. Meanwhile, the agency was growing and prospering, specializing in commercial and institutional risks. In 1976 it moved to even larger quarters at 135 St. Charles Street and shortly thereafter changed its corporate name to Gillis, Ellis & Baker, Inc. Then, in 1980, the company once again suffered the loss of its president by death. Vice-president Baker was named the agency's fourth president.

"It is worth noting," Mrs. Gillis told us, "that all of our principals have been a very real part of the community, with great concern for the city's welfare and growth. All three of our presidents have served on, and often chaired, boards of many of the area's charitable and cultural institutions. We are proud to have been a partner in the progress that New Orleans has made in recent years."

William A. Baker, Jr., CPCU, was elected president of Gillis, Ellis & Baker in 1980.

Gary E. Gillis, Jr. (1902-1957), founded the firm known today as Gillis, Ellis & Baker, Inc., in 1933.

Richard P. Ellis joined the company in 1952 and served as president from 1972 until his death in 1980.

HIBERNIA NATIONAL BANK

Hibernia Bank opened for business on Camp Street, New Orleans, September 1, 1870.

In 1870, five years after Appomattox, New Orleans was counting seven of its 11 banks among its casualties. Also, the city would wait another seven years before the end of Reconstruction, with a greedy hoard of carpetbaggers still on hand preying upon its economy.

Corruption, political graft, and wasteful extravagance abounded. For instance, expenses for a regular session of the state legislature never cost more than $100,000 before the war. But a carpetbagger session had just voted nearly a million dollars for 90 do-nothing days. The governor promised to look into this excess. But Henry Clay Warmoth was no lily-white. It was common knowledge that he had already banked a million dollars out of his $8,000 annual salary. Things looked pretty hopeless for New Orleans, already bankrupt.

Nevertheless, on April 30, 1870, 12 Irishmen met in the Camp Street law office of Thomas Gilmore. It was the first meeting of the board of directors of a new bank to be called "Hibernia." Patrick Irwin was elected president, at no salary, and Gilmore was retained as attorney. Others on the board were Thomas Fitzwilliams, Hugh McCloskey, Edward Burke, William Hart, Nicholas Burke, Edward Sweeny, Adam Thomson, John Henderson, Thomas McKenna, and Edward Conery. Quarters were found on Camp Street and a staff of 10 was hired and trained. Everything was in readiness for the bank's opening on September 1, 1870.

Both the *Picayune* and the *Times* gave the opening front-page notice, predicting success due to the "well-known citizens ... of highest integrity and standing" on the board. Their names, the paper went on, would place the Hibernia on a footing with the finest banks in the country. Being human, the highly complimented directors led in almost immediately over-subscribing the capital stock of $300,000.

Historians suggest the very name of the bank not be underestimated in appraising its success at this time. The last census had reported the city's population at 168,675, of which 41 percent was foreign-born. And half of this group was born in Ireland, which the ancient Romans called "Hibernia" before the time of St. Patrick. Alas, when the line formed on that first day to open accounts, no records were

In 1877 the bank moved a block and a half down Camp, between Common and Canal.

available to tell us how many in the line were Irish. It's a good bet they turned out.

However, it is a matter of record that Orleanians in general turned out. The bank's growth was continuous and sound. Its four moves, always to larger quarters, were to addresses that stand as milestones marking Hibernia's progress. The site of its first tiny office on Camp just off Gravier is now part of the New Orleans Chamber of Commerce's building. After seven years it moved a block and a half down Camp, between Common and Canal. This remained Hibernia's address for 27 years. In 1907, it built its third home on Carondelet and Gravier, with 13 stories that made it the city's tallest building. Sixteen years later this became the Carondelet Building when—on October 17, 1921—the bank's some 300 employees moved across the street to a fourth home. Called "The Hibernia Tower," a city guide book of the time tells us "it is the highest point in New Orleans. With its 24 stories, it is the only observation point in the city."

The Hibernia is proud of its tower, but more interested in the growth of the city it serves. Now, in the 1980s, it is with satisfaction that one can view on every side of this one-time observation tower many other buildings towering twice as high as its 1921 point of view. Also by 1921, Hibernia branch banks could be spotted as they began to appear on the city's panorama—the first downtown, a second uptown, a third in Algiers, until by 1981 they numbered 15.

More recently, Hibernia's enduring pride in its tower has been evidenced by its adoption as the corporate symbol of the bank in 1979. Martin C. Miler, the bank's president at this time, remarked in his 1979 Christmas message to his fellow employees that the symbol was adopted because "it represents Hibernia to many generations of New Orleanians, which is why we chose it as our corporate identifier in this marketplace." Miler also commented in his letter, "We have again

Twenty-seven years later, in 1907, Hibernia built its third home, on Carondelet and Gravier. Its 13 stories made it the city's tallest building.

lighted the tower to reinforce our logo and our presence as a landmark institution on the skyline." The floodlighted tower has been highly complimented. (It deserves to be noted that the tower has served as the debut studio and antenna for the city's first television station in 1948, before those interfering higher-risers joined the skyline.)

But down on the ground Hibernia has always taken the view that things good for New Orleans were also good for the bank. From its early years, when Captain Eads's jetties reopened the Port of New Orleans, the Hibernia has played a front-running role in its development and in the foreign trade it has spawned. It is more than symbolic that a former president of Hibernia,

Rudolf S. Hecht, accepted the chairmanship of a group of civic leaders who in 1943 founded International House on Gravier and Camp, the first World Trade Center that numbered 30 worldwide by 1981.

As an institution that cut its baby teeth on the unsavory years of Civil War Reconstruction, it appears that the Hibernia must have been toughened to parry the onslaughts of any obstacles standing in the path of its Irish-oriented forward progress. And there have been a few of them. Floodings, hurricanes, strikes, two world wars—all of them have harrassed the New Orleans community since 1870. Then there was the Great Depression in the '30s. The Hibernia barely made it through with its name intact after reorganization subsequent to the Bank Holiday, but by 1959 president Wallace M. Davis was announcing the highest earnings in the bank's history.

And then, in emulation of that first board of directors who did so well in 1870, the directors of the Hibernia National Bank in 1973 inaugurated Martin C. Miler, a highly regarded young North Carolina banker, as Hibernia's new president. Seven years later the *Southern Banker Magazine* was chronicling Miler's leadership as "high performance banking," and characterizing the Hibernia as a "beehive on the Mississippi."

By all accounts it would appear that in New Orleans a venerable old bank is in progressive young hands. Not a bad way to close a generation gap.

On October 17, 1921, the bank moved across the street to its fourth, and current, headquarters.

D.H. HOLMES COMPANY, LTD.

This photograph of the facade of the D.H. Holmes Store on Canal Street was taken shortly after the merchant opened his business there in 1849. The company still occupies the same site, although the building has been greatly expanded.

"Meet me under the clock at Holmes'."

New Orleanians who grew accustomed to hearing their mothers and grandmothers make this arrangement with friends before donning hats and gloves for shopping expeditions may be surprised to learn that the clock at the entrance to the D.H. Holmes Company, Ltd., retail establishment at 819 Canal Street was not installed until 1913.

By that time the store had long since become a landmark. The emporium that Daniel Henry Holmes had opened at the site on October 15, 1849, had burgeoned into one of the South's busiest department stores.

Actually, the Ohio-born Holmes dated the start of his company from April 2, 1842, when he enlarged a dry goods and specialty shop at No. 22 Chartres Street. The enterprising merchant operated this store only during the cooler months, selling goods he accumulated on yearly buying trips to France and England. He put in long hours at this one-man business, staying open at night until after the opera in order that Creole belles and their American counterparts could browse before going home.

Now the Canal Street location is only one—and not the largest—of five Holmes stores in the New Orleans area, and of 14 in Louisiana, Mississippi, and Alabama. The group was built on the principles laid down by the innovative Holmes.

"Goods must come up to all claims," he ruled, and replaced or refunded the purchase price of any item that did not satisfy the buyer. The no-risk shopping policy remains in force today at all Holmes stores.

In 1848, Holmes began the home-delivery system, using his own carriage to send parcels to the wives of officers stationed at Jackson Barracks during the Mexican War. They told him they feared being waylaid if they carried their own packages. Later the delivery wagons bearing Holmes' name became part of the New Orleans scene.

During the Civil War, while New Orleans was occupied by federal troops, manpower was scarce and Holmes became one of the first merchants in the South to employ female sales personnel. Holmes was one of the citizens who petitioned President Hayes to remove federal troops after the war and end the Reconstruction period that cost New Orleans its place in the economic sun. The long postwar depression kept Holmes from taking his retail know-how into other markets.

Holmes died at the age of 82 on July 3, 1898, while on a buying trip to New York. In 1905, the Holmes heirs sold their stock to a group of New Orleans businessmen. Now more than 90 percent of the shares are owned by Louisiana residents. The largest bloc of stockholders includes the company's 4,500 employees.

Holmes' has earned a place in New Orleans tradition, along with Mardi Gras, red beans and rice, and All Saints' Day visits to the cemeteries. Remember when the singing of carols under the clock on Christmas Eve marked the end of the hectic Santa Claus shopping splurge?

Daniel Henry Holmes, founder of the D.H. Holmes Company, Ltd., is shown in a portrait painted at the time of the Civil War.

HOWARD, WEIL, LABOUISSE, FRIEDRICHS, INCORPORATED

was easy to spell and pronounce.) Since the latter two were seasoned brokers, the three founders came in as equal partners.

In 1950 Walter H. Weil, Jr., brought Weil & Company, specialists in municipal bonds, into the company,

Pictured here (from left to right) are Hunter Collins, Walter H. Weil, Jr., G. Shelby Friedrichs, Forres M. Collins, Paul T. Westervelt, John P. Labouisse, and (insert) Alvin H. Howard, the founders and early associates of Howard, Weil, Labouisse, Friedrichs, Incorporated.

G. Shelby Friedrichs and John P. Labouisse tossed a coin (a nickel) in 1946 to see whose name would be listed second in the title of the newest investment securities house in New Orleans. Labouisse won, and thus the firm was christened Howard, Labouisse, Friedrichs and Company.

There was no question about the *Howard.* Alvin H. Howard, just back from service in World War II, wanted to get into the stock-brokerage business, but had no experience. He put up $100,000 of the capital, while Friedrichs and Labouisse scraped up $10,000 each. (And Howard's name

which changed its name to the present form: Howard, Weil, Labouisse, Friedrichs. The other partners were painfully aware they needed Weil's guidance. In 1947 they handled a $100,000 bond issue for Lafourche Parish that bore the interest rate of one percent (in the 1980s, public, tax-free offerings return as much as 8 or 9 percent). The result was a hard-to-take $15,000 loss.

But the timing was nearly perfect for the launching of what in effect was a coalition of four families all with deep roots in New Orleans. The postwar boom was on, governmental agencies were rushing to finance public improvements with the proceeds of bond issues, and Louisiana was turning into the largest natural-gas-producing and second largest oil-producing state with new wells both onshore and in the Gulf of Mexico.

After absorbing the local NYSE firm of Viguerie, Hayne and Chaffe in 1969, Howard, Weil, Labouisse, Friedrichs and Company grew into a major operation. A member of the New York Stock Exchange and other exchanges, the firm has 320 employees, 19 branches scattered from New York to Midland, Texas, a net worth of $10 million, and annual revenues approaching $30 million.

Incorporated in 1971 and owned by its officers and employees, the firm is among the 100 largest investment companies in the country, and ranks among the top 20 in underwriting revenue bonds. In a recent year it managed or comanaged debt offerings of nearly one billion dollars.

Long experience has brought recognition of the company's expertise in oil and gas production and supporting activities. Twice-a-year seminars conducted by executives assigned to the oil industry attract securities analysts from three continents.

Friedrichs, now chairman of the board, recalls that the founders had to deal with extremely conservative New Orleans investors. "Historically, they put their money into real estate and municipal bonds," he explains. "We had to educate our clients to know that good common stocks were good investments, too." An influx of oil industry people has brought some changes in investment attitudes. "We've got some high fliers now," Friedrichs remarks.

Labouisse remains as director emeritus. Howard and Weil have died. In an evolution to bring younger men into positions of authority, John B. Levert, Jr., became president, chief executive officer, and chairman of the executive committee.

Friedrichs must have had memories of the 1947 bond debacle when the firm recently served as principal comanager in the underwriting of bonds of the Louisiana superport, an offshore unloading facility for giant oil tankers. The face amount of $450 million made the issue the largest in history for revenue bonds.

ROLAND HYMEL AND ASSOCIATES

Roland J. Hymel, Jr., CLU, is cited in Who's Who in Finance and Industry *for his pioneering work in tax-sheltered trusts. He is the founder of the Roland Hymel Agency, Roland Hymel and Associates, and Fringe Benefit Administrators.*

At no time in the history of civilization has financial planning been of greater use and importance than it is in the United States today. The marriage of taxation and inflation has fostered an economic environment in which success, defined in terms of material acquisition and wealth, is dependent as much upon one's talent for keeping what one makes as upon making it in the first place. The sprawling tangle of laws and regulations has elevated effective money management from the status of a pastime to that of a profession. Preserving one's income and assets now presumes more than a passing familiarity with the laws governing income and estate taxation and the methodologies of accounting, investment analysis, and insurance planning.

This dilemma has given rise to a new breed of professional—part lawyer, part accountant, part investment and insurance advisor—whose

Above and right
Staff experts and specialists serve as integral resources for each associate when addressing his or her client's special needs and problems. Pictured from left to right are Steven T. Ahrons, CFP, equities and investment manager; Ann T. Bond, J.D., CLU, director, estate analysis department; and Richard H. Watson, Jr., EBPS, president, Fringe Benefit Administrators.

specialty it is to help money-makers keep more of what they make and make more of what they keep.

Every industry and profession has had its visionaries, men and women whose faculty or good fortune it has been to anticipate trends before their less-gifted contemporaries. One such progressive thinker is New Orleanian Roland J. Hymel, Jr., CLU.

An accomplished athlete in high school and college, Hymel majored in marketing and minored in accounting at Loyola University, graduating in 1953 to become one of the leading salesmen for the then-infant IBM Corporation. A few years later, still a young man in his twenties, Hymel wrested a plum franchise from more experienced competitors, becoming general agent for the New Orleans agency of the State Mutual Life Assurance Company of America, one of the nation's oldest and most esteemed life insurance companies. His office, then in the Pere Marquette Building, occupied only a modest 1,000 square feet, and his production

for that year rounded off at a respectable one million dollars.

After a move to a Lee Circle location, he acquired the Canal Street Financial Planning Center with 44,000 square feet. Six years later, his New Orleans State Mutual agency produced better than $174 million in volume, distinguishing it as the largest producing franchise agency in the 136-year history of State Mutual.

Several years into the business, Hymel had gained the respect of his competitors and the admiration of his clients. In addition, he attracted a number of other strong-willed, independent thinkers like himself, who could readily appreciate what the progressive environment would mean for their abilities to serve and expand their clientele. Most came originally from other fields—law, accounting, stock and real estate brokerage, even advertising and public relations—but at heart, they were marketers and their products became their own unique versions of the Hymel message. By 1970, in addition to the main New Orleans office, Hymel had satellite offices in Baton Rouge, Houma, Thibodaux, Alexandria, and elsewhere throughout Louisiana. Today, his field associates alone number 40.

Equally as essential to his vision were staff-support people—experts and consultants—who would act as resources for himself and his fellow field professionals. Some were attor-

neys, certified financial planners, employee-benefit specialists. Others started with practical, on-the-job experience. Some held or later obtained multiple certifications, designations, and degrees.

These men and women are impressive in their own rights. Among them, Richard H. Watson, who was recruited straight from college, is president of Fringe Benefit Administrators, another firm in the Hymel trinity. Beginning with a prodigious talent for computer programming and later certification as an employee-benefit specialist, Watson was groomed and soon developed as the stabilizing pragmatic complement to Hymel's whirlwind creativity.

Ann T. Bond, J.D., CLU, accountant, was one of the first women with such broad credentials to be attracted to the business in general and to the energy of the Hymel operation in particular. Several years of experience with the Internal Revenue Service Department in both the income and estate and gift taxation divisions made her particularly well-suited to pioneer Roland Hymel and Associates' estate-analysis service.

In his search for antidotes to the business world's ills, Hymel often taxed his own and his associates' capacities to their limits. The consequence was that Roland Hymel and Associates, the foundation of the tripartite organization and the most widely

known of Hymel's three firms, has earned an unparalleled reputation for innovation in the business and professional communities.

"Most of our clients are business and estate owners," says Hymel, "who have some or all of the pieces to the

Individuals holding the Chartered Life Underwriters designations are recognized as professionals, well-versed in financial planning. Thirteen RHA associates are CLUs already and others are enrolled in the CLU program. Among those who have already received their CLU designation are (front row, left to right) Avera L. Mays; Steven T. Ahrons, CFP; Verna C. Corriveau; Charles P. Carriere III, J.D., CPCU; Paul K. LeBlanc; (second row, left to right) Hilton J. Michel, Jr.; Ann T. Bond, J.D.; Lawrence H. Hennessey, Jr.; Patrick A. Hymel, J.D.; Roland J. Hymel, Jr.; (back row) Noel "Butch" Baum. Missing at time photograph was taken were Travis E. Nichols and W. Howard Woodyard.

The Financial Planning Center at 2475 Canal Street is the home base of the Hymel companies. Its 44,000 square feet houses the offices of many of the associates and various equipment, including two computer systems and a terminal hookup to a third system.

success puzzle. They've probably had some help in putting parts of it together. What they need now is someone to help them integrate all those components and loose pieces. Over the past two decades, we've developed an organization with the manpower, instrumentation, and know-how to do just that." The long list of prominent clients, which includes the proprietors of the famous Brennan's Restaurant, the Batt brothers of the Pontchartrain Beach Amusement Park, and several well-known political figures, are testament to that claim.

INTERNATIONAL-MATEX TANK TERMINALS

Eighty-two bottles lined up on a cabinet shelf offer evidence that anything that flows can be stored or handled in the sprawling Mississippi River terminals operated by an international company in which a New Orleans family was founder.

Each bottle contains one of the different liquids that have been brought into the facilities of the International-Matex Tank Terminals at Avondale on the west bank and St. Rose on the east. The fluids range from fish oil to naphtha, from carbon black to diesel fuel.

The array is in the office of Thomas B. Coleman, managing partner, a member of the family, which in 1975 merged its International Tank Terminals with Matex, operated by the van Ommeren family interests of Rotterdam, the Netherlands. The

Fleecy clouds form a backdrop for tanks and pipes at the International-Matex Tank Terminals facility on the Mississippi River at St. Rose, Louisiana.

amalgamation gives the partnership 15 deepwater terminals in Asia, Europe, and North America, adding up to a total tank capacity of 40 million barrels.

At the Mississippi River terminals, liquids can be stored in tanks with a capacity of up to half a million barrels, or interchanged through a maze of pipes among sea-going vessels, barges, railroad cars, and trucks. There are facilities for heating such products as tallow, which can be piped only at high temperature. Canning and drumming services also are offered. The Avondale and St. Rose terminals bring business to the Port of New Orleans that would be lost without the capabilities provided.

The van Ommeren interests date back to 1839. James J. Coleman, Sr., founded International Tank Terminals in 1938 after acquiring the Avondale site from an oil company. He built the St. Rose terminal, then established tank centers at Mobile, Alabama; Karachi, Pakistan; Chittagong, Bangladesh; and Ulsan, Korea, before entering into the van Ommeren partnership.

The elder Coleman was one of the moving spirits in the building of the In-

At the company's Mississippi River terminals, liquids can be stored in tanks with capacities of up to half a million barrels each.

ternational Trade Mart, which he has served as president and general counsel. He was involved in the 35,000-acre New Orleans East development, participated in the building of the New Orleans Hilton Hotel, and has interests in condominiums and an office building scheduled to be erected on the riverfront.

With his sons, Jimmy Jr., Tommy, and Peter, and his daughter and son-in-law Dian and Tom Winingder, he has begun the construction of three large office buildings on Poydras Street across from the Louisiana Superdome. A graduate of the Tulane University School of Law, the senior Coleman established the law firm of Coleman, Dutrey & Thomson in 1937. He is the senior partner.

LEON IRWIN AND COMPANY, INC.

Since 1895, many have said that "Leon Irwin is a name that means insurance in New Orleans." Three persons carrying the name of Leon Irwin have headed the firm of Leon Irwin and Company, Inc., since its founding in 1895, and each has made a strong effort to have the name of the firm synonymous with insurance and community service.

Through the 86 years since the firm began, there have been numerous occasions which have called on the full support of the citizens of the community to restore damage and overcome hardships. Mississippi River flooding, hurricanes of immense proportions, the yellow fever epidemic, the impact of wars and armed conflict—Spanish-American, World War I, World War II, Korean Conflict, and Vietnam—have all called upon the individual and united efforts of the citizenry for unselfish effort. No industry has been called upon to respond more in time of disaster than the insurance industry, and Leon Irwin and Company has been involved locally in responding to the needs of its customers through six years of the 19th century and 81 years of the 20th century.

The firm's founder, Leon Irwin, established a precedent of community

Pictured below are a century of corporate presidents. From left to right they are Leon Irwin, the founder; Leon Irwin, Jr., his son; and Leon Irwin III, grandson of the founder.

involvement and service beyond the scope of normal insurance business requirements. His son, Leon Irwin, Jr., and his grandson, Leon Irwin III, have followed that precedent over the years in various community activities. Likewise, the personnel of the firm have always been heavily involved in the civic, service, religious, and social life of the community. Examples of the community involvement of the three generations heading the firm include service as president of the Board of Commissioners of the Port of New Orleans, director of Host International, Inc., member of the Board of Administrators of the Tulane Educational Fund (advisory), and former general agent of the John Hancock Mutual Life Insurance Company, by Leon Irwin, Jr.; chairman of the Downtown Development District and Special Assistant to Mayor Moon Landrieu by Leon Irwin III. Leon Irwin and Leon Irwin, Jr., were both honored by being selected as Rex, King of Carnival, the father in 1928 and the son in 1954.

After founding the firm and heading its operations for 46 years, Leon Irwin died in 1941, and his son, Leon Irwin, Jr., headed the firm for the next 26 years. During his tenure as president, the firm disposed of its office building at 736 Union Street in the central business district after almost 60 years' occupancy, and moved to what is now the K&B Plaza, formerly the John Hancock Building, at Lee Circle. The firm occupies most of a floor in the building and employs some 45 people in various aspects of the insurance operation.

In 1975, Leon Irwin, Jr., became chairman, and his son, Leon Irwin III, assumed the presidency of the firm. At this writing, the agency has over 7,000 accounts providing insurance of all types to many of the businesses in the area and to a large number of individuals. The firm represents some of the leading insurance companies in the nation, including the Chubb Group, The Travelers, The St. Paul Companies, Continental Insurance Company, United States Fidelity & Guaranty Company, The Home Insurance Company, Aetna Insurance Company, American International Group, and Fireman's Fund. It also operates an excess and surplus lines division which places special insurance risks for other agencies through Louisiana. The firm was distinguished in early 1981 when it was selected as exclusive agent for the Fireman's Fund FAMEX program, which involves exclusive agent authority for writing national franchise accounts in a 9-parish area surrounding New Orleans.

Leon Irwin and Company, through its family leaders, has seen New Orleans grow and develop from the post-Civil War city of 1895 to one of the modern, emerging metropolitan leaders of the "New South" about which so much is written today. Throughout the changes of time, the problems resulting from disasters of all types, and the need to innovate to keep up with change, Leon Irwin and Company has continued to grow and expand its base of serving the insurance needs of the area. It is today one of the larger locally-owned insurance agencies in New Orleans and Louisiana, and its principals take pride in their involvement in the changes that have taken place in the city. The future of cities and the insurance industry is very exciting, and it can reasonably be expected that Leon Irwin and Company will be heavily involved in that future. The traditions of the company will continue—as has been the case since 1895—a tradition of providing service to its customers and the community.

S. JACKSON & SON, INC.

S. Jackson reportedly chartered a vessel to bring the first shipment of Brazilian coffee into the Port of New Orleans. It happened while Jackson (the name Stonewall was legally bestowed by an aunt in honor of the Confederate hero, but the recipient used only the initial) was employed in the 19th century and earliest years of the 20th by the importing firm of Hard and Hand.

For a 5-year period beginning in 1891, he was assigned to Mexico as a buyer. Accompanied by an armed guard because his saddle bags were stuffed with silver dollars, he rode into the countryside to purchase coffee beans from the farmers.

He returned to New Orleans as

Represented in this photograph are three generations of the Jackson family. Elizabeth Orme Jackson, great-granddaughter of the founder of S. Jackson & Son, Inc., recently joined the firm as a clerk. Her grandfather, J. Norcom Jackson, is chairman of the board; and her father, J. Norcom Jackson, Jr., is the company's president.

manager, then in 1902 founded his own company. It has become S. Jackson & Son, Inc., and ever since has been providing the kind of special services to importers and exporters that keep New Orleans in the front rank of the world's seaports.

Jackson served coffee roasters by arranging for custom clearance, sampling, weighing, drayage, storage, and shipment of imports. The company still performs the same functions, but has broadened its activities to include other commodities as well as coffee, and to handle exports. It had a significant part in making New Orleans a major port for tea imports.

The founder's only son, J. Norcom Jackson, entered the business in 1914, then left to form the General Shipping Corporation. The trucking concern hauled coffee from the wharves to rail sheds for loading into freight cars. Upon Jackson's death in 1927, the son became president of his company. A few years later the General Shipping Corporation was absorbed.

When the volume of coffee shipments into New Orleans soared during World War II, S. Jackson & Son became one of the first agencies to load the bags directly into rail cars at

shipside. Trucking was no longer needed, and the subsidiary firm was terminated in the early '40s.

J. Norcom Jackson, Jr., began work in 1950 as a messenger during school vacations, then earned experience in the warehouse. A graduate of Tulane University, he became president in 1967, when his father moved up to chairman of the board.

Under the leadership of the founder's grandson, the company has multiplied its activities for exporters, handling legal and logistic details for shipments to many parts of the world. A 100-year-old building at 755 Magazine Street was renovated and is the focal point for operations.

Among the 35 S. Jackson employees are a dozen who know Spanish and two who are fluent in French. They make out the detailed entry forms required at foreign ports, a complicated task that would stump most customers if they had to do it themselves. Jackson relies on computers for most of the detailed paperwork and record keeping.

A fourth generation Jackson has joined the firm as a clerk. She is Elizabeth Orme Jackson, daughter of the president.

PETER JUDLIN, INC.

When the father of the founder of this company left his native Alsace-on-the-Rhine for New Orleans-on-the-Mississippi, he left a historic troubled land for land even more unsettled—geographically, that is.

For openers, this young immigrant's French first name of "Jean Baptiste" coupled with the German surname of "Judlin" aptly illustrates how evenly divided was ancient Alsace, which dates back to the Roman Empire. For hundreds of years it has swung back and forth as a province of the two nations it borders. Sometime before 1850, Judlin opened a grocery store on a street called Levee, alongside a river that has swung from side to side for thousands of years, washing away land on one bank and depositing new land on the opposite bank. More recently the Army Corps of Engineers has had to build a massive concrete wall to halt Ol' Man River from washing away the site of Judlin's grocery, as well as the entire French Market. In 1870, the name of Levee Street became Decatur.

In 1902 Peter Louis Judlin founded the company that bears his name.

But Jean Baptiste Judlin lived out his life in his home behind his grocery, raising a son and two daughters. Sometime prior to 1887 Peter Louis Judlin, his son, was in business with his brother-in-law on the Carondelet Canal near Claiborne, and 12 blocks back from the river. Louis Mestier and Peter Judlin's business was selling wood, coal, lime, sand, shells, and lathes—building supplies primarily. They had three schooners to bring in these supplies from sources across the lake. After 1891, when Peter bought out the Plaswirth building supply business at 2311 North Rampart and Louis continued the business on the canal, both companies used the schooners, two of which were named "Josephine Mestier" and "Mabelee Judlin." These must have been the names of the wives of Louis and Peter, but the Judlin family can't be sure. The family is certain, however, that the schooners were in use until 1915, when the company began to retire mules and acquire trucks.

Peter Judlin died in 1917, and his son, Peter Jr., became president for a number of years, to be followed by his younger brother, Walter D. Judlin. The firm had now moved a few blocks down the street to larger quarters at St. Claude and Montegut, where it would remain for 52 years, and where ready-mix concrete would become its main order of business.

In 1975, following the death of Walter D. Judlin, the third generation took over management in the person of Walter D. Judlin, Jr., who had been active in the company since 1932. So he had more than enough experience to supervise the company's move, in 1977, to its present, acres-large site on Old Gentilly Road at Read Road. There was need for more space to accommodate new modern equipment and a larger fleet of vehicles.

The future is also assured of Judlin continuity in its management, as the picture here of president Walter D. Judlin, Jr., would indicate. He is shown flanked by the fourth generation—both of them great-great-grandsons of founding father Peter Louis Judlin, and both of them already on the payroll accruing years of experience.

Shown center, Walter D. Judlin, Jr., became company president in 1975. Flanking him are his cousin, Foster Gery (left), and his son, Richard John Judlin (right), representing the fourth generation of family leadership in the business.

LAKE LAWN METAIRIE CEMETERIES & FUNERAL HOME

Among America's most beautiful and historical cemeteries is New Orleans's Metairie.

"The only architecture in New Orleans," Mark Twain has said, "is in its cemeteries." Obviously, the architecture Twain meant was the beautiful marble and granite structures of classical antiquity he had seen abroad.

As a matter of fact, in New Orleans cemeteries, especially in Metairie, there are more replicas of ancient Egyptian, Greek, and Roman architecture, lavishly illustrated with statuary, than in any cemetery anywhere in America. It is a beautiful and historic place to visit, as Henri Gandolfo makes abundantly clear in his book, *Metairie Cemetery, An Historic Memoir*. Its publication, by the proprietors of the cemetery, is scheduled coincidentally with the publication of this book. Henri is the living resident historian of Metairie, and what other American cemetery outside New Orleans can match that?

Stewart Enterprises, Inc., proprietor of Metairie, is somewhat matchless on its own account. Almost accidently the Stewart family, as the Acme Realty Company, made its debut into the cemetery and stone construction business in 1910, when it acquired the St. Vincent de Paul Cemeteries far down-town in New Orleans. The property consisted of three old cemeteries and an equally antiquated marble shop. Because the properties weren't salable, the Stewarts decided to improve them. To accomplish this the Acme Marble and Granite Company, Inc., was formed early in the 1930s. Not only were the cemeteries converted into attractive assets, but the Stewarts acquired other cemetery interests, and expanded their marble and granite works. For several years the company was active in the memorial and commercial construction business.

Then, in 1949, Frank B. Stewart, Sr., president of Acme, realized the potential of another large burial facility for New Orleans. Land was acquired adjacent to Metairie Cemetery, and Lake Lawn Park Cemetery and Mausoleum had its beginning in 1950. The original mausoleum has been ex-panded many times since then. Also in the 1950s, a second generation of Stewarts became active in the company, and soon Stewart know-how in their field became such that they were offering their services to other southern cemeteries to develop and sell community mausoleum properties. Before long their services were being sought nationally, then internationally. Their Acme Marble and Granite Company in 1981 was licensed as general contractors and designers, qualified to do business in 36 states and two Canadian provinces. The company brings to its clients the expertise gained in 70 years in the cemetery field and is the largest cemetery development firm in the nation.

Frank B. Stewart, who continued his father's work, also had the foresight to sire two most capable and enterprising sons—Albert II and Frank B. Stewart, Jr., who took over as president upon his father's death in 1966. It was Frank Stewart, Jr., who acquired the Metairie Cemetery in the late 1960s, with all of its 152 acres. Then, on a small portion of its undeveloped 30 acres they dedicated the Lake Lawn Metairie Funeral Home on Sunday, June 23, 1979. Headed by leaders of all faiths, 3,000 attended dedication ceremonies of the Funeral Home and Chapel.

During the construction of the funeral home, the 1874 funeral home

The magnificent Lake Lawn Metairie Funeral Home represents a growing national trend, combining cemetery and funeral home to provide greater economy to families in need.

The all-faith chapel in the Lake Lawn Metairie Funeral Home, which seats 300.

firm of Jacob Schoen and Sons, Inc., became coventurers with the Stewarts. This new facility of Stewart Enterprises, Inc., has met with overwhelming favor. It offers many advantages of combined cemetery and funeral home services at one location.

The decor and interior design and appointments are outstanding. For New Orleans it follows a national trend where chapel, funeral home, flower shop, even crematory are located within the cemeteries they principally serve. It provides savings, convenience, and ease of planning—indeed,

a common-sense answer to those who wanted something done about the high cost of final arrangements.

Another example of this national trend are the Restland, Laurel Land, and Singing Hills properties in Dallas, Texas, recently acquired by Stewart Enterprises, Inc. Said to be the largest privately owned cemetery operation in the United States, its 600-plus acres include two major cemeteries, both with community mausoleums, and three funeral homes. In the Dallas area,

Lake Lawn Park is considered the South's finest cemetery and mausoleum. Perpetual care is included in every mausoleum crypt arrangement.

over 4,000 families call on these Stewart cemeteries each year.

And speaking of mausoleums, named for King Mausolus who got the first 353 B.C. model, it is unlikely his royal person was as well accommodated as those for whom Lake Lawn's scientifically sealed vaults are acquired, and payable at far less then the "king's ransom" of old.

To provide the wide range of services Stewart Enterprises offers, a total of 13 corporate subsidiaries have been marshaled. In addition to those mentioned, others range from International Stone & Erectors, Inc., to Estate Assurance Company. The first, besides handling all commercial and mausoleum stonework for Stewart and its subsidiaries, has provided and installed stone facing for 30 high-rise buildings, such as the Superdome, One Shell Square, the new Pan American Life building, and the Tulane Library, as well as others in Houston, Chicago, Augusta, Cincinnati, Minneapolis, and many other cities.

As president Frank B. Stewart, Jr., in his foreword to Henry Gandolfo's Metairie book has said in quoting William Gladstone: "Show me the manner in which a nation or community cares for its dead and I shall measure with mathematical exactness their tender mercies toward their people and their respect for the laws of the land."

Certainly Mr. Stewart's company has taken a lead in providing this community all manners of doing this, and gathering a lot of New Orleans history in the process. You can start with duelling master Pepe Llula who once owned, and today lies buried in, St. Vincent de Paul Cemetery, which introduced Albert L. Stewart to the cemetery business. Then there are so many historic figures among those approximately 40,000 who are interred in Metairie Cemetery, now nearly 200 years away from the time it began as a racetrack.

But that's history, and Henri Gandolfo tells of that in his book of memoirs.

LOUISIANA GENERAL SERVICES, INC.

This company has had three beginnings. The first, in 1927, was a humble start as the gas department of a New Orleans area utility company. In that year the Louisiana Power & Light Company purchased assets from the West New Orleans Light & Traction Company—assets which amounted to 584 gas customers in Arabi, Gretna, and Metairie. To these then-small communities, all outside the New Orleans city limits and all using manufactured gas, LP&L almost immediately was able to add 1,095 more customers acquired in northern Louisiana. Also, by 1928, natural gas had replaced the less-efficient manufactured product.

This company, actually the gas division of the Louisiana Power & Light Company, spent the next 32 years increasing this nucleus of 1,679 gas customers to nearly 100,000 in communities throughout the state. Expansion was slow at first. Laboriously digging trenches with picks and shovels to lay the gas mains was slow work. And slow, too, was the settlement of vacant lands on the outskirts of New Orleans, as well as other communities. But, finally, led by the rapidly developing petrochemical industry in Louisiana, plants began to spring up on the river and other waterways, and residential areas for workers appeared like magic in former truck farms and cow pastures. Also, there came a new awareness of the efficiency of natural gas as fuel, and the economy of the then-limitless supply. In increasing numbers, plants as well as homes were piping it in.

By 1960 things were prospering in the gas business. However, the Federal Securities and Exchange Commission had ordered utility companies providing service to more than one community to limit themselves to provid-

In the early years of this gas company, oxen power was used to lay gas pipes in areas not yet residential.

ing but one service. Under this order, the Louisiana Power & Light Company was divested of its gas properties.

The stage was set for the second beginning of the Louisiana General Services, Inc. In 1960 it was called Louisiana Gas Service Company, a separate entity, investor-owned and listed on the American Stock Exchange. It became popularly known in the metro area as "LGS."

In the ensuing years, LGS developed rapidly. By 1969, two en-

tirely new companies had been formed, with others planned. To accommodate such diverse development, there was need for a parent organization. Thus the third, and greatest, beginning was when Louisiana General Services, Inc., became the corporate name of a now-major company that had its start as a small gas department serving 584 customers. Its gas service now rings the city of New Orleans, spreading far and wide throughout the state to serve over 230,000 residential and industrial customers.

Under the leadership of president John S. Ingersoll and an energetic board of directors, expansion afield has been outstanding. It ranges from a full-service life insurance firm to a pipeline enterprise serving its distribution concern; there's even an exploration company to find more gas. The LGS growth pattern continues. Perhaps the Louisiana General Service Company, Inc., sums it up best when it terms itself a "company of companies."

The main office of Louisiana General Services is located on the Westbank Expressway in Harvey.

THE LOUISIANA LAND AND EXPLORATION COMPANY

A century after the Louisiana Purchase, oil was discovered in Louisiana. That was in 1901, the year that Edward Wisner began to fulfill his dream of reclaiming swampland south of New Orleans for an agricultural bonanza. He bought over a million acres for as little as 11 cents an acre.

But, alas, Wisner died in 1915, and his ambitious project died with him. Ultimately, through foreclosure, the majority of his land holdings, over 600,000 acres, became the property of H.H. Timken, president of the Timken Roller Bearing Company.

In 1926, Timken teamed with Colonel E.F. Simms, who held some one million acres of state mineral leases in the area, to form Border Research

Corporation. The young firm's aim was to locate petroleum deposits beneath the Louisiana marsh. Following reorganization less than a year later, the company became The Louisiana Land and Exploration Company headed by Ernest B. Tracy, who served as president for nearly two decades.

Early efforts by the company to tap the mineral riches beneath the marsh proved futile. Then, late in 1928, Texaco paid $1.8 million for the rights to drill on LL&E's property, with the stipulation that royalties would be paid if oil was discovered. Needless to say, the swampland began to yield its wealth of black gold, and LL&E began that period during which most of its income was derived from royalties.

It was in the 1960s, under the leadership of Ford M. Graham, that LL&E began to put its royalty earnings

The type of worldwide operation in which The Louisiana Land and Exploration Company is involved is exemplified by ODECO's "Ocean Voyager" in the turbulent North Sea.

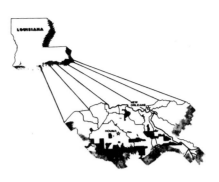

This schematic map of coastal southeastern Louisiana illustrates the vastness of the company's operations. Black areas indicate the original properties of Edward Wisner, now owned by The Louisiana Land and Exploration Company.

to work. Aggressive activities such as the acquisition of offshore leases, expansion of exploration worldwide, and the development of industrial real estate were important strides for an organization that was to become one of the nation's major producers of oil and gas.

The 1970s began with one of the most significant domestic petroleum discoveries, the Jay Field, and the creation of another subsidiary, the Louisiana Land Offshore Exploration Company. The year 1972 marked the election of John G. Phillips as chief executive officer. Subsequently, a major refinery was constructed at Mobile, Alabama, and the company expanded its area of interest to include other minerals, primarily copper and coal.

The present officers—Phillips, chairman of the board; E.J. Langhetee, Jr., vice-chairman; and E.L. Williamson, president—have led the company to compile a record of continued growth and prosperity.

Today there are some 3,000 LL&E employees staffing 21 offices worldwide. The firm's 1980 contributions to the nation's energy supply amounted to over 21 million barrels of liquid petroleum products and 116 billion cubic feet of natural gas. Gross revenues exceeded one billion dollars and capital expenditures totaled some $371 million.

McILHENNY COMPANY

OF AVERY ISLAND

By John Chase

Edmund McIlhenny, pictured here at the time of his wedding, was born into those spicy and flavorful decades preceding the Civil War, when the country was still young, when so many young Americans were enacting exciting roles, so richly steeped in romance and derring-do. It is among these that young Edmund stands out for what he accomplished before, during, and after that war. Small wonder he has left us all a spicy and flavorful *sauce piquante* of his own invention. For more than a century it has made his an unforgettable name. His story is unforgettable, too.

Perhaps it all happened because he had romantic parents. Who else can boast of a father who rescued his beloved from the confinement of a "female seminary," properly chaperoned by a maiden aunt he brought along. The three eloped to Lancaster, Pennsylvania, where the chaperone witnessed the marriage of John McIlhenny to Ann Newcomer.

Avery Island, Louisiana, home of Tabasco pepper sauce and the family who created it and still manages the industry.

After a Philadelphia honeymoon, the couple settled in Hagerstown, Maryland. Here John practiced medicine, until he contracted a fatal disease from a patient—not uncommon in those days before Pasteur discovered germs. His death was in 1832, but not before he had sired nine sons. Edmund, age 17 and the second eldest, soon decided to go to work and help his mother care for and educate his seven younger brothers. We know all this because, years and years later, Edmund dictated it to his daughter, Sara, who has left the record. But the record is unclear as to how soon Edmund went to work, and where. It seems realistic that in nearby Baltimore, his mother's hometown, friends would find work for an unskilled 17-year-old. Telephoneless banks always needed messengers. Then, when things got tough—there was a panic in 1837 severely felt in the East—it could have been his banker employers who gave him a letter in-

troducing the bright and experienced young man to colleagues in New Orleans. Edmund could have been in his early twenties then, and no longer a messenger.

Although he probably arrived in New Orleans much earlier, his name first appears in the city directory in 1846, listing him as a bookkeeper at the Bank of Louisiana and living in the suburbs on Euterpe Street near Magazine. His name continued so listed, at various suburban addresses, until 1855. In those nine years Edmund McIlhenny had become an important man in New Orleans. He was agent at the Bank of Louisiana, in charge of the paper money the bank was obliged to print and keep at par value, such as the $20 bank note shown here. Besides the bank's main office at Royal and Conti streets (also shown), he kept in touch with its branches at Baton Rouge, Donaldsonville, St. Francisville, Alexandria, and St. Martinville. He was constantly traveling, and always when in Baton Rouge he was welcomed at the home of his friend, Judge Daniel Dudley Avery, on the northwest corner of Convention and Lafayette streets. Mary Eliza, the Judge's eldest daughter, was much attracted to the handsome banker, 22 years her senior. She often declared it her secret that she would marry him when grown.

In New Orleans, Edmund's bachelor quarters were at No. 12 Exchange Place, across the street from the Boston Club then housed in the Merchant's Exchange. He was on the governing committee of the Orleans Club, world famous for its lunches with seven courses of wild game, as well as vice-commodore of the Southern Yacht Club. Summertimes he was a "regular" at Pass Christian, as were many members of the Yacht

Club. He was much in demand as a judge at regattas, but on July 4, 1853, he declined. His yacht called *Secret* was in the race and it won. In all probability Mary Eliza Avery, who attended boarding school on the Gulf Coast, witnessed this race. It was no secret to her why Edmund called the boat *Secret,* nor was it any joking, make-believe secret that she would marry her banker when she grew up. Six years after this race, in Baton Rouge on June 30, 1859, at age 21 she did, indeed, become Mrs. Edmund McIlhenny, and his cottage at Pass Christian was the scene of their month-long honeymoon.

It was common knowledge from a book entitled *How to Get a Rich Wife* that Edmund McIlhenny was worth over $100,000 at the time of his marriage. Besides his salary at the bank, besides what the state paid him to function as secretary of the Office of the Board of Currency, a sort of state board to which all banks were obliged to file monthly reports, Edmund's personal investments in real estate had been successful. His banking career

was during what has been described as "the golden period of commerce in New Orleans." Louisiana banking during the time Edmund was a banker has also been termed "enlightening," and management of banknotes during this period served as a model to the federal government after the Civil War, when the United States began the issue of legal tender other than specie—paper money, that is. Perhaps one observer

has best described the banks and this golden age of commerce just before the Civil War: "Of this economy the banks were certainly a great part, but they did not affect it so much as they were affected by it."

However, it was against this backdrop that Edmund played out his "from rags to riches" banker role of some 25 years, depending on whether he made his debut as a teenager, as Sara McIlhenny has indicated, or after 20 as has been suggested. In New Orleans, he bought Mary Eliza a fine house—No. 41 on then-fashionable North Rampart Street—but their residence there was cut short in 1862, when a Union fleet under Farragut, with General "Spoons" Butler aboard, entered the river. Butler's regime would end up in possession of Edmund's priceless collection of uncut gems and bronze and silver pieces. Because of their active participation in the war, supplying the Confederates with Avery Island salt, newlywed McIlhenny and all his wife's relatives had to make a hasty, strategic withdrawal to Texas for the duration.

The harsh years of the Civil War and Reconstruction which so divided the country would only serve to further unite the Avery and McIlhenny families of Louisiana—first for wartime security, then in mutual respect and regard for each other. Names of the children of Mary Eliza Avery McIlhenny and Edmund McIlhenny rather eloquently testify to this, with eight of their nine christened with a middle name of "Avery."

Of the two families, the Averys were first in Louisiana. Dr. Dudley L. Avery arrived in time to serve as medical officer at the Battle of New Orleans. In 1837 his son married the daughter of John Craig Marsh, who had purchased the north end of an island in 1818—

Edmund's Bank of Louisiana, at Royal and Conti streets, is now the Tourist Center. This drawing by Clarence Millet is from Stanley Clisby Arthur's "Old New Orleans." It is reproduced here by permission.

Edmund's bachelor quarters at No. 12 Exchange Place, then known as "the street of the fencing masters." The building was still standing in 1981.

an island later to be called "Avery." Much later his son-in-law—the future Judge Daniel Dudley Avery—bought the other half. Never formally named, it was first called "Salt Island" because of its salt, then "Petit Anse," after the

At right is the thoroughly modern Tabasco plant at Avery Island in production since 1980, replacing a smaller 1910 plant. Below is shown the "laboratory," where Edmund McIlhenny's experiments produced the now-famous Tabasco pepper sauce.

bayou that almost encircled it. Curiously, it was never called "Marsh Island" after its first owner who built the first house and lived there raising sugarcane. Instead, it ended up being called "Avery Island" when the family his daughter married into became its most frequent and steady visitors.

It was 1862 and Civil War time when John Marsh Avery, a son of Judge Daniel and Sarah Marsh, was there with workmen to enlarge the briny spring to provide more salt for the Confederacy when a shovel struck rock salt 20 feet down. Immediately, two things resulted. Avery Island, it became apparent, was no normal island. Almost round, its 2,500 acres rose 152 feet above the surrounding wet marsh, But the elevation, iceberg-like, was but the tip of a huge block of solid salt that extended down an incredible 50,000 feet below sea level—or marsh level, which is the same along coastal Louisiana. Beautiful, semitropical Avery Island with its shady groves of great oaks, all sat on top of a mineral-rich Louisiana salt dome of which the island's owners would one day share production.

The other result of this discovery—the first find of rock salt in all America—was to make Avery Island a prime objective of Yankee invaders already occupying New Orleans and Baton Rouge. On May 21, 1863,

Union General N.P. Banks dispatched a force to destroy the Confederate salt mine, which was accomplished. Before this, fortunately, Judge Avery had gathered his two families together to resume their strategic withdrawal over 100 miles into Texas.

Few records are left to tell us how the Judge's refugee group spent the two years they lived in the remote German community of Brenham 78 miles up present-day highway 290 from Houston on the way to Austin. Edmund McIlhenny became a Confederate colonel in the Quartermaster Corps, presumably to supply Confederate General Richard Taylor back in Louisiana resisting vastly superior Union forces. And how was material procured? Before leaving for Texas, the judge had converted over one million dollars into Confederate money, which even Edmund's 25 years of banking know-how could not maintain at par. Nor was Edmund getting his handsome banker's salary. In fact, General "Spoons" Butler had overdrawn the Bank of Louisiana of every cent it had in specie.

But Marshall, Edmund's brother, lived in the area. Through him the refugee group must have made friends, even Mexican friends, whose cuisine—so highly seasoned with red peppers—must have interested Edmund, gourmet that he was. Back in New Orleans, his friend Maunsell White had invented and even marketed a wine sauce for oyster eating, but little else

was known of pepper sauces in ante-bellum New Orleans or other parts.

With the war over, in the summer of 1865 the Avery-McIlhenny families returned to a war-torn Avery Island. It was a travel-weary party of seven who took up residence in the old Marsh home. At this point in the life of Edmund McIlhenny he had reason to be despondent. Through no fault of his own, he was penniless. Oh, he had property, as did the judge. But the judge and his wife owned Avery Island. Here he was, a man of 50 being supported by his wife's folks. It's the kind of thing that could bother a man, so Edmund McIlhenny sat down and invented Tabasco pepper sauce.

Of course it wasn't that easy. Nor are the facts of how he started it all easy to come by. It is a great American legend that must remain legendary in the telling. Nobody knows how he got the first peppers, or where a lifelong banker got the idea that the world was waiting for a good pepper sauce. Most of all, how could he have suddenly become so qualified a chemist.

Most repeated is the legend that the peppers were found in the kitchen garden of the Marsh house, having survived the vandalism of the Yankee soldiers. The peppers are a rare variety of the Capsicum group, less harsh than cayenne with its ground pods and seeds. It is pretty well established they were of Mexican origin, but not necessarily from the Mexican state of Tabasco. Both the state and McIlhenny's peppers appear to have originated with an Indian word meaning "land where the soil is humid." Edmund picked the word because of its sound. Another legend tells of a soldier named Gleason who brought the peppers back from Mexico at the time of the Mexican War; McIlhenny planted them and made pepper sauce for the family for years. Sounds good, only the Mexican War was in 1846, before Edmund married Mary Eliza Avery. It's just as likely Edmund brought them back from Brenham, Texas, in 1865, because he had tasted them in Mexican cooking there.

But how did Edmund know he should crush the peppers, remove foreign matter, salt the mash, then let it age for three warm seasons in wooden barrels? How did he know the final mixture should be roughly one-third cured mash, and two-thirds vinegar? How did he know the real secret would be not to hurry?

The point is that somehow he knew, and when he died in 1890, the formula of Tabasco was fixed forever, and its reputation had been established. His son John, who had been called back from Harvard to assist his father in promoting Tabasco, became the company's second president. But not for long. In 1898 he was off to join Teddy Roosevelt's Rough Riders, charge up San Juan Hill, and win the Spanish-American War. When John moved to Washington in 1906 to accept appointment as a U.S. Civil Service commissioner, his brother Edward took the reins and presided over the company for more than 40 years.

"Mister Ned," as Edward McIlhenny was widely known, took over a $100,000 business in 1898, which continued steady growth. A naturalist of international reputation, he established Jungle Gardens, an extension of Bird City which helped halt a threatened extinction of the egrets. His dedication transformed Avery Island into one vast wildlife sanctuary and a tourist attraction with few equals. On the business side, worthy of mention, during his administration, on April 3,

1906, the name "Tabasco" was firmly registered as a trademark for pepper sauce by the U.S. Patent Office. It has made of the company's product a dictionary word; it is listed as "... Tabasco, a trade name for a pepper sauce." You can't get more exclusive than that.

In 1949 Mr. Ned's contributions to

Before Tabasco sauce shows up on your table in its famous bottle (see above), each barrel after aging is personally appraised before being blended with strong distilled vinegar and stirred for weeks. Below, president Walter McIlhenny is shown inspecting the mash.

the legacy his father left all McIlhennys came to an end. His nephew was elected to assume the responsibilities with orders to "carry on." Fortunately, Walter Stauffer McIlhenny, the nephew, had served with the U.S. Marines during World War II, retiring as a brigadier. Walter was used to taking orders. He was used to giving orders, too! Fortunately, this grandson of Edmund's was soon joined by a great-grandson, Edward McIlhenny Simmons, a college-trained naturalist.

Also available to this new president would be sophisticated, modern equipment plantwise, officewise, and otherwise. In time the company was able to bottle as many as 120,000 items daily of its ever increasingly popular pepper sauce, with 40 percent of its production going to foreign countries. Small wonder Tabasco sauce is now bottled in half a dozen countries with peppers grown in several others—all of which goes on under the eyes of experts sent out from Avery Island. And all of this has got to characterize the company's growth as "phenomenal."

Perhaps "Mr. Walter"—as all longtime workers on the Island call him—summed it up best when he said "plus ca change, plus c'est la meme

chose," which they say loses in the English translation. But not lost in any language is the thought that no matter how high sales may soar, Tabasco sauce quality—as Edmund corked it—remains still corked in those familiar little red bottles.

McMoRan OIL & GAS CO.

The corporate name of this company is an acronym formed by the initial letters of the names of its founders (left to right), W.K. McWilliams, Jr., James R. Moffett, and B.M. Rankin, Jr. Not since the "Tinker to Evers to Chance" days of the 1906 Chicago Cubs has there been such a winning trio.

nizing Moffett's potential, McWilliams hired him after college, and took him along in 1965, when they both left Dietrich to become independent geologists. Using the first two letters of their surnames, they organized a company named "McMoCo," which was shortly to become "McMoRan" when B.M. Rankin, Jr., resigned as one of the Hunt Oil Company's chief land-

ter definition: "The independents always have drilled most of the wildcats and thus made most of the major new-field discoveries. ... This primarily has been (because) the independents have the advantages of smallness and greater flexibility that have enabled them to make decisions and move more quickly than the large oil companies."

It isn't often a potentially great football star is awarded an athletic scholarship by a major university where he starred in education but just barely made the football team. Maybe there ought to be more undergraduates in colleges on athletic scholarships like James Robert Moffett, president and chief executive officer of this company.

But material like Jim Bob Moffett doesn't come along very often. Back in the 1950s, as a poor Houston boy, he did accept the opportunity of an athletic scholarship to the University of Texas, where he won honors in geology, receiving a bachelor of science degree, along with his letter for playing tackle on the football team between classes. Moving to New Orleans, he picked up his master's degree in geology at Tulane University, graduating magna cum laude.

It was during summer vacations in New Orleans that he worked as a roustabout for Howard Hughes's Dietrich Oil & Gas Company, where he caught the eye of W.K. McWilliams, Jr., Hughes's chief geologist. Recog-

men to join the new firm.

Because of his wide acquaintance in the industry gained during the years he traveled representing Hunt, Rankin was immediately named first president. But before McMoRan could perform the acknowledged wonders in wildcatting that were to come, it became necessary to increase its acquaintance among well-to-do investors anxious for tax shelters afforded by long-term investments in exploration for oil and gas. There was no better way to accomplish this than by going public. But how? McMoRan (all three of them) knew how. They journeyed to Utah and purchased a worn-out mining company, which was publicly held and traded over-the-counter. Changing its name from Horn Silver Mines Company to McMoRan Exploration Co., presto—they were a public company. In time the firm would become listed on the New York Stock Exchange.

"Wildcatting" has a dictionary definition meaning "an exploratory well drilled to discover deposits of oil or gas; a prospect well." President Rankin in 1971 was quoted with a bet-

Referring more particularly to his own firm, Rankin went on to say, "We've normally had the money to wildcat in areas where wildcatting is relatively expensive." This McMoRan advantage was to prove particularly true after 1974, when a younger president Moffett took over from president Rankin. Along with McWilliams, Rankin has remained on the board of directors. Although both of these men complete their signatures with "Jr.," Moffett is the baby of the trio. And what a baby. "Jim Bob was ready," the senior McWilliams commented when his protege was named president, and he was right. By 1977, fast-moving, tireless president Jim Bob had readied McMoRan for something called a "farm-in program."

All offshore Louisiana and Texas is checkered off in huge blocks which interested oil companies periodically lease from the federal government for five years by paying millions of dollars in so-called "bonuses." To be representative, the major oil companies eagerly bid for these leases. After drilling one or more unsuccessful ex-

Typical offshore drilling and production platform operated by McMoRan in the Gulf of Mexico.

ploratory wells, not always do their geologists recommend taking the risk of additional drilling—especially on the federal blocks.

Independents like McMoRan are in no position to come up with the enormous front-money costs of leases, but with a farm-in program, president Moffett explained, he could sort of sharecrop on a lease at his own drilling costs—a minor $3- or $4-million outlay—and when he strikes oil or gas the leasing company shares in the development cost and production.

To provide this service, Moffett organized the McMoRan Offshore Exploration Co., immediately nicknamed

MOXY. At the same time he rounded up four oil- and gas-hungry companies to stake MOXY to $60 million over a 3-year period to make the program pay off for all involved. MOXY received a management fee of 5 percent on all exploration costs, and earned a 30 percent interest in each successful well for which it paid 20 percent of the drilling costs.

Recently, McMoRan has been hitting an amazing 70 percent of the time it drilled a bit down to find oil or gas. This isn't altogether luck. McMoRan drillers are quarterbacked by an unusual amount of seismic study. They play this blue-chip underground game of hide-and-seek with great skill. CLK Corporation is a consulting group that works its magic exclusively for

McMoRan on its farm-in prospects in the Gulf of Mexico. Few independent consultants have CLK's experience and expertise, and fewer still receive the degree of cooperation and trust that CLK gets from MOXY. "We have constant verification of our hits and misses from MOXY's logs," says Hal Kuntz, CLK president. "We can refine our techniques better than others who can't confirm what they've predicted."

This revealing comment by CLK's Kuntz has been reported by the May 1980 issue of *Fortune* in an article by Alexander Stuart titled, "Jim Bob Moffett Beats the Odds in Wildcatting." Author Stuart gives a good account of what this company has accomplished in a scant 11 years since changing its corporate name from Horn Silver Mines to McMoRan. The article concludes with Moffett's comment on the company's "breathtaking assault on wildcatting averages." Says president Jim Bob: "You can only become a star once. We'd be kidding ourselves to think we can hit 70 percent of the time forever."

This book was published a year later than the *Fortune* article, and the time lapse makes its author sound peculiarly prophetic. "... If he can keep his ambition in check, if he doesn't plunge too deep," writes *Fortune*'s Stuart in a final word on Moffett's comment above, "it seems a fair bet Moffett's and McMoRan's star will keep rising for some time to come."

Eleven years earlier, speaking of McMoRan's long-range objectives, then-president Rankin had said: "Our goal is to become a $50- to $100-million petroleum company that will become less dependent on its ability to raise outside capital ..." Then, as this article you are reading was actually being put together, word came that Freeport Minerals Company and McMoRan Oil & Gas Co. had merged to form Freeport-McMoRan Inc. Already, the New York Stock Exchange trading symbol is "FTX." Other news will be forthcoming, but too late for reporting here.

MAISON BLANCHE

Few Orleanians alive today remember when the towering, terra-cotta white building of the Maison Blanche (MB) department store was not the landmark of New Orleans's world-famous Canal Street.

The building was built exactly 100 years after the street had its beginning—March 3, 1807—when the U.S. Congress recognized and confirmed the city's rights to the Commons around the colonial town, now the French Quarter, providing the city "shall reserve for the purpose, and convey gratuitously for the public benefit ... as much of the said Commons as shall be necessary to continue the Canal of Carondelet from its present Basin to the Mississippi River."

Needless to say, on October 21, 1907, when the store moved into its new building, that canal still had not been dug. Instead, its right-of-way in the street's center had come to be called "neutral ground." This recalled the City Charter of 1834, which divided New Orleans into two cities, each with its own city council. The French city was below Canal, and the American above, leaving the center of the street neutral. From this beginning, centers of all 2-lane streets in New Orleans have come to be called "neutral grounds."

But Maison Blanche has not stood there idly in its historical neighborhood. The store has made some history itself. For example, during World War I, the store, which had remained closed for the duration to save fuel, staged a parade on Armistice Day, November 11. Led by its founder and president, S.J. Schwartz, all the employees paraded down Canal Street. Six years later, Schwartz was the 1924 recipient of *The Times-Picayune* Loving Cup for his countless civic achievements.

The next year, the store joined with the Saenger Theater to put radio station WSMB on the air. Those last three letters in the station name (SMB) identify Saenger and Maison Blanche as its founders. Its studios have always been in the Maison Blanche building, and the two tall transmitter towers on its roof prompted a wag to inquire at the time, "Has Maison Blanche struck oil?"

The 1920s was an eventful decade for Maison Blanche. One exciting day in November of 1926, over 7,000 people crowded the store to try out the city's first escalators.

Then, on March 4, 1938, misfortune struck. Fire broke out on the top floor, and the store had to be shut down for a full week to clean up the mess. But the establishment that survived war and the Great Depression was able to withstand the devastating fire, as well.

In 1942, MB opened its first suburban store. Others soon followed. But New Orleans's Central City, on both sides of Canal, is the city's prime tourist attraction. When the Superdome was added to this, New Orleans found that tourism had become its second largest industry. And now with a World Fair in the wings, it behooves Maison Blanche to stand tall on its historic corner, as it has for so many years, to beckon countless more visitors. Because they're on the way.

Maison Blanche has been the landmark of New Orleans's world-famous Canal Street since 1907.

MANHEIM GALLERIES

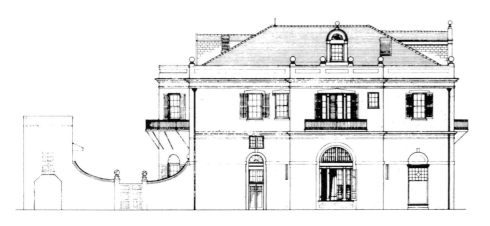

1919 occupied three floors and the slave quarters of the del Campo Townhouse at 409 Royal Street, and

A.G. Manheim, and his grandchildren, Ida Manheim, James Manheim, and Edward L. Weitz, who comprise today's third generation of Manheims. Following in the quality tradition of Bernard, they continue to maintain one of the world's finest and most comprehensive collections of art and antiques in New Orleans, as well as two Manheim Galleries in Dallas.

During the latter years of his life Bernard Manheim became an ardent collector of Orientalia—especially jade carvings. Much of the collection he secreted in a small room on the second floor of Latrobe's bank building. Following Bernard's death in 1967, his children brought the fabulous collection of jade carvings together and,

Austrian-born Bernard Manheim moved to England at 13, where he learned woodworking. His skill found employment, and he remained for several years. But it was cold there. That's why Manheim, still a young man, migrated to New Orleans where it is seldom cold. His first employment was directing 100 workmen making period furniture in the rear building of the Brulatour Courtyard.

Soon his savings enabled him to buy a small shop in Royal Street. But the "antique" shops of New Orleans in the early years of the 20th century were not satisfying to Bernard Manheim, who had seen some of the great antique houses of Edwardian London. In New Orleans, shops were filled with remnants of furniture dispersed from the great antebellum sugar and cotton plantation houses upriver, which had been impoverished by the Civil War. Little of the furniture dated before the 19th century and much of it was ponderous Victorian pieces, mass-produced in the city itself.

Not wanting to deal in what seemed to him to be "secondhand furniture," Manheim established connections in England, France, and elsewhere in Europe to import genuine 18th-century antiques to New Orleans. He traveled to the Continent to select personally much of the stock, which by

With good reason, guidebooks exclaim over Latrobe's Conti Street design of his bank, shown at top. Around the corner on Royal Street (at right), his exquisite doorway bids Manheim customers welcome. (Drawing by Benjamin Latrobe.)

overflowed, as early as 1929, into the banking rooms, boardroom, and cashier's living quarters at the 1820 building at 403 Royal Street. That structure, La Banque de l'Etat de la Louisiane, had been designed by Benjamin Henry Latrobe, one of the designers of the United States Capitol at Washington, D.C.

For La Banque's principal banking room, Latrobe replicated a room he had created in the Capitol, a domed salon, magnificent in design and proportions. Because of a previous tenant, the building had already become known in New Orleans as "the antique dome" and Bernard Manheim's selection of works of art and antique furnishings, "many previously owned by noble families of Europe," soon turned the Manheim Galleries into "the largest and most comprehensive collection of antique English, Continental, and Oriental furnishings, porcelains, paintings, silver, and jade" in New Orleans.

The magnificent collection of the Manheim Galleries has been maintained by Bernard's heirs, his son,

in 1969, displayed it in the directors' boardroom of the bank, a semicircular salon renamed the Manheim Jade Room—one of the great jade resources of the world. Adjoining are several galleries of Chinese ceramics and porcelains, some dating from the Sui Dynasty (A.D. 589-618).

The Manheim Galleries at 403-409 Royal Street in New Orleans are indeed a modern-day tribute to the indomitable spirits of Benjamin Henry Latrobe and Bernard Manheim, two immigrant sons of America dedicated to fine quality and noble works in design.

MARTIN EXPLORATION COMPANY

The adventurers and empire builders who were lured to New Orleans before the Louisiana Purchase poled their way down the Mississippi River in flatboats and keelboats. More than a century and a half later, Ken G. Martin made his arrival in a broken-down 10-year-old 1953 Chevrolet filled with wife, babies, and little else. He also was seeking his fortune, but the magnitude of the goal he would ultimately develop would have flabbergasted those colonial frontiersmen.

Martin, a geologist, was sent to New Orleans in 1963 to work for Amoco. Ten years later he formed his own company—Martin Exploration Company—"on a shoestring." By 1978 his firm was gambling in southern Louisiana for stakes that dwarfed the national budget of 1803, the year of the Purchase. He put his New Orleans-based company into the race to explore for natural gas in the newly opened Tuscaloosa Trend, and by mid-1980 was competing in the Trend, well for well with such industry giants as Shell, Chevron, Gulf, and Amoco. By late 1980 the company's exploratory effort had been so successful that the future net income from a mere 5 percent of its Tuscaloosa leases approximated $3 billion. Moderate success in developing its remaining acreage would soon make Martin Exploration one of the country's richest privately owned oil companies.

When a Chevron well near Baton Rouge blew out under tremendous pressure from the Tuscaloosa Sand in late 1977, Martin recognized what he calls "the kind of chance that today comes once in a lifetime." He shoved all of his chips into the pot, using every dollar he could borrow to outbid the major companies in acquiring oil and gas leases in the heart of the Trend, a 100-mile by 25-mile layer of shallow-water sandstone deposited in southern Louisiana by a river system 100 million years ago. Today this sandstone is buried from 15,000 to 25,000 feet below sea level.

How did a geologist earning $10,000 a year 12 years ago become such an important factor in the development of the Tuscaloosa Trend, which some studies indicate might provide enough natural gas to increase the country's reserves by one fourth? How could his wholly owned company, which has only 17 employees, hold leases on 160,000 acres (10 percent of the total) in the most promising portion of the Trend and compete

Ken G. Martin, operator of the Martin Exploration Company, has struck it rich in the Louisiana natural gas deposits of the Tuscaloosa Trend.

successfully with companies having thousands of employees?

The story began when the elder son of Glenn "Abe" Martin, legendary football coach at Southern Illinois University, entered Louisiana State University in 1954 on an athletic scholarship and studied geology. He later won a graduate degree at the University of Texas and went to work for a major oil company.

Transferred to New Orleans in 1963, Martin devoted his energy to learning all that he could about oil and gas exploration in southern Louisiana. In January 1968 he forsook the security of a regular job and joined two associates to form Kenmore Oil Company, which had only $20,000 for the acquisition of leases. By the time the firm was disbanded at the end of 1972 and the partners went their sepa-

rate ways, Kenmore Oil Company was rated one of the 50 most successful domestic oil companies. From this experience Martin learned he had the skills to play his own hand in the high-stakes oil game.

In March 1973, he obtained a loan of $80,000 on his home in a New Orleans suburb, and launched Martin Exploration. The only stockholders were —and remain—Martin, his wife, and their children.

By the year's end Martin had put together 15 drilling deals for Dow Chemical, which needed gas for its Louisiana plants, and his company was on its way. Then came the Arab embargo of late 1973, and a quick rise in the price of oil and gas, making it profitable to drill in areas that had been marginal before. Accepting the full risks himself rather than selling off shares, Martin exploited the opportunity by plowing back his profits and even borrowing all he could against future profits. By mid-1978 his company had risked $100 million in borrowed funds.

When Chevron's Tuscaloosa well blew out at 21,346 feet and spewed gas at the astounding rate of 140 MMCF per day (one million dollars per day at today's prices) in late 1977, Martin moved quickly. "Being the only bureaucracy in the company, once I was confident I knew what was going on, we borrowed heavily and began buying leases," he recalls. "I didn't have to try to explain it to an accountant, and then work my way up through the hierarchy."

Crucial to his decision was his knowledge of southern Louisiana. "If this find had been in Texas or Wyoming, we would not have had the nerve to go in," he admits. "But this was our territory." He maintains his headquarters in New Orleans because of the proximity to the company's holdings, all of which are located in south Louisiana.

Martin knows better than most that the oil and gas business is not a one-way street to billions. In early 1978 one of his wells blew out, taking a year to bring under control at a cost of $20 million—all out of Martin's pocket because he had no insurance. His company was driven to the brink of bankruptcy, but only one employee deserted what many surmised was a hopeless cause. Those who stayed have profited, since each is cut in for a share of the income from Martin's successful wells.

Martin rewarded his family by acquiring one of New Orleans's grand antebellum mansions when the profits began to roll in. He has also become very supportive of cultural and charitable activities in the metropolitan New Orleans area, among other things having underwritten the costs to build a library and light the football field at St. Martin's Episcopal School in suburban Metairie.

But he has no illusions. "Every time I leave in the morning I think, 'It could all be gone tomorrow.' With everything at risk, you can't let up. But I believe I function best when I'm hip deep in alligators.

"You know, not many independents can compete with the majors, one on one, and few even try. But we can today because of our position in the Tuscaloosa. That's what I call fun!"

All of this equipment was involved in a $20-million operation to cap a Louisiana gas well being drilled by the Martin Exploration Company.

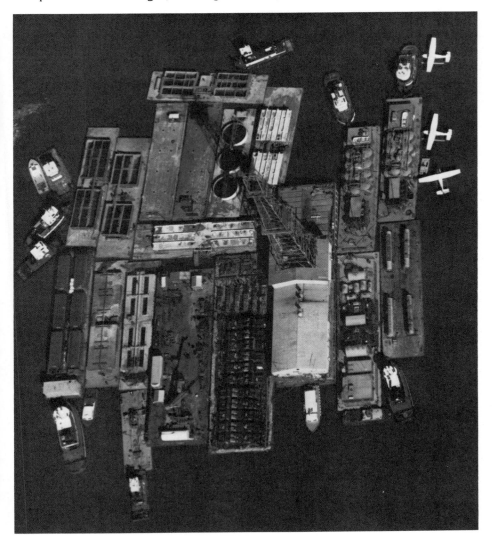

WALDEMAR S. NELSON AND COMPANY INCORPORATED ENGINEERS AND ARCHITECTS

Executives of Nelson and Company are (seated) Waldemar S. Nelson, president; Henry I. Madden, executive vice-president; (and standing, left to right) Tilghman G. Chachere, secretary; and Jerrel J. Freeman, Charles H. Weatherly, Leonardo A. Villalon, senior vice-presidents.

Waldemar S. Nelson graduated from Tulane University just in time to work with the U.S. Army Corps of Engineers, building cantonments, airfields, and other World War II training facilities. On one assignment he met an old Boy Scout colleague, John G. Bedell, also an engineer. They decided to team up as consulting engineers after the war.

As it happened, however, it was Bedell's father, who had been their scoutmaster on that earlier tour of duty, who initiated such a partnership. Colonel V.J. Bedell opened a New Orleans office in 1944. His son and Nelson joined him in 1945, and the three commenced a partnership on January 1, 1946.

In its first year of operation the firm outgrew its office on Camp Street and acquired an entire floor of a building on Union Street. Then, 10 years later, as the company was outgrowing this second home, tragedy struck. Colonel Bedell died suddenly in 1955, and his son had a fatal heart attack the following year. It was a busy time for Nelson, as he continued the firm's practice, completed a heavy work load, liquidated his deceased partners' interests in the business, and moved the company to larger quarters at 1200 St. Charles Avenue, which has remained its headquarters for 25 years. At the same time he incorporated the firm, bringing in as shareholders key engineers and architects of the staff.

From the outset the company built its practice on the principle of providing complete engineering service for a project within one office, thus offering its clients maximum coordination and efficiency in the design of facilities and administration of construction contracts. Because of the rapid growth of air transport following World War II, its early practice involved much airport design. With its location in New Orleans (the second largest port in the country) on the Mississippi River and Gulf Coast, the firm's practice has involved a great deal of marine work including wharves; locks; flood gates; levees; marine terminals; cargo-handling installations; channels; dredging; and offshore sulphur, oil, and gas installations. With the rapid growth of industries attracted by water transportation and abundant raw material supplies, the company's practice has typically involved work with petroleum refineries, ore processing plants, and factories for varied products.

This diversity in professional practice has required Waldemar S. Nelson and Company Incorporated to develop a large and versatile professional staff of 220 persons including civil, chemical, electrical, instrumentation, mechanical, process, and structural engineers; architects; scientists; and allied technical employees.

In 1980 the firm had over 700 clients with total construction value of projects amounting to $500 million. Many undertakings are large in scope, such as the $26-million East Bank Sewage Treatment Plant of the Sewerage and Water Board of New Orleans, pictured here. Nelson engineers and architects designed the plant and Nelson field personnel inspected the construction and administered the contracts.

Designed by Nelson engineers and architects, the East Bank Sewage Treatment Plant spans several city blocks.

NEW ORLEANS COLD STORAGE & WAREHOUSE CO., LTD.

Philip G. Kuehn is president of New Orleans Cold Storage & Warehouse Co., Ltd. Pictured with him here is the France Road complex, newest of the company's facilities.

TV weathermen, who admit they often have to make educated guesses in forecasting the weather, surely must envy the president of this cold-storage company and his three vice-presidents who manage the three complexes of the company. In the combined 3.7 million cubic feet of the Nashville Avenue, Airline Highway, and France Road complexes, management exercises complete control of the temperature. Night and day, winter and summer, it's always freezing the correct degrees to preserve foods properly.

Orleanians, with their historic appetite for rich food and drink, have been forever seeking ways to preserve the edibility of their Creole cuisine, if not its freshness. In antebellum days Orleanian housewives ignored New England pond ice of questionable sanitation being peddled in southern ports, but one of the first ice-making factories in the United States was built here in 1868. And 33 years later—on June 30, 1901—subscribers for the formation of a cold-storage company met. They appointed a board of directors, pledged $100,000 capital, and ordered an attorney to draw up a charter. Soon a 5-story building on Gaiennie Street opened for business. It's all in the minutes book.

By 1957, the New Orleans Cold Storage & Warehouse Co., Ltd., had moved from Gaiennie Street to more adequate quarters on Airline Highway, convenient to the railways and truck routes which move most perishable foods. In 1967 an even larger complex was built on the river at Nashville Avenue. And in 1973 Philip G. Kuehn was installed as its new president.

When the firm acquired Kuehn for its president, it got a rather remarkable man—one actually born in the cold-storage business, who had managed two similar companies before coming to New Orleans. It all began when his grandfather, a German emigrant to Milwaukee in the 1870s, bought the Wisconsin Cold Storage Company and placed his son, Kuehn's father, in charge. Eventually, Kuehn succeeded his father as president, then sold out to his brother in 1964. For a time he was vice-president and manager of the United States Cold Storage Company in Miami. "I've always liked the cold-storage business," Mr. Kuehn will tell you, "but I like it locked up. I didn't like Wisconsin's cold-storage winters. That's why I went South."

Kuehn had been in New Orleans seven years when the firm's third complex opened on France Road to service the port's largest container terminals at the industrial canal. Its picture is shown here. Inside, on every side, is evident the vastly improved and sophisticated equipment available for cold storages. It is hard to conceive of any more efficient cold-storage design and implementation anywhere. It is also designed for future growth.

The company advertises its complexes as "the three coldest places in town." They are very busy places, bustling to serve a generation that is living more and more in a Frozen Food Age.

NEW ORLEANS PUBLIC SERVICE INC.

Dedicated five years after New Orleans Public Service was incorporated in 1922, this 8-story building is still the executive and general offices of the utility company. Substantial modernization has kept the interior up-to-date.

This company, which was incorporated in 1922, literally bulges with some 46 previous streetcar, gas, and electric companies, of which it is the solitary remaining consolidation. Some of its predecessors have absolutely amazing stories to tell.

Take, for instance, the New Orleans & Carrollton Railroad, which began to roll 30 years after the Louisiana Purchase. As a railroad, its corporate birthday was February 9, 1833. That's when it was chartered to run from Canal Street to Bayou Sara by way of Baton Rouge. For some reason, when tracks-end was at Carrollton, it decided to stay in town and later became the St. Charles streetcar line. By 1973 it had run long enough to be listed on the National Register of Historic Places. Imagine a historic place that stops at every other corner. That famous streetcar line is only one of more than 40 transit routes (the

others are bus lines) comprising today's transit system, which carries more than 89 million passengers each year.

On January 1, 1824, Orleanians paid admission at James H. Caldwell's American Theater on Camp Street for their introduction to gas as an illuminant. Caldwell had imported a "gas-machine" from England for his theater to increase the candlepower of his whale-oil footlights. It did, and Orleanians (and Caldwell) were so impressed that in 1833 the legislature chartered the New Orleans Gas Light & Banking Company, with Caldwell in charge, to manufacture and sell gas. Two miles of cast-iron mains had been laid by August 9, 1834, when New Orleans struck a match to become the fourth U.S. city lit by gas. In 1928, natural gas from Louisiana wells replaced manufactured gas in Public Service's pipelines. Most cooking, water heating, and space heating in the city today is still by natural gas and the company serves more than 177,000 gas customers.

Public Service's corporate beginning with electricity came later because Thomas A. Edison came later. In 1882, the year after Edison built the world's first electric power plant in New York City, the Southwestern Brush Electric Light and Power Com-

pany contracted to light the streets of New Orleans with electricity. Mark Twain, who was visiting the city when the lights were turned on, reported that New Orleans was "the best lighted city in the Union . . . much better than New York."

The World's Industrial & Cotton Centennial Exposition in New Orleans in 1884 became a dazzling showplace of electric lighting and by 1886 there were three electric companies in town, with Edison himself a director of the third. It was the survivor that ultimately became "NOPSI," as today's company is usually termed.

NOPSI has pioneered in placing electrical facilities underground for improved urban appearance, not only downtown (in the early 1920s) but in new residential areas since the 1940s. The NOPSI electric system serves 194,000 customers and is interconnected with surrounding systems in three states as a part of the Middle South Utilities system.

But NOPSI's singular career may end soon. As this book goes to press it has been announced that NOPSI and Louisiana Power & Light Company had begun to develop a plan of consolidation of the two companies into one, with early 1982 as a target date.

A far cry from Caldwell's "gas-machine" of the 1820s are these three electric generating units of Public Service's Michoud Station, the company's largest. These units are currently burning natural gas as their primary fuel.

OCHSNER MEDICAL INSTITUTIONS

Dr. Alton Ochsner, world-renowned surgeon, gave his name to the medical institutions that have made New Orleans a major center for sophisticated medical care.

Outside the $100-million facility on the Jefferson Highway, the flags of the Latin American republics flutter in the breeze. Inside, soft southern accents blend with the liquid sounds of the Spanish language.

Modern, high-rise buildings create a melting pot every year for 200,000 patients who flock to the Ochsner Medical Institutions. Ten percent are Latins, and thousands of others are from Dixie, referred by hometown physicians to a regional court-of-last-resort for serious illnesses. Still others are residents of metropolitan New Orleans.

In almost four decades of operation, the Ochsner Clinic and Ochsner Foundation Hospital have been factors in reviving New Orleans's 19th-century standing as a major medical center, now international in scope. The institutions bear the name of Dr. Alton Ochsner, one of the giants of modern surgery, who in 1942 joined forces with four other colleagues on the Tulane University medical faculty in establishing the first major group practice in the South.

They opened the doors 25 days after the Japanese attack on Pearl Harbor. The clinic concept of providing patients with the diagnostic and treat-

Flags of the Latin American republics fly outside the complex of the Ochsner Medical Institutions.

ment skills of specialist physicians under one roof caught on immediately. In 1947, unable to find beds for all of its patients in existing hospitals, the group took over an abandoned wartime military hospital at Camp Plauche, near the Huey P. Long Bridge. They called it "Splinter Village," because it was a cluster of frame buildings connected by long, enclosed walkways.

The surroundings were rough, but the care was world class. Here Ochsner installed the pioneer recovery room for the early hours after surgery and the first family room where relatives of patients received special attention during the anxious period when an operation was in progress. Here, too, was established a hotel for patients and their kin. All the while, the clinic was pioneering in surgical advances and treatment therapies for cancer and heart disease.

The hospital was moved in 1954 to a sparkling, modern facility at 1516 Jefferson Highway, and in 1963 an ad-joining building was erected for the Ochsner Clinic. Both structures later were expanded to their present size. Part of the complex is Brent House, the modern version of the hotel.

From the start, patients from Central and South America made their way to the facilities. Some were sent by Latin doctors who had been students of Dr. Ochsner. Others were attracted by the diagnostic reputation of the clinic in the countries south of the border.

Over the years hundreds of doctors who served their internships and specialty residences at Ochsner have scattered over the United States, most of them in the South. They now are a major source of referrals. A postgraduate program helps to keep practicing physicians and surgeons abreast of medical advances. A research program sponsored by the Alton Ochsner Medical Foundation has made its contributions, particularly in the treatment of high blood pressure, all forms of cancer, and new techniques in heart surgery.

The Ochsner Clinic is a member of the "Big Six" association which includes the Mayo Clinic, the Cleveland Clinic, and other renowned American centers for medical referral. Today, 180 staff physicians practice in 36 medical and surgical specialties. In addition, 180 young, new doctors are obtaining their specialty training at the foundation.

PEREZ ASSOCIATES, ARCHITECTS

The home office for Perez Associates, Architects, was converted from an 80-year-old warehouse. The stairway, shown here, links all three floors. The dramatic effect was created by combining wood from the original warehouse with touches of marble.

The Piazza d'Italia has brought national and international attention to the Perez office. The piazza, called a masterly environmental celebration by some, while others consider it theatrical and out-of-place, epitomizes the design philosophy of the firm. "I believe in exposing yourself to criticism," says August Perez III, whose father founded the firm in 1940. Whereas Perez Jr.'s buildings are modern, conventional, and functional—the Tulane Medical Center, One Shell Square, and the Hale Boggs office building and court building, for example—Perez Associates' approach to architecture is more aesthetically exciting.

When Perez III inherited the firm in 1976, the office obtained several contracts for showpiece projects in the Central Business District and along the riverfront. Included was Canal Place, an office, retail, hotel, and condominium center that is creating an anchor at the foot of Canal Street. The Hilton Hotel addition, with con-dominiums atop the Julia Street Wharf, is the first new housing project of any kind downtown since 1900. The New Orleans Convention and Exhibition Center, the Louisiana Pavilion at the 1984 New Orleans World's Fair, is bringing the city into an equally competitive position in the national-convention and trade-show market.

Perez Associates' commitment to the revitalization of the old warehouse district, the CBD and Canal Street won the firm the commission of master architect planner for the world's fair. Perez's vision of the fair is one of green parks lining the Mississippi, giving the riverfront back to the people. And the old warehouses, transformed into an exciting neighborhood of offices and hotels, art galleries and restaurants, and apartments and condominiums, will become the Soho of the South.

One of Perez III's first actions as head of the firm was to move its headquarters from a 5-story Canal Street building developed by his father in 1960 to a sleekly converted 80-year-old coffee warehouse. The move was a symbolic effort to prove the firm's ambition to win awards for design excellence, and is a physical example of the design and renovation possibilities of the old warehouses. Only the painted white band atop the parapet, the skylight, and the new doors at the entrance lobby reveal new uses inside. The interior is like a huge piece of sculpture. Skylights, an atrium, diagonal walls, planes, muted colors and shadows, and exposed brick and beams create a dynamic and stimulating setting for each day's work.

This building in Harvey, on the west bank, was constructed for a Louisiana utility company. Simple in design, with dark window bands wrapping the facade, the facility is a fine example of corporate architecture.

PERLIS, INC.

In New Orleans, the Carnival Season begins on Twelfth Night and runs some 50 days through Mardi Gras to Ash Wednesday. In observation of this, Carnival organizations stage more formal balls than the 50 days of the season. That's why more evening wear is sold in New Orleans than in any other city in America, regardless of size.

Also in New Orleans, Rogers Perlis sells more men's formal wear than anyone—including more than 150 full-dress suits, the *costume de rigueur* of the Mardi Gras Ball. Although a colorful personality himself, Perlis will tolerate the selling of no pastel-colored, fur-collared, or flashy evening wear for men at his store uptown on Magazine and Webster streets.

It is an address in the heart of the uptown area—a century-old, conservative neighborhood of well-to-do and friendly residents. Perlis doesn't even advertise. These people learn much about worthwhile things from each other, and Perlis long ago was proven worthwhile. Now people flock to his store—even some who have been forced to move out of the neighborhood. This is an unusual business success, this clothing store for men and boys, which recently has added a women's wear section.

It all began when 21-year-old Rogers Perlis began selling clothing downtown. He fell in love with Dorothy Koehl, who was a fashion model and looked beautiful in her clothes. Could it have been that that was what first attracted her to the young salesman, whose life was already dedicated to getting people properly fitted into their clothing? Anyway, as the courtship went on, this talent of Rogers's endeared him to Dorothy. But, she declared to him, it was wasted if he continued working for others. She refused to marry him until he established his own business. Maybe this is only a family legend, but it gains considerable credence when it is learned

they were married July 28, 1940, eight months after he had opened his own store at 6058 Magazine Street.

Like all businesses with high hopes and low capital, this one called for long hours of hard work. No luxuries—just dedication and application, plus good luck and a touch of genius. The business was an immediate success; within six years Rogers and Dorothy had purchased a building on the corner of Magazine and Webster. Here Perlis would win his distinction as the "premier clothier of Uptown," from here they would send their two children—David and Sharon—to become the practicing attorneys they are today. Here, by 1980, their clientele was such that a store three times as large was built, with the old store torn down to become the paved parking lot.

In a recent interview, Rogers Perlis was quoted as saying, "I love to wait on the people, by gosh." And, by gosh, it is this unwavering tradition of personal service, now shared by a staff of nearly 50 that has been the secret of this store's success, as well as another Perlis store in a suburban shopping center, and a leased department in Gus Mayer's Carrollton store. Rogers Perlis has achieved all this and more.

In 1972 David Perlis relinquished his law practice to become executive vice-president of this family corporation, and Mrs. David Perlis later joined him to head up the Perlis women's departments. With David to manage the business, Rogers Perlis has achieved continuity. Now, undisturbed and uninterrupted, he can enjoy his hobby of waiting on the people.

And his clientele will just *love* that.

The original Perlis store opened on Magazine Street, New Orleans, in 1940. It was still located there in 1981.

Rogers Perlis (left) was joined in the family business by his son David in 1972.

PETERSON MARITIME SERVICES, INC.

Peterson Maritime preparing to respond to a hazardous material spill with the company's twin, off-loading lifesaving equipment from their emergency vehicle.

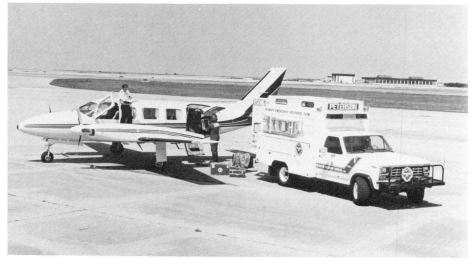

In 1972 Harold J. Pecunia resigned an executive position with a steamship agency to take over the operation and management of the company. At that time the name was changed to Peterson Maritime Services, Inc., and Pecunia subsequently became president and owner of the company. Associated with the maritime community ecutive charter.

Peterson also owns and operates Waterfront Transportation Corp. This firm provides water transportation to vessels at anchor in the port, utilizing a fleet of high-speed crew boats.

Many things have led to the booming expansion of the company, but intensified public and private awareness of the environmental dangers inherent in oil and hazardous material pollution was a major factor. The firm has invested heavily in technicians and equipment to fulfill the demands of successfully combating pollution by hazardous materials.

After many years of solving a myriad of problems, the entire operation is commonly referred to in the industry as "The Peterson Machine." Pecunia proudly comments, "We built it, we run it, and it works all over the world."

Harold J. Pecunia, president of Peterson Maritime Services, Inc.

Few people realize the many services required by the giant oceangoing ships from every imaginable port of the world calling at the Port of New Orleans to discharge and load cargo.

In 1960 Dean Peterson, a retired sea captain, realized a need for better and faster ship cleaning in his home port, New Orleans, and started Peterson Marine Service, Inc. He noted that vessels arriving in the port loaded with oil and scheduled to take on grain or other cargoes were costing thousands of dollars daily while unskilled ship crews made feeble attempts at properly cleaning cargo areas.

Since that time antiquated methods have been eliminated and replaced for the most part by highly specialized equipment and accomplished technicians. Through the years the Peterson operation expanded and today, as senior member of cleaning companies, the company provides ship and barge cleaning services throughout the Gulf with offices in New Orleans, Houston, and Mobile.

since 1953, Pecunia traveled worldwide discussing problems with ship owners, operators, and agents. He used imaginative planning coupled with the need for additional related services in the fields of oil pollution, hazardous materials waste, aviation, and product sales to catapult the company into one of the leaders in the industry.

Peterson has responded to major incidents requiring its expertise throughout the United States as well as internationally, such as the 1979 oil well blowout in Mexico. The largest hazardous chemical spill of PCP in U.S. history, caused by a ship collision in New Orleans, was successfully cleaned up by Peterson.

Due to the emphasis placed on emergency response and to better facilitate the needs of the various divisions, the company owns and operates helicopters, an executive twin-engine airplane, and an amphibian float plane. When not involved in company business these aircraft are available for ex-

PONTCHARTRAIN MOTOR COMPANY, INC.

It was during World War I that the automobile first came to be regarded as a practical means of transportation. In earlier days, it was called "the rich man's toy" by those not wealthy enough to own one. And prior to this, the horse had been the principal mobile unit on battlefields since the warring days of Alexander the Great.

French Field Marshal Joseph Joffre provided the best advertisement for motor cars in combat on September 9, 1914, when he ordered reinforcement for the Battle of the Marne rushed up in Paris taxicabs. The German drive was stopped, and the conflict lapsed into static trench warfare for four years. Historians consider this the turning point in World War I.

When America entered the war, the U.S. Army ordered Cadillacs for staff cars. It is against this background that young Bill Willkomm can be introduced—in the driveway of his Lakeview home, repeatedly taking the motor of his mother's Pierce-Arrow apart and putting it back together again. Neighbors, watching Bill at work, decided that Mrs. Willkomm was getting the best service job in New Orleans. This was the beginning of a great interest in automobiles that would become Willkomm's lifework, not to mention the lifework of his son and grandson as well.

Selling cars, and directing the sale of them, was to become his career. Contemporaries who knew him in the old days attest to the fact that nobody could sell cars like Bill Willkomm—with the possible exception of Field Marshal Joffre.

Willkomm had been asking General Motors for a Cadillac distributorship since 1932. Instead, he was put in charge of a floundering Chevrolet distributorship. "If you can sell 100 cars a month for five years, we'll make you a distributor," GM told him, thinking

Here, William J. Willkomm, Sr., is shown with one of the 6,000 Chevrolets he sold during the 1930s. Sharp-eyed readers will notice the price of this 1933 Chevrolet—it cost $640.

that would eliminate Willkomm's sales pitch. After all, the country was in the midst of the Great Depression. Who could sell 6,000 cars? Well, Willkomm did, and that's how he became president of Pontchartrain Motor Company, Inc., on September 5, 1937, with instructions to sell Cadillacs in New Orleans, as well as throughout southern Louisiana and Mississippi.

Pontchartrain Motor Company, Inc., is located at 701 Baronne, the same address at which Willkomm had gotten his start in the business in 1919, selling Cadillacs for Gus Revol. His first 14 years of operation were lucrative enough to enable him to buy the build-

ing in 1951.

In 1947, William J. Willkomm, Jr., came to work at 701 Baronne in the new-car department while still in college. He became a Cadillac dealer and president of Pontchartrain Motor Company, Inc., in 1964. Upon completing college in 1973, William J. Willkomm III came to work for the company. Today he is vice-president and general manager.

It does appear that Bill Willkomm, in addition to selling 6,000 Chevrolets to become a Cadillac dealer, has also provided substantial continuity for the business. His grandson, the vice-president, is also called Bill.

This is a 1980 view of Pontchartrain Motor Company's Cadillac showroom on Baronne Street. It replaced an earlier structure on the same site that dated from the 1930s.

POPEYES FAMOUS FRIED CHICKEN

© King Features Syndicate

Alvin Copeland, founder and president of Popeyes Famous Fried Chicken, is shown below. The character at left needs no introduction.

Among New Orleans's principal attractions are its restaurants, so many of which feature the spicy, seasoned Creole and Cajun cuisine—a historic blending of the culinary talents of colonial French, Spanish, and Negro cooks. It has long been popular in New Orleans and southern Louisiana.

This success story had its beginning on Tuesday, June 13, 1972, in the Cajun community of Chalmette where the Battle of New Orleans was fought in 1815. And where, 157 years later, Alvin Copeland had a fast-food restaurant, "Chicken-On-The-Run," which wasn't doing well.

But Copeland discovered that customers were lining up to buy his spicy Cajun-style chicken and not the regular kind. "Then," he will tell you, "I decided to shut down over the weekend of June 10-11, and alter the restaurant to sell only the Cajun-spiced fried chicken. Also, by next week I'd need a new name for the place." So, to relax and think about a name Copeland took his wife to a movie.

The French Connection was the movie they saw. In one of the scenes of this 1971 Academy Award-winning film, somebody yelled "Popeye's here!" when Gene Hackman, in his Popeye Doyle role, made a dramatic entrance. And that was when Copeland made an equally dramatic exit to wake up a sign painter. "Paint me a sign to read 'Popeyes Mighty Good Fried Chicken,'" he instructed his sleepy sign painter, who had the sign completed by Monday.

Today, Popeyes operates restaurants in 28 states, 60 cities; and several international openings are pending. Al Copeland's spicy New Orleans-style recipes for Cajun rice, fresh onion rings, and of course, that famous spicy chicken have helped make the Popeyes chain the third largest fried chicken operation in the world.

When Copeland's one Chalmette restaurant began to gross upward of $200,000 a year, and before some 300 restaurants grossed $200 million annually eight years later, the company reached an agreement with King Features Syndicate in New York, owner of the Popeye copyright. In return for royalty payments, the firm would have exclusive rights to use all the cartoon characters of the comic strip in the promotion of its fried chicken restaurants.

At the time of this writing, the president of the company was in Malaysia contacting new Popeye franchise holders, and a vice-president had just returned from Europe, where there is considerable interest.

In the United States, with three restaurants opening every week, 1,000 sold franchises being implemented, and new international business looming, Copeland's company is straining to exercise the tight controls he believes are vital. All restaurants are regularly visited and all new franchises must send personnel to training schools at the New Orleans home office. At all times the company's image and its excellent product must be maintained. All the restaurants receive the proper recipe for the fried chicken, and the secret *ingredient d'origin,* which makes it Popeyes Famous Fried Chicken.

Finally, in the New Orleans area, the *place d'origin* of all this, the Popeyes restaurant on Canal Street is the largest volume fried chicken restaurant in the world, grossing $1.5 million annually. Certainly the record of this organization well matches the ever-winning prowess of "Popeye the Sailor Man"—and, as far as is known, Copeland's people seldom even eat spinach.

PORT OF NEW ORLEANS

"There is on this globe one spot, the possessor of which is our natural and habitual enemy. It is New Orleans ..." Thus, on April 18, 1802, Thomas Jefferson began a letter to Robert Livingston. With James Monroe, he was in Paris with orders to buy the Port of New Orleans for $2 million.

With clairvoyance unmatched by any other U.S. President, Jefferson went on to write that "the produce of three-eighths of our territory must pass through New Orleans to market. It won't be long," he added, "before half of it would follow this route."

It is widely believed that this letter gave Livingston and Monroe the courage to accept Napoleon's offer to sell to the United States all of the 551,538,560 acres of Louisiana for $15 million. If these three founding fathers had lived a scant 50 years after the Louisiana Purchase, they would have seen downriver trade at New Orleans amount to $300 million and New Orleans become the greatest export port in the world. What happened after the Civil War made Jefferson's extravagant 1802 claims for Mississippi River shipping downright niggardly.

Soon, powerful towboats were pushing "tows"—the name for many barges lashed together in a single train—both up and down the river, and pushing those picturesque 19th-century steamboats out of the river trade entirely. Nobody knows how many barges there are in this inland waterway service. But there is general agreement that, lashed together stem to stern, there are more than enough to make a "barge-walk" from New Orleans upriver to Chicago. There's further agreement that some 15 to 20 percent of them can be seen in the New Orleans harbor on any given day.

This inland waterway action is the most fascinating part of the Port of New Orleans's operation, which has its

Every year, some 5,000 ships carrying nearly 44 million tons of cargo valued at $10 billion pull into the Port of New Orleans's more than 100 cargo berths. The city's central business district is in the background.

seagoing side as well. Every year, some 5,000 ships carrying nearly 44 million tons of cargo valued at $10 billion pull into the port's more than 100 cargo berths. Ships are in constant parade up and down the 115-mile stretch of the river to the Gulf— that is, all but about 25 percent of the 5,000. Those ships use the Mississippi River gulf outlet from the Gulf to the intracoastal canal and inner harbor. It's actually a man-made fourth mouth of the Mississippi. (See the map.)

These two phases of the port's commerce, inland and seagoing, are aptly emphasized by the ever-increasing container traffic. Planners for the port are looking forward to more and more efficient container and other modes of traffic, as they devise the port's increased facilities for the 21st century.

And, alas, there are no models to follow. Nowhere on earth is there another port with the fascinating peculiarities of the Port of New Orleans.

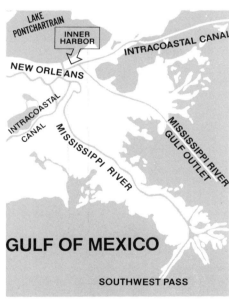

All but 25 percent of those 5,000 ships are in constant parade up and down the 115-mile stretch of the river to the Gulf. They use the Mississippi River gulf outlet from the Gulf to the intracoastal canal and inner harbor. It's actually a man-made fourth mouth of the Mississippi.

PRAGER INCORPORATED

When Bruno Prager emigrated to America from Plauen, Germany, in 1892, he was already an accomplished machinist. Arriving in New York as a dedicated craftsman, he had no trouble finding work and was hired immediately by Richard Hoe and Company, a respected printing-press manufacturer. Two years later, with a letter of commendation signed by Mr. Hoe, Bruno headed for New Orleans, where he continued to ply the machinist's trade. By 1897, he had saved $500, which he used to purchase the Novelty Machine Works, located at Tchoupitoulas and Girod streets. From that modest enterprise evolved Prager Incorporated, one of the South's largest, most reliable firms in the field of gear cutting, custom replacement parts, and major mechanical maintenance/repair service for the pulp, paper, textile, chemical, rubber, and other industries.

At the turn of the century, the Novelty Machine Works manufactured a number of different products. The company made bedsteads for Charity Hospital and faucets for wood cisterns that stored water for homes in the area. It produced frames for awnings widely used at the time. It built beer-keg cleaning machines and machines used for testing golf equipment.

Even with this kind of diversification, however, it was not long before the company came to be recognized as a specialist in the area of printing presses. The numerous New Orleans newspapers of that era, including the *Times Democrat*, the *Picayune*, the *States*, the *Bee*, the *Mascot*, and a German- and French-language paper, all used Prager craftsmen for installation or repair of their presses at one time or another.

As the years passed, Bruno was ably assisted by his two sons, Herman Prager, Sr., and Julius B. Prager II; the business prospered, resulting in the construction of a new, larger plant facility in 1922. Located at 472 Howard Avenue in downtown New Orleans, the original building continues to house the company's administrative offices and staff.

The first gear-cutting machine was purchased by the company in 1920; it is still in use today.

As the company grew and as the city's newspapers decreased in number, Prager began to diversify again. Changing the firm name to Prager Incorporated in 1931, by World War II the company had switched its emphasis to gear manufacture and repair and general machine repair. Following the war, two more members of the Prager family entered the business—Herman Prager, Jr., as an apprentice machinist in 1946, and J.B. Prager III, as an apprentice in 1951. They were followed by Thomas F. Ridgley in 1959.

The company embarked on an ambitious expansion program in the 1960s. Although Julius B. Prager II, the leader of the project, died in 1967, the third-generation family members, directed by Herman Prager, Sr., continued his important work in the succeeding years. A 22,000-square-foot storage facility on Constance Street directly across from Prager's shipping and receiving department was leased in 1971, providing the necessary additional space for pattern storage and completed projects awaiting shipment. In 1972, the firm acquired the Bishop-Edell Machine Works, a 17,000-square-foot plant adjacent to the Howard Avenue complex. The plant expanded Prager's line of services to include the rebuilding and overhauling of engines, compressors, and hydraulic pumps for the marine industry.

In 1979 a new addition of 12,000

In 1922 this was the new location of Novelty Machine Works. This building is still a part of the Prager Incorporated plant.

square feet completed Prager's expansion to encompass an entire square city block. Bounded by Howard, Magazine, Poeyfarre, and Constance streets, the plant facilities were renovated to connect the entire complex into one unit. The 1979 expansion maximizes efficiency on reducer repair, adds a modernized balancing and lapping department for high-speed gearing, and provides new testing facilities for reducers under power and magnetic particle inspection of finished gears and parts. The recent purchase of two buildings on Poeyfarre Street across from the main Prager plant will allow an additional 50,000 square feet for future expansion.

Throughout its history, the company has been known for its modern equipment, and acquisitions in recent years prove no exception. In 1979 the firm installed a Niles Gear Grinder, a high-precision machine that is the only one of its type in a job shop south of Chicago. The installation of a new 31-inch gear hobber and an 80-inch precision gear hobber in 1980 has elevated Prager's precision gear-cutting facilities to national prominence.

Prager Incorporated is organized into two divisions—the Gear and Pro-

The most recent addition in 1979 expanded the plant to an entire block. The exterior was updated and refurbished.

duction Division manufactures all new parts, shafts, gears, gear boxes, pinions, and pump parts; and the Marine and Repair Division specializes in the repair of equipment, rebuilding marine

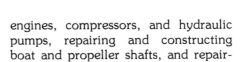

One of Prager Incorporated's newest additions, the Niles Gear Grinder has the capacity to grind gears to an accuracy of one ten-thousandth of an inch.

engines, compressors, and hydraulic pumps, repairing and constructing boat and propeller shafts, and repairing blowers and crank shafts.

The Prager company philosophy was summed up by former chief engineer Paul V. LeBlanc, who served the company for 56 years: "The will to serve, the determination to please, the knowledge to execute, our guarantee to satisfy, the pride of accomplishment." Present officers of the company include Herman J. Prager, Sr., chairman emeritus; Julius B. Prager III, chairman of the board; Herman J. Prager, Jr., president and chief executive officer; Thomas F. Ridgeley, vice-president and treasurer; and Elaine N. Prager, vice-president and secretary.

Prager's recent expansion and acquisitions demonstrate the company's faith in the city of New Orleans. As the company enters the 1980s, it will continue to provide customers the best in service and quality—as it has done since 1897.

PRESERVATION RESOURCE CENTER OF NEW ORLEANS

The Preservation Resource Center was established in 1974 as an organization that would be a resource for preservation-minded residents who were becoming more and more interested in New Orleans's historic inner-city neighborhoods. The Junior League provided the seed money for the foundation of the Preservation Resource Center of New Orleans, now an independent, self-sustaining organization that works full time to maintain the city's cultural and architectural heritage.

Patricia H. Gay, the director, describes the Center as an umbrella for 58 neighborhood and preservation associations, all with a common goal. Each organization is represented on the Preservation Resource Center Council, which meets monthly to discuss preservation matters and to be alerted to proposed zoning changes or other threats to building or neighborhood integrity.

The Center publishes the *Preservation Press of New Orleans,* 12 tabloid pages of news and articles of interest to supporters of the PRC. The *Press* has a circulation of 6,000, making it easily the most influential voice for preservation in the community.

In 1980 the Center began the restoration of a 3.5-story building at 604 Julia Street. It is one of 13 townhouses built in the 1830s on Julia Row, then an elegant neighborhood. In the present century the block between

This illustration shows the corner of Camp Street and Julia Row, an elegant neighborhood in the 1830s and '40s, now in the heart of the upper central business district. Although the area endured decades of neglect, it is experiencing restoration to its original ambience through the encouragement of the Preservation Resource Center.

St. Charles and Camp streets degenerated into a skid row, and 604 served as a flophouse. The PRC purchased and began renovating the house into an economically viable building with both commercial and residential tenants. The PRC office, along with the neighborhood revival program initially funded by Community Development, is located in this building.

The Preservation Resource Center's building at 604 Julia is only three blocks from the site of the 1984 World's Fair in New Orleans. Because of this proximity and because of the importance of this event to the city, the PRC keeps its membership well-informed of Expo '84 planning and development. The PRC was commissioned by Expo '84 to do an evaluation of the Warehouse District. This historical analysis and title research of properties, streets, and areas is an important service offered by the Center.

Other services include architectural tours of neighborhoods such as the Irish Channel and Jefferson City, providing brochures with maps and descriptions that enable sightseers to proceed on their own. The PRC trains guides for its architectural tours of New Orleans, tours conducted by bus which include two interior stops. A speakers' bureau provides knowledgeable lecturers for group meetings. A legislative review system keeps watch on proposed ordinances and laws regarding preservation, helping members to make their views known to city councilmen, state legislators, and congressmen.

The Center is supported by the dues of its members, by contributions, by small public appropriations, and by funds raised at such events as the Julia Jump, Holiday Home Tour, and a Jog for Julia. Center presidents have included Mrs. William Bell, Dr. John Ernst, Louis Koerner, Patricia Gay, Stanton Frazar, and Margie H. Villere.

The PRC offices are located at 604 Julia Row, a completely renovated townhouse which offers six units for lease as apartments, offices, or retail facilities.

RUBENSTEIN BROS.

Morris Rubenstein blinked in dismay when he pulled the top off the carton of neckties that he had ordered for the opening of Rubenstein's Haberdashery at 102 St. Charles Street on April 16, 1924. Every one of the 144 ties was light blue in color, a discouraging circumstance for a young proprietor who wanted to attract customers by offering a wide variety of merchandise. But his brother, Sam Rubenstein, had an idea.

The Prince of Wales (later King Edward VIII and then the Duke of Windsor) was making a state visit to the United States and was dazzling male America with his sartorial elegance. At Sam Rubenstein's suggestion, a commercial artist was employed to prepare display cards for the show windows. "Prince of Wales Blue," the cards proclaimed, and the whole shipment of ties was sold. Half a century later, Morris Rubenstein

Morris, Elkin, and Sam Rubenstein (left to right) stand in the original Rubenstein Bros. store, which opened at 102 St. Charles Street in 1924.

chuckles over "the honor we bestowed on the prince."

As chairman of the board, Morris Rubenstein still oversees the operations of Rubenstein Bros. menswear company. The main store is at Canal and St. Charles streets, occupying six buildings, one of which was the site of the original shop. The firm also has a branch in the Lake Forest Plaza mall. Sam Rubenstein still sees customers daily, as do his sisters, Dora and Gertrude Rubenstein. Another brother, Elkin, Morris's partner for many years, died in 1979. Elkin's sons, Andre and David, are presently managing the business, Andre as president and David as secretary-treasurer and merchandise manager.

Barely old enough to vote, Morris ventured into his own enterprise because he wanted to make enough money to get married. His capital was a total of $500, representing his savings and those of his fiancee, Helen Allenberg. Brother Elkin invested in the operation when the store was enlarged for the first time by the renting of an additional three feet of width. Although all of the Rubensteins spent a great deal of time on the sales floor, Elkin began to take a more direct interest in the areas of advertising and fi-

Today, the main Rubenstein Bros. store occupies six buildings at Canal and St. Charles streets, one of which was the site of the original shop.

nancing. It was at this time that Elkin and Morris began purchasing the properties which their business occupied.

From the start, Rubenstein's aimed at the patronage of students and young businessmen and professional men, always staying in the vanguard as fashions changed. "We listened to our customers," the chairman explains. "They taught us all we know. We have had to offer unusual items, something interesting with eye appeal. We have relied on impulse buying."

Today, selling to the sons and even the grandsons of its early clients, Rubenstein Bros. is one of the largest exclusive menswear stores in the nation, and one of the best known fashion leaders. The clothing store has continued to enlarge, and today includes specialized shopping departments such as the Madison Shop, for traditional and European fashions, and the Extra-Ordinary Man Shop, for tall and big customers who demand fashionable clothing.

In a flyer announcing the 1924 opening, Rubenstein said, "Come over and see what the men are wearing." Many New Orleanians still follow that advice. There are even longtime customers who fly in from Mexico and Central and South America to spend half a day shopping in the familiar store.

ST. CHARLES HOTEL

The stately entrance of the St. Charles Hotel is more than the way into a privately owned New Orleans hotel. It has been and continues to be completely furnished in quiet elegance to accommodate discriminating guests seeking surcease from the congestion and bustling crowds of the downtown.

The St. Charles Hotel's location on St. Charles at Jackson places it at the entrance to the city's famous Garden District, a historical residential neighborhood of gracious homes on spacious grounds, usually handsomely fenced in. This corner also marks the beginning of residential St. Charles Avenue, which is actually an extension of the Garden District four miles long and one street wide. In the early days of the 20th century, St. Charles was elegant all of its length. Homes like Mrs. Whitney's, which previously existed at the present site of the St. Charles Hotel, flanked both sides of "The Avenue."

In 1809, when the upper city limits were set at Felicity Street, city surveyor Barthelemy Lafon was subdividing several plantations from St. Joseph Street to Felicity. It was then that he designed present-day Lee Circle, so the uptown city streets would turn as the river turned. Also, Lafon gave those mythological names to many streets in this new neighborhood, among them the continuation of a wider St. Charles uptown from the Circle, which he named "Route of the Nayades." St. Charles Avenue would continue to be called for these river nymphs for the next 46 years.

St. Charles Avenue was still being called "Nayades Street" in 1833 when the legislature chartered both the city of Lafayette and the New Orleans & Carrollton Railroad. And it was Charles Zimpel, the railroad's surveyor, who ran the line of the wide street all the way to Carrollton, as Lafon had planned it, and laid his railroad track in the middle of it. This railroad hurried the settlement of the uptown. As the railroad crossed 11 plantations, 10 of the 11 plantation owners subdivided their lands and homeowners moved in. The 11th plantation remained unsettled, to become Audubon Park. Then, when this street called Nayades crossed Lowerline into Carrollton, it became "First Street," certainly an appropriate name. It has been the first—the premier—street of the uptown from the beginning.

Finally, on March 20, 1852, it was officially named "St. Charles Avenue" for every block of its length from Canal Street to Carrollton Avenue.

Rightfully, the New Orleans Public Service reckons the St. Charles Streetcar Line, established in 1833, as the corporate beginning of its transit division. Powered by steam, by mule, by compressed steam, by ammonia, it even had one car in 1866 that walked. It has always been an urban service and was the first to become an electric streetcar, on February 1, 1893. In 1973 it also became the first streetcar placed on the National Register of Historic Places, and is the oldest streetcar line in continuous service in the world. Today its fans have loudly petitioned the U.S. Postal Service to issue a St. Charles Avenue Commemorative stamp.

The St. Charles Hotel should be commended for advocating the preservation of St. Charles Avenue and the restoration of its charm of yesteryear, because in this era St. Charles Avenue is equally as historical and as nostalgically worthy as any of the other priceless relics of New Orleans's treasured past.

Built in the 1870s, the stately Whitney Mansion (below) was demolished in 1938 and the St. Charles Hotel (right) was built on the same block at St. Charles and Jackson avenues.

SCHWEGMANN GIANT SUPER MARKETS

The Schwegmann family has been in the grocery business in New Orleans ever since John Garret Schwegmann, a German immigrant, opened a store at the corner of Piety and Burgundy streets in 1869. The grocery later passed into the hands of his son, Garret A. Schwegmann, who was a fine businessman. Garret Schwegmann was well known not only as a grocer but also as a banker and part owner of a coffee company. Under his guidance the Schwegmann grocery business greatly improved and became firmly established.

In 1939 Garret Schwegmann rented the grocery to his brother John Schwegmann, Sr., and his nephews, John Schwegmann, Jr., Anthony Schwegmann, and Paul Schwegmann, and Wilfred I. Meyer, the best friend of John Schwegmann, Jr. It was at this time that a change to self service was made and the basic principle was formed upon which Schwegmann Super Markets operate; namely providing goods to the consumer at the lowest price possible and relying on large volume sales for a profit.

In 1946 the first Schwegmann Brothers Giant Super Market, founded

The familiar front of one of the 12 huge Schwegmann stores.

by John Schwegmann, Jr. (born 1911), opened on Saint Claude Avenue. By purchasing in large quantities and working on a low percentage of profit, the company has been able to offer consistently low prices.

However, the prices on many products were kept artificially high because state and federal Fair Trade laws allowed the manufacturer to dictate to the retailer what its product must sell for even though the manufacturer no longer owned the product. After a series of court battles which ended in

John G. Schwegmann founded the company in 1946.

1951 in the United States Supreme Court, a landmark decision in favor of Schwegmann Brothers Giant Super Markets struck down the Fair Trade laws. This decision has saved consumers throughout the United States literally billions of dollars over the years, as any retailer may now price merchandise below the manufacturer's suggested retail price. This is what free enterprise is really all about!

Through the years Schwegmann continued to campaign for consumer causes on state and federal levels. Two of the most notable were the price fixing of drugs and of liquor. In the case of the latter the Louisiana State Legislature passed a law making it mandatory for retailers to sell each bottle of liquor above a certain price; to sell cheaper was illegal. The other cause is Schwegmann's ongoing fight, spanning four decades, to eliminate the price fixing of milk. At this date Schwegmann's is still litigating certain aspects of this anticonsumer issue.

In 1979 the official name of the company changed from Schwegmann Brothers Giant Super Markets to Schwegmann Giant Super Markets.

Due to the support of its customers, Schwegmann Giant Super Markets over the years has been able to expand. Under the management of John Schwegmann, Jr., 10 stores were opened between 1946 and 1973. John F. Schwegmann represents the fourth generation of Schwegmann grocers in Louisiana.

T. SMITH & SON INC.

The day in 1981 this account was written, the Army Corps of Engineers reported waterborne commerce in the Port of New Orleans had topped New York with 167.1 million tons to New York's 163.6 million.

Another story in the same copy of the *Picayune* reported that coal would be providing more than half of the world's energy needs by the year 2000, and the United States had a limitless supply of coal. Actually, the story said the United States had a 300-year supply, which was certainly limitless for anyone reading the paper that day in 1981.

It was good news for New Orleans, its port, and especially for T. Smith & Son Inc., New Orleans-based stevedoring firm, as well as its oldest, biggest, and most resourceful. A year earlier the company had demonstrated how its high-speed revolver cranes had been loading sea vessels with coal in record-breaking times of 28 hours.

But this incident is nothing new for T. Smith & Son Inc., which has a century-long record of keeping up with the port's progress with stevedoring know-how as ships and the handling of them has so constantly changed through the years. In fact, Smith's only

error was that of its founder. Terence Smith, who arrived in New Orleans at the age of 13, was already an accomplished sail-maker, just when steam was making sailboats as dead in the water as sails had rendered Roman galleys.

But this teenage immigrant from County Caven, Ireland, lost no time adjusting; in fact, the whole port of New Orleans was experiencing a period of adjustment. Farragut's Yankee fleet had just steamed past outmoded Forts St. Philip and Jackson, historically rigged to stop only warships that sailed. Confederate New Orleans was a captured city. Commerce was nil; not only that but the river mouth was silting up. Even Farragut's bigger ships had to jettison coal to float up Southwest Pass. It would be 14 years before July 4, 1876, when Captain Eads would install his jetties in South Pass and ships would begin to come and go to New Orleans. In less than 10 years after that Terence Smith had organized the firm of Marsal, Delaney & Smith, a stevedoring company which Terence operated.

At the turn of the century, the firm's

In 1981, with nearly 100 million tons of coal coming downriver for shipment overseas, T. Smith's high-speed revolver cranes are shown lifting 63,000 tons of coal aboard ship in three and a half 8-hour shifts.

name became T. Smith & Son when William S. Smith, Sr., joined his father in the business. From the beginning this company had been well-aware of the ancient art of handling and stowing break-bulk cargoes, so vitally important in any stevedoring service. Along with strong management and a dedicated work force, the Smith operation has long demonstrated that it had the expertise and proper tools to handle the products and produce of the Mississippi Valley that pour downriver in infinite variety for shipment overseas. T. Smith & Son Inc. is particularly proud of its crewmen, many in the second and third generation who continue playing important roles in the company's growth and mutual prosperity.

Terence died in 1924 and William S. assumed management, to be followed in 23 years by the third Smith generation: Terence J., James E., and William S. Smith, Jr. Terence J. Smith, son of William, lived long enough to witness the beginning of great changes in stevedoring. A dramatic increase in the size of ships required investment in high-gantry, long-boom cranes.

Following World War II, the Smith company, which had a recognized reputation as fast, efficient stevedoring specialists, was literally deluged with demands for further services, heretofore not expected of stevedores. Wide diversification was called for, which resulted in the creation of Crescent Towing & Salvage Co. Inc., Glennon Drayage and Warehouse Co. Inc., Ship Service Inc., Fleet Service Inc., Smith Brothers Towing Co. Inc., Temiji Towing Co. Inc., along with an affiliate of the firm, Donegan Lumber Co. Inc.

Another new stevedoring chore, peculiar to New Orleans, was the containerization program—the "LASH" operation (a Port of New Orleans invention) which simply meant lifting entire barges aboard sea vessels. Along with the similar "Seabees," it required further investment by Smith in floating derricks, one of them an amazing

Cranes of T. Smith & Son Inc. have been lifting a long time. Back in the 1940s, this vessel was lifted aboard another vessel for shipment to the Orient by two T. Smith cranes.

structure with three cranes on one barge. Smith performs the whole operation in the river. No river barge ever wets the wharf. Smith loads the barges and takes them to the ship, where they are loaded on board by the ship's gantry crane. The whole fantastic performance seems to recall the classic boast of the 202 B.C. Greek physicist and inventor, Archimedes, who boasted in ancient Syracuse, "Give me where to stand, and I will move the earth."

Like his great-grandfather before him, James E. Smith has been around stevedoring since age 13, first as an office boy during vacations from school and full time since graduation from college in 1950. He was president of his firm when this book was published, as well as—unusual among stevedoring executives—a past president of the port's Board of Commissioners, and past chairman of the New Orleans Steamship Association.

His recent comments on the many-sided problems of stevedoring are interesting—how, in one year as the leading handler of heavy-lift cargo, the company handled 1.5 million tons of steel. "Steel is different," he said, "it comes in coils, plates, rods, and pipes of all dimensions and sizes. You would not want to put inexperienced people to work steel. Your accident rate would go out of sight. One group of longshoremen in the port handles nothing else."

Speaking of longshoremen, Mr. Smith recalls, in a single year his company's employment of them in the Port of New Orleans totaled 749,032 man-hours, not counting other employees in administration, towing, mooring, and maintenance. It is interesting that no ship's crew can tie up—mooring, it's called—at a foreign port. All wharves are different and

registered stevedores must provide the mooring service. Also, more recently this company has expanded to Texas with T. Smith & Son (Texas) Inc. Operations in Houston, Galveston, and Freeport have developed into a strong arm of the overall Smith operation.

But getting back to coal, the OPEC cartel already has European nations shifting away from tenuous Mid-East oil supplies to more reliable coal shipments from America and South Africa. The United States stands to reap strategic as well as economic benefits from this. In 1980, 90 million tons of coal were exported by the United States, which has the product and the potential to ship out over 200 million tons annually by the year 2000.

A number of Atlantic and Gulf ports are going to be used for this huge operation. It appears the miracles worked by the coal cranes of T. Smith & Son Inc. should indicate that the Port of New Orleans will be getting a fair share of this.

In 1981 this was the only one in the world— T. Smith's floating LASH and container loader, mounting three derricks on one barge. In the Port of New Orleans, birthplace of LASH (Lighter Aboard Ship), T. Smith has spawned such equipment to further expedite operations.

STANDARD MORTGAGE CORPORATION

The Marriott Hotel in New Orleans was originally financed by Standard Mortgage Corporation in 1972. The hotel was refinanced in 1978 to allow for a major addition.

Residents have to look up to see the impact of the Standard Mortgage Corporation's activities upon the skyline of New Orleans. Some of the city's tallest office buildings and largest shopping centers resulted from money funneled through the state's largest private mortgage banking company. No. 1 Shell Square, 225 Baronne, No. 1 Canal Place, and the Marriott Hotel were constructed with loans, of up to $50 million each, serviced by Standard. Regional shopping centers in Houma and Lafayette, Louisiana, as well as the Clearview and Lake Forest malls in New Orleans were also financed.

Yet the firm's president, Edgar A.G. Bright, is just as pleased with the influence the company has exerted in persuading large outside lenders to take mortgages on old-fashioned homes that make the residential neighborhoods distinctive. Ordinarily, insurance companies and pension funds prefer to lend only on new houses. "I like to think we have helped maintain the city's charm," Bright remarks. "We convinced investors that lending in New Orleans is different from making mortgage loans in other areas."

By the end of 1980, Standard was handling 17,000 mortgages in Louisiana with an aggregate value of $750 million. Including the operations of another Bright company in Atlanta, the Standard interests service loans totaling more than a billion dollars. The company, which also owns the Standard Mortgage Insurance Agency, has branches in Houma, Lafayette, Baton Rouge, and Shreveport.

Originally opened in 1925 as the Standard Bond and Mortgage Company, Inc., the firm dealt in residential mortgages until it was purchased in 1964 by Edgar A.G. Bright, Sr., and Edgar Bright, Jr., of New Orleans and Albert Earling of Milwaukee, the younger Bright's father-in-law. The senior Bright, a former King of Carnival, in his younger days was a cotton broker and president of the New Orleans Cotton Exchange.

The Brights expanded company operations to include mortgages on industrial and commercial real estate as well as on residential property. The Bright era began at a time when the state was starving for investment capital. Partly through Standard's efforts, the money began flowing in from such huge institutions as Metropolitan Life, Aetna Life, Connecticut General Life, and State Farm. The company's growth was spectacular. In 1964 mortgages being serviced totaled $84 million; by 1979 that figure had jumped to $600 million.

As a correspondent for insurance companies and other major investors, Standard brings together home buyers and real estate developers with cash-rich institutions, including savings banks, that seek conservative opportunities. On a day-by-day basis, Standard collects mortgage payments and pays taxes and insurance on properties.

In the residential mortgage field, Standard competes with homesteads and savings and loan associations. However, the homesteads mainly handle conventional mortgages, and Standard primarily handles Federal Housing Administration and Veterans Administration loans.

Edgar Bright, Jr., who became chief executive officer upon the death of his father, is convinced that his company will continue to channel needed outside capital into New Orleans. "The New Orleans area is very viable," he notes. "It's a great place to live. I am glad we have been able to help people own their homes here."

Pictured in front of Standard Mortgage Corporation's home office are (from left to right) Roy E. Lassus, in charge of loan servicing; Anthony Chimento, residential loans; Lowery W. Smith, income property loans; and Edgar Bright, Jr., chief executive officer.

DR. G.H. TICHENOR ANTISEPTIC COMPANY, INC.

Both Dr. Lister and Dr. Tichenor became interested in preventive medicine at an early age.

Dr. Lister grew up in England during the reign of Queen Victoria. In medical school he had become fascinated with cases of gangrene and mortification. Then, after graduation, he learned that microbes became tissue killers when exposed to air, and reasoned that the destruction of microbes with an antiseptic (*killing infection* in Latin) should restore life to flesh. In 1865 he performed an operation with sprays of carbonic acid. It worked. The patient recovered, and Lister became world famous.

Tichenor's story is different. He had always been interested in chemistry, and when the Civil War broke out he began making explosive guncotton for the Confederate Army, then enlisted himself. Several times he was wounded in combat, the last time severely in the leg. "It's bad," doctors at the Memphis hospital told him, "we

gotta cut off your leg, soldier. You got gangrene." That night, on his one good leg, Tichenor escaped from that hospital.

Secure in a friend's home, he mixed a batch of the antiseptic he had just concocted and commenced treating his leg. In a short time he was completely cured. This was in 1863, two years before Lister's discovery.

After patenting his antiseptic in 1883, he made several attempts to market the product during the following 22 years, but his efforts were largely unsuccessful. In 1905 Arthur D. Parker negotiated a contract with Dr. Tichenor to manufacture and market the antiseptic. This marked the beginning of the Dr. G.H. Tichenor Antiseptic Company, Inc., originally located at the foot of Canal Street on the site of the present International Trade Mart.

At the time he founded the present Dr. G.H. Tichenor Antiseptic Company, Arthur D. Parker was president of the Parker-Blake Drug Company. In later life he helped organize and served on the first board of directors of New Orleans Public Service. Upon his death in 1928, control of his business interests passed to his sons.

For three generations the volume of sales by the Dr. G.H. Tichenor Antiseptic Company has steadily mounted

throughout the South, especially in the larger cities. Today from its office and factory at 1700 Baronne Street the company is busily engaged in promoting the widespread popularity of this proven product nationwide.

As we have seen here, Dr. Tichenor's Antiseptic was a front-runner in preventive medicine and there is general agreement that the product has won favor wherever it has been sold. Check most any southern medicine cabinet.

At left is Dr. G.H. Tichenor, with A.D. Parker shown above. Mr. Parker founded the company that still markets Dr. Tichenor's Antiseptic.

TIDEWATER INC.

John P. Laborde is chairman, president, and chief executive officer of Tidewater Inc.

Had the pioneer Kerr-McGee rig, 45 miles off the coast of Morgan City in 1947, been a dry hole this page might not have been written.

But on November 14 the rig struck oil, touching off the greatest discovery since one Sunday morning in August 1858 when Colonel Edwin L. Drake in Titusville, Pennsylvania, was first to prove that there was oil underground somewhere but one had to drill for it. Drake's was the first such well in the world. In addition to bringing in oil it brought about a whole new age.

And just as that first well started something, so, too, did the first offshore rig. In no time at all, rigs from other companies dotted the Louisiana offshore, all of them in constant need of support—equipment, fuel, crew changes, many things. For a few years all sorts of craft were pressed into service. Surplus naval boats, oyster luggers, shrimpers, pleasure boats— everything that floated was huffing and puffing to serve a brand-new industry.

Meanwhile, a few men ashore in Morgan City and New Orleans were planning useful ways to adequately service offshore equipment and personnel in this strange, new environment. These men were the founders of Tidewater Inc. In a recent book by Charles L. (Pie) Dufour, sponsoring the commemoration of Tidewater's 25th anniversary, he tells of their enthusiastic and sometimes confused initial efforts.

Eventually, in downtown New Orleans they obtained a one-room office, with one boss, one employee, and one boat tied up somewhere. New Orleans has always been the corporate headquarters of Tidewater Inc. By 1981, the company occupied 13 percent of 350,000 square feet in a 24-story structure on Canal Street called Tidewater Place. The company is leasing agent, manager, and co-owner of this building.

As for boats, Tidewater founders designed the type now used by the entire support industry. By 1980 Tidewater Inc. was providing marine support service to the international offshore oil and gas industry throughout the world. By that year its fleet numbered 400, varying in size, power, and purpose. An estimated 50 percent of those operated off the U.S. Gulf Coast.

The Mire Tide belongs to Tidewater's fleet of towing-supply vessels, which serves the offshore oil and gas industry on a global scale. The Mire Tide is 190 feet long, has 4,300 BHP, and attains a maximum speed of 13 knots.

This initial theater of offshore drilling is still a front-runner. But fantastic planned increases in rigs and platforms worldwide indicate that Tidewater's fleet will have to double to handle its share of this phenomenal growth— especially with geologists telling us that 40 percent of the world's gas and oil reserves lie under offshore continental shelves, with only 10 percent explored by 1980.

In his book of Tidewater's first 25 years, Dufour is lavish in his praise of the company's leadership. And well he might be. In addition to providing the most support boats for the offshore industry worldwide, Tidewater has acquired its own domestic oil and gas exploration company. A third affiliated company, Tidewater Compression, Inc., provides air and natural-gas compression equipment and services in support of oil and gas exploration and production activities. Nor can the corporation's Indonesian production be overlooked. Over the years, drilling units operating offshore northwest Java and southeast Sumatra have continued to add their substantial part to the balance sheet of Tidewater Inc. which, according to the 1981 annual report to its stockholders, "is stronger than it has been in the entire history of the company."

THE TIMES-PICAYUNE THE STATES-ITEM

Only 34 years after the Louisiana Purchase brought New Orleans into the United States of America, two itinerant printers launched a new daily newspaper. They called it *The Picayune* because that was the street sale price, a picayune being a silver coin worth six and one-quarter cents, a holdover from the time when Louisiana was a Spanish colony.

Since January 25, 1837, the publication founded by Francis A. Lumsden and George W. Kendall has continued, under one title or another, to record the day-by-day history of the city. No matter what other names have been included in the masthead, most New Orleanians always called the paper *The Picayune*. They still do today, when the title is the *The Times-Picayune The States-Item*.

The Picayune early became the most quoted paper in America. Publisher Kendall, the first war correspondent to win journalistic fame, went riding off with the United States armies in Mexico. He sent back his dispatches by pony express and chartered steamboat, beating even official couriers with the news. Most other newspapers eagerly picked up *The Picayune*'s scoops.

Kendall and Lumsden turned over management of the newspaper to A.M. Holbrook and Samuel F. Wilson, who were in charge in the spring of 1862 when *Picayune* headlines announced the fall of the city to David Farragut's federal fleet. For most of the Civil War New Orleans was under bayonet rule, its newspapers subject to military censorship. The Yankees forced *The Picayune* to suspend publication from May 26 until July 9, 1864, because the newspaper printed an item from the Cairo, Illinois, *News* that turned out to be false. There was no way of checking on the news story because

This is the first issue of The Picayune, *predecessor of* The Times-Picayune The States-Item, *which appeared on January 25, 1837.*

the telegraph lines were out.

Holbrook became publisher after the death of Kendall in 1869. In 1872 he sold the paper to a group of 224 businessmen, who printed it "under the auspices of the merchants of New Orleans." The editor during this period, R.B. Rhett, Jr., of Charleston, South Carolina, killed a judge in a shotgun duel. Subsequently, Eliza Jane Poitevent, the poet Pearl Rivers, Holbrook's widow, became one of the first female publishers in the United States. She married George Nicholson, business manager.

Meanwhile, Edward A. Burke arranged the merger on December 4, 1881, of the *Times*, established on September 20, 1863, and the *Democrat*, founded on December 19, 1875. The *Times-Democrat* and *The Picayune* merged on April 6, 1914, into *The Times-Picayune*.

The Times-Picayune in 1933 acquired and continued to publish an afternoon paper, the *New Orleans States*, founded in 1880. In 1958 the *New Orleans Item*, established in 1877, was purchased and merged into *The States-Item*.

S.I. Newhouse, owner of a nation-wide group of dailies, purchased *The Times-Picayune* and *The States-Item* in 1962, pledging to leave editorial control in the hands of New Orleanians.

The first president of the Times-Picayune Publishing Company was Ashton Phelps. His grandson, also Ashton, became president and publisher in 1967. The latter moved up to chairman in 1979, and was succeeded as president-publisher by his son, Ashton Phelps, Jr. In 1980 the morning and evening papers were brought together by the younger Phelps into an all-day newspaper, serving readers around the clock.

Ashton Phelps, Jr., is the president-publisher of The Times-Picayune The States-Item.

WALDHORN COMPANY, INC.

*T'was in the Crescent City not long
ago befell
The tear-compelling incident I now
propose to tell . . .*

*In Royal Street at Conti, there's a
lovely curio shop,
And there, one balmy morning, it was
my chance to stop:*

Thus in the *Daily Picayune* on February 18, 1894, and countless syndicated papers nationwide, Eugene Field began his pioneer newspaper column in verse. Visiting in New Orleans, he had happened into the "curio" shop of Moise Waldhorn at 337-343 Royal Street, where then as now it was difficult to leave without acquiring at least some of the fascinating things available for purchase. In a later couplet of this 1894 column titled "Sharps and Flats," Field tells what happened that morning: "Two dainty silver salts, oh! there was no resisting them, and I blew in twenty dollars before 9 o'clock A.M."

Such unusual customer experiences at Waldhorn's are keepsakes of the firm, of which another, 12 years later at Christmastime, is memorable. Then,

Pictured here are the Waldhorn Shop on Royal Street and the company's president, Stephen A. Moses, standing beside the painting of his grandfather, longtime company president Samuel Waldhorn.

Josie Arlington, most famous of the infamous "madams" of Storyville, dropped by to purchase some Christmas presents for her "girls." Josie was no piker. She bought $684 of girlish jewelry for Santa Claus giving, according to Waldhorn's account ledger.

Moise Waldhorn arrived from Alsace-Lorraine in 1881 and opened his shop at Royal and Conti, before antique shops were so termed. Moise called his place "The People's Loan Office," actually a discreet pawn shop for the impoverished Creoles of the French Quarter. This was the time following the Civil War and Reconstruction, when many formerly wealthy Creoles were left destitute except for their jewelry. They brought it to Moise Waldhorn, alas, not to pawn but to sell. That is why circulars of a later date advertised for sale "rare collections from old Creole families." But before his death in 1910, Moise Waldhorn had firmly established his business as a curio-antique shop—the first one in New Orleans.

No less enterprising was his son, Samuel, who carried on the business for the next 61 years. Actually, Samuel Waldhorn became a New Orleans institution. Quite in character was his donation of a "sugar bowl" to the Sugar Bowl post-season football-game promoters, with no strings attached. It is what champion football teams have been competing for every New Year's Day since 1934. But Waldhorn's doesn't give away everything, as Eugene Field laments in his poem.

This solid silver wine cooler, crafted in London in 1831, became the symbol of the annual Sugar Bowl football game a century later when it was donated to the game promoters by Samuel Waldhorn.

Located on the same corner since 1881, Waldhorn's is a 4-generation operation, and flourished during Samuel's long and worthwhile leadership. Presently the store is operated by two of Moise Waldhorn's great-grandchildren, Stephen A. Moses as president and Nancy Kittay as vice-president. They are both indebted to Samuel Waldhorn for the years of training he gave them, but they have made some changes, including more-frequent buying trips, attracting new and younger customers, and restoring Waldhorn's historic 18th-century building. There, they recently gave a large party to celebrate the firm's 100th anniversary. It is interesting to note that among the guests present were third- and fourth-generation customers and suppliers doing business with Waldhorn's.

Today, Waldhorn's has a large and constantly changing collection of period antique English furniture, accented by lovely Chinese and English 18th- and 19th-century porcelain. The sugar bowl was chosen from their well-known antique silver collection. Also to be found in the store is a fascinating array of antique American and English gold and precious-stone jewelry. Combining the best of the old with efficient, modern business management, the city's oldest antique store looks forward to its next 100 years.

WALK, HAYDEL & ASSOCIATES, INC. ENGINEERS & CONSTRUCTION MANAGERS

Maybe Houston hasn't done anything for New Orleans lately, but New Orleans still appreciates what that city did for us back in the early 1950s.

That was when a Houston firm of engineers opened a branch office in New Orleans. The company looked around for bright, young, local engineers to staff such an office, signing up several people, including a Tulane University engineering graduate named Haydel, and another named Walk, a product of the LSU School of Engineering.

However, the Houston firm didn't find enough business, so they closed their New Orleans branch and left town. But they had introduced Frank H. Walk to Gerald M. Haydel, who went into business for themselves. And that's what the Louisiana petrochemical industry—forever in need of expansions and new installations—is so appreciative about. In the first 20 years after its founding, the consulting design-engineering firm of Walk, Haydel & Associates, Inc., has compiled a staggering list of completed projects for satisfied clients, including just about all of the big names in the energy business. The firm has just finished the largest oil refinery in the world ever to be built at one time; it's located at Garyville, on the Mississippi River above New Orleans. While south of New Orleans, Walk, Haydel people are performing design work on the onshore installation to handle the tremendous oil import from LOOP, the Louisiana Offshore Oil Port, the only U.S. deep-water port for those huge crude-oil carriers (VLCCs).

In 1956, this impressive company of professionals had its beginning when the two founding fathers and equal owners shook hands and formed a partnership, which became a corporation in 1965. In 1970 and each year since, the authoritative *Engineering*

Shown here are Gerald M. Haydel (left) and Frank H. Walk, the equal partners who direct Walk, Haydel & Associates, Inc.

News-Record included the organization among the first 100 of the nation's leading 500 design firms.

Walk, Haydel's main office in New Orleans, a 9-story building purchased by the firm in 1975, is now filled with 30 key officials directing the work of some 500 men and women, all highly trained in the engineering-architectural areas of the computerized technocracy of these latter years of the 20th century.

However, not all of those who comprise the company's multimillion-dollar annual payroll are always at the aforementioned Carondelet Street office. Many are busy around the corner at the firm's Special Projects Office on Baronne Street. Other employees are staffing two busy branches in Mobile and Baton Rouge, while still others are out in the field involved in WHPMM—that's the Walk, Haydel Project Management Method, which ensures the completion of capital projects on time and within budgeted costs.

"When we founded our organization," Frank Walk tells us, "most work for large industry was done by design-construction firms, or by each industry's staff. Jerry and I saw a need and a market for us. The New Orleans area was becoming the petrochemical base of the world. We were in the right place at the right time." Maybe so. Many people have been in the right place at the right time, but all people aren't Frank Walks and Jerry Haydels. As alumni, they even proved that LSU and Tulane *teamed together* are winners.

The huge oil refinery at Garyville, upriver from New Orleans, is one of the company's many projects. This is perhaps the world's largest oil refinery built at one time.

STAN WEBER & ASSOCIATES, INC.

The painfully shy part-time photographer had no premonition, of course, that Fate was knocking on his door when a sales manager neighbor asked him in the early 1960s to spend a Sunday afternoon showing houses to buyers who were flocking to the just-opened Terrytown subdivision on the west bank.

Twenty years later, that photographer no longer takes pictures of children for a living. He is the chairman of the board of Stan Weber & Associates, Inc., by far the largest real estate firm in Louisiana. By 1980 Stan Weber, Jr., had built an organization with 19 offices and 1,200 associates. He had the help of his wife, Beth; his son, Stan "Skip" Weber III; and Reetsie Hicks, whose feminine intuition has been vital in keeping track of the details in an operation that produces transactions totaling more than $200 million a year.

Weber learned from his experience in Terrytown that his soft-sell approach inspired confidence in home buyers. He joined an old-line firm as a full-time salesman in time to play a role in the growth of the New Orleans area. When he opened his own company in 1966, he knew the action was in the suburbs, and first concentrated his efforts there.

In 1970, Skip Weber came home from Vietnam, where he had been awarded a chestful of medals as a tank platoon commander. He arrived on a Saturday night and went to work for his father on the following Monday morning. Within two years, Skip had become one of the company's most productive salesmen. In 1976, at the age of 30, he became president while his father assumed the chairmanship.

Skip Weber credits his father's Puritan work ethic and entrepreneureal spirit for the firm's

success. "We reversed the experience of the old-line companies, which started in the central city and expanded to the periphery," he recalls. "We first conquered the suburbs, then moved into the center."

The firm instituted professional training courses for its employees. "This is a people business, and we want our managers and salesmen to know how to deal with people. We teach them to listen," Weber explains. "The companies that survive and thrive have to stay up to date. The approaches that were successful in the 1960s won't necessarily work now."

In an era of high property prices when young couples find difficulty raising the cash for down payments on homes, companies must be creative in arranging financing. A second mortgage may be needed, a "wrap-around" may be created, or other techniques may be thought out to, for example, reduce the couple's monthly payment.

Skip Weber has shaped the real estate company to meet the challenges of the 1980s, when significant changes in marketing strategy are expected to take place. He looks for competition from national firms that are buying out local enterprises and branching out into new areas. He faces the future with confidence. "We're in the growing Sun Belt," he reminds. "New Orleans is scheduled to have a World's Fair in 1984. We'll have two new bridges to facilitate traffic over the river. We like the prospect."

Stan Weber (seated) and his son, Stan "Skip" Weber III, have directed the development of the most active real estate firm in the New Orleans area.

WHITNEY NATIONAL BANK OF NEW ORLEANS

In the city and the state there was good news and bad news at the time the Whitney opened for business on November 5, 1883, to serve the New Orleans community.

Captain James Buchanan Eads had completed his jetties at the river's mouth, and the port of New Orleans was born again. The state legislature had moved back to Baton Rouge, and the city was busily planning the Cotton Centennial Exposition.

However, a representative of the gas company called at city hall to explain he would have to turn off the street lights if the long-overdue gas bill wasn't paid. Meanwhile, newly elected Mayor William J. Behan was at his

bank making a personal loan of $100,000 to meet the city hall payroll.

Nor was there much good news statewide. Louisiana was recovering from one of its worst floods. By a count of two to one, voters had just approved a new state constitution which reduced the governor's pay from $8,000 to $4,000.

Perhaps the founding fathers of the Whitney might have chosen a more auspicious time for their bank's beginning. But the century-long performance of this solid financial institution has proven very good news for the people of New Orleans, whom it has served so long.

Humble, indeed, was the Whitney's beginning that year. With little notice, it opened with 11 employees in rented rooms at 637 Gravier Street. It began to compete for business with a dozen already established and presumably prospering banks.

Over its first 100 years, the Whitney's main office could always be found in the 600 block of Gravier Street, although its third home—the present main office—would list its post office address as 228 St. Charles Street. Built in 1911, this large building absorbed the first address, near the present bank's Gravier Street entrance. Whitney's second home, prior to 1911, still exists at 619 Gravier. It functions as the safety deposits division of the main bank. Also, by 1981 Whitney could count 13 other addresses, locations of its branches citywide.

At its centennial, the bank can certainly take comfort in the respect it has received over the years from its customers. An example of this is the $67 million of deposits in 1929, at the peak of the boom. It contrasts with $79 million in 1933, in the midst of the Depression. That figures out as $12 million worth of confidence in the Whitney National Bank of New Orleans by its depositors.

At the close of 1980, the bank's 98th year of service, the Whitney posted total resource figures in excess of $1.7 billion with capital accounts

totaling more than $157.4 million and deposits of more than $1.4 billion. The bank had a loan portfolio of $897.6 million—funds at work building a greater Louisiana. With cash equivalents in excess of $700 million, the Whitney is well prepared to meet the challenges of today's economy and well girded for growth opportunities of the 21st century. It is truly a great bank for a great city!

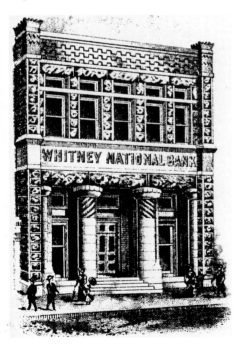

This rendering shows the Whitney's second home in greater detail, as Orleanians of the Gay '90s knew it.

The Whitney's third home, the present main office, has been a familiar landmark to Orleanians since 1911. In contrast, its smaller second home can be seen alongside it at the lower right. (Drawing by Morris Henry Hobbs.)

CARL E. WOODWARD, INC.

This office building project (above) is just one example of Carl E. Woodward's design-build expertise. Carl E. Woodward (inset) was the company's founder and first president.

A man is remembered for a lot of things. Back in 1913 Carl E. Woodward, a Tulane architect undergraduate, kicked a 52-yard field goal for Tulane that remained a record for as many years as the yards he kicked. He was graduated from Tulane just in time for World War I.

Then, in 1923, he founded this company, which has already recorded more years than its founder's field goal record. And Carl E. Woodward, Inc., is still going strong. It all happened like this:

On January 27 of that year, Thomas B. Denegre, a fellow veteran of Woodward's, joined him in chartering a firm to design and build homes. Woodward put up the architectural know-how to do that, but Denegre put up the $5,000 capital and that made him president. However, within five years Denegre sold his interest to his friend, and the charter was amended to read what it has been ever since—Carl E. Woodward, Inc. For the next 14 years the firm prospered. Then came World War II, and Colonel Woodward was recalled to active duty. The firm voted to suspend its business for the business of winning the war.

Then came the company's second birthday—February 1, 1949. It actually was reborn. Woodward was back, the corporate name of the firm was legally and firmly established as Carl E. Woodward, Inc., and Woodward had acquired a Butler Manufacturing Company dealership. This would make available to future CEW customers the economy of prefabrication. With its second birthday, the firm began directing its activities to commercial and industrial design-build construction, a further economy to CEW customers. The firm was faring well in the hazardous gamble of the construction business. It would do even better in 1955, when Woodward drew an Ace.

After being reborn in 1949, company records cite the coming of Armand "Ace" LeGardeur as the "third main event in Carl E. Woodward's history." LeGardeur will tell you he was green when he presented himself to Woodward for employment, but 26-year-old Ace, already a Yale graduate and a veteran of Korea as an army engineer, was green with the energetic, ambitious freshness of youth. In three years he was vice-president; in another six, president and chief executive officer. At that time chairman of the board Carl E. Woodward had this to say: "The present-day success is due mainly to the untiring and diligent efforts of Ace LeGardeur."

Corporate records can attest to that statement, citing that company revenues of a few hundred thousand dollars in 1955 were upward to $30 million in 1980. A scant half-dozen employees now number over 300, with qualifications among them in all the phases of expertise to listen to a client's needs, plan what he wants, and build it for his occupancy, and all within budgeted costs. The management team now includes Robert H. Grehan and Paul H. Flower as vice-presidents, and a complete sales and administrative team. Since 1970 CEW has been an "open shop" contractor, utilizing both union and nonunion subcontractors based on merit.

Most of all, the success of a design-build firm like CEW, Inc., is gauged by its completed projects. They are found all over town, most of them with contract amounts in the millions of dollars—how different from the old days when a smaller firm could qualify to build only smaller buildings.

Carl E. Woodward, Inc., has indeed come a long way, from the 1950s and a one-room office in the Vincent Building on Commercial Alley to the present domicile at 1019 South Dupre Street. "Yes," LeGardeur recalls, "the office space and the building elevator were barely big enough for the two of us back then and the largest contract ever was 'Swede' Woodward's decision to buy his own building and move out of the downtown area."

PATRONS

The following individuals, companies, and organizations have made a valuable commitment to the quality of this publication. Windsor Publications and the Preservation Resource Center of New Orleans gratefully acknowledge their participation in *New Orleans: An Illustrated History.*

Abry Brothers, Inc.*
Coleman E. Adler & Sons, Inc.*
American Security Bank, N.A., Washington, D.C.
Arnauds Restaurant*
Audubon Construction Corporation
John P. Barnes
John R. Batty
Bauerlein, Inc.*
C.F. Bean Corporation*
Becker & Associates, Inc.
Mr. and Mrs. Bryan Bell
Bernard and Nungesser, Inc.
Bisso Towboat Co., Inc.*
Boh Bros. Construction Co., Inc.*
E.G. Boh Forest Products, Inc.
Brennan's
Burnett & Company, Inc.
Canal Barge Company, Inc.*
Canal Place*
Joseph C. Canizaro Interests*
Dr. and Mrs. Michael E. Carey
John H. Carter Co., Inc.
Chart House Inc.*
Chevron U.S.A. Inc.*
Children's Hospital*
Clark Maritime Associates, Inc.
The Clothes-Horse, Inc.
Control Technologies, Inc.
Cooper Stevedoring Company, Inc.*
Dalton Steamship Corporation*
Dameron-Pierson Company, Ltd.*
Delta Steamship Lines*
Carlo Ditta, Inc.*
Dixie Machine Welding and Metal Works, Inc.
Dixie Printing & Supply Co., Inc.

Douglas-Guardian Warehouse Corporation
Drumm and Associates, Inc.*
Brooke H. Duncan
Eckco Fabricators, Inc.
Exxon Company, U.S.A.*
Favrot and Sons*
Gervais F. Favrot Company*
First Homestead Federal Savings & Loan Association*
First National Bank of Commerce*
Fischbach and Moore, Incorporated
Fitzgerald Advertising, Inc.*
C.B. Fox Company
French Market Corporation
Gallagher Transfer and Storage Company, Inc.*
George Engine Company, Inc.*
Gertrude Gardner, Inc., Realtors®*
Gillis, Ellis & Baker, Inc.*
Gulf Fleet Marine Corporation
Hellenic American Agencies, Inc.
Hibernia National Bank*
D.H. Holmes Company, Ltd.*
Howard, Weil, Labouisse, Friedrichs, Incorporated*
Roland Hymel and Associates*
International-Matex Tank Terminals*
Leon Irwin and Company, Inc.*
S. Jackson & Son, Inc.*
Peter Judlin, Inc.*
J.M. Key
Gordon H. Kolb Developments, Inc.
Lake Lawn Metairie Cemeteries & Funeral Home*
Landmark Motor Hotel
Louisiana General Services, Inc.*
The Louisiana Land and Exploration Company*
Louisiana World's Fair
Matt McGoey
McIlhenny Company of Avery Island*
McMoRan Oil & Gas Co.*
Maison Blanche*
Manheim Galleries*
Marine Engineering, Inc.
Martin Exploration Company*

Mechanical Construction Company of New Orleans, Inc.
Mercy Hospital, New Orleans
Waldemar S. Nelson and Company Incorporated* Engineers and Architects
New Orleans Cold Storage & Warehouse Co., Ltd.*
New Orleans Museum of Art
New Orleans Public Service Inc.*
Ochsner Medical Institutions*
Oosterhuis Industries, Inc.
Perez Associates, Architects*
Perlis, Inc.*
Peterson Maritime Services, Inc.*
Pontchartrain Motor Company, Inc.*
Popeyes Famous Fried Chicken*
Port of New Orleans*
Prager Incorporated*
Roldex International, Inc.
Rubenstein Bros.*
St. Charles Hotel*
Schwegmann Giant Super Markets*
T. Smith & Son Inc.*
Jahncke Spooner Associates Architects/Planners, Inc.
Standard Mortgage Corporation*
Mr. and Mrs. John A. Stewart, Jr.
Sunbelt Constructors
Dr. G.H. Tichenor Antiseptic Company, Inc.*
Tidewater Inc.*
The Times-Picayune The States Item*
Waldhorn Company, Inc.*
Walk, Haydel & Associates, Inc.* Engineers & Construction Managers
Hughes Walmsley & Company
Stan Weber & Associates, Inc.*
Mr. and Mrs. John G. Weinmann
Westinghouse Electric Corporation
Whitney National Bank of New Orleans*
Carl E. Woodward, Inc.*

*The histories of these companies and organizations appear in "Partners in Progress," beginning on page 225.

SELECTED BIBLIOGRAPHY

Articles

Drew, Christopher. "Hard Times Were Hardest on Blacks." New Orleans *States-Item*. October 27, 1929.

_____ and Pope, John. "Nightmarish Memories of Crash Still Haunting Orleanians." October 27, 1979.

Dufour, Charles L. "The Fall of New Orleans." *Louisiana History*, vol. 2, no. 2 (Spring 1961).

Haas, Edward F. "New Orleans on the Half-Shell: The Maestri Era, 1936-46." *Louisiana History*, vol. 13, no. 3 (Summer 1972).

Heleniak, Roman. "Local Reaction to the Great Depression in New Orleans, 1929-1933." *Louisiana History*, vol. 10, no. 4 (Fall 1969).

Jackson, Joy J. "Prohibition in New Orleans: The Unlikeliest Crusade." *Louisiana History*, vol. 19, no. 3 (Summer 1978).

Kemp, John R. "Politics and the Depression." New Orleans *States-Item*, November 2, 1979.

Kurtz, Michael L. "Earl Long's Political Relations with the City of New Orleans: 1948-1960." *Louisiana History*, vol. 10, no. 3 (Summer 1969).

Pope, John. "New Orleans Danced as Market Fell." New Orleans *States-Item*, October 24, 1979.

Reinders, Robert C. "A Wisconsin Soldier Reports from New Orleans." *Louisiana History*, vol. 3, no. 4 (Fall 1962).

Roland, Charles P. "Louisiana and Secession." *Louisiana History*, vol. 19, no. 4 (Fall 1978).

Schweninger, Loren. "A Negro Sojourner in Antebellum New Orleans." *Louisiana History*, vol. 20, no. 3 (Summer 1979).

Tansey, Richard. "Prostitution and Politics in Antebellum New Orleans." *Southern Studies*, vol. 18, no. 4 (Winter 1979).

Books

Asbury, Herbert. *The French Quarter; An Informal History of the New Orleans Underworld*. New York: Alfred A. Knopf, 1936.

Carter, Samuel III. *Blaze of Glory: The Fight for New Orleans, 1814-1815*. New York: St. Martin's Press, 1971.

Caughey, John Walton. *Bernardo De Galvez in Louisiana, 1776-1783*. Berkeley: University of California Press, 1934.

Chase, John. *Frenchmen, Desire, Good Children*. New Orleans: Robert L. Crager and Company, 1949.

Christovich, Mary Lou; Toledano, Roulhac; Swanson, Betsy; and Holden, Pat. "The American Sector (Faubourg St. Mary). New Orleans Architecture," vol. 2. Contains essays by Samuel Wilson, Jr., and Bernard Lemann. Gretna: Pelican Publishing Company and The Friends of the Cabildo. 1972.

Clark, John G. *New Orleans, 1718-1812; An Economic History*. Baton Rouge: Louisiana State University Press, 1970.

Costa, Myldred Masson, trans. *Letters of Marie-Madeleine*

Hachard, Ursuline of New Orleans, 1727-1728. New Orleans: 1974.

Davis, Edwin Adam. *Louisiana; A Narrative History.* rev. ed. Baton Rouge: Claitor's Publishing Division, 1971.

Dufour, Charles L. *Ten Flags in the Wind: The Story of Louisiana.* New York: Harper and Row, 1967.

Giraud, Marcel. *A History of French Louisiana.* vol. 1. Translated by Joseph C. Lambert. Baton Rouge: Louisiana State University Press, 1974.

Haas, Edward F. "The Southern Metropolis, 1940-1976." *The City in Southern History.* Edited by Blaine A. Brownell and David R. Goldfield. Port Washington, New York: Kennikat Press, 1977.

_____. *DeLesseps S. Morrison and the Image of Reform; New Orleans Politics, 1946-1961.* Baton Rouge: Louisiana State University Press, 1974.

Hair, William Ivy. *Bourbonism and Agrarian Protest; Louisiana Politics, 1877-1900.* Baton Rouge: Louisiana State University Press, 1969.

Jackson, Joy J. *New Orleans in the Gilded Age; Politics and Urban Progress, 1880-1896.* Baton Rouge: Louisiana State University Press, 1969.

Kemp, John R. *Martin Behrman of New Orleans: Memoirs of a City Boss.* Baton Rouge: Louisiana State University Press, 1977.

Kendall, John Smith. *History of New Orleans.* 3 Vols. Chicago and New York: Lewis, 1922.

Kirk, Susan Lauxman; and Smith, Helen Michel. *The Architecture of St. Charles Avenue.* Gretna: Pelican Publishing Company, 1977.

LaBree, Ben, ed. *The Confederate Soldier in the Civil War, 1861-1865.* Louisville, Kentucky: 1895.

Liebling, A.J. *The Earl of Louisiana: The Liberal Long.* New York: Simon and Schuster, 1961.

Macdonald, Robert R.; Kemp, John R.; and Haas, Edward F. *Louisiana's Black Heritage.* New Orleans: Louisiana State Museum, 1979.

Mclure, Mary Lilla. "Development of Political Parties and Factions to 1860." *Readings in Louisiana Politics.* Edited by Mark T. Carleton, Perry H. Howard, and Joseph B. Parker. Baton Rouge: Claitor's Publishing Division, 1975.

Nolte, Vincent. *50 Years in Both Hemispheres.* New York: Redfield, 1854.

Olmsted, Frederick Law. *A Journey in the Seaboard Slave States with Remarks on Their Economy.* New York: Dix, 1856.

Reed, Merl. "Boom or Bust—Louisiana's Economy During the 1830's." *Readings in Louisiana Politics.* Edited by Mark T. Carleton, Perry H. Howard, and Joseph B. Parker. Baton Rouge: Claitor's Publishing Division, 1975.

Reinders, Robert C. *End of an Era, 1850-1860.* Gretna: Pelican Publishing Company, 1964.

Reynolds, George M. *Machine Politics in New Orleans, 1897-1926.* New York: Columbia University Press, 1936.

Rightor, Henry. *Standard History of New Orleans, Louisiana.* Chicago: Lewis Publishing Company, 1900.

Robin, C.C. *Voyage to Louisiana.* Translated by Landry O. Stuart, Jr. New Orleans: Pelican Publishing Company, 1966.

Rose, Al; and Souchon, Edmond. *New Orleans Jazz; A Family Album.* rev. ed. Baton Rouge: Louisiana State University Press, 1978.

Samuel, Ray; Huber, Leonard V.; and Ogden, Warren C. *Tales of the Mississippi.* New York: Hastings House Publishers, 1965.

Siegel, Martin, ed. *New Orleans: A Chronological and Documentary History.* Dobbs Ferry, New York: Oceana Publications, Inc., 1975.

Sindler, Allan P. *Huey Long's Louisiana: State Politics 1920-1952.* Baltimore: Johns Hopkins University Press, 1956.

Taylor, Joe Gray. "The Warmoth Administration." *Readings in Louisiana History.* Edited by Glenn R. Conrad. New Orleans: Louisiana Historical Association, 1978.

_____. "The Kellogg Era." *Readings in Louisiana History.* Edited by Glenn R. Conrad. New Orleans: Louisiana Historical Association, 1978.

_____. *Louisiana Reconstructed, 1863-1877.* Baton Rouge: Louisiana State University Press, 1975.

Tindall, George B. "The Emergence of the New South, 1913-1945." *A History of the South,* vol. 10. Edited by W. H. Stephenson and C.M. Coulter. Baton Rouge: Louisiana State University Press, 1967.

Wilds, John. *Afternoon Story: A Century of the New Orleans States-Item.* Baton Rouge: Louisiana State University Press, 1976.

Williams, T. Harry. *Huey Long.* New York: Alfred A. Knopf, 1969.

Wilson, Samuel, Jr. *Benjamin Henry Boneval Latrobe: Impressions Respecting New Orleans.* New York: Columbia University Press, 1951.

_____. and Lemann, Bernard. "The Lower Garden District." *New Orleans Architecture,* vol. 1. Compiled and edited by Mary Lou Christovich, Roulhac Toledano, and Betsy Swanson. Gretna: The Friends of the Cabildo and Pelican Publishing Company, 1971.

Exhibition Catalogues

Hardy, D. Clive. *The World's Industrial and Cotton Centennial Exposition.* New Orleans: The Historic New Orleans Collection, n.d.

Louisiana Purchase. Louisiana State Museum, n.d.

Manuscript Collections

Louisiana State Museum. Beebe Papers.

_____. Kenner Papers.

_____. Nathaniel Cox Letters.

_____. Webb Diaries.

Unpublished Papers

Douthit, Leo Glenn. "The Governorship of Huey Long." Unpublished M.A. thesis, Tulane University, 1947.

Frazar, Luther E. "The Constitutional Convention of 1921." Unpublished M.A. thesis, Louisiana State University, 1935.

ACKNOWLEDGMENTS

This history of New Orleans is not the work of any single individual, but is the product of the dedicated efforts of many people and organizations over the last two years.

Innumerable services and great encouragement have been proffered by several New Orleans historical groups and their staffs, especially the Historic Collection's Director (and former Preservation Resource Center President) Stanton M. Frazar, and Curator John H. Lawrence. John was tireless in locating, selecting and captioning the hundreds of old and new illustrations appearing in this volume. I also wish to thank the Louisiana State Museum Historical Center, particularly Curator Edward F. Haas and staff members Rose Lambert and Joseph Castle and the book's sponsor, the Preservation Resource Center of New Orleans. I would especially like to single out three members of that organization: Patricia Gay, Ann Masson, and of course Mary Lou Christovich, who wrote the excellent chapter on preservation. Contributions from William Trufant, President of the Louisiana Historical Society; D. Clive Hardy, Archivist at the University of New Orleans; and Suzanne Ormond, also were appreciated.

I am deeply indebted to Samuel Wilson, Jr., architect and architectural historian, and Charles "Pie" Dufour, historian and longtime columnist for the States-Item, for reading the manuscript and making helpful suggestions.

I wish to thank the staff of Windsor Publications, especially Editor-in-Chief Lissa Sanders, who saw the book through conception to printing; as well as Textual Editors Randall Smoot and Taryn Bigelow, who are probably qualified to teach New Orleans history by now. Much gratitude is also due

John Chase, John Wilds, and the many New Orleans firms and organizations who purchased pages in the "Partners in Progress" section, thus making this book economically feasible and helping to round out the business history of New Orleans. I know that the firms and the writers of the chapter join me in acknowledging the essential role Windsor's Karen Story played in the editorial direction of the chapter.

Finally, I want to thank my wife, Betty, and my daughter, Virginia, for their patience throughout.

John R. Kemp

The illustrations in this volume came from many sources—obvious and obscure, public and private. The following individuals and organizations contributed greatly toward the visual content of this book. Their assistance is greatly appreciated.

Stanton M. Frazar, Director of the Historic New Orleans Collection, allowed great freedom of access to the pictorial holdings of that institution, which immensely simplified my task of selecting appropriate illustrations. The Collection's Chief Curator Dode Platou, and Curators John A. Mahe II and Rosanne McCaffrey were also very helpful in suggesting pieces for illustrating this book. Robert R. Macdonald, Director of the Louisiana State Museum offered his assistance and that of his staff, notably Vaughn Glasgow, Chief Curator; John Burton Harter, Curator; and Amy Husten, Registrar, in locating important illustrations from the museum's holdings. Colin Hamer, Head of the Louisiana Division of the New Orleans Public Library, and Wayne

Eberhard of the same division were helpful in providing information and illustrations concerning recent political history. John Bender, Director of the Public Information Office of the City of New Orleans, provided access to the vast pictorial holdings relating to the operation of the mayor's office over the past 30 years. Charles Ferguson, Managing Editor; Jack Davis, City Editor; and Warren Nardelle, Librarian of the Times-Picayune/States-Item made available to me the photographic files of the newspaper. Their assistance is deeply appreciated. Pat Aymard of the Louisiana Historical Association's Confederate Museum permitted access to the holdings of that institution. William Slatten, President of the New Orleans Levee Board, was extremely cooperative and supportive of this project.

Robin Boylan, who did nearly all of the contemporary color photography that appears in this book, deserves special recognition for the zeal and enthusiasm he displayed in undertaking this assignment.

I also wish to thank Ann Masson and Patricia Gay of the New Orleans Preservation Resource Center for their confidence in me and their whole-hearted support. John Kemp, author of the text, never failed in his encouragement and helpful suggestions for illustrations. Picture Editor Teri Davis Greenberg of Windsor Publications kept me on schedule, and gave me clear direction throughout the project.

And finally, a special thanks to my wife, Carol, who through long hours, and with stacks of photographs and caption sheets spread out all over the house, understood it all and made everything fall into place.

John H. Lawrence

THIS BOOK WAS SET IN
SOUVENIR AND BENQUIAT BOOK CONDENSED TYPES,
PRINTED ON
80 LB. MEAD DULL ENAMEL
AND BOUND BY
WALSWORTH PUBLISHING COMPANY.
COVER AND TEXT DESIGNED BY
ALEXANDER D'ANCA
LAYOUT BY
JERI BERMAN